graphic arts
fundamentals

by

JOHN R. WALKER

Bel Air High School
Bel Air, Maryland

South Holland, Illinois
THE GOODHEART-WILLCOX COMPANY, INC.
Publishers

NATIONAL PORK PRODUCERS COUNCIL

Example of four-color process printing by the lithographic or offset printing process. Taken from the textbook Guide To Good Food by Velda Largen.

8405

Copyright 1980
by
THE GOODHEART-WILLCOX CO., INC.

No part of this book may be reproduced in any form without violating the copyright law. Printed in U.S.A. Library of Congress Catalog Card Number 79—24182. International Standard Book Number 0—87006—288—3.

23456789—80—54321

Library of Congress Cataloging in Publication Data

Walker, John R
Graphic arts fundamentals
Includes index.
1. Graphic arts--Technique. 2. Communication--Audio-visual aids. 3. Commercial art. I. Title.
NC1000.W34   338.4'7'686   79—24182
ISBN 0—87006—288—3

INTRODUCTION

The graphic arts include the processes and techniques used to produce the printed word and the printed illustration. With them, you are able to record ideas, thoughts and beliefs. This permanent record will benefit future generations. Were it not for the printed word, you might still be living as your ancestors did during the Dark Ages.

The aim of GRAPHIC ARTS FUNDAMENTALS is to help you learn about the basic graphic arts areas. Numerous photographs, drawings, charts and diagrams are shown to make it easy for you to understand many of the more complex graphic arts processes.

GRAPHIC ARTS FUNDAMENTALS will acquaint you with the designing, production and sale of products and services of the graphic arts industries. You will be expected to take part in and develop skills in many of these areas.

GRAPHIC ARTS FUNDAMENTALS may challenge you to further your studies. Perhaps you will like one area well enough to make it your life's work. Career opportunities in this interesting field are found in all parts of the nation. Wages are above average and fringe benefits are very good.

GRAPHIC ARTS FUNDAMENTALS is well suited for a full year's program. With careful selection of its content, it can be adapted to nine, twelve and eighteen-week programs.

John R. Walker

Four-color printing makes this illustration attractive and appealing.
Taken from the textbook Modern Metalworking by John R. Walker.

CONTENTS

WHEAT FLOUR INSTITUTE

Good example of four-color printing shows variety of baked goods.
Taken from the textbook Guide To Good Food by Velda Largen.

Unit 1

HISTORY OF THE GRAPHIC ARTS

Objectives

This is a short account of the 6000 year history of graphic arts.

By studying this unit, you will understand how the craft of making identical copies of words and pictures developed from the clay tablets of the Babylonians (about 4000 B.C.) to the computer controlled printing devices of today.

PRINTING is the art of making many identical copies of words and pictures. The craft is more than 6000 years old. Johann Gutenberg did not invent printing; he improved it.

The Babylonians were among the first to keep printed records. They pressed picturelike symbols, called CUNEIFORM writing, onto tablets of moist clay and wax. Fig. 1-1.

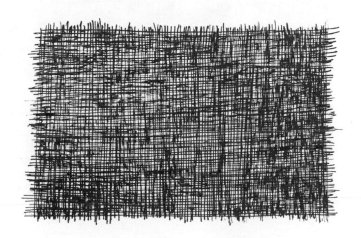

Fig. 1-2. The stringy fibers of the papyrus plant were laid at right angles to one another and pressed flat. The "sheet" was then rubbed with a flat stone or a bone to make a smoother writing surface.

water and vinegar. Another layer was laid on top of the first but in the opposite direction, Fig. 1-2. The two layers were hammered or pressed with a smooth stone to mat the fibers together and to make a surface smooth enough for writing. The remaining parts of the papyrus plant were used to make other grades of writing material. The lowest grade was used to wrap fruit and vegetables for shipment to market.

A scribe (writer) hand lettered information on the sheet. Books were made by tying or pasting several sheets together. The joined sheets were rolled into a SCROLL, Fig. 1-3.

FIRST PAPER MADE

PAPER was first made in China in A.D. 105. A scholar and government official named Ts'ai Lun was looking for something better than silk or other cloth to write on. The search led to the inner bark of the Mulberry tree. The bark could be pounded into a smooth pulp. This pulp was spread over a smooth, flat surface. When it had dried, the surface was polished with a stone burnisher. This made it less like a blotter and easier to write on.

Later, it was learned that rags and cloth could be beaten into a pulp. This too made fine paper.

Fig. 1-1. Early records were pressed in clay. Inscriptions on this cylinder refer to restoration of an Egyptian temple between 604 and 561 B.C. (Metropolitan Museum of Art)

About 5000 years ago, the Egyptians developed a paperlike material made by splitting the stalk of the papyrus plant into paper thin strips. Only the center portion of the strips were used. The thin strips were placed on a wet board. The exposed surface was coated with a thin wheat paste made with muddy

Fig. 1-4. Church music was hand lettered on parchment in the eleventh century.

Fig. 1-3. Ancient texts were prepared on rolls of paperlike material and stored in wooden containers. Left. Egyptian Twenty-first Dynasty funerary customs papyrus roll "Book of the Dead" is from the tomb of Nany, a ruler of Egypt. Above. Wood case was carved to hold papyrus roll at left. It is about 25 in. (635 mm) high. (Metropolitan Museum of Art)

Fig. 1-5. Religious scribes reproduced ancient books by hand (Gutenberg Museum, Mainz)

These hand lettered books took a long time to produce. It was common practice to chain them to storage shelves and reading tables to prevent their loss, Fig. 1-6.

Printing from woodcuts was not widely done in Europe until early in the 1500s, Fig. 1-7. The woodcuts were made by hand.

FIRST PRINTING IN EUROPE

Johann Gutenberg, Fig. 1-8, enters history in 1445. This is when he invented movable metal type for printing, Fig. 1-9. This refinement changed the way of reproducing written messages and thereby affected the whole world.

The idea of printing from movable type was not new. For about 150 years, the Chinese and Koreans had used movable type made from clay. But, due to the nature of their languages, each piece of type had to be a complete word. So

China also produced the first book in A.D. 868. It was printed from wood blocks. Known as the "Diamond Sutra," it was a selection of Buddhist scriptures. The pages were assembled to form a paper roll more than 16 ft. long.

Paper was brought to Europe during the Crusades. This was some time in the late 1100s. Until that time, PARCHMENT and VELLUM were used as writing materials, Fig. 1-4. Parchment was made from sheepskin and vellum from calfskin. Hard-working religious scribes (monks) hand lettered each book. Both religious works and classics were copied, Fig. 1-5.

the method was abandoned. Gutenberg cast single letters in metal. For this, he is generally credited as being the father of modern printing.

Gutenberg produced about 50 printed works. Yet, his fame is based on the *Gutenberg Bible*. It is also known as the 42-line bible since most pages had 42 lines of type.

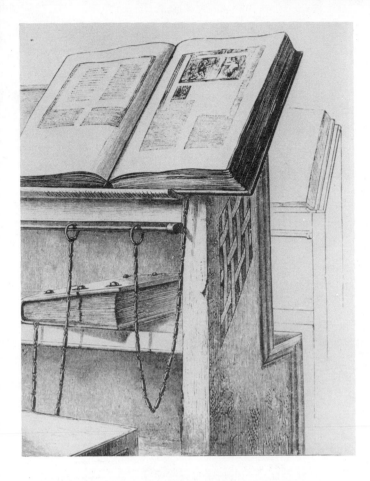

Fig. 1-6. Early hand-lettered books were so scarce that they were chained to storage shelves so they could not be stolen.

Fig. 1-8. Johann Gutenberg's invention of movable metal type affected the entire world. (Gutenberg Museum, Mainz)

Gutenberg's press was fashioned after the wine press then in common use, Fig. 1-10. It had a heavy wooden frame. An upright screw passed through a threaded hole in the cross beam. The paper being printed was placed over the inked type form. Turning the screw with a long handle brought the PLATEN (a smooth flat plate) down on the paper. Reversing the screw raised the platen so the printed sheet could be removed.

PRINTING IN AMERICA

The Reverend Jose Glover brought the first printing press to North America in 1638. Located in Cambridge, Massachusetts, it was associated with Harvard College.

Reverend Glover hired an English immigrant, Stephen Daye, and his two sons to operate the press. Daye was not a printer. He was to manage the printing office and keep the press in repair. His sons were to be the printers.

Matthew Daye, one of the sons, published *The Whole Book of Psalms* in 1640, Fig. 1-11. This was the first book printed in America.

Fig. 1-7. This wood engraving was made in Europe during 1423. (Gutenberg Museum, Mainz)

There were few printers in early colonial times. Paper was too scarce. But printing grew rapidly after David Rittenhouse began to make paper in Pennsylvania. He set up the first paper mill near Philadelphia in 1690. He had learned papermaking in Holland.

The first newspaper was printed at the beginning of the Eighteenth century. The *Boston Newsletter* was started in 1704. It was forced to stop printing 72 years later.

The most famous of the early American printers was Benjamin Franklin, Fig. 1-12. He learned the trade from his brother James. The firm, B. Franklin, Printer, was founded in 1728. It was located in Philadelphia.

In the same year, the firm printed the first issue of what was to be known as the *Pennsylvania Gazette.* The Gazette was later published as the *Saturday Evening Post. Poor Richard's Almanack* was another well-known publication of Franklin's. See Fig. 1-13.

Less well known are the contributions of women to printing in America. They were active both as managers of printing establishments and as skilled printers.

Anne Franklin was a printer for the colony of Rhode Island. Her most important work was a 340 page collection of colonial laws but she also produced many pamphlets. She and her two daughters were known to be competent and accurate compositors.

Fig. 1-10. How Gutenberg's print shop was thought to look. It can be seen at the Gutenberg Museum, Mainz, West Germany.

Fig. 1-9. Early printing methods. Upper left. Metal is cast in a mold similar to one devised by Gutenberg. Upper right. Gutenberg set his type in much the same way. Bottom. Printing form set from early metal type. (Gutenberg Museum, Mainz)

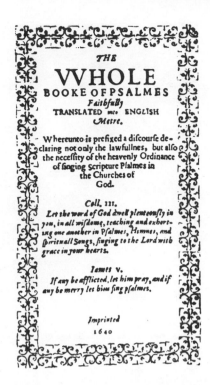

Fig. 1-11. Cover of first book published in America in 1640.

Fig. 1-12. Benjamin Franklin was the most famous of all early American printers. (The Franklin Institute)

Fig. 1-13. Cover from copy of Benjamin Franklin's Poor Richard's Almanack. (The Franklin Institute)

A native of Connecticut, Mary Katherine Goddard was an expert compositor who became manager of a printing business. From 1775 to 1784 she was the publisher of the *Maryland Journal,* a weekly newspaper.

Anne Catherine Green, born in Holland but raised in Maryland, became a printer. She published the *Maryland Gazette* from 1767 until her death in 1775.

Maria Edes of Bangor Maine was a compositor in her father's shop. He printed the *Kennebac Journal* (Augusta) and the *Bangor Gazette.* The time was around 1820.

Mary Crouch set up a printing house in Salem, Massachusetts in 1780 to publish the *Salem Gazette and General Advertiser.*

EARLY PRINTING EQUIPMENT

Just what were the early print shops like? The presses were only slightly different in shape from Gutenberg's press, Fig. 1-14. Some working parts were made from iron. The heavy

Upon the death of her husband, Margaret Draper became proprietor of the *Massachusetts Gazette and Boston Weekly Newsletter.* It was the first newspaper to be published in the American colonies.

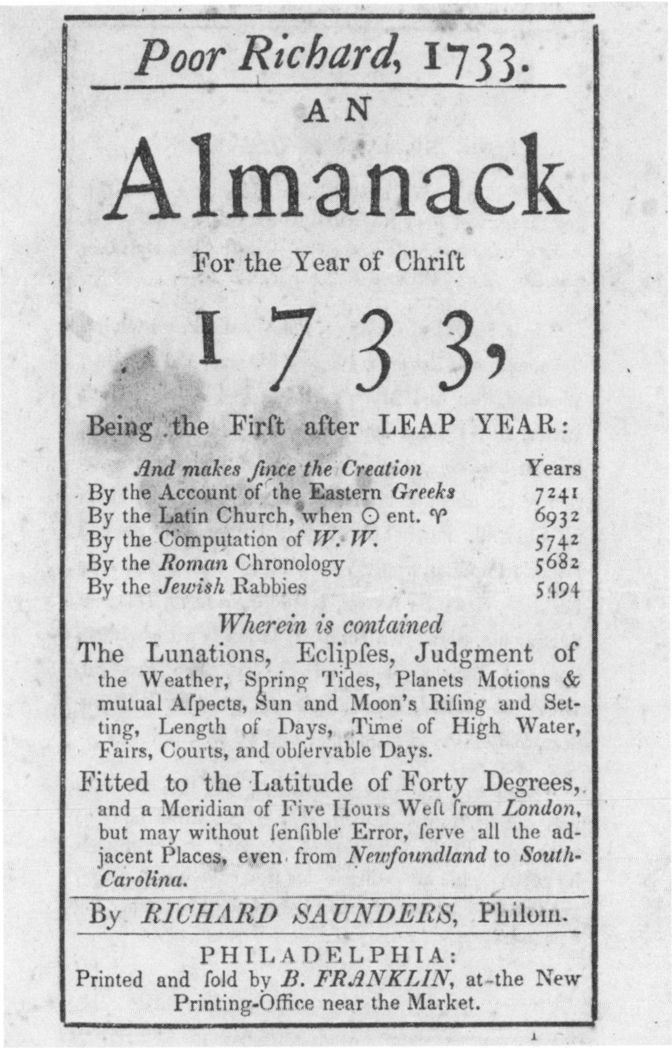

Fig. 1-14. Early American printing presses looked like this.
(The Smithsonian Institution)

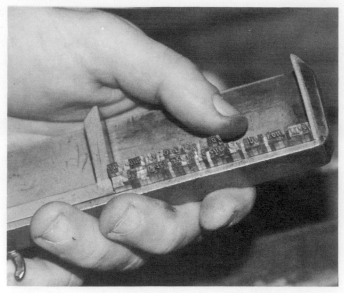

Fig. 1-16. Type was hand set in a device called a "stick."
(Colonial Williamsburg)

frame was still wood. They were now braced between the floor and the ceiling. This helped the press withstand the forces applied during the printing operation.

Type was cast in hand-cut brass molds, Fig. 1-15. The single pieces of type were set in a device called a STICK, Fig. 1-16. A good printer could set about two characters a second.

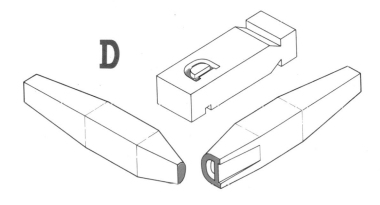

Fig. 1-15. Type was individually cast in brass molds.

Ink was made from boiled linseed oil, lampblack and varnish. Dabbers (stuffed leather balls, attached to wood handles) were used to put ink on the type. See Fig. 1-17.

The corrected type form was locked in an iron frame known as a CHASE, Fig. 1-18. This type of frame is still used today to hold metal type for printing.

PRESS OPERATION

Two persons were needed to operate the press, Fig. 1-19. Each had a specific job to do. One handled the paper. The other inked and worked the press controls.

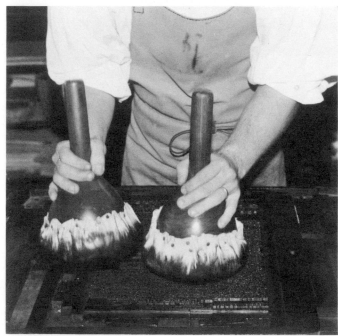

Fig. 1-17. Type forms were inked with "dabbers" made from leather and stuffed with rags.

A good printing team could produce up to 2000 printed sheets a day. A workday was 10 hours long.

Printers were skilled workers. They were paid about $14 for a six day work week.

PRINTING PROGRESS

The nineteenth century saw the start of the newspaper era in the United States. Newspapers were published in most of the settled areas of the nation.

Fig. 1-18. This type form was locked in an iron frame called a chase. (Colonial Williamsburg)

The nineteenth century was also the mechanical age for introducing new printing equipment. New graphic arts techniques were discovered. Others were refined or put into commercial use.

Papermaking machinery was invented. Paper became more plentiful and less costly.

ADVANCES IN RELIEF PRINTING

All-metal presses were produced. One in wide use was the Washington Hand Press, Fig. 1-20. A slightly changed version of this press is still used for display purposes.

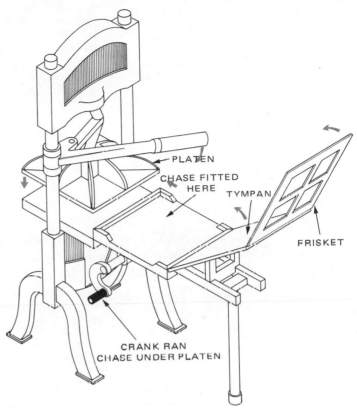

PLATEN
CHASE FITTED HERE
TYMPAN
FRISKET
CRANK RAN CHASE UNDER PLATEN

Fig. 1-20. The Washington Hand Press was one of the first all-metal printing presses.

Fig. 1-19. Operating the early press was a job for two. One person had to have clean hands to put the paper in the press and remove it after it was printed. (Gutenberg Museum, Mainz)

Fig. 1-21. Early sheet fed printing press was hand powered. (Gutenberg Museum, Mainz)

Fig. 1-22. Rotary press of 1846. It could print 4000 to 5000 sheets an hour. (Gutenberg Museum, Mainz)

Fig. 1-23. Ten press operators fed paper into the 10 cylinder newspaper press of 1855. It was developed by Richard M. Hoe.

Fig. 1-24. Web presses are designed to take paper off a roll. Press operator is preparing next roll. It will begin to feed into press while the press is running. Most modern web presses print by lithography. (Rand McNally & Co.)

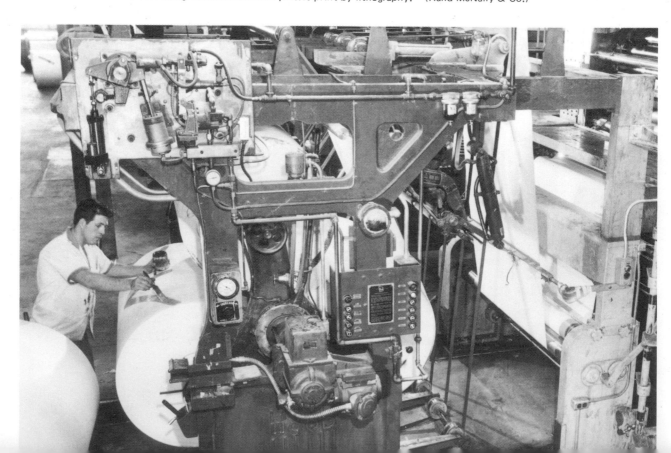

The sheet fed press, Fig. 1-21, was developed in this period. Some were steam powered. Later versions of the press printed 4000 to 5000 sheets an hour, Fig. 1-22. This was quite an advance over the 2000 sheets printed a day by the hand press.

During the second half of the nineteenth century, PHOTOGRAPHY was first used in the graphic arts. With photography came PHOTOENGRAVING. This technique allows drawings, pictures and letters to be reproduced by printing.

At mid-century, the rotary press was perfected. Type was fitted to a revolving cylinder. Steam was used to power it. One model printed up to 20,000 sheets an hour, Fig. 1-23.

The web press was invented at about the same time. This press printed on both sides of the paper. Paper was supplied in roll form, Fig. 1-24.

Ottmar Mergenthaler patented the Linotype in 1884. This machine was the first to set type mechanically, Fig. 1-25.

Fig. 1-26. The first litho printing was done from flat, porous stones. Top. Stone had to be quite thick. Bottom. A close-up of work drawn on an early litho stone. This was the work of a late nineteenth century apprentice who practiced drawing scrolls that would be used to embellish stocks and bonds.

plastic and paper printing plates. Today, much of our printing is done this way. The process can print on almost any surface — metal, wood, paper or plastic, Fig. 1-27.

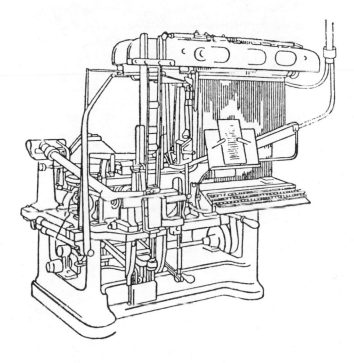

Fig. 1-25. This early Linotype machine was the first line casting machine to set type for a newspaper. The newspaper was the New York Tribune and the year was 1886.   (Mergenthaler Linotype Co.)

FLAT SURFACE PRINTING

LITHOGRAPHY (lih-thawg'-ruh-fee) is the art of printing from a flat surface. It was invented in 1798 by a Bohemian playwright. The process is based on the principle that water and grease do not mix. At first, lithographic printing was done from flat, porous stones. See Fig. 1-26.

Early in the twentieth century, OFFSET LITHOGRAPHIC printing was developed. The flat stone was replaced by metal,

Fig. 1-27. With offset lithography it is possible to print on just about any surface — metal, wood, plastic and paper.

Inkless printing was invented in the 1930s. The correct name for it is XEROGRAPHY (zee-rawg'-ra-fee). Many office copying machines use this principle, Fig. 1-28.

Fig. 1-28. Xerography machine makes copies instantly without ink. (Van Dyk Research Corp.)

By 1950, phototypesetting machines were in use. This equipment can now be controlled by computer. Type can be "set" photographically at the rate of 10,000 characters per second, Fig. 1-29. The colonial printer set two characters per second!

Printing presses now print up to 100,000 full color pieces an hour. See Fig. 1-30.

A computer controlled LASER (lay-zer) is now being employed to make letterpress and offset printing plates directly from pasteups. The plates are made in minutes, Fig. 1-31. No negatives, photoengravings, chemicals or water are needed. There is no air or water pollution.

The device, however, is as simple to operate as an office copier. See Fig. 1-32.

The computer controlled laser has also been developed to produce color separations up to 16 x 20 in. (406-508 mm) for letterpress, lithographic or gravure printing, Fig. 1-33. The device can make the color separations larger or smaller than the original copy. This process is described in Unit 14. It is called "separation" because each of three special filters is used to record only one color on a film.

The laser is also used to cut precision dies, Fig. 1-34. These dies cut paper and plastic to shapes other than the usual square or rectangle, Fig. 1-35. The cutting is done after the material has been printed.

The carton manufacturers, greeting card and advertising firms are the chief user of dies in the printing trades. Samples of die cut products are shown in Fig. 1-36.

Fig. 1-29. Phototypesetting machine. Top. Copy is scanned or keyed (typed) to make a tape. Text immediately appears on the video screen ready for layout. Operator can position copy on screen to match layout wanted. Center. Closeup of keyboard and video display screen. Bottom. Phototypesetter. Copy is "set" on this machine. (Harris Corp., Composition Systems Div.)

Fig. 1-30. Hantscho two-unit web press accepts 54 in. wide rolls of paper. It prints and folds 12,000 copies of a 96 page form per hour. (Rand McNally & Co.)

Fig. 1-31. Printing plates are made in minutes by the computer controlled laser. No negatives, photoengravings, chemicals or water are needed. There is no air or water pollution. (Laser Graphic Systems Inc.)

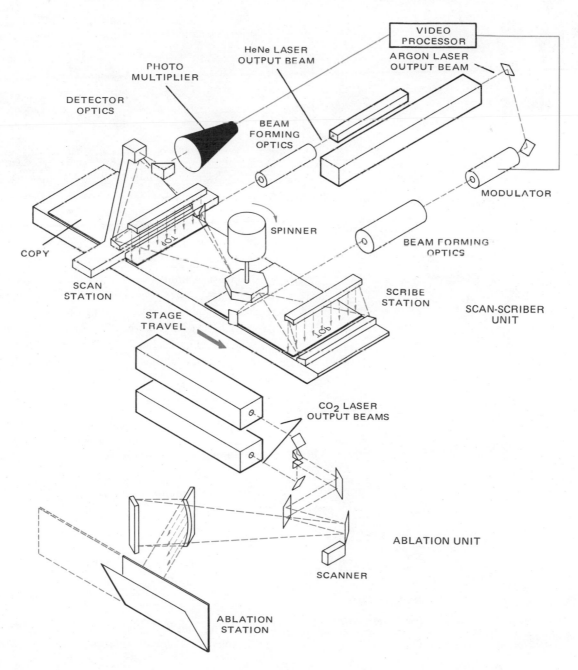

Fig. 1-32. Laser platemaking equipment is used by several newspaper publishing firms. (Elmira, New York Star-Gazette)

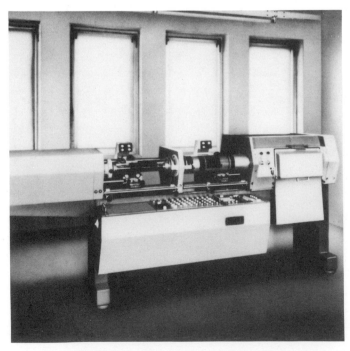

Fig. 1-33. Computer controlled lasers have also been developed to produce color separations for letter press, lithographic or gravure printing. (HCM Corp.)

Graphic arts industries are expanding. New ideas are being introduced to lower production costs. It is thought that the graphic arts industries will be using almost 100 million tons of paper each year by the year 2000. With this growth will come many new and interesting jobs. You may want to consider one of them for your future.

TEST YOUR KNOWLEDGE - UNIT 1

Write your answers to these questions on a separate sheet of paper. *Do not write in this book.*

1. Printing is more than _____ years old.
      1000   2000   3000   4000   5000   6000   8000

2. Records were kept on _____ and _____ tablets by the Babylonians.

3. The Egyptians wrote on a paperlike material made from the _____ reed.

4. Information was written on this material by (record the correct answer):
   a. Calligraphers.   c. Printers.   e. Scribes.
   b. Inkers.   d. Scholars.   f. Writers.

Fig. 1-34. Computer controlled laser diecutter. Controls are at left. Laser is contained in the rectangular box above table.

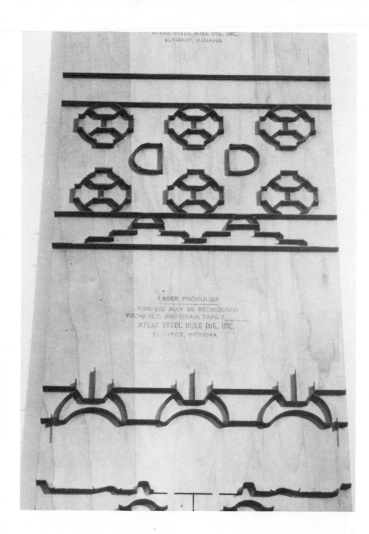

Fig. 1-35. Laser cuts required pattern in plywood; then steel cutting blades are shaped and fitted into the cuts. (Atlas Steel Rule Die, Inc.)

Fig. 1-36. Examples of die cut printed matter.

5. The _____ invented paper.

Babylonians	Egyptians	French
Chinese	English	Germans

6. The _____ printed the first book. It was printed from _____.

7. Why were the first books chained to the storage shelves and reading tables?

8. Parchment was a writing material made from _____.

9. Vellum was a writing material made from _____.

10. Johann Gutenberg is generally credited as being the father of modern printing because he (record the correct answer):

   a. Made woodcuts by hand.
   b. Invented an inexpensive way to make paper.
   c. Invented movable metal type.
   d. Invented movable type made from clay.
   e. None of the above.

11. Describe the printing press that was used by Gutenberg. Make a sketch if it will help you answer easier.
12. The first printing press was brought to North America in 1638. It was located in _____ .
13. There were few printers in early colonial times because (record the correct answer):
    a. It was very expensive to set up a print shop.
    b. Paper was scarce.
    c. The government did not allow them to set up shop.
    d. All of the above.
    e. None of the above.
14. Who is thought to be the most famous of early American printers?
15. His printing house was located in _____ .
16. His firm printed the first issue of the *Pennsylvania Gazette.* It is still being published as ___ _____ _____ _____ .
17. Name two women who were printers in colonial times.
18. Why was type "proofed" after it was set?
19. Two persons were needed to operate early printing presses. What was the job of each person?
20. A good printing team could make up to _____ impressions during a 10-hour work day. Since these printers were highly skilled workers, they received _____ dollars for a six day work week.
21. During the nineteenth century steam powered printing presses were developed. The sheet fed cylinder press printed _____ to _____ sheets per hour.
22. List four of the other printing processes that were developed during the nineteenth century.
23. Xerography was invented in the 1930s. It is an _____ printing process that is widely used in office copying machines.
24. Equipment is now available to set type photographically at the rate of _____ characters per second. Colonial printers set type at the rate of _____ characters per second.

THINGS TO DO

1. Research cuneiform writing and prepare an example on a clay or wax tablet similar to those made by the Babylonians.
2. Research and prepare an example of a scroll of the type used in ancient Egypt.
3. Make a working model of an early printing press.
4. Prepare an outline on the history of papermaking.
5. Benjamin Franklin was famous for his many quotations that appeared in *Poor Richard's Almanack.* Research them and make a pamphlet of them.
6. Read the autobiography of Benjamin Franklin.
7. There were many other early printers who became famous. Prepare a report on at least two of them.
8. Early printers used PRINTERS' MARKS to identify their products and to assure quality. Research these marks and draw several examples of them on posters. The poster should be no smaller than 10 in. (254 mm) square.
9. Samuel Clemens, better known as Mark Twain, was also a printer. Read his book *Roughing It* and prepare an outline on his experiences and adventures as a printer.
10. Visit a newspaper printing plant.
11. Visit a local printing office.
12. Visit a museum or restoration that has examples of early printing on display. Historical areas like Williamsburg, Virginia, and places like the Smithsonian Institute and the Franklin Institute have fine examples of print shops as they were during colonial times.

Fig. 2-1. Many different kinds of workers are needed in this paper mill. Engineers, quality control personnel, technicians, chemists, mechanics and environmentalists get involved in papermaking. Note how clean the working conditions are. (Westvaco Corp.)

Unit 2

CAREERS IN GRAPHIC COMMUNICATION

Objectives

This is a survey of some of the many career possibilities in the field of graphic communications.

Through this unit you will become familiar with career opportunities in graphic communications. You will be able to list many of the occupations. Some may fit your own interests or aptitudes. Perhaps you will be encouraged to seek employment in this challenging field where women and men can compete on equal terms for jobs.

Have you ever considered working in graphic communications? As an industry, it offers a wide choice of jobs. These jobs are located in all parts of the United States. They are found in large cities and small towns.

Jobs in graphic communications offer many advantages.
1. Pay is generally above average.
2. Working conditions are comfortable.
3. Most firms offer good fringe benefits and job security.
4. There are opportunities for promotions and advancement.
5. These jobs are little affected by recessions and layoffs.

Do you like to work with your mind and hands? Thousands who are skilled in the printing crafts — press operators, compositors, process camera operators, bookbinders and machinists work to transfer ideas, words and images into printed form. See Fig. 2-1. The printed word affects almost every part of our daily lives.

Do you like to work outdoors? The paper industry needs biologists, botanists and horticulturists. Their job is to produce better trees in greater quantity to be made into paper, Fig. 2-2.

Do you have creative talents? Writers, artists and illustrators create the words and images that are to be printed.

These are only a few of the many jobs that can be found in graphic communications. No matter what your interest, there may be a job to suit you.

CATEGORIES OF JOBS

Jobs in graphic communications fall into the following general categories.
1. Creative. These men and women create the ideas, words,

Fig. 2-2. Biologist, botanists and horticulturists work to produce better, faster-growing trees for the paper industry.

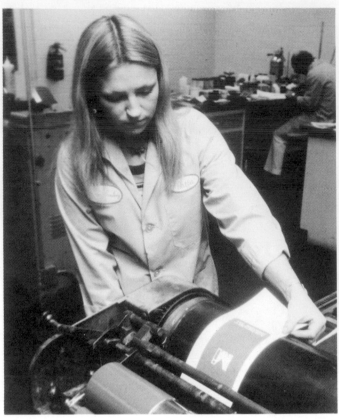

Fig. 2-5. Chemists of many specialties are needed to develop improved inks, paper and photographic materials that will not damage the environment. This woman is developing a new ink formula.   (NAPIM)

Fig. 2-3 Editors prepare copy for the printer.

artwork and photographs that are put into printed form. Editors, Fig. 2-3, reporters, artists, illustrators, writers, package designers, Fig. 2-4, and commercial photographers are but a few of the positions in this category.

Schooling varies from several years training in a trade or technical school, to two or more years of college.

Fig. 2-4. Packaging is an important sales tool. Artists, illustrators, package designers, writers and photographers are needed in this phase of the graphic arts.

Fig. 2-6. Mechanical, chemical and electrical engineers design and develop new graphic arts equipment. Left. Electronic typesetter is fast and easy to operate. (Harris Corp., Composition Systems Div.) Right. Four-color offset press produces printing of outstanding quality while operating faster than older presses. (Veritone Co., Inc.)

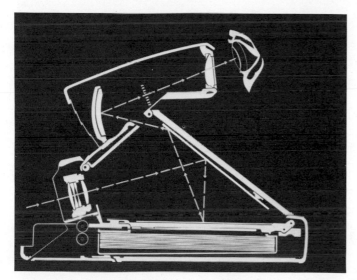

2. Professional. The graphic communications industry is in the greatest technological revolution ever known. Chemists of many specialties are needed to develop better inks, paper and photographic materials. See Fig. 2-5. Biologists and ecologists are employed to reduce pollutants while developing methods for reclaiming and recycling water, chemicals, paper and solvents.

Challenging positions are open for engineers — mechanical, chemical and electrical — to design and develop new graphic arts equipment, Fig. 2-6.

Physicists and mathematicians are working on such things as three-dimensional photography and adapting laser technology to the graphic arts, Fig. 2-7.

A bachelor's degree is usually the minimum requirement for entering a profession. However, some women and men have been able to enter the professional ranks without a degree after several years experience as technicians. They

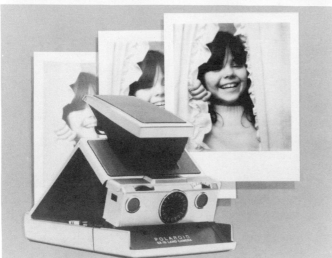

Fig. 2-7. Physicists and mathematicians research and develop new ideas for the graphic arts industry. Top. Diagram was made of instant developing developing film and camera that was to use it. Bottom. Camera and instant film as eventually developed. (Polaroid Corp.)

Fig. 2-8. Quality control is an important part of the graphic arts. Here a quality control technician is checking press sheets to be sure printed product meets color standards. (Diversified Printing Corp.)

are required, however, to take some college-level courses.

3. Technicians. Some technicians test new ideas and equipment. Some work with engineers to make new equipment practical. Other technicians work as estimators, data processing experts, computer specialists and in quality control, Fig. 2-8. Technicians are also employed to install, repair and maintain electronic equipment used in graphic communications, Fig. 2-9.

Technicians, for the most part, must have two or more years of college or technical school training. Many women find this area of graphic communications challenging and are making it a career.

4. Skilled craftworkers. Those who work at skilled printing crafts are the backbone of the industry. They put the ideas, words, photographs and illustrations into final printed form. There are hundreds of different jobs in the skilled category. See Fig. 2-10 through Fig. 2-17. Included are compositors, proofreaders, press operators, color matchers, bookbinders, platemakers, machinists, electricians and process camera operators to name but a few of the positions.

Many skilled persons learn their trade during four or more years of apprenticeship. This training includes study with experienced craftworkers on-the-job. Part of this time is also spent in a classroom studying English, mathematics, science and other related subjects.

The Armed Forces are another way to get training in

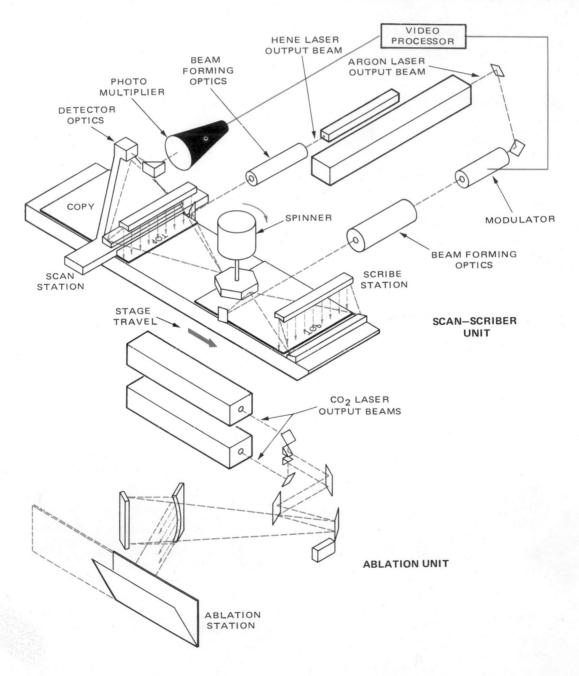

Fig. 2-9. Equipment like this laser platemaker, which produces plates for offset or relief printing, is installed, maintained and repaired by technicians.

Fig. 2-10. Compositors set type using a variety of equipment. Left. This woman is operating a composing unit for a strike-on typesetting system. Right. This operator works on a unit that justifies lines and makes corrections electronically. (Melbourn, Florida, Today)

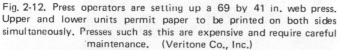

Fig. 2-11. Dot etcher checks values of four-color process negatives. (Veritone Co., Inc.)

Fig. 2-12. Press operators are setting up a 69 by 41 in. web press. Upper and lower units permit paper to be printed on both sides simultaneously. Presses such as this are expensive and require careful maintenance. (Veritone Co., Inc.)

Fig. 2-13. Film stripper prepares negative film attaching them to flats so that plates can be made for printing. This is a highly skilled job. (Ferris State College, Big Rapids, Mich.)

Fig. 2-14. Press operator in training. He is setting up a small offset press. (Cheney State College)

Fig. 2-15. Making pasteups of pages for a daily newspaper. Some of the pages will be run in four colors.   (Melbourn, Florida, Today)

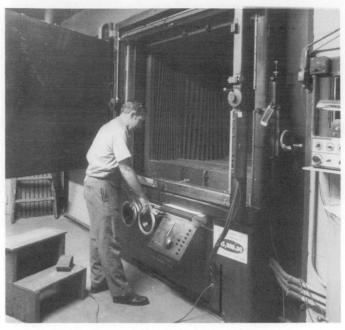

Fig. 2-16. Camera operator prepares camera for new exposure. (Veritone Co., Inc.)

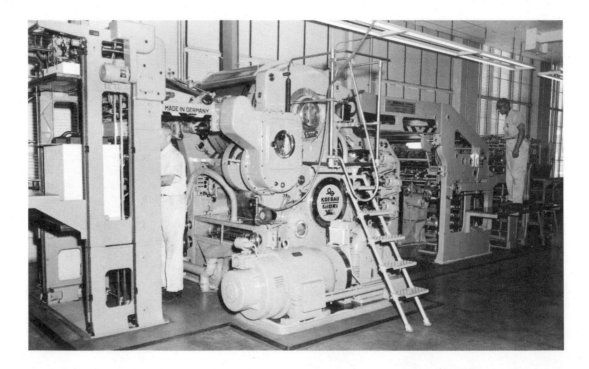

Fig. 2-17. Gravure press printing U.S. currency. Press operators served a four or five-year apprenticeship.
(U.S. Bureau of Engraving and Printing)

some areas of the graphic arts. It would be to your advantage to start your training in the industrial arts, industrial education or vocational-technical programs in your school.

5. Sales. These are the men and women who sell printed products, Fig. 2-18. Others in this category sell equipment and supplies to the graphic arts industries.

Sales training is frequently an in-plant program. Knowledge of the graphic arts is helpful.

6. Management.Managers have the policy and decision-making role in graphic communications. They decide how their company will reach its carefully determined goals. Management also is responsible for maintaining good morale among their employees.

Many of the men and women in management have degrees in business administration. Others in this group have come up through the ranks. They often start as craftworkers and learned all aspects of the business.

Fig. 2-18. Sales people market the printed products.

7. Education. Teaching, Fig. 2-19, is a satisfying career. It is a field students too often overlook. The teacher of industrial arts, industrial education and technical education is in a most fortunate position. It is a challenging career that offers freedom not found in most professions.

Four years of college level training is required. Experience in the graphic arts is not a prerequisite, but will prove helpful. Credits toward teacher certification are often given for experience in the trade.

FINDING MORE INFORMATION

More information on graphic arts occupations is to be found from books, associations and educational institutions. The closest source of information is the guidance office of your own school.

Almost all community colleges have career information centers. The centers can furnish a broad range of occupational information.

State employment office are another excellent source of information. These offices can tell you about local opportunities for employment. Local graphic arts union headquarters can tell you where apprenticeship training is offered.

LITERATURE ON JOBS

Many of the jobs in graphic arts are listed and described in the OCCUPATIONAL OUTLOOK HANDBOOK. This book, published by the U.S. Department of Labor, may be found in the school guidance office or in your local library. Check the reference section of the library for other books on printing and publishing careers.

ASSOCIATIONS

There are a number of association and trade organizations serving the graphic arts industry. Any of them may be contacted for literature about a specific occupation. Libraries have directories of associations with current addresses. Ask the librarian for help in locating them.

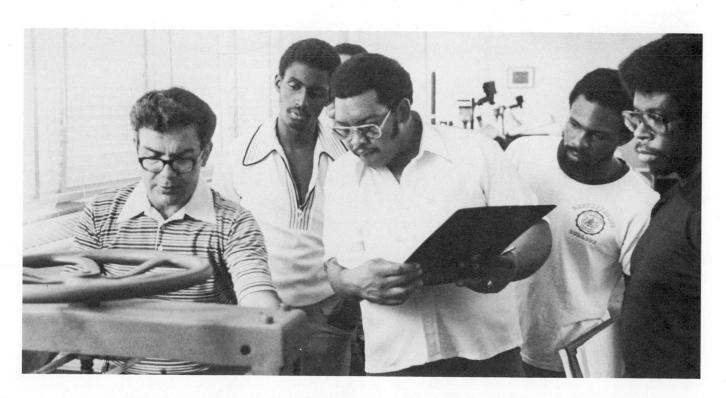

Fig. 2-19. Teaching is a very satisfying profession. Statistics show that there will be a steady demand for Industrial Education teachers in most parts of the United States.   (Cheney State College)

The following organizations will respond to inquiries about specific occupations and most will send literature if the request is made on school stationery:

The United States Department of Labor
  Bureau of Labor Statistics
Graphic Arts Technical Foundation
American Newspaper Publishers Assoc.
Book Manufacturers' Institute, Inc.
Printing Industry of America, Inc.
Gravure Technical Assoc.
Graphic Arts Research Center
  Rochester Institute of Technology
National Association of Printers and Lithographers
Screen Printing Association, International
In-Plant Printing Management Assoc.
International Association of Printing House Craftsmen

TEST YOUR KNOWLEDGE - UNIT 2

1. What are some of the advantages of working in graphic communications?
2. List the categories of jobs in graphic communications. Briefly describe each.
3. Name three sources of information about graphic arts occupations.
4. Many of the jobs in graphic arts are listed and described in _____ _____ _____ _____.
5. In addition to information found in books, you can write to _____ and _____ asking for specific information about job opportunities.

THINGS TO DO

1. Prepare a list of occupations that have been made possible directly or indirectly by the graphic arts industries.
2. Invite a speaker from the State Employment Office to discuss, with your graphic arts class, employment opportunities in the local graphic arts industries.
3. Study the Help Wanted columns in daily papers for two weeks. Prepare a list of the graphic arts jobs available, the salaries offered and the minimum requirements for securing the positions. Also list how often additional benefits, such as insurance and hospitalization, are mentioned.
4. Secure job applications from various nearby and local industries. Summarize the information they request.
5. Study the information on the graphic arts occupations in the government publication, OCCUPATIONAL OUTLOOK HANDBOOK. Summarize the information and make it available to your class.
6. Contact engineering societies and arrange to borrow a few of their films on the engineering profession.
7. Prepare a list of the graphic communication industries within a specified area and classify them according to the types of graphic arts work they perform. What graphic arts occupations are represented?
8. Have a representative from the employment office of a large printing firm discuss with your class what the company expects from its workers.
9. Visit a local printing plant or newspaper and observe employees at work. Prepare a list of the different occupations that were observed.

Unit 3
GENERAL SAFETY

Objectives

This unit emphasizes the importance of developing safe work habits.

After reading it you will be aware of the precautions you must take when working and studying in the graphic arts lab. You will learn how to dress, how to handle chemicals, how to use the machines and what to do when accidents do happen.

Graphic communications labs are designed to be as safe as possible. Even so, machines and tools can cause serious injury if you are not careful. Safety, then, becomes a full time concern. While working in the lab, you are responsible not only for your own safety but also for the wellbeing of persons working around you.

If you work at it, safety becomes a habit. Part of working safely is never taking chances; the penalty for an unsafe moment may be permanent injury.

GENERAL SAFETY RULES

The first safety rule should be to observe the safety rules drawn up by the instructors. They are concerned about your safety too.

Safety will be stressed throughout your experience in the graphic arts. So too, will safety be stressed throughout your textbook. You will be reminded of safety practices whenever you become engaged in an activity or process that presents some potential hazard. However, certain safety practices are basic to all graphic arts activity. Study them well and observe them.

PROPER DRESS

Dress properly for the job. Avoid loose fitting clothing. Keep sleeves rolled up. Remove ties, rings and other jewelry.

An apron or snug-fitting shop coat will protect clothing. Wear approved safety glasses.

BEHAVIOR

The graphic arts lab is not a safe place for pranks or horseplay. Tricks and mischief can be dangerous for you. They may cause injury to others, as well.

Avoid running in the lab. You could stumble or collide with another student who is operating a machine.

IF YOU ARE INJURED

Get prompt attention for cuts, bruises and other injuries. Do this no matter how minor the injury seems to be. Report all accidents to your teacher. None are so trivial as to be ignored.

USING SOLVENTS AND CHEMICALS

Grease and solvent-soaked cleaning rags ignite easily and burn rapidly. Dispose of them in safety containers furnished for that purpose, Fig. 3-1. Never store them in your locker.

Many solvents and chemicals are used in the graphic arts. Read labels carefully, Fig. 3-2. Use them with care. Know what to do should you spill or splash them on yourself or your clothing.

Wear plastic or rubber gloves when there is danger of getting chemicals on the skin. Make sure the gloves are clean both inside and outside. Check them for cracks or leaks.

Avoid contaminating the outside of chemical bottles. They may be touched later on with the bare hands.

Wash after using chemicals and solvents. You may need to wash your hands several times during some class periods. Protect them by applying a good hand cream after each washing. This helps prevent chapping and cracking that lead to skin problems. Above all, avoid the use of harsh, abrasive

Fig. 3-1. Place solvent-soaked rags and paper in approved metal safety containers. (Eagle Manufacturing Co.)

Fig. 3-2. Read labels on containers before using their contents. Carefully follow those instructions.

Fig. 3-3. Plunger type container stores and dispenses solvents safely. (Eagle Manufacturing Co.)

Fig. 3-4. Wash presses only with an approved cleaning fluid. (Cheney State College)

Fig. 3-5. Return solvents and chemicals to proper storage after use. Be sure doors are kept closed at all times. It is open here to display the special containers designed for safe storage of solvents and chemicals. (Eagle Manufacturing Co.)

soaps. Avoid cuts and abrasions by working carefully around tools and paper.

Use solvents only in well ventilated areas. Where possible, store them in a PLUNGER CAN, Fig. 3-3. Excess fluid drains back into the can. The wire mesh screen acts as a fire baffle against accidental ignition of the can's contents.

Do not wash printing presses with gasoline, Fig. 3-4.

Store solvents and chemicals in metal cabinets, Fig. 3-5. Be sure cabinet doors are closed after the material is stored.

See your instructor before using liquids stored in unmarked containers. Never try to find what is in the can by breathing in the fumes, Fig. 3-6.

Fig. 3-6. Student designed safety poster emphasizes how not to find out what is in an unmarked container.

Wipe up oil, solvents and chemicals spilled on the floor. Slippery floors could cause injury to someone.

MACHINE SAFETY

Machines used in the graphic arts have moving parts. The paper cutter has a very sharp cutting blade, Fig. 3-7. DO NOT USE POWER EQUIPMENT UNTIL:

1. You have been taught how to use it.
2. You have permission from your teacher.
3. All guards and safety devices are in place.

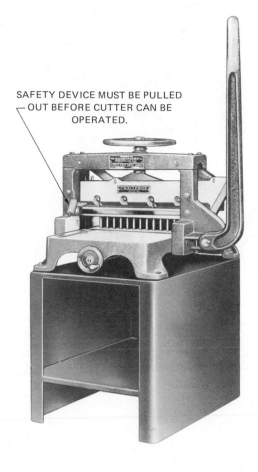

SAFETY DEVICE MUST BE PULLED OUT BEFORE CUTTER CAN BE OPERATED.

Fig. 3-7. Hand operated paper cutter. Safety features require that two hands be used when cutting paper. Only one person should operate a paper cutter at a time. (The Challenge Machinery Co.)

Only one person should use a machine at a time. The confusion that may result when more than one person operates a piece of equipment can cause serious injury.

	PRESSURIZED WATER	LOADED STREAM	CO^2	REGULAR DRY CHEMICAL	ALL USE DRY CHEMICAL
Class A Fires Paper, wood, cloth, etc. Where quenching by water or insulating by general purpose dry chemical is effective	Yes Excellent	Yes Excellent	Small surface fires only	Small surface fires only	Yes Excellent Forms smothering film, prevents reflash
Class B Fires Burning liquids (Gasoline, oils, cooking fats, etc.) where smothering action is required.	No Water will spread fire	Yes Has limited capability	Yes Carbon Dioxide has no residual effects of food or equipment.	Yes Excellent Chemical Smothers fire	Yes Excellent Smothers fire prevents reflash
Class C Fires Fire in live electrical equipment (Motors, switches, appliances, etc.) Where a non-conductive extinguishing agent is required	No Water is a conductor of electricity	No Water is a conductor of electricity	Yes Excellent CO^2 is a non-conductor leaves no residue	Yes Excellent Non-conducting smothering film. Screens operator from heat	Yes Excellent Non-conducting smothering film. Screens operator from heat

Fig. 3-8. Chart shows what fire extinguisher should be used for different types of fires. Know where the fire extinguishers are located in the lab. Learn how to use them.

SLOGANS AND SUCH

Know where the fire extinguishers are located. Be aware of how they are to be used, Fig. 3-8.

Paper can cause bad cuts. Handle it with care.

Keep in mind the following safety slogans:

1. Think before acting.
2. Safety is a full time job.
3. It hurts to get hurt.
4. Remember the ABCs of safety—Always Be Careful.

TEST YOUR KNOWLEDGE - UNIT 3

1. Safety is a _____.
2. How should you dress when working in the graphic arts lab?
3. Avoid running in the lab. You might _____.
4. What should be done about cuts, bruises and burns received in the graphic arts lab?
5. Why should grease, oil, solvents and chemicals be wiped from the floor if spilled?

6. Use solvents only in _____ _____.
7. Rags that are oil or solvent soaked should be stored in:
   a. A metal locker.
   b. Special safety containers.
   c. Metal trash cans.
   d. Any kind of closed container.
8. Avoid operating machines until (list three conditions):

THINGS TO DO

1. Devise an accident prevention program for your school's graphic arts lab.
2. Design a bulletin board on safety in the graphic arts lab.
3. Invite the local fire company to demonstrate the proper way to use the fire extinguishers in the graphic arts lab.
4. Identify the locations of the fire extinguishers in the lab in some noticeable manner.
5. Invite a safety engineer to describe to the class the scope of duties and responsibilities assigned to safety experts in industry.

Unit 4
BASIC PRINTING PROCESSES

Objectives

This unit provides an introduction to the basic printing processes.

After reading it you will understand how the different printing processes reproduce the printed word. You will also be able to describe the characteristics that distinguish each of the processes.

Transferring an image from one material to another material is called printing. This process plays an essential role in visual communications, Fig. 4-1.

Printed matter is produced by eight basic processes.
1. Relief printing.
2. Planographic printing.
3. Intaglio printing.
4. Stencil printing.
5. Photographic printing.
6. Heat transfer printing.
7. Xerographic printing.
8. Ink Jet printing.

Each process will be described in more detail in later units. All except ink jet printing (at the present time) can produce printed matter in single colors and in full color. The first three methods account for most printed matter produced each year.

RELIEF PRINTING

Relief printing is also called LETTERPRESS, Fig. 4-2. The printing surface is raised above the nonprinting surface. Those parts of the raised surface which reproduce words are called type. Parts which reproduce drawings or photographs are called ENGRAVINGS or CUTS. See Fig. 4-3.

Fig. 4-1. The United States alone prints more than a half billion books each year. Without printing there would be few books, newspapers or colorful packaging. Not many people would be able to read and write. These are only a few of the products that rely on printing.

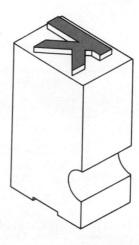

Fig. 4-2. In relief printing, the printing surface is raised above the nonprinting areas. This is shown on piece of foundry type.

33

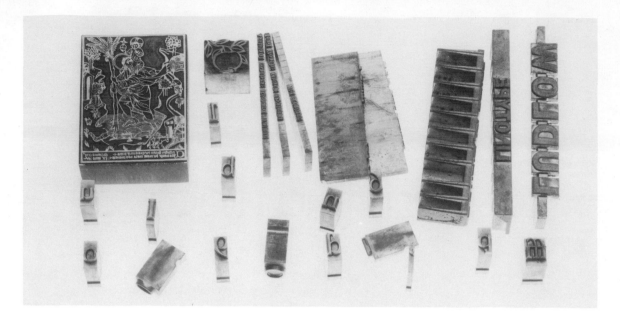

Fig. 4-3. Hand set type has single letter on each piece. Machine type has whole words or lines on one piece. Illustrations for relief printing, upper left, are made by a photographic and chemical technique. Chemicals eat away area which will not print.

Fig. 4-4. Rubber stamp prints from raised surface like metal type.

Ink is put on the raised surface during printing. It is then transferred to the paper. The printing plate or form holding the printing surface is also called the IMAGE CARRIER. A rubber stamp, Fig. 4-4, is a familiar example of relief printing. The image carrier is mounted on a wooden handle.

Many newspapers and magazines are printed by letterpress. They may use metal image carriers. See Fig. 4-5.

PLANOGRAPHIC PRINTING

The planographic process prints from a flat surface, Fig. 4-6. There is a good chance that the work sheets and test

Fig. 4-5. This metal half cylinder is called a stereotype plate. It is used in printing many newspapers and magazines. Notice how the printing surfaces are raised above the nonprinting areas.

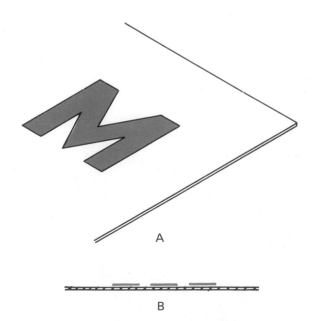

Fig. 4-6. Planographic printing is done from a flat surface. Printing area is not raised above nonprinting area. A—Top view. B—Edge view.

papers you use in school were printed by a planographic process called SPIRIT DUPLICATING, Fig. 4-7. The image is placed on the surface of a DUPLICATOR MASTER SHEET.

Fig. 4-7. Many of your test papers and work sheets are printed on a spirit duplicator. (Standard Duplicating Machine Corp.)

Another of the planographic printing processes is known as LITHOGRAPHY or OFFSET. The term OFFSET is most often used. It is so called because the image is first received by a blanket and transfers to the sheet to be printed. This book was produced by offset.

Offset printing is based on the fact that grease and water do not readily mix. Printing is done from thin metal, paper or plastic plates, Fig. 4-8. The image or printing area is usually put on the plate by a photochemical process.

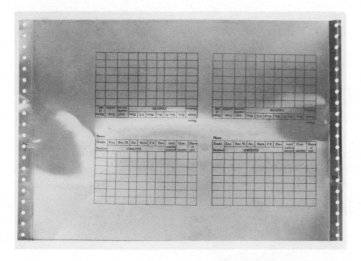

Fig. 4-8. This thin metal plate is used as an image carrier in offset printing. The darkened areas are ink receptive.

The image area on the plate is processed so the greasy ink sticks to it but water runs off. It "receives ink but repels water." The nonimage area of the plate is processed to pick up

and hold water but not ink. Thus, it is said to "be receptive to water but repels ink." Ink will not adhere (stick) to the nonprinting area while that area is covered with a thin film of moisture.

The offset press, Fig. 4-9, maintains a balance between water and ink. This insures that only the image area will print.

Fig. 4-9. Offset press. Note flat printing plate and blanket cylinder. (Fairchild-Davidson Div., Fairchild Camera and Instrument Corp.)

INTAGLIO PRINTING

In intaglio printing, the image area is below the area that does not print. See Fig. 4-10. Ink is applied to the entire surface of the printing form. It also fills in the recessed image

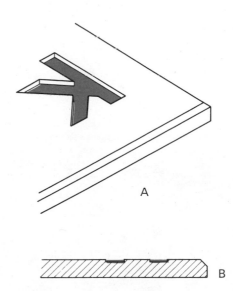

Fig. 4-10. Intaglio printing is the opposite of relief printing. The image being printed is below the nonprinting areas. A—Top view. B—Edge view shows depressed image areas.

area. However, ink is removed from the nonprinting area as it is wiped or scraped by a thin, sharp blade called a DOCTOR KNIFE, Fig. 4-11. When paper is pressed against the printing form, it picks up the ink remaining in the recessed image area. Thus, the image is left (printed) on the paper.

Gravure is the term used when photography and a chemical process are used to make the recessed image area. Many newspaper inserts and catalogs are produced by this method, Fig. 4-13.

Fig. 4-13. These are a few of the more familiar products printed by the gravure process.

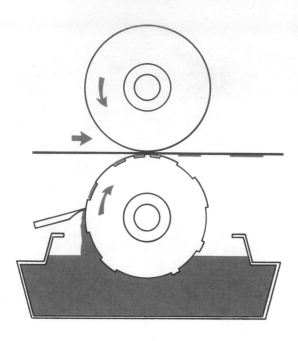

Fig. 4-11. Doctor knife removes ink from nonprinting areas of a gravure cylinder.

GRAVURE is another name for intaglio. Intaglio has come to mean that the image area is made by engraving, etching or scratching. Our paper money and some stamps are made by this technique, Fig. 4-12.

STENCIL PRINTING

In stencil printing, the lettering or design to be printed is cut out of thin material (sheet metal, plastic or paper). Ink or paint is then forced through the cut-away portion onto the material being printed. See Fig. 4-14, for stencil printing in its simplest form.

Fig. 4-12. Paper money and some stamps are printed by the intaglio process.   (Bureau of Printing and Engraving)

been mechanized as shown in Fig. 4-16. Objects of varied shapes can be printed by the screen process technique. A few of them are shown in Fig. 4-17.

Fig. 4-14. Stencil printing in its simplest form. Paint or ink is brushed or sprayed through a design cut in stiff paper.

SCREEN PRINTING is another form of stencil printing. It is also known as SILKSCREEN PRINTING, SCREEN PROCESS and SCREEN PROCESS PRINTING. A hand cut or photographically prepared film stencil is adhered (stuck) to a screen mounted on a frame. The screen may be make of silk, dacron, nylon, polyester or stainless steel wire mesh. Printing is done by forcing special paints through the cut-away image area. A SQUEEGEE is used, Fig. 4-15. Screen printing has also

Fig. 4-15. Screen printing is done by forcing special paints through the cutaway image area using a squeegee. The material in which the design has been cut is attached to a fine mesh screen of fabric or metal.

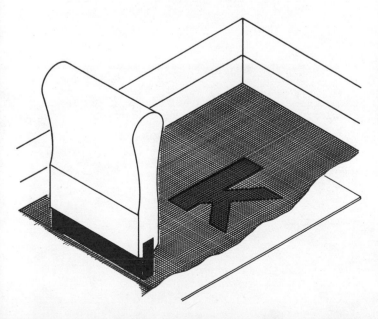

Fig. 4-16. Screen printing is mechanized with a screen printing press. (American Screen Printing Equipment Co.)

Fig. 4-17. Screen printing works well on uneven surfaces and products having irregular shapes.

PHOTOGRAPHIC PRINTING

A photograph is a picture drawn with light rays. The process requires a CAMERA, FILM and a LIGHT SOURCE, Fig. 4-18. Chemicals are needed to bring out the image on the

Fig. 4-18. Equipment needed to take a photograph.

the exposed film is removed from the camera, Fig. 4-20. Photography is important to the graphic arts. Most printing processes would be very limited without it.

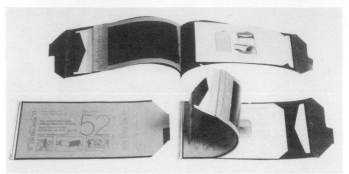

film. This is known as developing. The film is called a NEGATIVE. It is the opposite of a black and white photograph. Dark areas print white while clear areas print dark. More processing is needed to make a POSITIVE print (picture) of the image, Fig. 4-19.

In photographic processing, a series of carefully controlled steps produce a print. However, there is a rapid photographic process that can produce a black and white print in 15 seconds. A color print needs 60 seconds. Timing starts when

Fig. 4-20. Top. This camera develops its own pictures. Bottom. Black and white prints can be made in 15 seconds. Color prints require slightly more time. (Polaroid Corp.)

Fig. 4-19. A strip of negatives and a positive print made from one of them.

HEAT TRANSFER PRINTING

Heat transfer or sublimation printing is not a new process. However, not until recently has the technique grown rapidly. Today, heat transfer printing is used to print fabrics.

Have you ever used a pressing iron to print a novelty design on your T-shirt, Fig. 4-21? If so, you have used heat transfer printing.

Fig. 4-21. An example of heat transfer printing. Hot iron causes inks to become a gas and form image on cloth.

Modern heat transfer printing starts with a special ink and, in some cases, special paper. The design or pattern is printed on the paper usually by a gravure process. The paper can be a special thermoprinting type, film coated paper, or a ground wood, clay coated type. Use either sheet or roll stock.

The dried, printed image is placed over the cloth and heat is applied. At about 350 deg. F (199 C) the ink goes from a solid to a vapor (sublimates). This causes the dyes to go into the fibers of the cloth and color them.

A heat transfer printing machine is shown in Fig. 4-22. It is capable of printing 3281 ft. (1000 m) of cloth per hour. A skilled operator is needed to supervise and adjust the machine.

XEROGRAPHY

Xerography (pronounced ze-rog'-ra-fee) prints from dry materials. No fluids are used. The process uses an electrostatic charge (stationary electric charge) to duplicate an original written, drawn or printed image, Fig. 4-23.

Xerography is based on the principle that like electrical charges repel and unlike charges attract, Fig. 4-24.

Fig. 4-23. Xerography is a dry printing process. (Van Dyk Research Corp.)

Fig. 4-22. A heat transfer printing machine. Design is printed on continuous roll of cloth. (Herbert Kannegiesser Corp.)

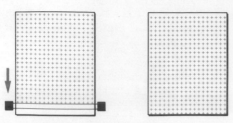

A. LIGHT-SENSITIVE PLATE OR DRUM BECOMES ELECTRI-CALLY CHARGED AS IT PASSES UNDER WIRES. PLUS MARKS REPRESENT POSITIVE CHARGES.

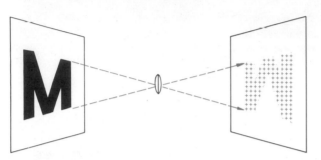

B. IMAGE PROJECTED THROUGH LENS ONTO CHARGED PLATE. CHARGES REMAIN IN IMAGE AREA BUT ARE DRAINED AWAY WHERE LIGHT STRIKES.

 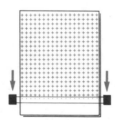

C. NEGATIVELY CHARGED TONER OR DRY INK STICKS TO THE IMAGE AREA.

D. PAPER RECEIVES POSITIVE CHARGE FROM PLATE.

PAPER

SELENIUM PLATE

E. POSITIVELY CHARGED PAPER PICKS UP TONER FROM PLATE.

F. HEAT FUSES IMAGE TO SURFACE OF PAPER.

Fig. 4-24. Sequence followed in xerographic printing.   (Xerox Corp.)

The xerographic process makes a copy exactly duplicating the original. It is clean and dry. The copy can be enlarged or decreased in size if desired. Full color copies can be made on color copying xerographic machines.

The main use of xerographic printing is to make inexpensive duplicate copies. However, offset printing plates can also be made by this process.

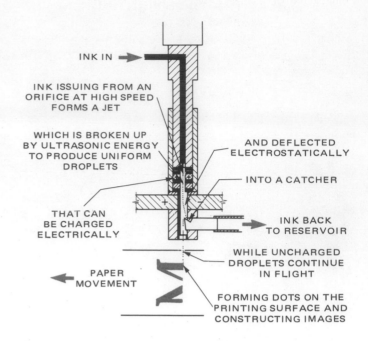

INK IN

INK ISSUING FROM AN ORIFICE AT HIGH SPEED FORMS A JET

WHICH IS BROKEN UP BY ULTRASONIC ENERGY TO PRODUCE UNIFORM DROPLETS

AND DEFLECTED ELECTROSTATICALLY

INTO A CATCHER

THAT CAN BE CHARGED ELECTRICALLY

INK BACK TO RESERVOIR

PAPER MOVEMENT

WHILE UNCHARGED DROPLETS CONTINUE IN FLIGHT

FORMING DOTS ON THE PRINTING SURFACE AND CONSTRUCTING IMAGES

Fig. 4-25. Printing head of the ink jet printing system. It is the newest of the printing processes.   (Mead Digital Systems, Inc.)

MEAD DIJIT IMAGE SYSTEM

A Demonstration of its Flexibility

Store on-line up to **8 Fonts** of 255 characters each

FONT 1: 7 X 12 Matrix, medium & **bold** face

FONT 2: 12 PT. Archer, medium & **bold** face

FONT 3: 18 PT. Archer, medium & **bol**

FONT 4: 36 PT.

FONT 5: One of several available bar codes.

FONT 6: Other special character sets, including

FONT 7: jumbo numerals and rotated alphanumerics

FONT 8: are also available.

Fig. 4-26. Samples of work produced by the ink jet process. Both characters and line images can be printed. It is a non-contact printing process. No type or printing plates touch the paper.
(Mead Digital Systems, Inc.)

INK JET PRINTING

Ink jet printing, Fig. 4-25, is a non-contact printing process. No printing surfaces such as type, plates made by photographic means, or film are needed.

Copy to be printed is prepared by computer. A minicomputer in the ink jet printer controls ink jets in the printing head. On command, microscopic droplets of ink emerge from the jets to print characters and images, Fig. 4-26.

The printing head is a series of single jets, Fig. 4-27. Up to 1280 jets spaced at 0.0083 in. are in the printing head.

The ink droplets are created in the system. They are either permitted to impact on the moving web of paper, or are deflected into a reservoir when no printing is desired. Deflected ink is reused. Printing is done in one pass of the paper under the ink jets.

The process, as developed by one company, is known as DIJIT (Direct Image by Jet Ink Transfer). However, the most common name for it appears to be ink jet printing. Its greatest use is in direct mail printing, personalized book publishing and addressing systems.

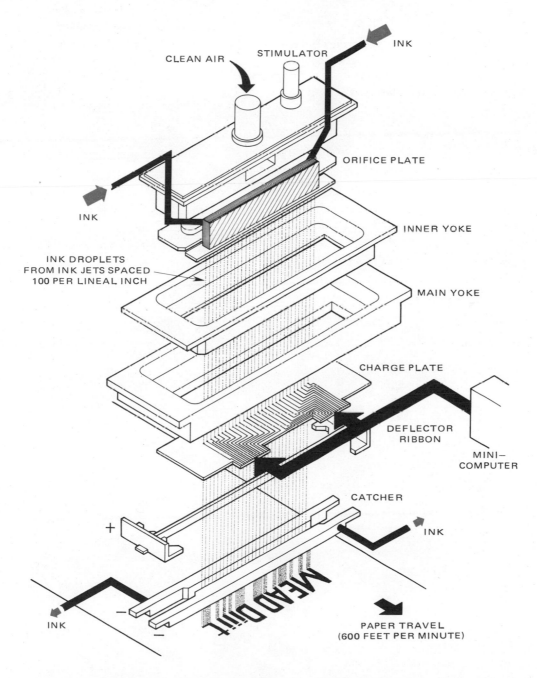

Fig. 4-27. A generalization of how the ink jet printing process works. Ink is forced through tiny jets that are located one-eighth to 1/4 in. above the paper web that travels at 600 feet per minute. Each jet and droplet is controlled by a mini-computer. (Mead Digital Systems, Inc.)

TEST YOUR KNOWLEDGE - UNIT 4

1. List the eight basic printing processes. Describe each briefly.
2. A rubber stamp is an example of _____ printing.
3. What type of printing is based on the principle that grease and water do not readily mix?
4. What printing process is employed in the printing of paper money?
5. In the _____ process, ink or paint is forced through a thin material where the image area has been cut away.
6. A _____ is a picture that has been drawn with light.
7. What printing process is often used to print fabric?
8. The printing process that is based on the principle that like electrical charges repel and unlike charges attract is called _____.
9. What printing process uses a thin flat metal, paper or plastic plate?
10. The process is also known as _____ and _____ printing.

THINGS TO DO

1. Collect examples of the eight basic printing processes. Label each example.
2. Visit a small local print shop. What printing processes are used in the shop? Ask the printer to give you samples of work that might be done on a typical day.
3. Construct a large model of a piece of type.
4. Display an example of a T-shirt on which the design has been printed by the heat transfer printing process.
5. Secure an example of a full-color illustration duplicated on a xerographic color copying machine.
6. Gather material on the seven basic printing processes for the graphic arts lab's technical reference file.
7. Get copies of printing magazines like GRAPHIC ARTS BUYER, INLAND PRINTER or PRINTING IMPRESSIONS. Look them over. Mark with paper clips articles that relate to work being done in the school's graphic arts lab.

Unit 5
RELIEF PRINTING

Objectives

This unit describes the materials, tools and processes involved in printing from a raised surface.

After reading it you will be able to describe and do such operations as hand typesetting, imposition (assembly) of copy, makeready, press operation, press maintenance and block printing. You will also understand the processes that produce machine set type, line and halftone illustrations, electrotypes and stereotypes.

In relief printing, a raised surface transfers images from a metal, plastic or rubber printing form onto the material being printed. See Fig. 5-1.

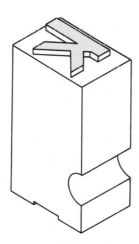

Fig. 5-1. Relief printing is done from a raised surface. The nonprinting area of a piece of type is below the printing surface.

Because nonprinting portions of the form are lower, they do not pick up ink. Likewise, being lower, they do not touch the surface being printed.

Most relief printing surfaces are made by pouring molten (hot, liquified) metal into a suitable mold. The mold cavity (hole) has a reverse image of a single type character as shown in Fig. 5-2. Other metal and plastic relief printing surfaces are made by an etching process that eats away the nonprinting surface.

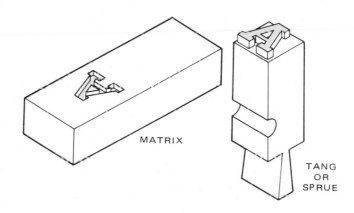

Fig. 5-2. The mold cavity has a reverse image of a single type character.

Whenever type is assembled into words or sentences it is called COMPOSITION. Setting type by pouring molten metal into a mold is called HOT METAL COMPOSITION.

When the type characters (FOUNDRY TYPE and MONO-TYPE) are set by hand, the process is called HAND COMPOSI-TION. When a whole line of characters is cast at one time it is called MACHINE COMPOSITION.

Besides composition, relief printing involves:
1. Imposition. This is the arranging and locking up of typeforms.
2. Presswork. In this process, the press is prepared. The typeform is placed in the press and made ready for printing. Finally, the job is run.
3. Platemaking. This process converts photographs and art-work to relief printing forms. Chemicals and photography are usually used. However, hand tools can be used to make simple printing plates.

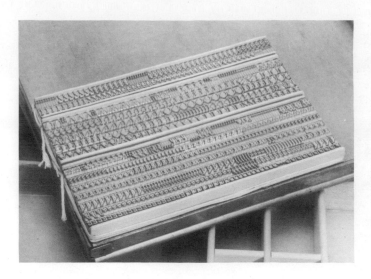

Fig. 5-3. Complete font of 18 point hand set type contains letters, numbers and punctuation marks.

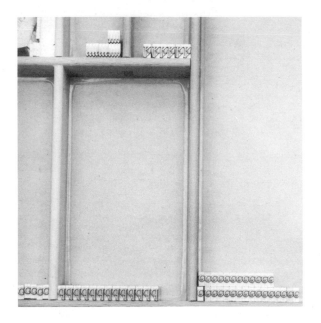

Fig. 5-4. The quantity of each character in a font varies according to how often it is used.

You will learn about all these processes in this unit. Some are too difficult or technical to be attempted at this point. But you will learn to set type by hand and print it on small letter press equipment.

HAND COMPOSITION

Hand set type is cast in metal. Each letter (character) is separate. Manufactured from molten (melted) materials that are allowed to harden in a mold, the type is usually purchased as a "set" which is known as a complete FONT.

A font includes CAPITAL (caps) and LOWER CASE (l.c.) letters and figures of one style and size of type, Fig. 5-3. There are several of each character since the same letters appear over and over again in a printed message. There will be a larger number of some characters such as the letter "e" because it is used more often than a "k", for example. See Fig. 5-4.

These single type characters are assembled in a COMPOSING STICK, Fig. 5-5. After use, the type is DISTRIBUTED or put back into the type case for storage.

MEASURING TYPE

The basic units of the measure in type composition are the POINT and PICA, Fig. 5-6. Twelve points equal one pica. There are about six picas or 72 points to the inch. One point equals .01384 in. (0.35 mm).

1 inch	=	72 points (approximate)
12 points	=	1 pica (exactly)
6 picas	=	1 inch (approximate)
5 1/2 points	=	1 agate (exactly)

Fig. 5-6. Basic units of measurement used in graphic arts are the point and the pica. Inches are also used for large dimensions.

Point and pica measurements are made with a LINE GAUGE, Fig. 5-7. Type sizes are measured in points, Fig. 5-8. There are a number of traditional sizes, Fig. 5-9.

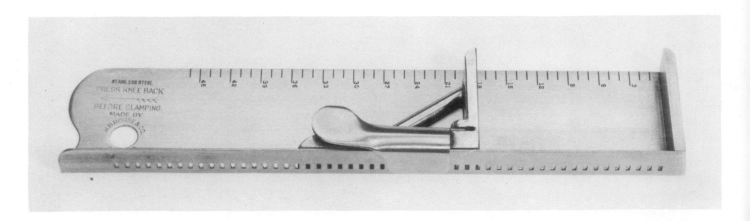

Fig. 5-5. Composing stick has adjustable stop called a knee. Numbers on edge mark length of line in picas.

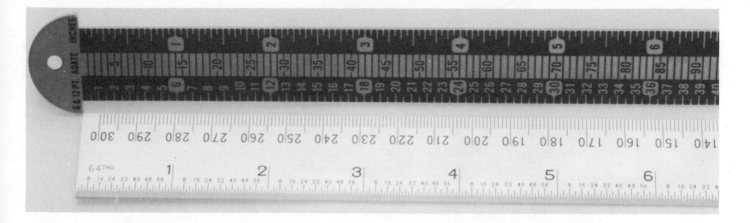

Fig. 5-7. One style of line gauge. Note comparison with English-metric rule.

Fig. 5-8. Type is measured in points. This is a piece of 72 point type. Measurement is always taken on the body of the type as shown.

TEXT or BODY type is used to compose general reading matter. Such type is 12-point or smaller. When larger than 12 points it is called DISPLAY type. The parts of a type character are shown in Fig. 5-10.

METRIC MEASURE

Foundry and hot type are not expected to change to the SI metric system. It is likely that the point system will remain in use for relief printing. Type height, 0.918 in., will simply convert to 23.32 mm.

CLASSIFYING TYPE

A complete range of sizes in one type style is called a SERIES, Fig. 5-11. Two or more series of a typeface having similar characteristics are known as a FAMILY of type, Fig. 5-12. A type family has the same name. They are of the same basic design. However, each of the type series that make up the family varies slightly. Different type faces, as long as they are in the same family, can be used together in a LAYOUT. They will produce a pleasing and harmonious design.

Typefaces are grouped into several easily identified classes, each class has a name, as shown in Fig. 5-13.

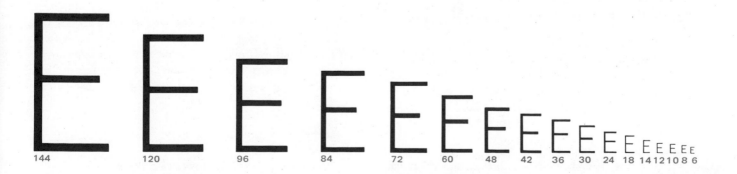

Fig. 5-9. Type is made in several traditional sizes.

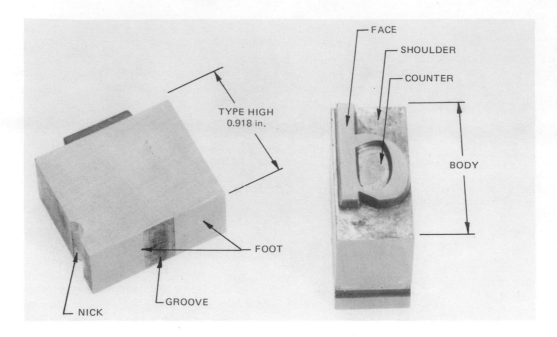

Fig. 5-10. Parts of a piece of foundry type.

6 ABCDEFGHIJKLMNOPQRSTUVWXYZABCDEFG
8 ABCDEFGHIJKLMNOPQRSTUVWXYZ
10 ABCDEFGHIJKLMNOPQRSTU
12 ABCDEFGHIJKLMNOPQR
14 ABCDEFGHIJKLMNOP
18 ABCDEFGHIJKLM
24 ABCDEFGHI
30 ABCDEFG
42 ABCDE
48 ABCD
60 ABC

Fig. 5-11. A complete size range of one type face style is called a series.

THE CALIFORNIA JOB CASE

Foundry type is stored in a shallow drawer called a California job case. It is divided into three main sections each having a number of smaller compartments. The case holds an entire font of one size and style of type, Fig. 5-14. Each type character has its own compartment. The LAY OF THE CASE

Helvetica Light
Helvetica Light Italic
Helvetica Medium
Helvetica Bold
Helvetica Med. Italic
Helvetica Bold It.
 Helvetica Med. Outline

Fig. 5-12. Two or more series having similar characteristics are known as a family of type.

refers to the location of each letter, figure, punctuation mark and space in the case, Fig. 5-15.

The right third of the case holds CAPITAL LETTERS. Capital letters are also called UPPER CASE letters.

The other two-thirds of the case stores LOWER CASE letters, figures, punctuation marks, LIGATURES, spaces and quads. A ligature is one piece of type, Fig. 5-16, having more than one type character on it. Lower case letters are stored according to how often they are used. Often-used characters are grouped together.

There are many styles of typecases. Special cases are designed to hold:
1. Type fonts that have no lower case letters.
2. Fonts make up of caps and small caps of the same type style and body size, Fig. 5-17.
3. Cuts (plates used in printing illustrations).

PACK MY BOX WITH FIVE|
Pack my box with five dozen|123
OLDSTYLE (GOUDY OLDSTYLE)

PACK MY BOX WIT|
Pack my box wit|123
MODERN (CRAW MODERN)

PACK MY BOX WITH FIVE|
Pack my box with five|1234
SQUARE SERIF (STYMIE MEDIUM)

PACK MY BOX WITH FIVE DOZ|
Pack my box with five dozen|123
SANS SERIF (LYDIAN)

Pack My Box With Five Dozen | *1234*
CURSIVE OR SCRIPT (LYDIAN CURSIVE)

Pack My Box With Five D|123
TEXT OR OLD ENGLISH (CLOISTER BLACK)

Pack My Box With Five|123
OCCASIONAL OR DECORATIVE (MURRAY HILL BOLD)

Fig. 5-13. Seven classes of type with a face representative of each class.

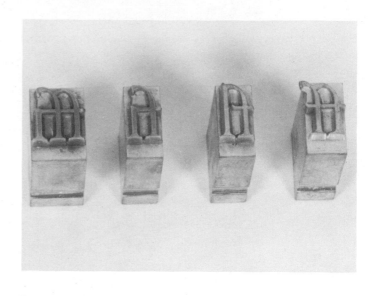

Fig. 5-16. Ligatures contain several narrow letters on one piece of type.

LEADERSHIP

Fig. 5-17. Small caps have the same face style and are on the same size body as caps, but are smaller than regular capital letters.

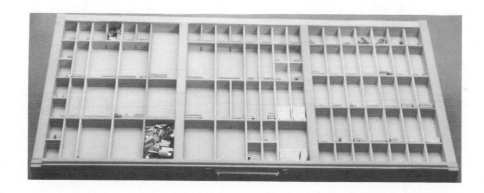

Fig. 5-14. The case is laid out to hold an entire font of one size and style of type.

Fig. 5-15. The lay of the case refers to the location of the letters, figures and spaces in the case.

ffi	fl	5-EM	4-EM	⌐	k		1	2	3	4	5	6	7	8		$	¢		[	]	(	)
j													ff	9								
	b	c	d	e		i	s	f	g		fi	0		A	B	C	D	E	F	G		
?																					
!															H	I	K	L	M	N	O	
	l	m	n	h		o	y	p	w		EN Quads	EM Quads									
z																					
x								;	:		2-EM and 3-EM Quads		P	Q	R	S	T	V	W		
q	v	u	t	3-EM Spaces		a	r	.	-				X	Y	Z	J	U	&	ffl		

Type cases are stored in TYPE BANKS, Fig. 5-18. Locate the case you plan to use. See Fig. 5-19 for proper removal. After sliding out the typecase, place it on the slanted top of the type bank, Fig. 5-20.

Be sure it is held by the rail on the top of the bank before you let go of the typecase. Take your time. Can you imagine the work needed to clean (put the type back where it belongs) a case that has been PIED (spilled)?

SPACING MATERIALS

The lines of text in this book are known as SOLID MATTER. Usually, when solid matter is composed, each line is set flush (even) on both margins. See Fig. 5-21. Each line must, therefore, be exactly the same length. Each must fit snugly in the composing stick. This is accomplished by JUSTIFICATION. A line is justified by increasing or decreasing the size of spaces between words.

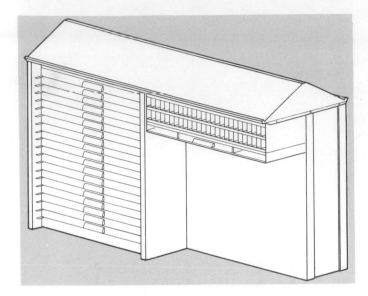

Fig. 5-18. Typecases are stored in type banks.

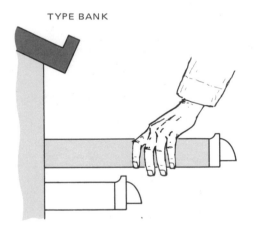

Fig. 5-19. Before removing a typecase from the bank, pull out the typecase just below it about 6 inches. It will support the typecase you plan to use if it should slip from your grasp while it is being withdrawn.

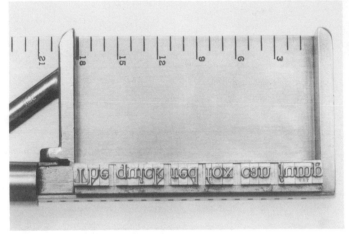

Fig. 5-21. Type set flush to both margins is said to be "justified."

Quads and Spaces

Quads and spaces are pieces of metal used for justification. Being shorter than type, they do not print. See Fig. 5-22 to compare sizes. Spaces are thinner than quads.

The EM QUAD is square in any size of type. It is the basic unit for other spaces and quads. Paragraphs are indented with quads. They are used to fill in blank space at the end of a paragraph.

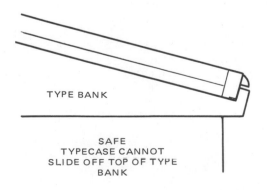

SAFE
TYPECASE CANNOT
SLIDE OFF TOP OF TYPE
BANK

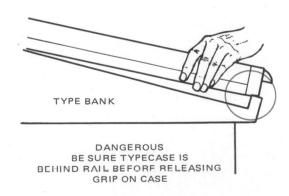

DANGEROUS
BE SURE TYPECASE IS
BEHIND RAIL BEFORE RELEASING
GRIP ON CASE

Fig. 5-20. Make certain the typecase is caught behind the rail on the top of the type bank.

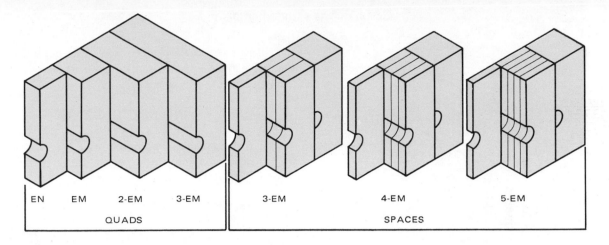

Fig. 5-22. Spaces are thinner pieces than quads. See how they compare in size. Note that a 3-em space is one-third of an em wide but a 3-em quad is 3-ems wide.

Line length determines how many quads to indent a paragraph. An em quad or a 2-em quad will do for most jobs, Fig. 5-23.

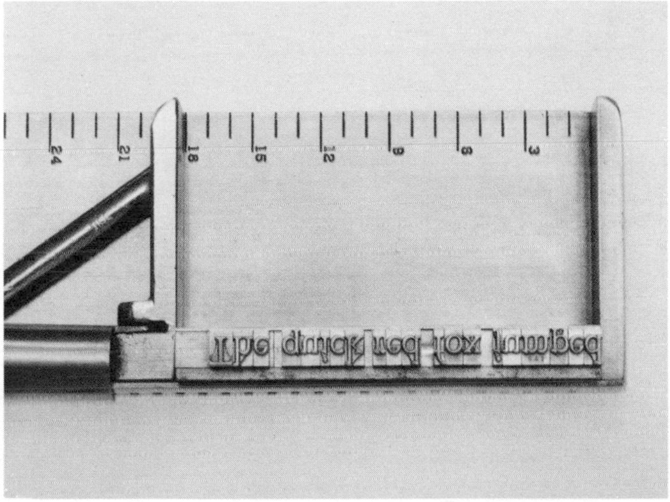

Fig. 5-23. Type size determines the number of ems to indent a paragraph. This line is indented 1-em.

The EN QUAD is half the thickness of the em quad. It is the spacing used between words set in all capital letters.

A 3-EM SPACE is one-third as thick as an em quad. It is normally the spacing used between words set in lowercase letters. If the last word does not fill the composing stick, expand the line by removing the 3-em space and substitute a combination of 4-EM and 5-EM SPACES. HAIR SPACES are thin pieces of copper and brass. They are also used to space out and justify a line of type. Each California job case contains a full set of spaces and quads, Fig. 5-24.

Leads and Slugs

Leads and slugs are metal strips placed between lines of type to add space. Leads are thinner being 1 and 2 points thick. Slugs are generally 6 points thick. See Fig. 5-25. A cutter, Fig. 5-26, is used to cut any length slug needed.

DEMON CHARACTERS

The demon characters are letters, figures and punctuation marks that look alike. Since type is set and read upside down,

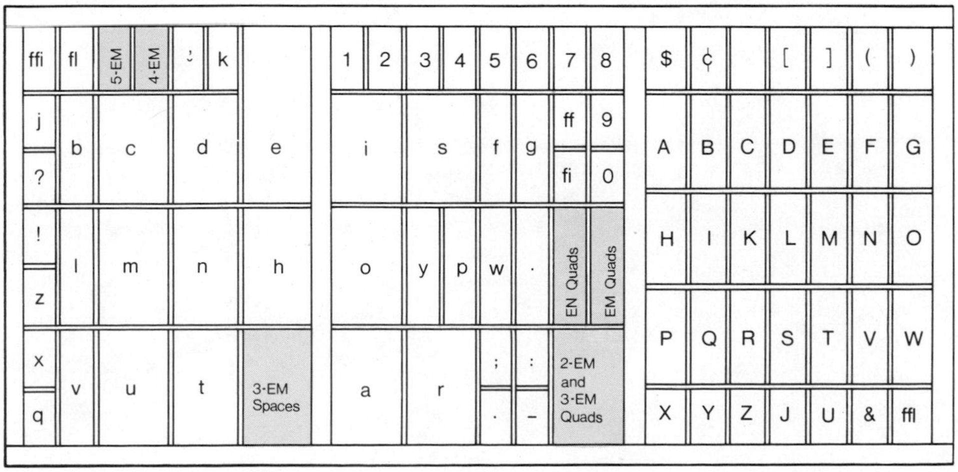

ffi	fl	5-EM	4-EM	·	k		1	2	3	4	5	6	7	8		$	¢		[	]		(	)
j	b	c	d	e			i	s	f	g		ff	9		A	B	C	D	E	F	G
?												fi	0								
!	l	m	n	h			o	y	p	w	·	EN Quads	EM Quads		H	I	K	L	M	N	O
z																					
x	v	u	t	3-EM Spaces			a	r	;	:	2-EM and 3-EM Quads		P	Q	R	S	T	V	W
q										·	−			X	Y	Z	J	U	&	ffl

Fig. 5-24. The California job case has special compartments for quads and spaces.

49

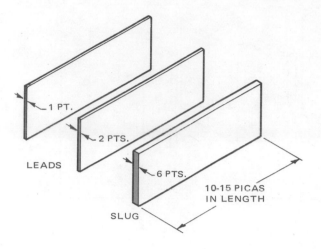

Fig. 5-25. Leads and slug are thin and thick line spacing materials.

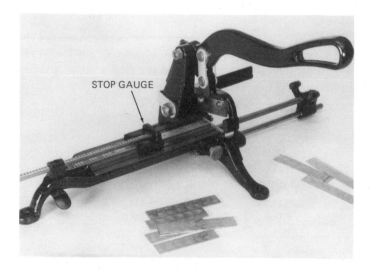

Fig. 5-26. Lead and slug cutter. Stop gauge is adjustable.

the demon characters may cause the printer confusion. Carefully study Fig. 5-27 so you will become familiar with how they look as they are set.

HAND SETTING TYPE

The first step in hand composition is to decide the line length. Adjust the composing stick to the correct pica setting. See Fig. 5-28.

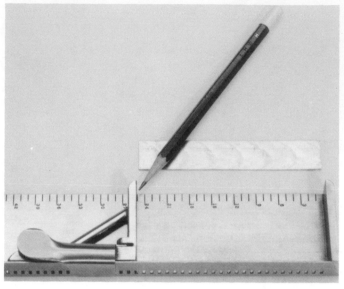

Fig. 5-28. Adjust composing stick to desired pica setting. The piece of metal shown is a slug. It will be placed in the stick to support the type. Pencil points to line length setting of 25 pica.

Secure a slug the same length as the stick setting. Place it in the stick up against the closed side.

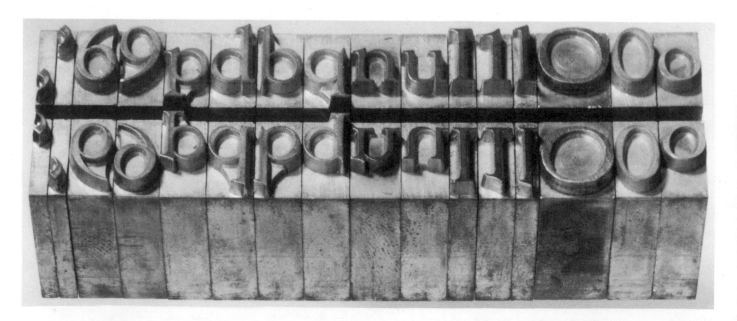

Fig. 5-27. Demon type characters. The type characters at bottom are shown as they look when set in the stick. Upper line shows how demon characters will print.

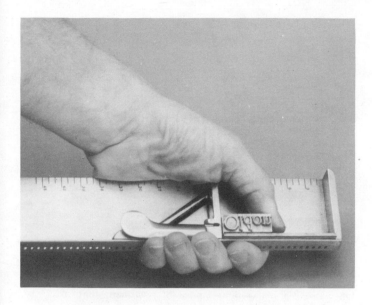

Fig. 5-29. Hold the type in the stick with your thumb.

Fig. 5-30. Set type with the type faces up and the nicks toward the open side of the stick.

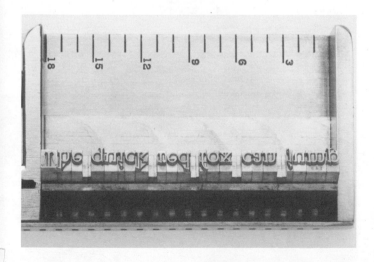

Fig. 5-31. A properly justified line of type when tipped at an angle, will not fall over or become misaligned.

Holding the stick as shown in Fig. 5-29, begin to set type. Arrange the type in the stick from left to right. The faces should be up and the nicks toward the open side of the stick. See Fig. 5-30. The thumb is pressed against the last piece to prevent the type from falling over.

JUSTIFYING TYPE

Each line of type must be justified before the next line is set. Add spacing as described under *Quads and spaces,* this unit. Check line snugness by placing the stick on a level surface. Then tip the justified line, Fig. 5-31. It should be tight enough to keep itself in this position but still loose enough so it can be moved back as one unit.

DIVIDING WORDS

There are times when a word must be divided at the end of a line. Divide a word only between syllables as recommended in a dictionary. Place a hyphen after the syllable break at the end of the line. The rest of the word is set on the next line.

Avoid hyphenating more than two successive lines. Single syllable words cannot be divided. There is no space between a syllable and the hyphen. There is no space between a word and a punctuation mark.

SPACING TYPE

Spacing is placed around printing for better appearance and to make it easier to read. It is used in several situations.

1. LINE SPACING puts distance between lines of type. Body type is referred to as being set solid or having one or more points of spacing. Thickness of the spacing depends upon the space available in the layout and the size of the type. The larger the type or the wider the line the more space must be placed between lines. See Fig. 5-32.

This body of type is set solid. This means that no leading (space) has been inserted between lines. Type may be set solid if the line length is not too long. There is a small amount of space between the lines because the foundry type characters are placed on a body which is somewhat larger than the type.

This sample has one point of leading. A 1 point lead has been placed between the lines. Leading adds white space in printing making the type appear lighter and more airy. If lines are longer, the added space makes for easier reading. Does this copy seem easier or harder to read than the copy set solid?

In this paragraph, a 2 point lead has been placed between lines. This book has been set in 10 pt. type with two points of leading. Even more space can be placed between lines, particularly if the width (measure) is greater. However there is a limit to the width a line should be. Long lines tend to be hard to read.

Fig. 5-32. Line spacing adds white space between printed lines.

2. LETTER SPACING puts space between individual letters. This may be done for better appearance. Words set in capital letters may need to be letter spaced to make them appear to be evenly spaced, Fig. 5-33. Letter-spaced words must have additional space between them or they will seem to run together.

WALTER
AS ORIGINALLY SET. NO SPACING BETWEEN LETTERS

WALTER
LETTERS SPACED.

Fig. 5-33. Letter spacing type makes letters appear to be evenly spaced.

3. WORD SPACING is done to make type more readable or to make lines justify. Normally a 3-em space is placed between words. If the line will not justify, more or less space can be used.

CENTERING LINES OF TYPE

Some printing must be centered in the stick. This is done by placing an equal amount of space material on each side of the line after it has been set. (Work carefully to avoid pied type.) Place thinner space materials near the type. The quads are placed to the outside as shown in Fig. 5-34.

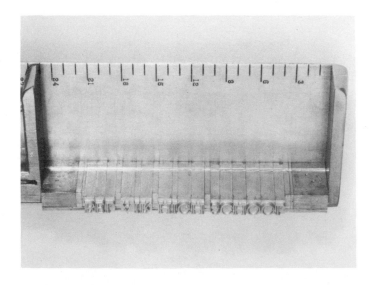

Fig. 5-34. When centering type line, place thinner space material near the type.

DUMPING THE STICK

Until you have acquired some skill, empty your stick after it has become one-half to three-quarters full. Printers call this dumping the stick. Do not forget to place a slug against the last line before dumping.

Place the stick on a GALLEY, Fig. 5-35. Grasp the type as shown in Fig. 5-36. Press the third finger of each hand against the ends. This will prevent pied type.

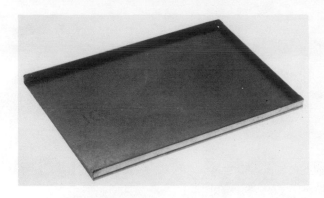

Fig. 5-35. Galley is used for storage of type matter until it can be printed.

Fig. 5-36. When dumping the stick, grasp sides of form with thumbs and forefingers. Press third finger against each end.

Slide the type off the stick onto the galley. Move it to one corner as shown in Fig. 5-37.

After all lines have been composed, the type (or typeform) is ready to be tied. Loose type would pie easily and is hard to handle.

Fig. 5-37. Place type in one corner of galley. Hold it in place with wood or metal blocks called furniture.

TYING

Get a piece of light-weight cord long enough to go around the typeform four or five times. Start at one corner and wrap the cord clockwise around the typeform. Let the first loop overlap the starting end of the cord. This holds the cord in place and frees the left hand to hold the form. Wind the cord tightly around the typeform. Each wrap should be just above the last one.

Tuck the cord end down between the loops and the form. Use a tool called a MAKEUP RULE to do this. Leave a short end exposed above the loops, Fig. 5-38. This will hold the type in place and the cord can be removed easily when the form is readied for printing.

Fig. 5-39. Proof press is inked by hand. Roller at right is pulled over inked form and paper. Small box at left is called an ink plate.

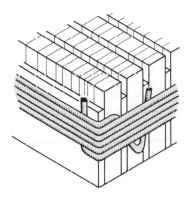

Fig. 5-38. The printer's knot keeps cord tight but can be quickly released by pulling up one end of cord.

PULLING A PROOF

Mistakes and errors can occur no matter how carefully you think you have set the type. These errors must be found because they can change the entire meaning of a word or sentence.

A PROOF must be pulled (taken) to find these errors, or omissions and to discover damaged type. The proof is pulled on a PROOF PRESS, such as the one shown in Fig. 5-39.

Use a BRAYER, Fig. 5-40, to ink the form. The brayer gets a supply of ink from the INK PLATE on the proof press. Roll the ink out evenly with the brayer before transferring it to the typeform.

Position the galley with the inked form at a slight angle on the proof press bed, Fig. 5-41. This will prevent the type from tipping over as the impression cylinder passes over it.

Caution: A metal plate is used with some proof presses to bring cuts up to type height. Be sure this is removed before taking your proof.

Always return the brayer to the ink plate. Be sure it is placed on its feet. This will lift the roller from the plate preventing a flat spot in the roller.

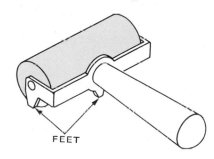

FEET

Fig. 5-40. Brayer is used to ink relief printing forms.

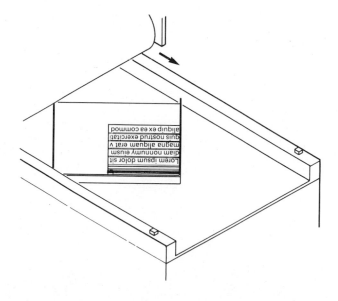

Fig. 5-41. Place galley with inked form at a slight angle on proof press bed. This will prevent type from tipping.

Carefully lay a piece of paper over the inked form. Gently pull the press cylinder over the form to transfer the ink to the paper.

A sloppy proof usually indicates too much ink was used. Surplus ink must be removed from the ink plate. Place a sheet of paper over the ink plate and roll the brayer over it. Re-ink the type and pull another proof.

Clean the form using a cloth dampened in solvent. If there is a great deal of ink on the type, use a soft brush and solvent to remove it. Wipe away surplus solvent with a dry cloth pad. Remove the galley and type from the proof press.

SAFETY PRECAUTIONS

1. Never place type, spaces, leads or slugs in your mouth. They contain a large percentage of lead. You could develop lead poisioning if you swallow enough lead.
2. Never throw type. You might hit someone causing painful injury.
3. Ink and solvent soaked cloths should be placed in a metal safety can. Do not put them in a trash can nor in your locker.

PROOFREADING

Proofreaders compare proofs with the original copy. They then use PROOFREADERS' MARKS, Fig. 5-42. These are a kind of "shorthand" to tell the COMPOSITOR what corrections must be made. (The compositor is the person who sets type.) The proofreading marks are placed on the margin of the copy and in the text. The proof is sent to the COMPOSING ROOM for correction.

Printed matter must have no mistakes. Proofreaders must be very accurate in finding and correcting them. They must compare every word in the proof with the original copy. Punctuation marks, spelling, hyphenated words and spacing must be checked.

After the form is corrected, pull a second proof. This proof must also be checked. Repeat these steps until all corrections are made. Then, the typeform is ready to be printed. It may be stored for later use or placed in the press. Type waiting to be printed is called LIVE MATTER.

CORRECTING HAND-SET TYPE

Correction of errors starts with untying the typeform. Simple corrections can be made right in the galley. This includes changing punctuation marks and letters of the same size — "u" for "n" and "b" for "d", for example.

When a complete word is left out, the line of type must be returned to the composing stick. Corrections of this kind may require rejustifying several lines to get enough room to insert

	PROOFREADERS' MARKS				
∧	INSERT CORRECTION NOTED IN MARGIN	✓/✓	INSERT QUOTATION MARK	∿	UNDER LETTER OR WORD MEANS "BOLD FACE"
✗	DEFECTIVE LETTER	/?/	INSERT QUESTION MARK	○	SPELL OUT (CIRCLE ABBREVIATION)
///	STRAIGHTEN LINE	(!)	INSERT EXCLAMATION POINT	stet.	LET IT STAND, RETAIN
w.f.	WRONG FONT	/=/	INSERT HYPHEN	out s.c.	SEE COPY FOR OMISSION
✓	CORRECT SPACING	(/)	INSERT PARENTHESES	tr.	TRANSPOSE LETTER OR WORD
#	INSERT SPACE	[/]	INSERT BRACKETS	lc.	CHANGE TO LOWER CASE
¶	PARAGRAPH	$\frac{1}{m}$ or $\frac{2}{m}$	1-EM OR 2-EM DASH	caps	CHANGE TO CAPS
⊥	PUSH DOWN SPACE	⌒	CLOSE UP, NO SPACE	s.c.	CHANGE TO SMALL CAPS
⊙	INSERT PERIOD	⌣	LESS SPACE	ital	CHANGE TO ITALICS
,/	INSERT COMMA	[	MOVE WORD OR LETTER LEFT	rom.	CHANGE TO ROMAN LETTERS
:/	INSERT COLON	]	MOVE WORD OR LETTER RIGHT	∿∿	EQUALIZE SPACING
;/	INSERT SEMICOLON	ꝯ	TURN REVERSED LETTER	Qu or?	IS THIS CORRECT?
✓	INSERT APOSTROPHE	ꝺ	TAKE OUT, DELETE		

Fig. 5-42. Proofreaders' marks are symbols every printer understands.

the missing word. Separate the line to be moved from the rest of the lines by placing several slugs on each side.

When all lines have been corrected, return them to the galley in right order. Retie the form and pull another proof.

HOW TO DISTRIBUTE TYPE

When a typeform is to be reprinted it is left STANDING. That is, it is not distributed. However, most jobs must be distributed after they are printed. The typeform, in such cases, is called DEAD MATTER.

Before distribution can begin, type must be cleaned with solvent and returned to a galley. Nick side should be visible, Fig. 5-43. The type must be distributed in the correct type case. To be sure this is done, check the following by comparing pieces of type with those in the case:
1. Type size.
2. Type style.
3. Matching nicks in type body.

Never match type by only one of the above. All three must correspond.

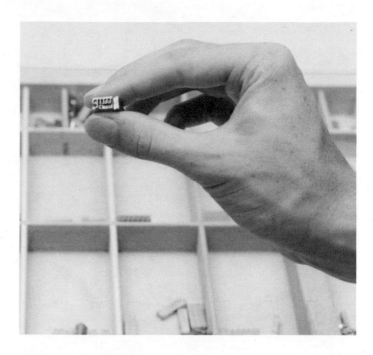

Fig. 5-44. Distribute one word at a time.

As you gain experience it may be easier to distribute several lines at a time, Fig. 5-45. Hold the type in your left hand. Use light pressure on the type to prevent it from dropping. Use the right hand to pick up the type for distribution. If you are left-handed, reverse this procedure.

Fig. 5-43. Return type to the galley nick side up for distribution.

Until you have gained experience, it will be easier to distribute type if the form is left in the galley. Place the galley beside the typecase. Remove one word at a time and distribute it as in Fig. 5-44.

Never throw type back into the case. It can be damaged. Carefully drop the smaller type into their proper compartments. Type sizes 18 point or larger should be placed, not dropped, when it is distributed.

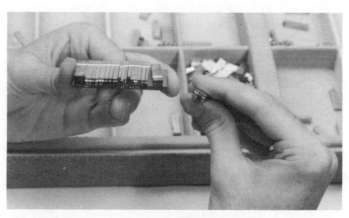

Fig. 5-45. With some experience, it may be easier to remove several lines at a time from the galley. Try to distribute a word or syllable at a time. Mentally spell out the word or syllable as you drop each character.

Distribute all type and space material. Finally, separate the leads and slugs according to thickness and length. Return them to storage, Fig. 5-46.

RULES

Rules are pieces of type metal that print as lines, Fig. 5-47. They can also be used to make up charts as in Fig. 5-48. Rules can be made of type metal or brass and are different widths. A fine line is made with a HAIR LINE RULE which has a body thickness of 2 points, Fig. 5-49. Thicker lines are made with rules having a full face.

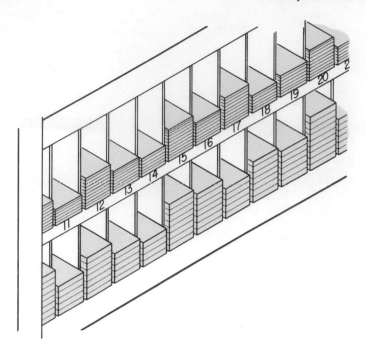

Fig. 5-46. Storage rack separates lead and slug by length and thickness.

LEADERS

Leaders are pieces of type metal in quad body size. Made in many point sizes, they print evenly-spaced dots or short dashes. See Fig. 5-50.

To test your knowledge of hand composition, refer to Test Questions 4 through 29 at the end of this unit.

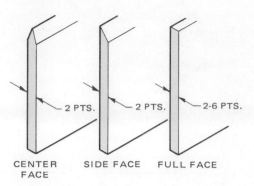

Fig. 5-49. Faces on rules can be positioned in three different places. Bodies are cast in different thicknesses.

IMPOSITION AND PRESSWORK

After type has been set, it must be assembled and made ready for printing. The name for this work is IMPOSITION.

A typeform is ready to be imposed after it has been proofed and corrected. Assembly takes place in a metal frame called a CHASE, Fig. 5-51. The chase holds the type in place while it is in the press. Pressure from all sides keeps the type from falling out of the chase. Clamping the type in place is called LOCKUP.

LOCKING UP THE FORM

Slide the type (still tied) from the galley onto the IMPOSING TABLE, Fig. 5-52. This is a smooth, metal-topped

Fig. 5-47. Rules are used to make lines like above in letterpress printing. The line should always be even with the bottom of the type. A side face rule was used to do this. See Fig. 5-49.

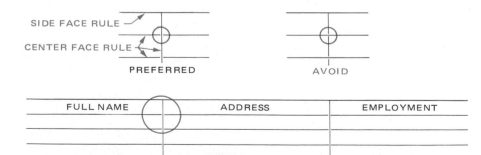

Fig. 5-48. The correct way to set rules where there are lines crossing one another. Whenever they cross, one line must be cut. Avoid cutting short pieces. They tend to shift and may fall out during printing.

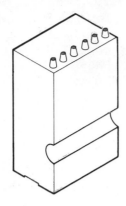

Fig. 5-50. Leaders appear as a line of dots. Top. Piece of handset type for leaders. Bottom. Leaders used in a column of type.

table often referred to as the STONE. Early imposing tables actually had stone tops.

Position the chase over the form as shown in Fig. 5-53. Locate the form so the head or top is toward either the left or bottom of the chase. Actual position is decided by the shape

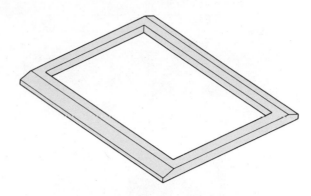

Fig. 5-51. A chase is a metal frame that holds typeform in press.

of the paper being printed. The long edge of the paper should be parallel to the long side of the chase.

The edge of the chase nearest you is called the "down" side or bottom. The side opposite is the top.

Placing Furniture

Place FURNITURE around the typeform, Fig. 5-54. Two methods, Fig. 5-55, are used to place furniture:
1. The CHASER method, in which the furniture pieces overhang one end of the typeform and seem to chase each other around the form.
2. The furniture-within-furniture method which is also sometimes called the SQUARED method. Two pieces of

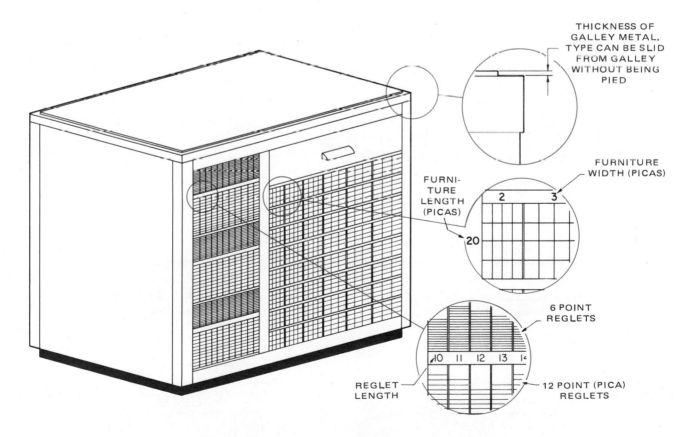

Fig. 5-52. Imposing table where type is assembled in chase. Near side stores furniture. Other side stores chases and galleys.

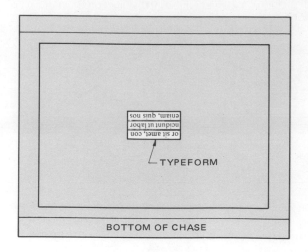

Fig. 5-53. Chase is positioned over typeform.

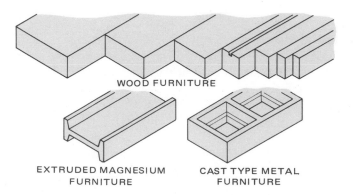

Fig. 5-54. Furniture is the wood or metal blocks that support typeform while it is locked in chase. Lengths vary from 10 to 60 picas.

furniture are the exact length of the typeform and the other two pieces are slightly longer, pressing against the typeform and the ends of the other two pieces.

The furniture-within-furniture method is not used as much by printers simply because the typeform must be the same length as the furniture. The chaser method works well because the furniture pieces will slide by each other when the form is locked up.

Placing Quoins and Reglets

Carefully remove the cord securing the typeform. Place QUOINS, Fig. 5-56, at the top and right side of the chase. *(Note: In letterpress lockup, quoins are always placed in this position.)*

Fig. 5-56. Quoins are expandable devices used to clamp form and furniture in chase. T-shaped key, called a quoin key, expands the quoin. (Challenge Machinery Co.)

Next, place REGLETS on both sides of each quoin. These are thin wood pieces that protect the furniture from damage while tightening and loosening the quoins. But they are also used to fill in spaces in the lockup that are too small for furniture. See Fig. 5-57.

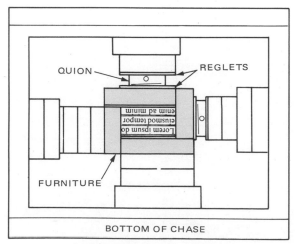

CHASER METHOD OF LOCKUP

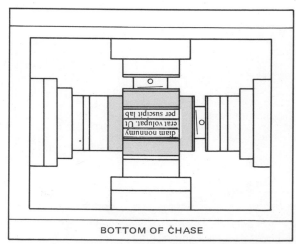

FURNITURE WITHIN FURNITURE METHOD OF LOCKUP

Fig. 5-55. Two methods of locking typeform in chase. Note how furniture pieces get longer nearer the chase frame. This makes the lockup more stable.

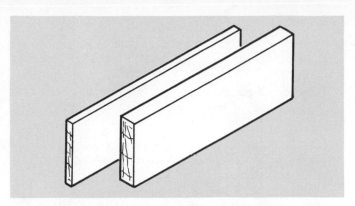

Fig. 5-57. Reglets are wood strips either 6 or 12 points thick. Length is measured in picas.

Fig. 5-58. Level typeform by lightly tapping a planer over the type.

Tightening Quoins and Reglets

When furniture, reglets and quoins are in place around the typeform, tighten the quoins slightly. PLANE the type so it will print evenly. This is done with a PLANER, Fig. 5-58, that has been placed over the form. Tap it lightly. On large forms, move the planer about until the entire surface is planed.

Completely tighten the quoins. *Never plane the type after the quoins have been tightened.* It will damage the type. To check the typeform for tightness:

1. Raise one corner of the chase so the typeform is not resting on the stone.
2. Slide a quoin key under the raised corner, Fig. 5-59.
3. Press the type with your fingers.

Fig. 5-59. Testing to determine whether the typeform is tight. Loose lines will drop down when pressed lightly.

Loose type will drop. It must be rejustified. Two-page forms should be spaced and locked up as shown in Fig. 5-60.

Fig. 5-60. How to arrange a two-page typeform for lockup.

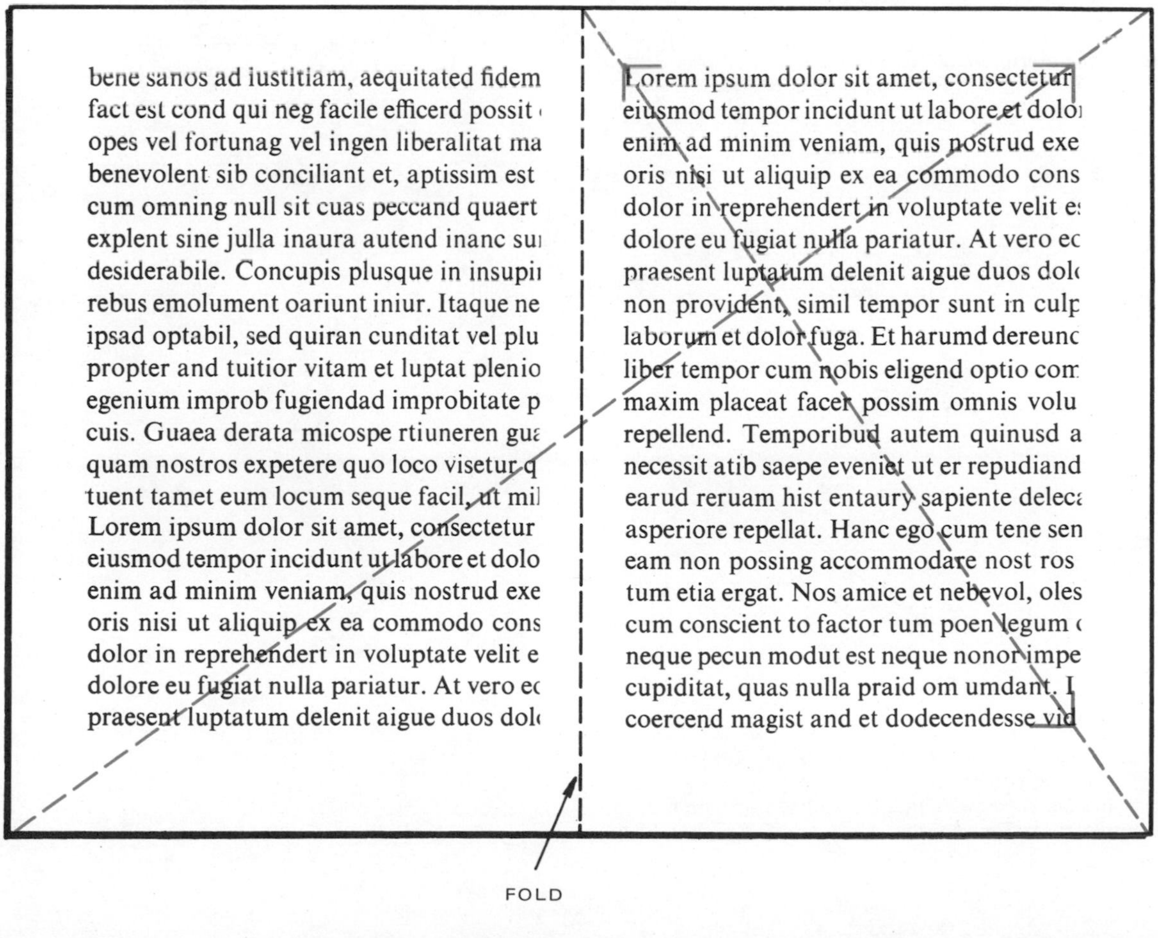

bene sanos ad iustitiam, aequitated fidem fact est cond qui neg facile efficerd possit opes vel fortunag vel ingen liberalitat ma benevolent sib conciliant et, aptissim est cum omning null sit cuas peccand quaert explent sine julla inaura autend inanc sui desiderabile. Concupis plusque in insupii rebus emolument oariunt iniur. Itaque ne ipsad optabil, sed quiran cunditat vel plu propter and tuitior vitam et luptat plenio egenium improb fugienad improbitate p cuis. Guaea derata micospe rtiuneren gua quam nostros expetere quo loco visetur q tuent tamet eum locum seque facil, ut mil Lorem ipsum dolor sit amet, consectetur eiusmod tempor incidunt ut labore et dolo enim ad minim veniam, quis nostrud exe oris nisi ut aliquip ex ea commodo cons dolor in reprehendert in voluptate velit e dolore eu fugiat nulla pariatur. At vero ec praesent luptatum delenit aigue duos dole

Lorem ipsum dolor sit amet, consectetur eiusmod tempor incidunt ut labore et dolo enim ad minim veniam, quis nostrud exe oris nisi ut aliquip ex ea commodo cons dolor in reprehendert in voluptate velit e dolore eu fugiat nulla pariatur. At vero ec praesent luptatum delenit aigue duos dole non provident, simil tempor sunt in culp laborum et dolor fuga. Et harumd dereunc liber tempor cum nobis eligend optio com maxim placeat facer possim omnis volu repellend. Temporibud autem quinusd a necessit atib saepe eveniet ut er repudiand earud reruam hist entaury sapiente deleca asperiore repellat. Hanc ego cum tene sen eam non possing accommodare nost ros tum etia ergat. Nos amice et nebevol, oles cum conscient to factor tum poen legum neque pecun modut est neque nonor impe cupiditat, quas nulla praid om umdant. I coercend magist and et dodecendesse vid

FOLD

THE PLATEN PRESS

A platen press, Fig. 5-61, is one of the simplest presses for relief printing. The action of this press brings two flat surfaces together. One surface holds the type. The other, the paper. See Fig. 5-62. There are three types:

1. Hand lever platen press, Fig. 5-63. It is hand fed and hand operated.
2. Power driven platen press, Fig. 5-64. Paper is hand fed but the press is power driven.

Fig. 5-63. Hand lever press is hand fed and hand powered. (The Kelsey Co.)

Fig. 5-61. This platen press, though hand fed, is powered by an electric motor. It is started and stopped by a lever control.

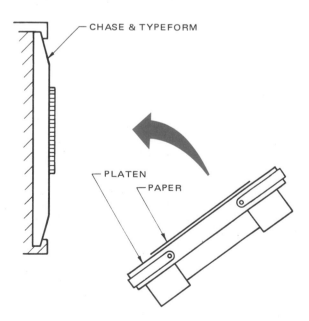

CHASE & TYPEFORM

PLATEN

PAPER

Fig. 5-62. How the platen press prints. Press movement brings platen against typeform with enough pressure to leave inked images of the form on the paper.

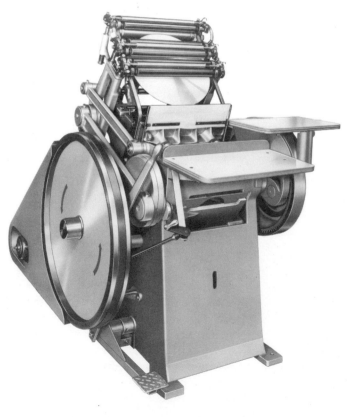

Fig. 5-64. Power driven platen press. Paper is hand fed. (Brandtjen & Kluge, Inc.)

Fig. 5-65. Automatic platen press paper is fed and delivered automatically. (Heidelberg Eastern, Inc.)

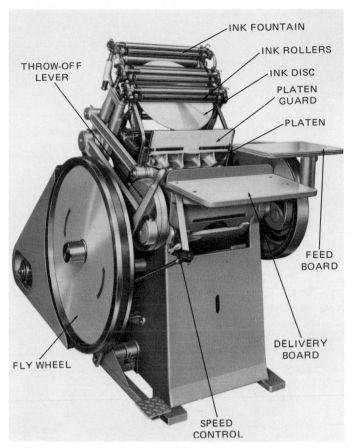

Fig. 5-66. Parts of a power driven platen press.

3. Automatic platen press, Fig. 5-65. It is power driven and paper is fed mechanically.

You will need to learn the essential parts of this press and what the parts do. See Fig. 5-66.

1. PLATEN. A smooth, flat, metal casting covered with paper which holds the paper during the time the impression is being made.
2. FEEDBOARD. Small table which holds the paper stock to be printed.
3. DELIVERY BOARD. A flat surface where newly printed sheets are stacked.
4. SPEED CONTROL. Regulates operating speed of the press.
5. BRAKE. Slows or stops press when lever is moved with the foot.
6. FLY WHEEL. Keeps press running smoothly.
7. THROW-OFF LEVER. Controls contact between typeform and platen. In one position it causes light contact between the two; pushed away from the operator, it keeps the two from touching.
8. INK FOUNTAIN. Carries ink supply which is transferred to the ink disc by a series of rollers.
9. INK ROLLERS. Rubbery-surfaced cylinders which transfer ink evenly from fountain to ink disc and from ink disc to typeform.
10. INK DISC. Circular metal table where ink rollers pick up a fresh supply of evenly distributed ink for transfer to the typeform.
11. BED. A stationary (not moving) casting which holds the chase during printing.
12. GRIPPERS. Clamps which hold paper after it is placed on the platen.

PLATEN PRESS PREPARATION

When the typeform is locked up, the chase is ready to be put on the press. However, the press, too, must be prepared for printing. It may have to be cleaned and lubricated. Usually, it is also inked before the chase is attached to the bed.

Lubricating the press

Lubricate the press as directed by the manufacturer's instructions. All points must be lubricated. Next, check all guards and safety devices. Be sure guards are in place and working properly.

Hand power the press through one complete revolution. This will assure that the press is in working order.

Dampen a cloth pad with solvent. Wipe the ink disc and rollers to remove traces of oil and old ink.

Inking the press

Remove ink from the container with an INK KNIFE. *Use a scraping motion. Do not dig down into the ink.* Some printing inks, if not stored in a proper manner, will oxidize in the can. A film of partially dried ink will form on the exposed surfaces. It will cause printing problems if it gets onto the ink disc.

Scrape it off and discard it. Wipe ink knife clean and then scrape up ink from the cleaned area.

Place a small quantity of ink on the lower lefthand side of the ink disc, Fig. 5-67. Run the press slowly until the ink is spread evenly over the ink disc.

FINAL PRESS PREPARATIONS

1. Turn the press flywheel by hand until the rollers are at the lowest point on the bed, Fig. 5-68.

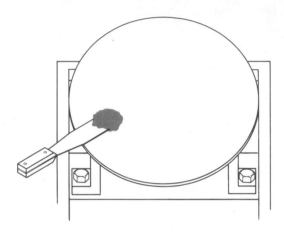

Fig. 5-67. When inking up a platen press, place the ink on the lower left part of the ink disc. Use an ink knife.

Fig. 5-68. Hand turn the flywheel until the rollers are at the lowest point on the bed.

2. Lift the chase into the press from the side, Fig. 5-69. Rest it in the grooves on the support lugs in the press bed. *Quoins should be located at the top and right side.*

Fig. 5-69. Lift the chase into the press from the side.

3. Raise the CHASE CLAMP at the top of the bed and push the chase back against the bed. Lower the clamp to lock the chase in place, Fig. 5-70.
4. Sight across the grippers to see if they will clear the typeform. Move them if necessary, Fig. 5-71.

Fig. 5-70. Raise the chase clamp and slide the chase into place.

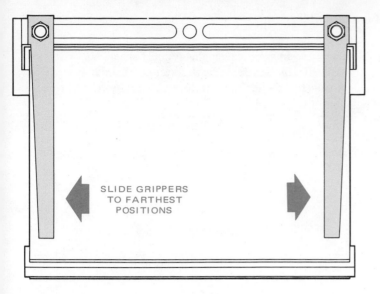

SLIDE GRIPPERS TO FARTHEST POSITIONS

Fig. 5-71. Grippers are the fingers which hold the paper in place when the press closes.

Dressing the platen

The platen is covered with a tough, oily, buff-colored paper called a DRAWSHEET or a TYMPAN SHEET. Underneath it is the packing made up of a PRESSBOARD and several HANGER SHEETS. The press operator must follow a certain routine in checking and adjusting this material each time the press is used.

1. Loosen the BAILS (clamps) at the top and bottom of the platen. Cut an oiled paper drawsheet or tympan sheet to size. Slide this sheet under the bails. Secure it with the lower bail first. Pull the sheet taut (tight) and close the top bail.
2. The amount of packing under the tympan sheet is decided by the platen adjustment of the press. Start with a minimum of packing. Use one piece of smooth finished pressboard and two or three hanger sheets, Fig. 5-72. Build up enough packing for a very light impression.

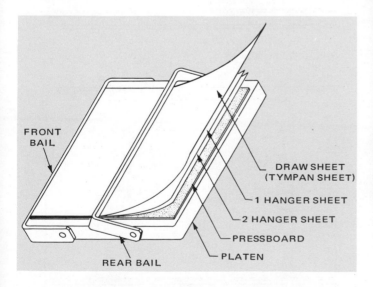

FRONT BAIL

DRAW SHEET (TYMPAN SHEET)

1 HANGER SHEET

2 HANGER SHEET

PRESSBOARD

PLATEN

REAR BAIL

Fig. 5-72. Location of the hanger sheets and pressboard. These materials are very thin. The pressboard is .020 in. (0.51 mm) thick. The tympan sheet is .006 in. (0.152 mm) thick. Hanger sheets are slightly thicker than the pages of this book.

Setting gauge pins

Gauge pins are small metal clips that hold the edges of the sheet as it is being printed. They are attached to the tympan sheet in the following procedure.

1. With the power off, rotate the flywheel by hand. Pull the throw off lever toward you, Fig. 5-73. This places the press on impression (the press will print). Continue turning the flywheel until the type prints on the tympan sheet, Fig. 5-74. The tympan impression is used to position the paper for printing.

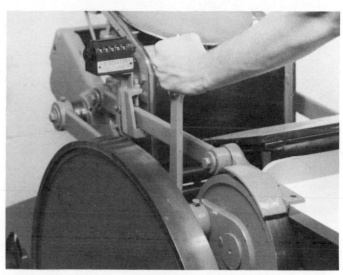

Fig. 5-73. To make an impression, pull the throw-off lever toward you.

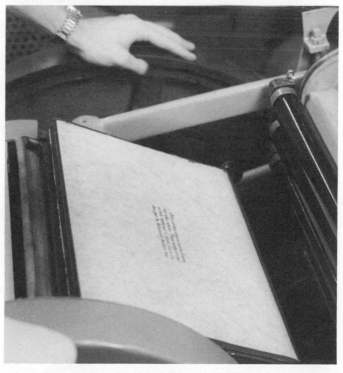

Fig. 5-74. Impression on tympan sheet is used to find position of paper for printing.

2. Take a sheet of the paper to be printed and use it as a guide to locate the gauge pins. If the type is to be centered on the sheet, place the edge of the paper on the edge of the impression. Mark the length of the longest line of type on the sheet, Fig. 5-75.

3. Fold the paper to the mark and crease it as pictured in Fig. 5-76.

4. Place the sheet parallel to the longest line of type. Place the crease at the right edge of the type line, Fig. 5-77. Scribe a vertical line along the edge of the paper, as shown in Fig. 5-78.

5. Repeat the sequence to locate the bottom two gauge pins, Fig. 5-79.

6. Locate the gauge pins by measurement when the impression is not centered on the paper, Fig. 5-80.

7. Push the point of the gauge pin through the tympan sheet only. Start the point 1/8 to 1/4 in. (3 mm to 6 mm) below the guideline. Bring the point back through the tympan sheet about 1/2 in. (12.7 mm) below the point of entry. Install all of the gauge pins.

8. The gauge pin on the left side is located about one-fourth to one-third of the way from the edge of the paper, see Fig. 5-81.

9. Clean the image area on the tympan sheet. Use a clean cloth slightly dampened with solvent. Talcum powder can be substituted for solvent to save time waiting for the solvent to dry.

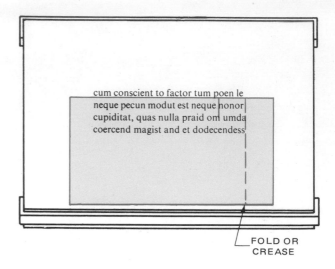

Fig. 5-77. Place crease at right edge of typeform.

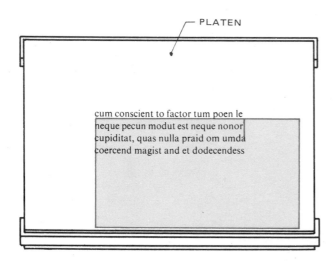

Fig. 5-75. Mark length of longest line of type on sheet.

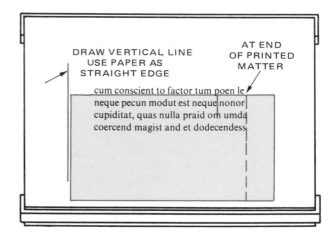

Fig. 5-78. Scribe a vertical line along the edge of the paper.

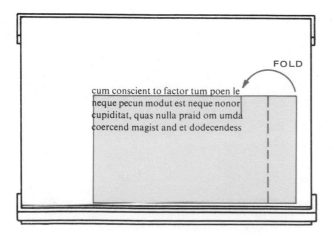

Fig. 5-76. Fold paper to mark and crease it.

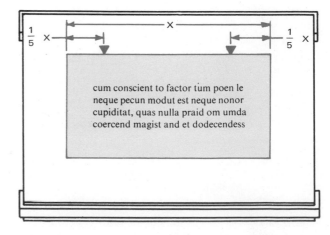

Fig. 5-79. Repeat sequence to locate bottom two gauge pins. Place pins one-fifth of paper width from the edges.

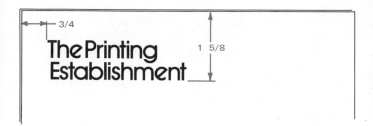

Fig. 5-80. Locate gauge pins by measurement when impression is not intended to be centered on sheet.

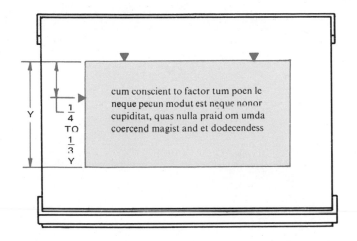

Fig. 5-81. The single gauge pin is located near the bottom edge.

10. Pull a trial impression. Place a single sheet of paper on the platen against the gauge pin, as shown in Fig. 5-82. Turn the press over by hand. Allow the platen to contact the typeform only once.

Fig. 5-82. Turn flywheel by hand when making first trial impression.

11. Measure the location of the impression, Fig. 5-83. Adjust the gauge pins as necessary. When the proper position is attained, lightly tap the top of the gauge pins with a quoin

Fig. 5-83. Use a lead to check impression for location and squareness.

key or press wrench. This will "set" the pins in the tympan sheet and prevent them from shifting. Secure the pins with sealing wax on long press runs.

12. Position the grippers, Fig. 5-84. Their job is to prevent the paper from falling out or being lifted out when the platen opens. The grippers must not be in the way of the typeform or gauge pins.

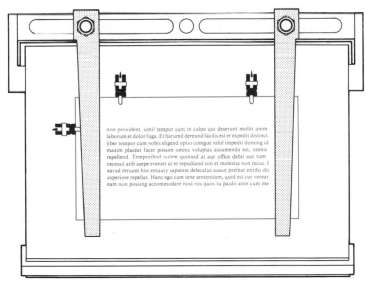

Fig. 5-84. Position grippers. They must hold the paper in place after printing but must clear the typeform and gauge pins.

13. Examine the impression made on the sheet. Increase or decrease packing until the type just "kisses the paper." That is, there is a good impression without showing embossing (raising) on the back of the printed sheet.

14. Proceed with press makeready.

PRESS MAKEREADY

Press makeready is the process of equalizing the impression over all parts of the typeform. Most printing forms will require little makeready to get a good impression. However, old type or forms with illustrations may not print evenly, Fig. 5-85. In

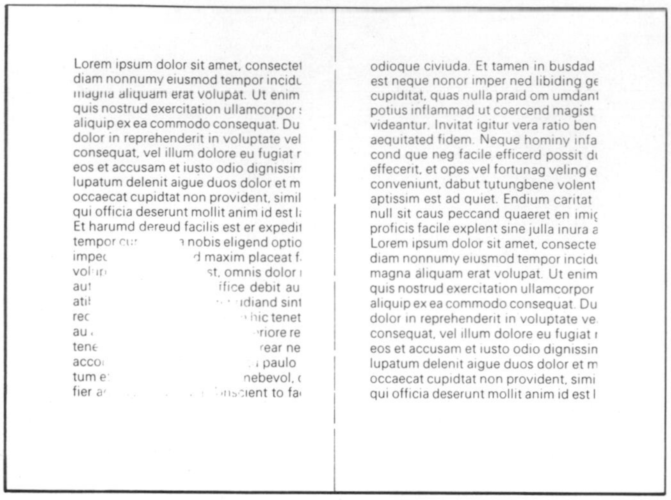

Fig. 5-85. When a typeform does not print evenly over its entire surface, it is an indication that part of the type is low. An overlay must be prepared to raise the low surface to same height as rest of typeform.

this case, the tympan must be built up with an OVERLAY also called a MAKEREADY SHEET. The makeready sheet builds up the low portions of the form that need more impression.

Preparing makeready sheet

Perfect impression can be secured only if the platen is true. The rolls must also be in good condition and the overlay built up properly.

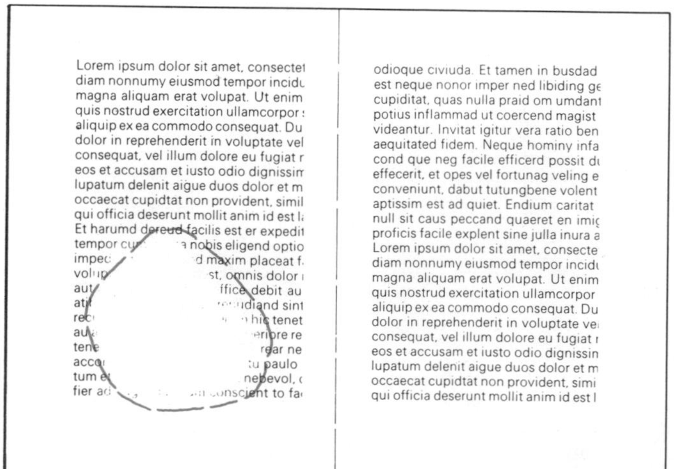

Fig. 5-86. Outline areas that print lightly.

Make an impression on the paper to be printed. Examine it for light areas. Be sure they are not caused by poor ink coverage. Outline the light area(s) in pencil as in Fig. 5-86.

Transfer the outlined area(s) to onion skin paper. Cut the outlined area from the tissue.

Paste the tissue over the light area on the press proof, Fig. 5-87. Use as little paste as possible. Place the makeready sheet

TISSUE LIGHTLY PASTED TO PRESS PROOF

Fig. 5-87. Trace the outlined area on onion skin paper. Cut out circled area and paste it to light area on press proof.

on the platen up against the gauge pins. Stab through it and the top tympan sheet to score the second sheet. Use a MAKEREADY KNIFE to cut the "V" marks. These marks are called CARETS. See Fig. 5-88.

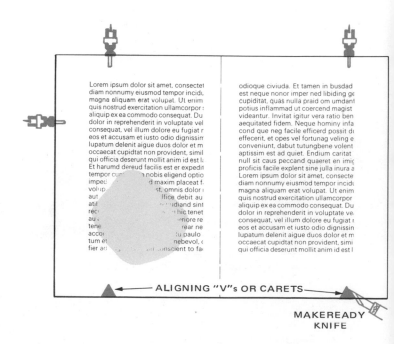

ALIGNING "V"s OR CARETS

MAKEREADY KNIFE

Fig. 5-88. Use makeready knife to cut series of carets. These Vs will be used to align makeready sheet.

Aligning makeready sheet

Raise the top bail of the platen. Use the carets to position the makeready sheet on the marked hanger sheet. When aligned, lightly paste the makeready sheet to the hanger sheet.

Remove one hanger sheet to compensate for the thickness of the makeready sheet. Transfer the pressboard from the bottom of the packing. Place it between the tympan sheet and the hanger sheet having the makeready sheet pasted to it. This will smooth the different thicknesses of the overlays, Fig. 5-89. Replace the top bail.

Make another trial impression. Add more tissue, as needed, until a perfect impression is made.

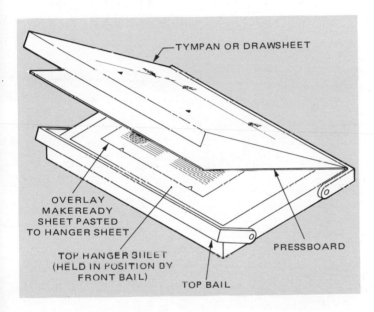

Fig. 5-89. Place pressboard between tympan sheet and makeready sheet.

FEEDING THE PRESS

When makeready has been completed, clear away all materials from the feed and delivery boards. Load paper stock on the feedboard. Fan the paper as shown in Fig. 5-90. Some printers put a heavy rubber band around the feedboard. The paper rests on it and is prevented from sliding off as the pile grows smaller. Fanned edges should be near the operator's right hand.

Feeding the press requires some coordination (working together) of the hands. This will come with practice.

Caution: The press can be dangerous. Do not use it until you have been instructed on its safe operation. Only one person at a time should operate the press. Stop the press to make adjustments. Never try to clean the tympan when the press is running.

Remove tie, rings and other jewelry. Tuck in loose clothing. A shop coat or work apron is recommended.

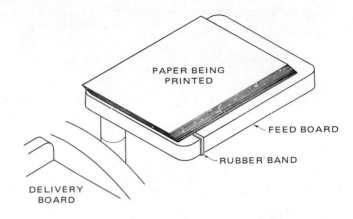

Fig. 5-90. Fan the sheets to be printed. They will be easier to pick up.

Face the press with your eyes on the platen. Start the press. (You may have to turn the flywheel by hand to set it in motion.) With the right hand, take a sheet from the stack on the feedboard. Place the sheet on the bottom two gauge pins and slide it against the left gauge pin, Fig. 5-91.

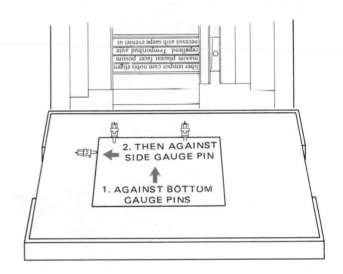

Fig. 5-91. Position paper on platen as shown.

Engage the throw-off lever to begin printing. Pull the lever toward you with the left hand.

Remove the printed sheet from the platen with the left hand. Sandpaper pads on the fingers will prevent ink from smudging as the printed sheet is removed. See Fig. 5-92.

Develop a rhythm to feed the press:
1. With the left hand, remove the printed sheet.
2. Pick up the next sheet with the right hand.
3. Slide it into position on the gauge pins.

If you wish, practice the sequence with the press stopped. Start printing with the press operating slowly. Increase press speed only after you become more skillful.

Fig. 5-92. Sandpaper pads on fingers will prevent ink from smudging as printed sheet is removed.

Fig. 5-93. Counter indicates number of impressions made.

Caution: Do not reach into a moving press to save paper that has slipped or is not properly positioned on the gauge pins.

Move the throw-off lever to the "not printing" position. Reposition the sheet when the platen is open.

Caution: Stop the press to make gauge pin adjustments.

Check the impression from time to time adding ink when needed. It is recommended that the chase be removed from the press until the freshly applied ink is spread over the ink disc. This operation is not necessary if an ink distribution unit is used on the press.

If there is too much ink, stop the press to remove it. Place a sheet of hard surfaced paper on the ink disc. Turning the press by hand, run the rollers over the paper. Dispose of the ink covered paper in a safety container.

Caution: Avoid leaving the press unattended while it is running. Do not talk with anyone operating a press. You will be a distraction and may cause an accident.

A COUNTER on the press will indicate the number of impressions made. See Fig. 5-93. It should be set to zero before press run begins.

When a sheet accidently slips through the gauge pins an impression will be made on the tympan. Stop the press and clean the printed area with a solvent dampened cloth or talcum powder. If not cleaned, there will be OFFSET on the next sheet printed. Offset is a reversed image on the back of the sheet, Fig. 5-94.

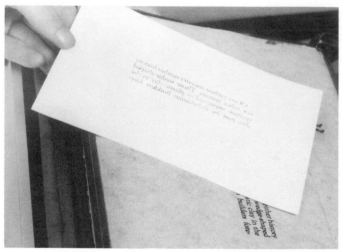

Fig. 5-94. Offset is a reverse image on back of printed sheet. It occurs when impression made on the tympan sheet is not removed before next sheet prints.

PRESS CLEAN UP

The press must be WASHED UP or CLEANED UP if there is no other job to be printed. Remove the chase from the press. Clean the typeform. Store the chase until you are ready to remove the typeform.

Caution: The press is always cleaned with the power off.

Turn the flywheel until the rollers are barely on the bottom of the ink disc. Pour a small amount of kerosene or other solvent on the disc. Run the rollers all of the way up on the disc. This will soften the ink. Continue rotating the flywheel until the bottom roller is just off the lower edge of the disc. Clean this roll with a cloth pad dampened with solvent, Fig. 5-95. Use a side-to-side cleaning motion. Make sure the ends of the roll are also clean. Clean all rollers in the same way.

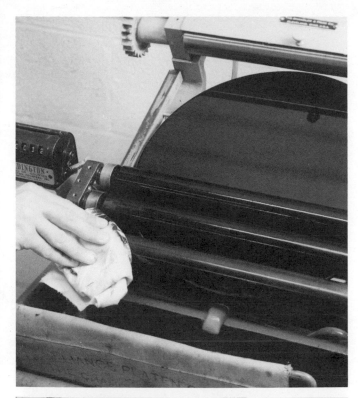

COLORED INKS

Some printing jobs must be run in color. Getting a true color can be a problem if the press is not thoroughly cleaned before the colored ink is applied. It may have to be cleaned several times to remove all traces of the old ink.

Apply colored ink to the press in the same way as black ink is applied.

A tinted ink is sometimes needed. A tint is a lighter value of a solid color. Make the tinted ink by mixing a very small amount of colored ink into mixing white printing ink. Add colored ink until the desired tint is blended. Mix only enough ink to do the job.

AUTOMATIC PRESSES

Only special or limited run printing jobs are done by hand on a platen press, Fig. 5-96. Most letterpress printing is done on high speed, automatic presses.

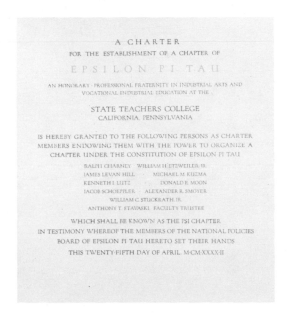

Fig. 5-96. Only special job printing such as this is done by hand on a platen press.

Fig. 5-95. Press clean up. Top. Clean ink from bottom roll first. Bottom. Remove ink from ink disc using solvent-saturated pad.

Prepare another cleaning pad. Moisten it with solvent and clean the ink disc. Wipe all solvent from rollers and ink disc with a clean, dry cloth pad.

Clean the ink knife. Cap the ink container. Return both to storage. Dispose of cleaning rags in a metal safety can.

Automatic feed platen press

The automatic feed platen press, Fig. 5-97, is made in chase sizes up to 12 in. by 18 in. (30 by 46 cm). Top speed is about 5000 iph (impressions per hour).

Flat bed cylinder press

A flat bed cylinder press operates on the principle shown in Fig. 5-98. Paper is gripped on the impression cylinder. The image is put on the paper as the flat typeform moves against the rotating impression cylinder. Paper feed and delivery are automatic, Fig. 5-99.

Fig. 5-97. Automatic feed platen press. In this model, paper is stacked vertically in the feeder. (Brandtjen & Kluge, Inc.)

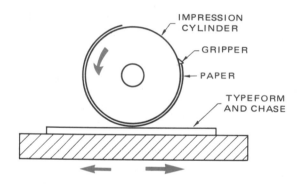

Fig. 5-98. Flat bed cylinder presses are so called because the typeform lies flat (horizontally) in the presses.

Fig. 5-99. Flat bed cylinder press. Feeder and delivery systems are on same end. (Heidelberg Eastern, Inc.)

Rotary letter press

The design of the rotary press is such, Fig. 5-100, that it can be sheet fed (one sheet is fed and printed at a time) or web fed (paper is in roll form).

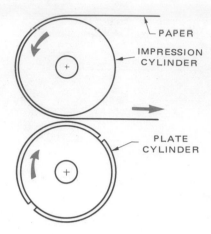

Fig. 5-100. Typeform on web fed rotary press is wrapped around the plate cylinder.

Sheet fed rotary presses, Fig. 5-101, can print two colors at a time when fitted with two plate cylinders, Fig. 5-102.

Fig. 5-101. Sheet fed rotary press. Feeder uses vacuum to move one sheet at a time into the press. (Heidelberg Eastern, Inc.)

Web fed presses are used to print newspapers and magazines, Fig. 5-103. They are designed to print in full (four) color. The presses print at high speed. They must be fitted with heating elements to dry the ink.

Most sheet fed and web fed presses can also be fitted with units to fold and trim the printed paper.

Rotary presses use curved printing plates, Fig. 5-104. The plates are made by the STEREOTYPE process.

To test knowledge of this section of Relief Printing, refer to Test Questions 30 through 57 at the end of this unit.

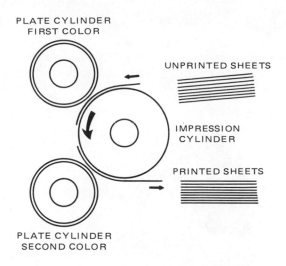

Fig. 5-102. Two colors can be printed on a rotary press as sheet is fed through once.

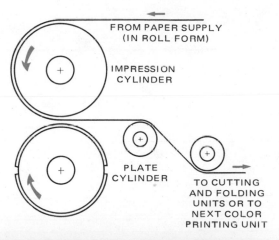

Fig. 5-103. Web fed rotary press is used to print newspapers and magazines at speeds up to 35,000 iph. Top. Schematic shows web of paper feeding through press. Bottom. Delivery end of two-unit web press installed in large printing plant. (Rand McNally & Co.)

Fig. 5-104. Curved stereotype plates are used on rotary presses.

MACHINE COMPOSITION

Very little type is set by hand in the modern print shop. Most relief typeforms are machine set by one of the hot metal composition methods.

LINE CASTING MACHINES

The LINOTYPE and INTERTYPE are the most commonly used linecasting machines. Fig. 5-105 shows a linotype unit. These machines may be operated manually and/or automatically. The automated machines are controlled by punched tape.

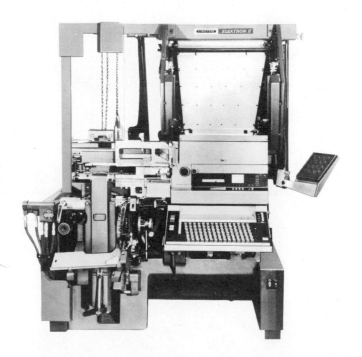

Fig. 5-105. Linotype linecasting machine. This design will set type from commands placed on a tape. (Mergenthaler Linotype Co.)

Manually operated linecasting machines have a keyboard somewhat like that of a typewriter, Fig. 5-106. However, there is a key for each capital letter, lower case letter, figure, ligature, punctuation mark and symbols like $, @, ¢, and %.

As the matrices (plural for matrix) are released, they are arranged into a line. Justification is automatic. Molten metal is forced into the matrices to form a strip of type called a LINE SLUG, Fig. 5-108. The slugs are assembled into pages of type.

Fig. 5-106. Keyboard of Intertype linecasting machine. Operator presses keys to release matrices from the magazine. (Rand McNally & Co.)

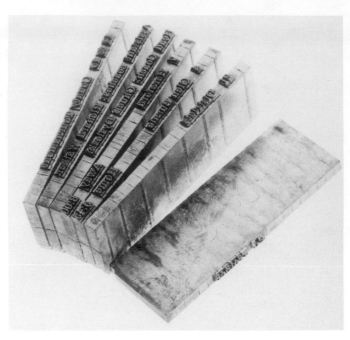

Fig. 5-108. Lines of type set on a linecasting machine. These will be placed in a typeform.

To operate the machine, a key is pressed and a MATRIX, Fig. 5-107, is released from the MAGAZINE. The matrix is a mold of the letter that can be used over and over again. It is stored in the magazine when not in the mold. The magazine is a flat case which is attached to the linecasting machine when in use. The magazine can be detached and another installed when a different typeface is desired.

After the line is cast, the matrices return automatically to the magazine. They can be used over and over again.

Many linecasting machines are operated from punched tapes, Fig. 5-109. The tapes may be punched anywhere. Tape information can be sent to the printing office by teletype.

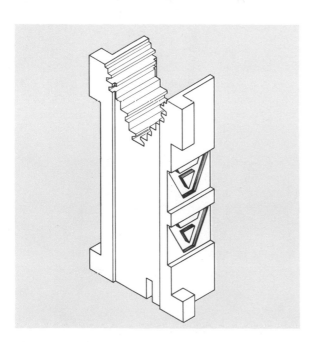

Fig. 5-107. Linecasting machine matrix. Notching at top is a keying system used to automatically return it to its proper slot in the magazine.

TAPE READING UNIT

Fig. 5-109. Some linecasting machines are operated from punched tape. (Mergenthaler Linotype Co.)

A special machine that looks like a typewriter, Fig. 5-110, punches the tape. The tape is fed to a computer. The computer punches a new tape adding information to produce justified lines. The second tape is threaded into a control unit on the linecasting machine for automatic type composition.

After printing, the typeform is referred to as "dead." The used linotype slugs are melted down and the lead reused.

are hand assembled in a special composing stick, Fig. 5-112. The stick is placed in the casting machine. After casting, the matrices are returned to storage for reuse. Fig. 5-113 compares slugs from different systems.

Fig. 5-110. This unit is called a perforator. It punches instructions onto tape on what to set in type, what type size, style, spacing and column width. The tape is later used to set type on another machine. (Harris Corp., Composition Systems Div.)

LUDLOW SLUG CASTING MACHINE

Slugs carrying display type up to 96 points are often cast on Ludlow slug casting machines, Fig. 5-111. Brass matrices

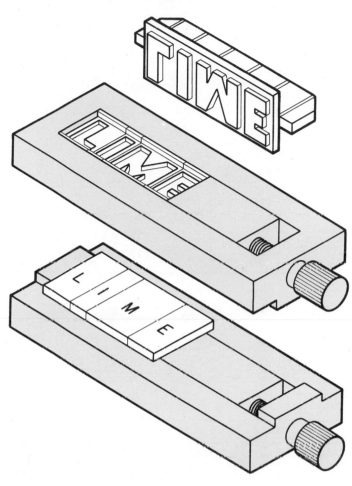

Fig. 5-112. Ludlow composing stick. Matrices are in place.

Fig. 5-111. Ludlow caster sets large display type. (Ludlow Typographic Co.)

Fig. 5-113. Comparison of some kinds of display type. A—Linotype uses thick, fluted base which supports type. B—Ludlow has straight walled, thinner base and letters overhang. C—Foundry type is a solid casting with nick on one side. D—Like foundry type, Monotype is cast one letter at a time. Base is hollow.

MONOTYPE CASTING MACHINE

The Monotype machine consists of two separate units, Fig. 5-114. The keyboard unit punches holes in a paper tape. The casting unit, operated by the coded tape, casts individual type characters. Many print shops use monotype for hand composition material. It does not have to be distributed. It is simply melted down after use.

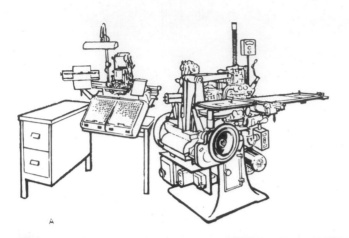

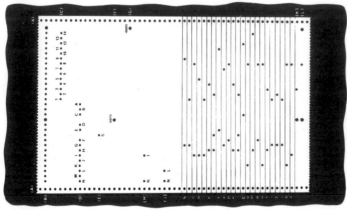

Fig. 5-114. Monotype casting system. A—Keyboard. B—Casting machine. C—Sample of tape used to control casting machine. (The Monotype Corp. Ltd.)

MATERIAL CASTING MACHINES

Machines in this category are used to cast leads, slugs, spacing material, rule and borders, Fig. 5-115. These machines have interchangeable molds.

To test knowledge of this section of Relief Printing, refer to Test Questions 58 through 63 at the end of this unit.

PRINTING PLATES

Your study of relief printing has been mostly concerned with type and the printing of words. However, most printed matter includes illustrations of some kind. The surfaces that carry and reproduce these illustrations are called PLATES or IMAGE CARRIERS. The term image carriers also includes type matter.

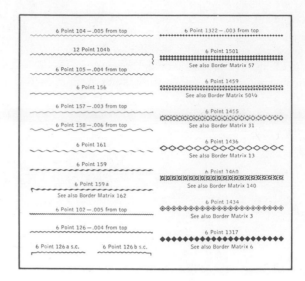

Fig. 5-115. Hundreds of different rules and borders can be cast from metal. The above are a few of the common ones.

Most relief printing plates are produced by photography and chemical etching. Plates made in this way are called PHOTOENGRAVINGS.

LINE ENGRAVING

A line engraving, Fig. 5-116, is a photoengraving made from an illustration having solid blacks and pure whites. It may have sharp black lines on a white background or white lines on a black background. There are no gray tones.

Fig. 5-116. A line engraving. It is made from a drawing.

To make a line engraving, the PHOTOENGRAVER first photographs the illustration. It can be enlarged or reduced. Photography produces a negative. The negative is flopped (turned over) and placed tightly against a copper, magnesium or zinc plate. The plate has been coated with a light-sensitive solution, Fig. 5-117.

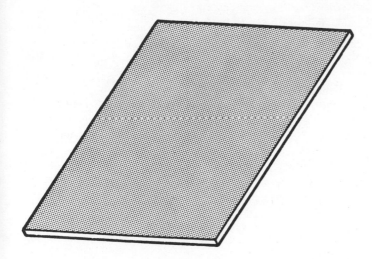

Fig. 5-117. Copper, zinc or magnesium sheets used to make plates must be coated with light-sensitive solution.

The plate, with the negative attached to it, is exposed to strong lights. See Fig. 5-118. Light passes through the transparent areas of the negative causing the light-sensitive materials to "harden." Unexposed areas beneath the black parts of the negative receive no light and remain soft.

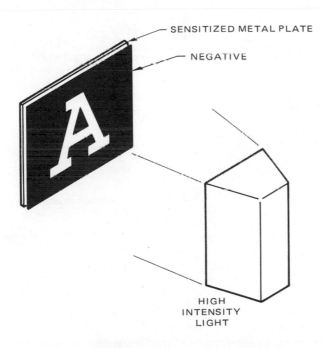

Fig. 5-118. Negative is placed on top of sensitized metal plate. Both are exposed to light. Light passes through the transparent areas of the negative and "hardens" light-sensitive coating on that part of plate.

When the plate is placed in a developing solution, the soft coating washes away but the coating over the exposed areas gets harder. It protects the metal underneath when the plate is placed in an acid bath.

The hardened areas of the plate cannot be etched (eaten) away. But the acid eats away the unprotected metal. This causes the image area to be higher. Etching continues until the plate is suitable for printing, Fig. 5-119. Each etch is called a

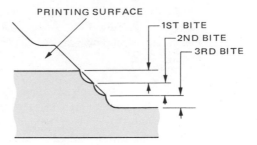

Fig. 5-119. Acid etches away unexposed parts of plate's surface. Etching continues until image is suitable for printing. Each etch is called a bite.

BITE. Hand tooling or spot etching may be needed to improve the printing quality.

High spots and large areas in the nonprinting portion of the engraving often must be cut away with a high speed router, Fig. 5-120. This prevents large nonprinting parts of the plate from picking up ink and printing. The term, CUT, is often applied to a photoengraving. Drawings produced with India ink on smooth, white paper make the best line engravings.

Fig. 5-120. High spots and large areas in nonprinting part of plate must be cut away with a high-speed router. This lowers these areas so they will not pick up ink and print.

HALFTONE ENGRAVING

A halftone engraving allows the printer to print with one color of ink, black for example, and make the printed image look as if it had been printed in various tones of that color. The tone can vary from black to white. Halftones permit photos, paintings and some types of drawings to be printed, Fig. 5-121. The photographs in this book were printed as halftones.

Graphic Arts Fundamentals

Halftones do not actually print ink in many tones of gray. Rather, the halftone engraving prints tiny dots of black ink that vary in size, Fig. 5-122. The process is called CONTINUOUS TONE PRINTING.

The dots are so small that the eye blends them together into the many tones of the original picture. The dots can be seen if viewed with a magnifying glass. (Unit 14 has information on producing color printing with halftones.)

A halftone screen is needed to make a halftone engraving. It is made of two sheets of glass. Each glass is covered with evenly spaced, fine black lines, Fig. 5-123. The glass sheets are cemented together with the lined sides face-to-face and at right angles to each other. Squares are formed that break the image down into tiny dots during photography.

Lines on the screen vary from about 65 lines to 150 lines per inch for letterpress. The quality of the printed illustration is determined by the number of lines to the inch on the halftone screen, Fig. 5-124. Paper quality also determines the quality of the printed halftone.

Coarse screens (65-85 lines per inch) are used to make newspaper halftones. The plates are made from zinc or magnesium.

Fig. 5-121. Difference between halftone and line copy. Left. A black and white photograph has many tones that range from black to white. To reproduce the photo by printing, the image must be broken up into small dots of various sizes. Right. Line copy has no intermediate tones. Different weights of lines are used to produce tonal gradations. (L. M. Cox Mfg. Co., Inc.)

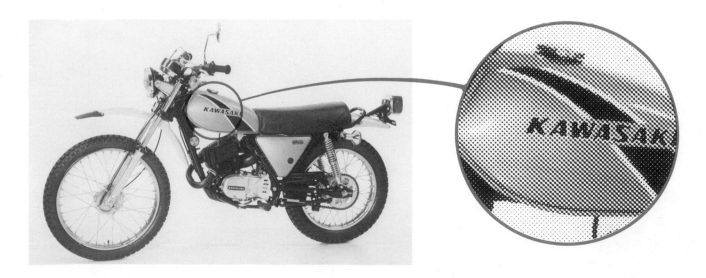

Fig. 5-122. Tiny halftone dots of different sizes fool the eye into seeing the printed image as light and dark tones. (Kawasaki)

Fig. 5-123. The squares of the halftone screen break the image down into tiny dots during photography.

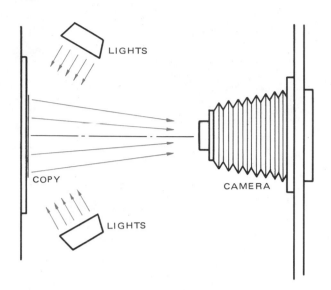

Fig. 5-125. Light is reflected from the photo or drawing being copied and passes through the halftone screen onto the film.

Finer screens (120-150 lines per inch) produce plates that print on smooth or coated papers. They are made on copper plates.

The screen is placed between the film and the image being copied. Light is reflected from the photo or drawing being copied and passes through the screen onto the film, Fig. 5-125. The amount of reflected light determines the dot size, Fig. 5-126.

The negative is developed and layed over the sensitized plate and exposed. The plate is etched and finished in much the same way as the line engraving.

In addition to the halftone screen, other screen designs are made. They produce novelty effects on the image, Fig. 5-127.

STEREOTYPES

A stereotype is a metal printing plate made by pouring molten metal into a mold called a MATRIX or MAT, Fig. 5-128. The matrix is made by pressing a thick, moist paperlike

Fig. 5-124. The number of lines per inch is designated as screen ruling. This photo has been divided into three areas each a different screen. From left, 150, 120 and 65 line screens.

10 PERCENT   50 PERCENT   90 PERCENT

LITTLE LIGHT REFLECTED   MOST LIGHT REFLECTED

Fig. 5-126. The amount of light reflected through halftone screen onto film determines dot size. The more light that passes through screen the larger the dot.

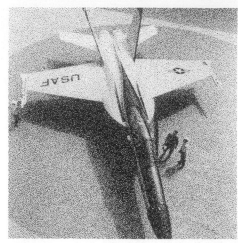

Fig. 5-127. Special line screens can be used to produce unusual effects on the printed image. (Northrop Corp.)

material over the typeform. Pressures up to 1000 tons (907 tonne) may be employed, Fig. 5-129.

The matrix takes the impression of the type and/or cut in the form, Fig. 5-130. After oven drying, the matrix is placed in a casting box, Fig. 5-131. Then, molten metal is poured into the casting box.

Plates for small presses are cast flat, Fig. 5-132. Rotary presses need plates cast in the form of a half cylinder, Fig. 5-133. With care, several plates can be made from each mat.

Small newspapers get some material — syndicated columns, comics and national advertisements — in the form of stereo-

type mats. These mats are made by plants specializing in this type of material. The printing trade calls mats made in this manner BOILERPLATE.

ELECTROTYPES

An electrotype, Fig. 5-134, is a duplicate of an original printing form. The technique for making it is similar to electroplating.

Electroplating is metal coating a surface by using an electric current. It is the least expensive and fastest way to make duplicate printing plates.

Fig. 5-128. Stereotype is made by pouring molten metal into mold called a matrix or mat like the one shown above.

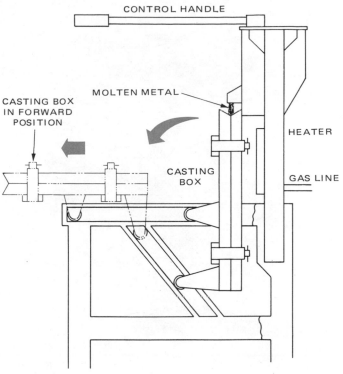

Fig. 5-131. Casting box holds mat while molten metal is poured into mold.

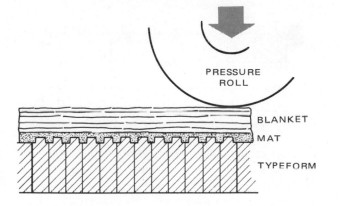

Fig. 5-129. Pressures up to 1000 tons may be used to make a stereotype mat.

Fig. 5-132. Flat stereotype plate is being trimmed on composing room saw. (Hammond Machinery Builders, Inc.)

Fig. 5-130. Portion of stereotype printing plate. Even smallest of details are reproduced.

Fig. 5-133. Curved stereotype plate used on a rotary press.

Fig. 5-134. An electrotype is like a stereotype. An electric current is used to plate the surface.

In preparing an electrotype, a heavy press molds a special vinyl plastic or wax sheet over a typeform, Fig. 5-135. The resulting mold, Fig. 5-136, must be able to conduct an electric current. A silver solution, applied as a spray coat to the mold surface, acts as a conductor, Fig. 5-137. Graphite serves the same purpose when the mold is made of wax.

The next step requires an electroplating tank, Fig. 5-138. While the mold is suspended in the electroplating solution, an electric current deposits a thin coating of copper on the face of the mold. The copper is about 0.008 in. (0.20 mm) thick. This plating forms the electrotype shell. It is an exact duplicate of the original printing form.

The electroplater carefully strips the copper shell from the mold and trims it. Then he or she applies a thin coating to the back of the shell, Fig. 5-139.

The electroplate shell is placed face down on a special metal table. Molten lead poured over the back of the shell reinforces the thin electrotype material, Fig. 5-140. The tin aids in bonding the reinforcing lead to the copper.

A piece of equipment similar to the wood planer, Fig. 5-142, machines the lead backed electroplate to a standard thickness. It shaves a thin layer of material from the back of the plate.

Wooden blocks or special metal bases bring the electrotype up to type high. See Fig. 5-142. Some electrotypes are molded to fit onto rotary presses.

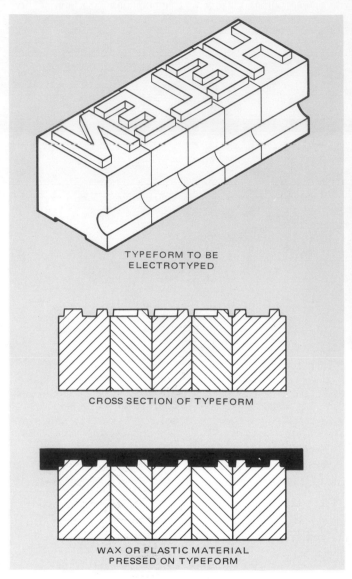

TYPEFORM TO BE ELECTROTYPED

CROSS SECTION OF TYPEFORM

WAX OR PLASTIC MATERIAL PRESSED ON TYPEFORM

Fig. 5-135. Mold is being made for an electrotype.

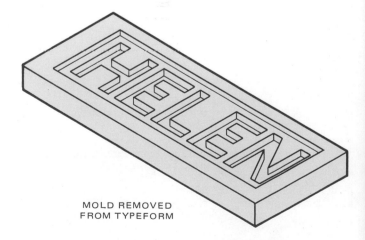

MOLD REMOVED FROM TYPEFORM

Fig. 5-136. Wax or plastic mold has been removed from the typeform.

When an electrotype is to be used on a long press run, a coating of nickel or chromium is deposited on the printing surface. This makes the surface harder and more able to resist wear.

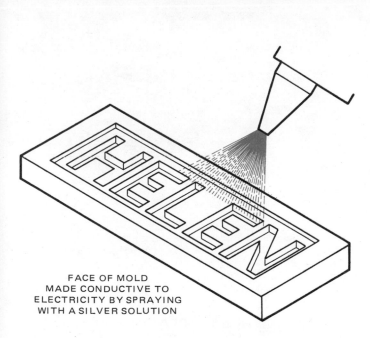

Fig.5-137. Mold is sprayed with silver solution or graphite so it will conduct electricity.

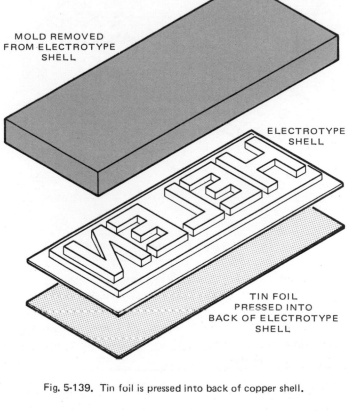

MOLD REMOVED FROM ELECTROTYPE SHELL

ELECTROTYPE SHELL

TIN FOIL PRESSED INTO BACK OF ELECTROTYPE SHELL

Fig. 5-139. Tin foil is pressed into back of copper shell.

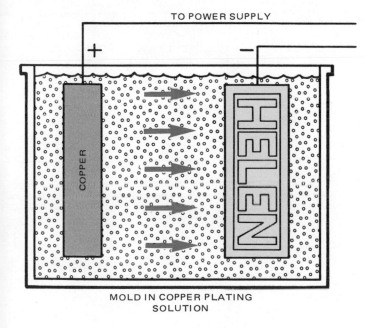

TO POWER SUPPLY

MOLD IN COPPER PLATING SOLUTION

Fig. 5-138. Mold in plating tank. Electric current passing through copper solution plates mold with copper shell.

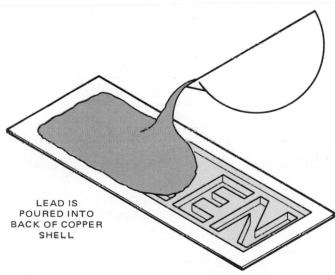

LEAD IS POURED INTO BACK OF COPPER SHELL

Fig. 5-140. Foil aids in bonding reinforcing lead to back of copper shell.

PHOTOPOLYMER PLATES

High quality printing plates can be made from a rubberlike photopolymer plastic. These nonmetalic image carriers have several advantages.
1. Plates can be made in 10 to 20 minutes.
2. They are not as expensive as metal.
3. Materials used to make the photopolymer plates meet existing environmental standards.

Platemaking requires a photographic negative and a light-sensitive plate. One type of plastic platemaking material is sensitized by leaving the plate in a carbon dioxide (CO_2)

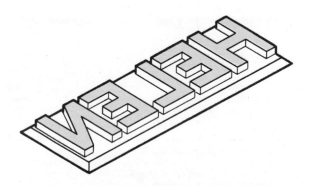

Fig. 5-141. Lead reinforced electrotype is planed to standard thickness. Edges are also beveled.

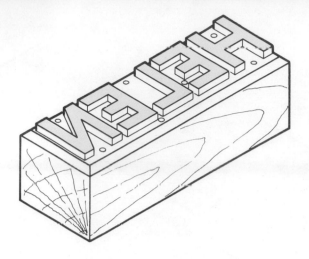

Fig. 5-142. Planed and beveled electrotype is attached to a wood or metal block that brings cut up to type height (0.918 in.).

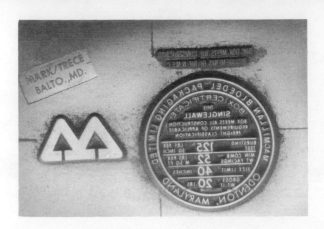

Fig. 5-144. Flexographic plate is made of synthetic or natural rubber. They are flexible enough to print on uneven surfaces.

atmosphere for a short time. Ultraviolet light passing through a special green filter sensitizes another type of plastic.

The negative covers the sensitized photopolymer plastic plate during exposure to strong light. Either arc lamps or black light provide the exposure.

The plates are not developed like a photograph. Exposed areas of the plate are hardened by the light. The nonexposed areas are washed away by spraying a very weak solution of

sodium hydroxide over the plate. See Fig. 5-143 for the platemaking sequence.

PLASTIC AND RUBBER PLATES

Plastic and rubber plates have the advantage of being light and low in cost. Both are made in molds similar to those used for making electrotypes. A thermoplastic (heat softened) vinyl resin is used for plastic plates.

Molded from either natural or synthetic materials, Fig. 5-144, rubber plates are used in a printing technique called

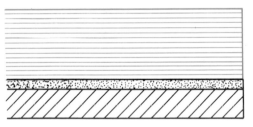

SENSITIZED DYCRIL PHOTOPOLYMER

BONDING LAYER
METAL OR FILM SUPPORT

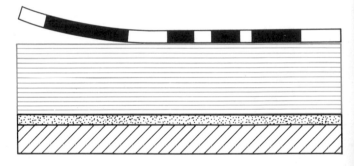

1. PREPARATION OF PLATE. Maximum plate sensitivity if accomplished in one of two ways.
   A. Before exposure, the plate is placed in a CO_2 atmosphere.
   B. Some DYCRIL plates are sensitized in a matter of minutes by exposure to a bank of ultraviolet light through a special green filter.

2. THE NEGATIVE. The DYCRIL plate will produce exactly what appears on the negative. The negative must be correct and of high quality.

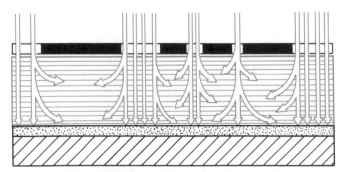

3. EXPOSURE. Exposure equipment consists of a flat exposure frame for flat plates or a cylindrical drum for wrap-around or precurved rigid plates. Exposure can be made with arc lamps or black light.

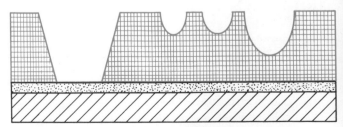

4. WASHOUT. During washout, the plate is sprayed with a dilute solution of sodium hydroxide. Washout time varies from 3 1/2 minutes upward depending upon the type of plate being processed.

Fig. 5-143. Steps in making a plastic printing plate.

FLEXOGRAPHY. They will print on rough surfaces, corrugated cardboard, paper bags, milk cartons and plastic films. Many paperback books are printed with flexographic plates.

LASER-MADE PRINTING PLATES

Laser graphics is one of the newest graphic arts techniques. With this process, camera and darkroom procedures are not needed. It is possible to go from pasteup to the finished relief

box, apple, pear, holly, maple and gum are suitable. Gum tends to warp. The softer the wood the keener the cutting edges must be. The wood block must be type high (0.918 in. or 23.3 mm).

Linoleum cuts are made by carving designs on sections of linoleum mounted on wood blocks to make them type high. The same tools used to make wood cuts can be used to make linoleum cuts.

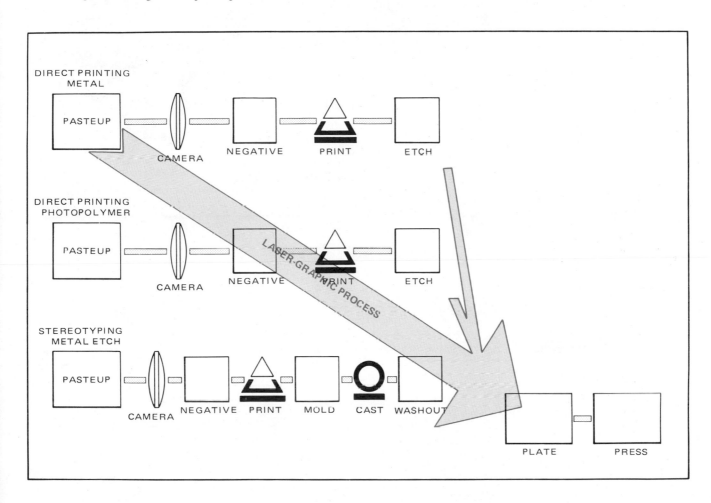

Fig. 5-145. No camera or darkroom procedures are needed to make printing plates by the laser technique. The laser etches are exact reproduction of pasteup directly onto printing plate.

printing plate, Fig. 5-145. The pasteup is made from text set by phototypesetting machines, drawings and photographs.

WOOD CUTS, WOOD ENGRAVINGS AND LINOLEUM CUTS

Until photography was invented, all illustrations printed were made from wood cuts or wood engravings. Fig. 5-146 shows some examples.

There is a difference between a wood cut and a wood engraving. The wood engraving is a design cut in wood with gravers, Fig. 5-147. The wood cut is made with gouges and knives, Fig. 5-148. A wood cut is usually made on the face of the wood. End grain is capable of finer details and wood engravings are made on it, Fig. 5-149. Close-grained wood like

Wood cuts and wood engravings are still used to illustrate limited edition books, greeting cards and as art prints. Linoleum cuts are popular in industrial arts classes, art classes and craft work, Fig. 5-150.

HOW TO MAKE WOOD AND LINOLEUM CUTS

Prepare the design. The first one should be as simple as possible. Remember, the design is reversed when it appears in print. To print the correct way, the drawing must be made in reverse on the wood or linoleum block.

Select a section of smooth, close-grained wood. Cut it type high. Linoleum is sold already mounted on wood and is very close to type high.

Fig. 5-146. Illustrations can be made of wood. Left. Wood engraving. Right. Wood cut.

If you are placing your design in a linoleum block, spray a coat of flat white paint on the printing surface, Fig. 5-151.

Fig. 5-147. Wood engravings are cut with gravers of different shapes.

Allow the paint to dry. Nothing needs to be done to the wood block other than to make sure its edges are square. The printing surface should be sanded smooth with fine sandpaper.

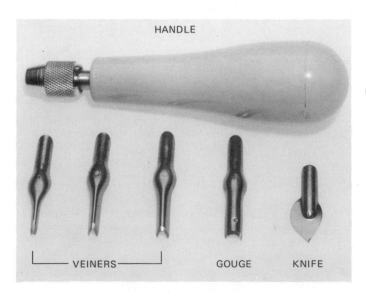

HANDLE

VEINERS   GOUGE   KNIFE

Fig. 5-148. Wood and linoleum cuts are made with gouges, veiners and knives. Blades are interchangeable.

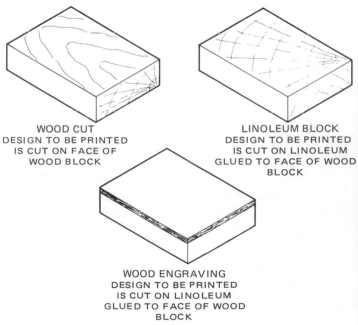

WOOD CUT
DESIGN TO BE PRINTED
IS CUT ON FACE OF
WOOD BLOCK

LINOLEUM BLOCK
DESIGN TO BE PRINTED
IS CUT ON LINOLEUM
GLUED TO FACE OF WOOD
BLOCK

WOOD ENGRAVING
DESIGN TO BE PRINTED
IS CUT ON LINOLEUM
GLUED TO FACE OF WOOD
BLOCK

Fig. 5-149. Wood cuts are made on the face of a wood block. Wood engravings are cut on the end grain. Linoleum blocks are cut in heavy linoleum that has been mounted on a wood block to make it type high.

Fig. 5-150. Suitable wood cut designs. Left. Student designed Christmas card made with a linoleum block. Center. Wood cut used to decorate the introduction page of a privately printed book of poetry. Right. A book illustration made from a wood block.

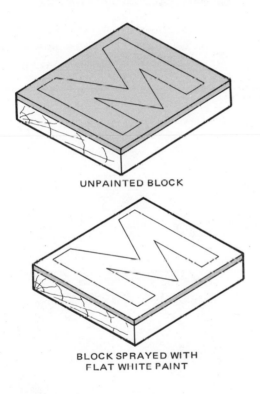

UNPAINTED BLOCK

BLOCK SPRAYED WITH
FLAT WHITE PAINT

Fig. 5-151. Linoleum block should be sprayed with a flat white paint. The design, when drawn on its surface, will be easier to see.

Transfer the design to the wood or linoleum. There are several methods for doing this.

1. If the design is already reversed, place carbon paper between the design and the block. Use masking tape to hold the design and carbon in position. Transfer the reversed design to the block.

2. Draw the original design with a soft lead pencil. Place the design face down on the block and tape it in place. Rub over the back of the design. When this technique is used, the design does not have to be drawn in reverse.

3. If you have a design that is not reversed, place a piece of carbon paper on the back side, carbon side up. Trace the design, flop it and proceed as in No. 1 above.

Go over the transferred design with India ink. Fill in the areas that are to print. Place a bench hook on the table to hold the block while it is being cut, Fig. 5-152.

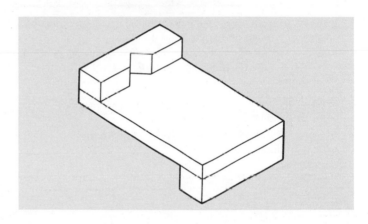

Fig. 5-152. Bench hook holds linoleum block during carving.

Caution: Do not try to hand hold the block while it is being cut. A slip of the cutter can cause a serious injury.

Sharpen the cutters. Then outline the design with a knife or fine veining tool. Use various sizes of gouges to remove large nonprinting areas. Work slowly. It is almost impossible to correct a mistake. Keep the cutters sharp.

Avoid undercutting the printing surface. Maintain a bevel *away* from the printing surface, Fig. 5-153.

Pull a proof. Wipe the ink from the block before it dries. *Do not use a solvent.* Carefully examine the proof. It may be necessary to touch up some areas of the cut. Unwanted printing areas must be removed, Fig. 5-154. See Fig. 5-155 for the proper sequence in making a wood or linoleum cut.

Regular printing inks can be used to print a wood or linoleum cut. However, special inks are made which produce a much better print with less tendency of the paper to stick to the cut. "Slurring" (ink smears on the paper) occurs when sticking paper has to be pulled from the cut.

Paper made especially for printing cuts produces better prints if dampened slightly. A separate block must be used for each color in a multicolor design.

To test knowledge of this section of Relief Printing refer to Test Questions 64 through 73.

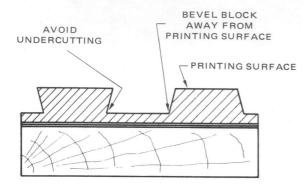

Fig. 5-153. Avoid undercutting printing surfaces. Edges will crumble or split off ruining the illustration.

TEST YOUR KNOWLEDGE – UNIT 5

1. Prepare a sketch of a piece of type showing how relief printing is done.
2. Making relief printing surfaces by pouring molten metal into a mold is called _____ _____ composition.
3. Composition is the technique of _____ .

Fig. 5-154. Check over the proof. Remove unwanted areas that print.

Hand Composition

4. Hand set type is cast as _____ characters.
5. A complete font of type includes _____ and _____ of one style and size of type.
6. Why does the quantity of each character in a font vary?
7. Type is hand set in a:
   a. Brayer.
   b. Chase.
   c. Composing stick.
   d. Galley.
   e. Job case.

  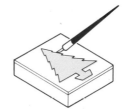

MAKE FULL SIZE DRAWING OF DESIGN

USE CARBON PAPER TO TRANSFER DESIGN TO LINOLEUM BLOCK

FILL IN DRAWING WITH INDIA INK

 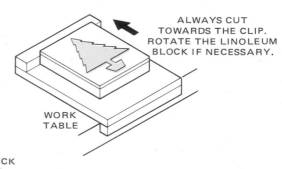

SPRAY INKED DESIGN WITH CLEAR PLASTIC SPRAY TO PREVENT DESIGN FROM WIPING OFF WHEN CLEANING PRINTING INK FROM BLOCK AFTER PULLING PROOF.

ALWAYS CUT TOWARDS THE CLIP. ROTATE THE LINOLEUM BLOCK IF NECESSARY.

WORK TABLE

Fig. 5-155. Follow these steps to make a wood or linoleum cut.

8. How many points in a pica?
9. A complete size range of one typestyle is called a serif. True or False?
10. List five classes of type faces.
11. The right third of a California job case holds _____ letters. These letters are sometimes called _____ letters.
12. Type cases are stored in _____ .
13. When are leads and slugs used?
14. Type is set from _____ to _____ .
15. List some of the demon characters.
16. Why are they called demon characters?
17. An em quad is equal to:
    a. 4 ems.
    b. Half an em.
    c. One-fourth em.
    d. Twice the width of an em.
    e. The square of any type size.
18. An em quad is _____ an em quad.
19. A 3-em space is _____ as thick as an em quad.
20. What are hair spaces?
21. What does the term justify mean?
22. Removing type from the stick is called _____ .
23. A galley is a tray for storing type until it can be printed. True or False?
24. Type is known as pied when it has been _____ .
25. A _____ is pulled to check a typeform for errors and mistakes.
26. What is a brayer?
27. List three safety precautions that must be observed when setting type by hand.
28. Before putting type back in a typecase, three things must be checked to be sure the type is returned to the proper case. What are they?
29. Rules are used to make _____ on printed matter.

Imposition and Presswork

30. Lockup refers to _____ the typeform in a metal frame called a _____ .
31. Prepare a sketch showing a correct chaser method of lockup.
32. Prepare a sketch showing a correct furniture-within-furniture lockup.
33. How are reglets used?
34. What is a quoin and how is it used?
35. Avoid planing a typeform before quoins have been tightened. True or False?
36. How can you check whether a typeform is locked up tightly?
37. Name and briefly describe each of the three types of platen press.
38. After the press has been lubricated, the next step would be to check all _____ and _____ devices.

MATCHING TEST. Match the terms in the first column with the phrases in the second column. In the blank space place the letter of the phrase which best describes the term. Do not write in the text. Use a clean sheet of paper.

39. ____ Rollers.
40. ____ Ink disc.
41. ____ Grippers.
42. ____ Platen.
43. ____ Tympan sheet.
44. ____ Hanger sheets.
45. ____ Bails.
46. ____ Packing.
47. ____ Gauge pins.
48. ____ Fan.
49. ____ Feedboard.
50. ____ Counter.
51. ____ Tinted ink.
52. ____ Offset.

a. Used to position the paper for printing.
b. Hold the tympan sheet to the platen.
c. Sheets under tympan sheet.
d. Holds paper to be fed into press.
e. A light hue of a solid color ink.
f. Spreading paper to make it easier to pick up for printing.
g. Prevents printed sheet from sticking to typeform.
h. Takes ink from ink disc and puts it on the typeform.
i. Holds the gauge pins.
j. Sheets under tympan sheet.
k. Holds the supply of ink.
l. Reverse image on back of printed sheet.
m. Tells number of impressions made.
n. Paper is printed on this surface.

53. Building up the platen so light areas of a proof will print darker is called _____ .
54. Prepare a sketch showing how a flat bed cylinder press works.
55. Prepare a sketch showing how a rotary press operates.
56. List the two types of cylinder presses.
57. The rotary printing press uses _____ printing plates.

Machine Composition

MATCHING TEST. In the blank alongside each word in the left column place the letter of the phrase that best describes the word. Do not write in the text. Use a clean sheet of paper.

58. ____ Line slug.
59. ____ Matrix.
60. ____ Magazine.
61. ____ Monotype.
62. ____ Ludlow.

a. Cast as individual characters.
b. Holds the matrices.
c. Strip of type containing several characters.
d. Casts type up to 96 points.
e. Mold of type character.

63. One advantage of machine composed text is that the type does not have to be _____ . It is _____ .

Printing Plates

64. Most relief printing plates are made by a _____ and _____ _____ .

65. A _____ _____ is made from a drawing with sharp black lines on a white background. There are no gray tones.
66. Explain the steps in making the line engraving.
67. A _____ _____ engraving permits the printing of a photograph where the tones vary from black to white.
68. The printing surface of the above plate is made up of tiny _____ that vary in size. The eye _____ them together into the many tones of gray of the original photograph.
69. How is a stereotype printing plate made?
70. An _____ is a duplicate of an original printing form.
71. List three advantages of the plastic printing plate.
72. How does a wood cut differ from a wood engraving?
73. List the steps in making a wood cut or a linoleum cut.

THINGS TO DO

1. Make a large model of a piece of type.
2. Make models to the same scale of quads and space material.
3. Have your instructor assign you a typecase containing 10 or 12 point type. Note the typecase number and the size and the name of the typeface in it. Study the lay of the case. Check the case to be sure the type and space materials are distributed properly.
4. Secure discarded printed material (old magazines, books and advertisements) and cut from them examples of the following typefaces.
   a. Oldstyle.
   b. Modern.
   c. Square serif.
   d. Sans serif.
   e. Occasional or Novelty.
   f. Cursive or Script.
   g. Text or Old English.
   Carefully paste your examples of a sheet of paper 8 1/2 by 11 in. Put your name on the sheet and turn it in to your instructor for credit.
5. Get a copy of the daily paper. Proofread several columns on the front page. Use proofreaders' marks to note mistakes and omissions. Put your name of the page and turn it in to your instructor for credit.
6. Clip examples of initial letters from discarded printed matter. Mount them neatly on a sheet of paper 8 1/2 by 11 in. Put your name on the paper and turn it in to your instructor for credit.
7. Secure examples of the various types of relief printing image carriers: foundry type, Monotype, linotype slug, Ludlow slug, line engraving, halftone engraving and stereotype. Mount them on a display panel. Neatly label each example.
8. Visit a local newspaper office. Request permission to spend time with the proofreaders. Note how they work. Prepare a report on what you have observed.
9. Visit a local printing firm. Observe the sequence of operations from placing the order to delivery of the finished printing job. Secure copies of the various forms that are used for routing the job. Prepare a report on what you have observed.
10. Contact a local printing firm. Request examples of the work they do. Make the samples available to the class for examination.
11. Secure examples of wood cuts, wood engravings and linoleum cuts. Do not cut the examples from the books but rather make copies of them on a copy machine.
12. Secure a cut or block of wood at least 15 by 25 picas. Demonstrate how to lock up a job by the chaser method and by the furniture-within-furniture method. Have your instructor check your work.
13. Research the history of the linotype line casting machine.
14. Research the history of the platen press.
15. Clean and lubricate the power-driven platen press. Prepare it for printing. Do not ink the press.
16. Secure 50 to 100 sheets of scrap paper at least 5 by 8 in. Locate gauge pins in the center of the platen press. Use the paper to practice feeding the press. Start with the press at slow speed. Increase speed as you get experience.
17. Visit a local printing firm. Request to visit the machine composition area. Write a report on what you observe.
18. Visit a local printing firm. Request to visit the pressroom. Prepare a report on what you have observed.

Unit 6
LITHOGRAPHY OR OFFSET PRINTING

Objectives

This unit is an overview of how printing is done when the image area is level with the printing plate's surface.

You will learn how type and illustrations are generated, assembled and converted into a printing plate. You will see how an offset printing plate uses ink and water to reproduce the plate image on paper. You will be able to recognize the tools and equipment, name their parts and describe their operation. Given the use of tools and equipment, you will be able to produce simple offset printing.

Lithographic or offset printing uses no raised printing surfaces. Both the printing and nonprinting areas are on the same level or plane. That is why such printing processes are also called PLANOGRAPHIC (one plane) printing, Fig. 6-1.

Fig. 6-1. Planographic printing is done from a flat surface. Image and non-image areas are on the same plane or level.

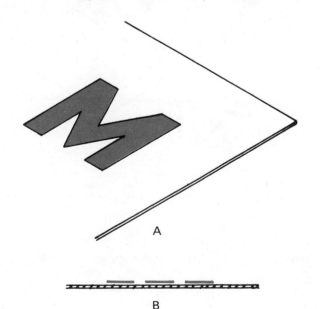

A

B

The first planographic printing was done from etched stone plates, Fig. 6-2. Thus came the name lithography which means "stone printing." Stone is still sometimes used. It is a hand printing operation employed most often as an art technique.

Fig. 6-2. This stone has a design etched in its surface for lithographic printing.

It would seem impossible that printing could take place when the type and pictures are not raised above other areas of the printing plate. *Planographic printing works because grease and water do not readily mix.*

The image or printing area is usually put onto the printing plate with photographic and chemical processes. A camera produces an image on a film negative while chemical solutions develop the image on both film and printing plate. The process is said, therefore, to be PHOTOCHEMICAL.

Printing areas on the plate are processed so they will accept ink (grease). Nonprinting areas are processed to be receptive to water. Ink will not stick to nonprinting areas when those areas are coated with a thin film of water, Fig. 6-3.

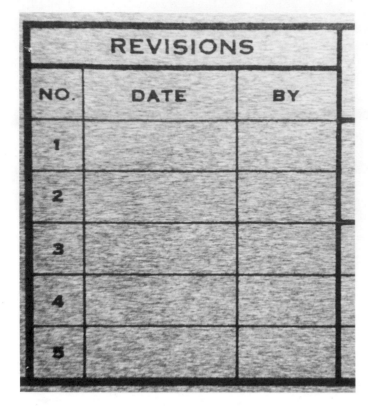

Fig. 6-3. Close-up view shows surface of an aluminum offset plate. Image was placed on a plate by a photochemical process. The image is treated to attract ink. Ink will not adhere (stick) to non-image areas as long as those areas are kept moistened.

Fig. 6-4. Offset is the term employed for planographic printing when the printing is done by a machine. (ATF/Davidson Co., Inc.)

Most modern planographic printing is done by the offset method. This is a machine operation, Fig. 6-4. The inked image on the plate (image carrier) is picked up by a rubber blanket. From the blanket the image transfers to the paper, Fig. 6-5. The image carrier can be a plate of thin metal, (aluminum), paper or plastic. See Fig. 6-6. Offset plates are low in cost. They can be made quickly.

The quality of offset printing is determined by many things or factors. Each will be described briefly. All of them depend on the technical skills of the workers or technicians who perform the various printing tasks.

IMAGE GENERATION

Image generation is the act of producing all parts of the printed message appearing in a printed job. Another term for it is COPY PREPARATION.

Unit 12, Typographic Design, describes how printed material is designed. In job printing the design is prepared before any copy is prepared.

A printed message may consist of type alone or it may include some kind of illustration. Type and illustrations are produced in several very distinct ways. Image generation, then, can be separated into two distinct parts. Each part has several processes:

1. Type composition — producing the letters and words.

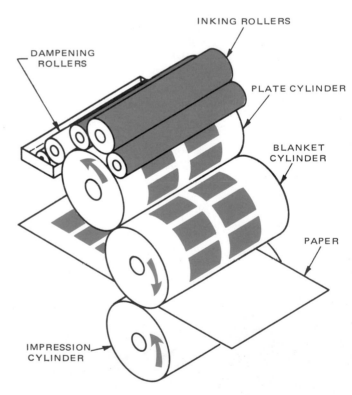

Fig. 6-5. Offset printing is a machine operation. With this planographic technique, ink is offset from a thin plate (image carrier) to a rubber blanket. From the blanket, the image (ink) is transferred to the paper.

   a. Hot type composition.
   b. Cold type composition.
2. Generating illustrations — producing and preparing art or photography.
   a. Manual image generation.
   b. Mechanical generation of illustrations (photographs).

Fig. 6-6. The image carrier is a thin metal, plastic or paper plate. (ATF/Davidson Co., Inc.)

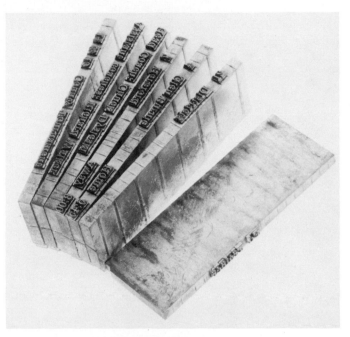

Fig. 6-7. Hot type composition uses individual type characters or entire lines of type cast from metal.

HOT TYPE COMPOSITION

Hot type composition is so called because it includes the generation (making) of both individual letters and lines of type from molten metal. Hand set (foundry) type is considered hot type because the letters, though now quite cool, were molten when originally cast. It is easier to see why machine set type, Fig. 6-7, is called hot type. It is cast in machines which heat the molten metal to about 500 deg. F (260 C) before forcing it into the type matrices (molds). (Unit 5, Relief Printing, has more information about hot typesetting methods.)

Being designed for use in relief printing, hot type must be adapted for use with a system such as planographic printing which prints from a flat surface. This is accomplished by making a black on white reproduction of the type. The type is inked and a high quality proof is taken of it. This is called a REPRODUCTION PROOF or REPRO. See Fig. 6-8. The proof is then pasted onto the layout. Later the layout is photographed. The film negative will be used in making the offset printing plate.

COLD TYPE COMPOSITION

Cold type composition includes all type-generating techniques that do not use metal type. Type can be created using one of the following techniques.

The Varigraph, Fig. 6-9, is a mechanical lettering instrument. A stylus, following a design cut into a metal or plastic

Fig. 6-8. These proofs made on smooth white paper, are called "repros." The repro is trimmed and pasted onto the layout.

Fig. 6-9. A mechanical lettering instrument. Many styles of lettering matrices are available. (Varitype Inc.)

matrix, (pattern), guides a pen to draw the image. India ink is used in the pen. Another type of mechanical lettering device is shown in Fig. 6-10.

Fig. 6-10. Leroy lettering equipment produces lettering manually.

Rub-on materials, Fig. 6-11, are also known as DRY TRANSFER MATERIALS. The lettering is transferred from the backing sheet by lightly rubbing over the design with a burnisher. This is done after the image has been positioned on the layout.

PRESSURE SENSITIVE MATERIALS, Fig. 6-12, offer lettering attached to a plastic support sheet. The layout person cuts the image away from the backing sheet. After it is positioned, a slight pressure will adhere it to the layout.

A wide selection of alphabets, symbols, illustrations, special effects images, lines and decorative borders are available in both rub-on and pressure sensitive materials, Fig. 6-13.

TAB TYPE, Fig. 6-14, is used to set headlines. Type comes in tab form. The layout artist places the tabbed letters and figures in a special composing stick. Spacing is done with blank tabs. Type is set from left to right as it would read. The letters

Fig. 6-11. Rub-on lettering. Left. Transfer letters are fastened down by placing the letter in position and burnishing the back of the sheet with a smooth object. Right. Removing the lettering sheet after the letter has been applied to the sheet. Guideline is erased after entire line of lettering has been applied.

Fig. 6-12. Dry transfer lettering. Left. Removing letter from lettering sheet. Right. Applying letter to layout. Guideline keeps type straight. It is cut away after entire line of lettering is positioned.

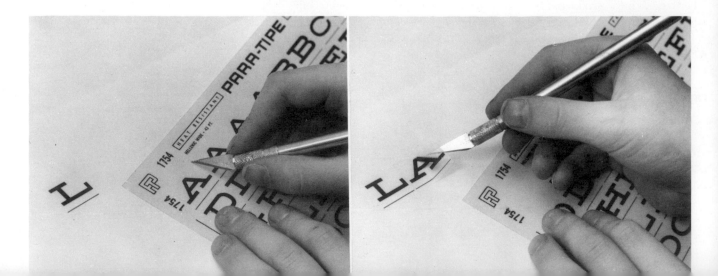

LEADERSHIP IN THE
18 leadership in the creat
LEADERSHIP IN
24 leadership in the

LEADERSHIP
24 leadership in
LEADERS
30 leadership

Leaders
LEADERShi
leadership in
Leadership In T

LEADERSHIP IN THE
24 leadership in the cre
LEADERSHIP IN
36 leadership in
LEADERSHIP IN THE
24 leadership in the
LEADERSHIP

Fig. 6-13. Preprinted lettering. Many styles and sizes are available.

Fig. 6-14. Tab type is used to set headline. The characters are furnished in tab form. Type characters, printed on heavy stock, are assembled in special composing stick shown.

Fig. 6-15. Direct impression or strike-on composition is generated on a typewriterlike device. (Royal Typewriter Co.)

are double faced (on both sides of the tabs). Tape holds the line together. The taped side is turned over and pasted or taped to the layout.

STRIKE-ON COMPOSITION

Strike-on composition is type matter generated by a machine like a typewriter. See Fig. 6-15. This technique is often referred to as DIRECT-IMPRESSION COMPOSITION.

The conventional typewriter can produce usable copy if a carbon ribbon replaces the regular cloth ribbon. An electric typewriter will produce copy that is more uniform in appearance than a manual typewriter. However, either machine is too slow for commercial work. Each line, moreover, must be justified manually, Fig. 6-16.

Semi-automatic systems, like the A-M Varityper, Fig. 6-17, have proportionally designed typefaces. (Not all characters take the same space. All characters on a regular typewriter are equally spaced). Copy must be typed twice for justified composition. Spacing is uniform throughout the line of text.

Other direct-impression machines are fully automatic, Fig. 6-18. They record copy on magnetic or punched tapes. Lines are not justified nor are words hyphenated. The tapes are coded and fed into a READER that drives a COMPOSER UNIT. Copy can be set at speeds up to 150 words per minute, Fig. 6-19. The text in this book was set by direct impression.

PHOTOGRAPHIC TYPESETTING

All photographic typesetters have the following in common, Fig. 6-20:
1. Master type font negatives.
2. Light source.
3. Light-sensitive film or paper.

In phototypesetting, the type fonts are on negative film. The individual characters are called PHOTOMATRICES. Typesetting takes place when a high intensity light shines through these matrices onto light-sensitive paper. Developing solutions bring out the image to produce copy that is ready for pasteup.

Justifying makes both sides of a — 0
column of type line/up vertically. — 1
Even/though/your/typewriter does — 3
not have/an/automatic/justifier, — 3
justifying/is/a/simple/two-step — 4
process that results in much neater — 0
looking columns, and a more profes- — 0
sional looking paper. —

Here is how it is done. /First, — 1
draw a/column on a sheet of paper; — 1
or set/the/right hand tab stop to — 2
column width. Then type your story — 0
completely through. DO/NOT extend — 1
copy over the right hand line. —

Justifying makes both sides of a
column of type line up vertically.
Even   though   your   typewriter does
not have   an   automatic   justifier,
justifying   is   a   simple   two-step
process that results in much neater
looking columns, and a more professional looking paper.

Here is how it is done.   First,
draw a   column on a sheet of paper;
or set   the   right hand tab stop to
column width.   Then type your story
completely through.   DO NOT extend
copy over the right hand line.

Fig. 6-16. Direct impression composition must be justified manually. Left. First step in justifying typewriter typesetting. Count number of letters each line is short. Indicate this on outside of the right hand margin line. Mark diagonal line at each point where additional spaces can be added. Right. Justified column. When done properly, both right and left margins are aligned.

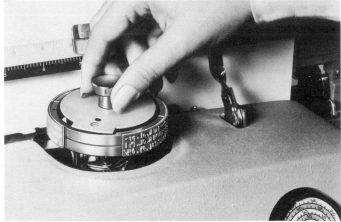

Fig. 6-17. Varityper is a semiautomatic composer with interchangeable typefaces. Left. Unit is slightly larger than a typewriter. Right. Interchangeable type font.   (A.M. International, Inc.)

Fig. 6-18. Copy is shown being prepared on the IBM Magnetic Tape Selectric Composer. A "draft" copy is first prepared on a recording unit. During the typing all machine functions are recorded on magnetic tape which can store about 4000 words or about a solid page of newspaper copy. Tape is placed in a reading unit (right) by the operator to set final copy.   (IBM Corp.)

Fig. 6-19. This copy was set on a tape controlled composing unit. It justifies lines, indents paragraphs and hyphenates words where needed.

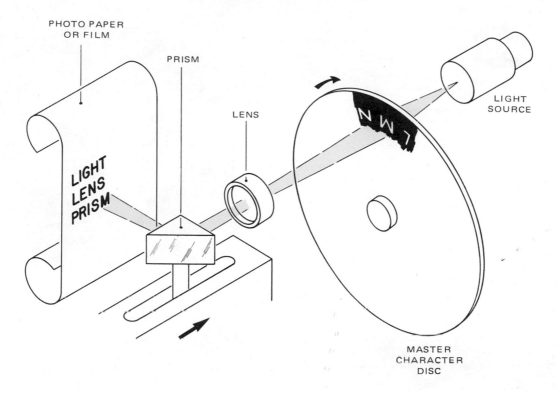

PHOTO PAPER OR FILM

PRISM

LENS

LIGHT SOURCE

LIGHT LENS PRISM

MASTER CHARACTER DISC

Fig. 6-20. Makeup of a typical phototypesetter always includes negative type fonts, light source and light sensitive material.

A series of lenses may be used to change type size. Exposed film or paper, after developing the drying, is ready for layout.

Phototypesetters like the one shown in Fig. 6-21 produce headlines and display lines. They can set type in sizes ranging up to 115 points. There is a variety of styles, Fig. 6-22. Letter spacing is controlled manually or semiautomatically, depending upon the machine.

On a DIRECT ENTRY PHOTOTYPESETTER, Fig. 6-23, all controls are at the operator's fingertips on a keyboard similar to that of a typewriter. Format data (type size, font selection, leading and line length) are continuously displayed on a video screen. The screen also displays the line being keyboarded (typed) and the line being set by the photo unit. Corrections can be made anywhere on the line being keyboarded.

Characters are generated from a master character font, Fig. 6-24. They can also be set electronically on the face of a cathode ray tube (CRT), Fig. 6-25.

COMPUTER AIDED COMPOSITION

Many phototypesetters are computer controlled. Information (input data) is entered into the computer at TERMINALS. These are keyboards similar to the one on a typewriter. As text is entered into the system, it can be seen at the bottom of the screen, Fig. 6-26. Copy moves up the screen as each line is filled. Later, any of the copy can be recalled to the screen for review or corrections.

Fig. 6-21. Some phototypesetters produce headlines and display type only. Top. The VariTyper headliner. (A.M. International, Inc.) Bottom. The StripPrinter Headline Maker. (StripPrinter, Inc.)

Fig. 6-22. Samples of type that can be set on the StripPrinter Headline Maker. Top. Type is exposed on white paper. Bottom. Type exposed on film.

Fig. 6-24. Master character font for direct entry phototypesetter shown in Fig. 6-23. It carries a film negative of 112 characters.

Fig. 6-23. Direct entry phototypesetter lets operator see "televised" copy of what is being typeset. (A.M. International, Inc.)

All inserts (additions), deletions (material taken out) or revisions can be made directly on the screen. There is no need for hand markup or typewritten copy. The system adjusts automatically for changes in the copy. It hyphenates and justifies lines from unjustified input. (Input is the copy that has been typed into the unit.) Copy is fitted, given a size and is positioned on the screen before it is actually typeset.

All text is stored in the computer memory bank until ready for use. There are no tapes to handle. Type matter is photo-composed at up to 150 lines per minute. Type sizes range from 5 to 72 points.

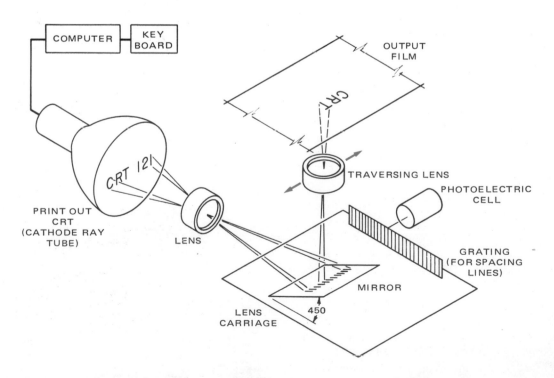

Fig. 6-25. One technique used to generate text from a cathode ray tube (CRT). In response to coded tape, selected lines of text form, one line at a time, on the CRT. Line is transmitted through a mirror-lens system and gets carefully positioned on output film.

Fig. 6-26. Input terminal for a computer controlled phototypesetter. (Today Newspaper, Melbourne, FL)

The next stage of development in computer-aided typesetting does away with pasteups. A computer controlled laser produces printing plates (relief or offset) from coded instructions. Text as well as line and halftone illustrations are reproduced. See Fig. 6-27.

GENERATING ART AND PHOTOGRAPHY

Copy other than type or some kind of lettering is often used in producing a printed message. Known as art, it can be generated in several ways.

MANUAL IMAGE GENERATION is material prepared by hand with a pen and ink, brush, charcoal or other art tools. See Fig. 6-28. India ink, drawn on a smooth, flat white paper is recommended for the best reproduction. Avoid pencil-drawn images. Pencil lines do not always photograph well.

CLIP ART, Fig. 6-29, is another source of ready-made artwork. Illustrations or designs can be purchased on sheets. They are cut from the sheet and pasted onto the layout. Designs are usually furnished in several sizes. Different seasonal and holiday themes are available in clip art form.

PHOTOGRAPHS are a common type of illustration used in printing. You can see many examples in this text. There are several sources for photography. You can take the photographs yourself or you can purchase them from freelance photographers, commercial photographers or photo services. The latter have catalogs from which you can choose the illustrations you want.

To test your knowledge of Image Generation, refer to Test Questions 6 through 9.

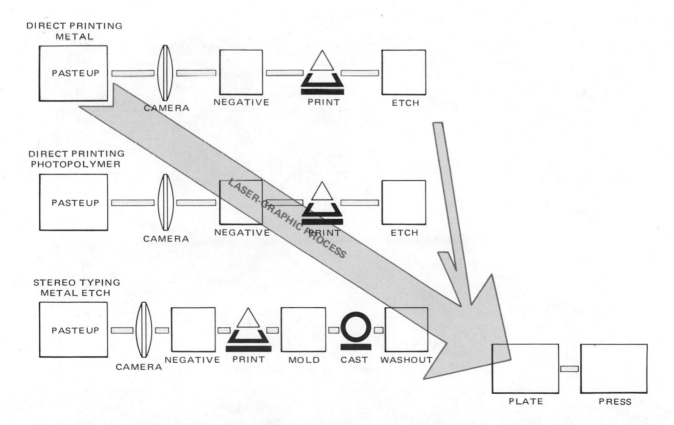

Fig. 6-27. Computer controlled laser can make offset printing plate directly from coded input data. No pasteup needs to be made.

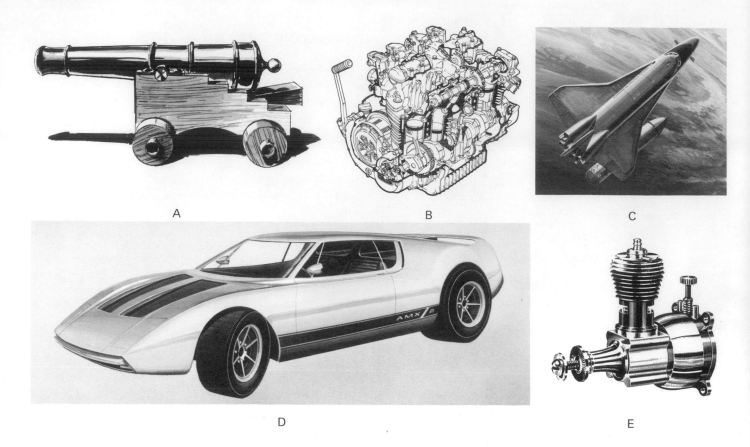

Fig. 6-28. There are many ways to produce illustrations by hand. A—Wash drawing. B—Pen and ink drawing. C—Brush drawing. D—Air brush. E—Scratch board.

Fig. 6-29. Clip art is another source of ready-made artwork. Illustration or design is cut from clip art sheet or book and pasted to layout. (Volk Corp.)

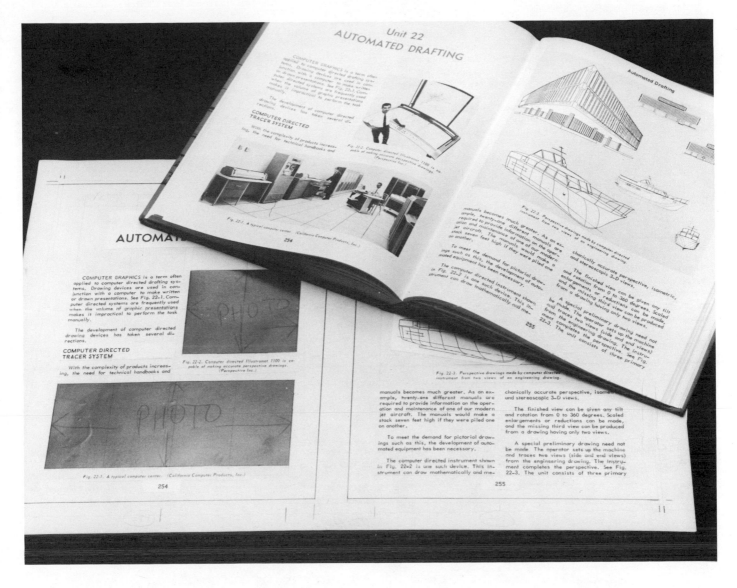

Fig. 6-30. Pasteup for two pages of drafting book. Note areas blocked in darker color for halftones (photographs).

COPY PREPARATION

The final assembly of camera-ready art and copy is called a PASTEUP, FINAL LAYOUT OR MECHANICAL. See Fig. 6-30. Making the pasteup is also know by the term IMAGE ASSEMBLY.

Since it will be copied photographically, the pasteup must be made accurately.

Line work, Fig. 6-31, must be clean, sharp and uniform. Locations for halftones are drawn with red or black KEY-LINES, Fig. 6-32, or blocked out with a black or red block, Fig. 6-33. These areas must be exactly the same sizes as the halftones being used.

The halftones will be fitted or keyed into the blocked out areas on the photo negative made from the pasteup. Often, only a single halftone is needed in a layout. If the pasteup is 100 percent printed size, a contact print of the halftone negative can be attached directly to the pasteup. Halftone positives are known as VELOXES.

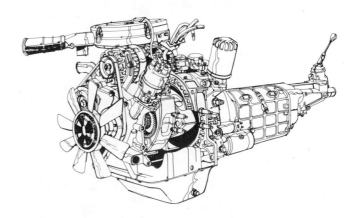

Fig. 6-31. Line work must be clean, sharp and uniform to be used on a pasteup. This is a pen and ink drawing of a Wankel internal combustion engine. (Mazda Motors Corp. of America)

rebus emolument oariunt iniur. Itaque ipsad optabil, sed quiran cunditat vel propter and tuitior vitam et luptat pler egenium improb fugienda improbitate cuis. Guaea derata micospe rtiuneren quam nostros expetere quo loco visetur tuent tamet eum locum seque facil, ut Lorem ipsum dolor sit amet, consectet eiusmod tempor incidunt ut labore et de enim ad minim veniam, quis nostrud oris nisi ut aliquip ex ea commodo co dolor in reprehendert in voluptate veli dolore eu fugiat nulla pariatur. At vero praesent luptatum delenit aigue duos non provident, simil tempor sunt in c laborum et dolor fuga. Et harumd dere liber tempor cum nobis eligend optio c maxim placeat facer possim omnis v repellend. Temporibud autem quinus necessit atib saepe eveniet ut er repudia bene sanos ad iustitiam, aequitated fidem. Neque hominy infant aut inuist fact est cond qui neg facile efficerd possit duo conetud notiner si effecerit, e opes vel fortunag vel ingen liberalitat magis conveniunt, da but tuntung e benevolent sib conciliant et, aptissim est ad quiet. Endium caritat praeser cum omning null sit cuas peccand quaert en imigent cupidat a natura facil explent sine julla inaura autend inanc sunt is parend non est nihil enim a desiderabile. Concupis plusque in insupinaria detriment est quam in his e

Ectamen nedue enim haec movere pellat sensar luptae epicur semper.

Fig. 6-32. Key lines can be used to locate halftones on a pasteup.

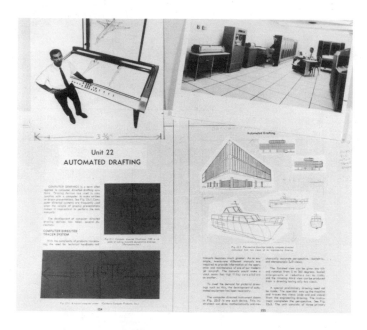

Fig. 6-33. Location of halftones can also be indicated with red or black blocks. Blocks must be same size as the halftones. They will show as clear windows in negative. Photographs are shown at top.

A printed piece may require several different illustrations. Some of them have to be enlarged or reduced in size to fit the layout. This will require SCALING and/or CROPPING of the illustrations.

SCALING

When the size of an illustration must be enlarged or reduced to fit a layout, both dimensions will change. The new size of one dimension will be known. However the new size of the

other dimension must be found. The methods for finding this out are known as SCALING. See Fig. 6-34, for the DIAGONAL LINE METHOD of scaling. A PROPORTIONAL SCALE, Fig. 6-35, is used when scaling is done mathematically. Line artwork can be enlarged or reduced in size by making a photostat, Fig. 6-36. (A photostat or "stat" is an inexpensive photographic print.)

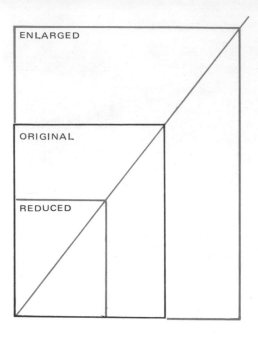

Fig. 6-34. The diagonal line method of scaling a photo or illustration. Draw parallel line. Where it meets diagonal line marks other dimension. Second line drawn at right angles to first will give new size.

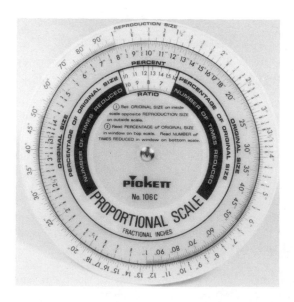

Fig. 6-35. Proportional scale. Calculates percentage that artwork has been reduced or enlarged and gives size of unknown dimension.

CROPPING

Cropping eliminates unwanted portions of an illustration, Fig. 6-37. Crop marks are made on the illustration to show the area that is to be printed.

Fig. 6-36. Artwork can be enlarged or reduced photographically. Resulting print is called a stat.

Fig. 6-38. Pasteups are made on a smooth, white heavy matte paper or illustration board.

THE PASTEUP

The pasteup is made on smooth, white, heavy matte paper or illustration board. Fig. 6-38. Light blue guidelines, Fig. 6-39, are often used to mark where images are to be placed. The film used in graphic arts photography is not sensitive to blue. Thus, the lines will not appear (reproduce) on the film.

Another aid for truing up the copy is the T-square. Fig. 6-40 shows a layout person using one.

ATTACHING ELEMENTS TO PASTEUP

Three methods of attaching elements to the pasteup have proven satisfactory.
1. Waxing. Pass the copy through a WAX COATER, Fig. 6-41. The coater rolls a thin layer of melted wax on the back of the copy. Press the waxed copy in place (with a clean hand roller or burnisher) to make the copy stick to the pasteup.

Fig. 6-37. Crop lines show the camera operator what part of the photo or drawing will be used. These marks should be placed in the margin as shown, never in the image area.

Fig. 6-39. Light blue guide lines are often used to help align copy and artwork. The lines do not reproduce on graphic arts film. Shown is a layout sheet used to produce the metalworking book pictured. (Lines were made black so they could reproduce here.)

Fig. 6-40. Align copy during pasteup with T-square.

Fig. 6-41. Waxer places thin coating of an adhesive wax on back of copy. Pressure will attach it to layout sheet.

Waxed copy does not have to be attached immediately.

2. Taping. Transparent tape, Fig. 6-42, (both single and double faced) can also be used to affix copy to the pasteup. With tape, however, it is difficult to reposition copy after it has been fastened.

Fig. 6-42. Copy and artwork can also be attached to pasteup with transparent tape.

3. Rubber cement. To apply rubber cement, Fig. 6-43, place copy face down on a clean sheet of paper. Brush a thin coat of rubber cement on the back of the copy. Keep the cement thinned to the proper consistency or it will dry too quickly. Excess cement will squeeze out around the edges of the element after it has been adhered. This surplus can be rubbed away with a clean finger or a rubber cement pickup.

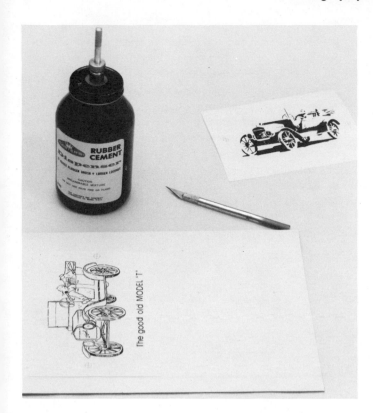

Fig. 6-43. Rubber cement will also attach copy and artwork to pasteup.

A tissue or acetate film oversheet, Fig. 6-44, will protect the pasteup during handling and storage. Also instructions can be written on the oversheet.

Fig. 6-44. Protective tissue or acetate film oversheet covers a pasteup during handling and storage. Instructions can be written on the tissue.

REGISTER MARKS

Register marks, Fig. 6-45, are used for alignment purposes when two or more elements of a pasteup are to be photographed and/or printed separately on the same job, Fig. 6-46.

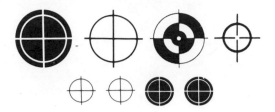

Fig. 6-45. Register marks are produced in several styles.

Fig. 6-46. Register marks aid in aligning multicolored artwork.

The printing will be in REGISTER if the marks are in perfect alignment when the complementary flats, one for each color, are stripped up, Fig. 6-47. (A flat is the film of the printing image after it is prepared for exposure of the printing plate.)

The good old MODEL "T"

Fig. 6-47. How register marks are used to align the two colors on this illustration.

To test your knowledge of Copy Preparation, refer to Test Questions 10 through 19 at the end of this unit.

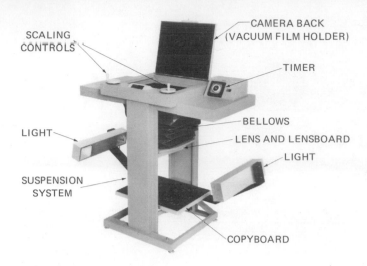

Fig. 6-48. Parts that make up a graphic arts camera. Lensboard and copyboard are movable.   (Gateco Products)

PHOTOCONVERSION

In photoconversion, the image assembled for printing is photographed on film and transferred to the printing plate. The photographic image is made on the film with a PROCESS CAMERA. (Unit 15, Photography, describes how a camera and film work.)

The process camera can copy the image same size, enlarge it or reduce it. The operator controls the size by the distance the copy is from the lens of the camera.

The camera is made up of several important parts:
1. A copyboard, to which the image is attached.
2. A lensboard, to which the lens is attached.
3. A lens, which is an arrangement of glass prisms to direct the reflections from the copy onto the film.
4. A camera back, a flat surface supporting the film.
5. Bellows, a hood stretching between the lensboard and the camera back. Its purpose is to keep outside light from ruining the film before the exposure is made.
6. Suspension system, a framework supporting all other parts of the camera.

Parts of a process camera are shown in Fig. 6-48. Cameras are designed either as VERTICAL or HORIZONTAL systems. See Fig. 6-49.

Caution: A process camera is an expensive piece of equipment. Use it carefully. If you are not sure how to adjust it, ask your instructor for assistance.

GRAPHIC ARTS FILM

All photographic films have the same basic construction. A base of clear polyester, acetate, glass or some other transparent material supports an emulsion of gelatin in which are suspended light-sensitive grains of silver halides. (See Unit 15, Photography, for additional information on film.)

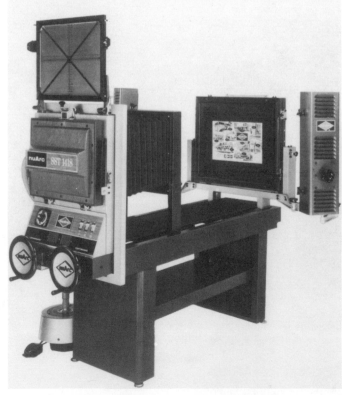

Fig. 6-49. Process cameras are of either the vertical or horizontal type. Left. In vertical camera, lensboard and copyboard are lined up vertically. Right. Lensboard and copyboard of a horizontal are lined up horizontally.   (nuArc Co., Inc.)

A special dye layer separates the emulsion from the base. Its purpose is to prevent light rays from bouncing back into the emulsion and spoiling the exposure.

Graphic arts films are of two types:
1. Panchromatic which is sensitive to all colors of light.
2. Orthochromatic which is sensitive to blue, green and yellow light but practically insensitive to red light.

MAKING A LINE NEGATIVE

Line copy is an image made up of solid lines and/or type. Fig. 6-50 illustrates different kinds of line copy. The image has no gray middle tones like those found on a photograph. When such material is photographed, the negative shows the lines and type as either opaque or perfectly clear areas, Fig. 6-51. (Opaque means no light can come through it.)

PREPARING THE CAMERA

1. Clean the glass cover on the copyboard of the camera.
2. Center the copy on the copyboard, Fig. 6-52. Guidelines on the copyboard correspond with similar lines on the film holder.

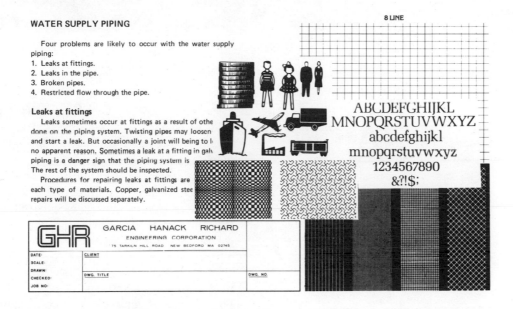

Fig. 6-50. Typical examples of line copy. There are no gray middletones like those found in a photograph.

Fig. 6-51. When exposed and developed, a line copy negative shows lines and type as perfectly clean areas.

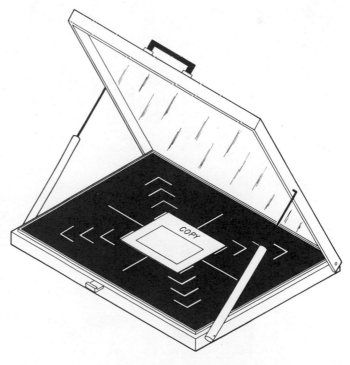

Fig. 6-52. Use guidelines on copyboard to center copy.

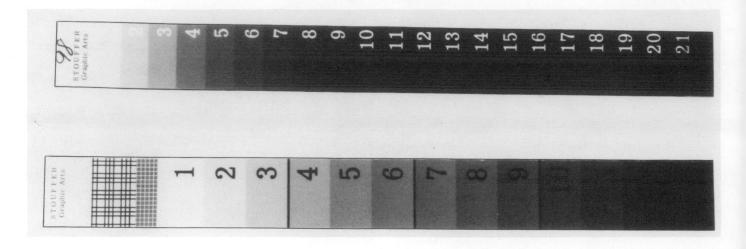

Fig. 6-53. Sensitivity guides are also known as gray scales. Top. Platemakers' sensitivity guide. Bottom. Camera operators' sensitivity guide.

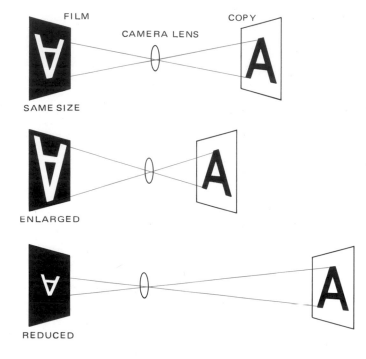

Fig. 6-54. Image size on negative is determined by how far copyboard is from film.

3. Place a SENSITIVITY GUIDE (also called a GRAY SCALE) on the copy as near center as possible. See Fig. 6-53. Avoid covering any part of the copy with the guide.
4. Close the copyboard cover.
5. Move the camera lights until the copy is evenly lighted.
6. Adjust the camera for the size the copy is to be reproduced on the negative. (Copy can be enlarged, reduced or made the same size as the original.) Image size on the negative is determined by how far the copyboard is from the film, Fig. 6-54.

Many cameras have SCALING CONTROLS, Fig. 6-55, to establish the percentage of reduction or enlargement. For example, if copy is to be photographed full size (100 percent), set the scaling controls to 100 percent. Scaling controls would be set to 50 percent if copy is to be reduced to half size (50 percent).

Some cameras have a ground glass screen fitted on the film back, Fig. 6-56. An image of the copy will be projected on the glass screen if the lens is opened and the camera lights turned on. Focus can be checked by examining the projected image with a 6 or 10 power magnifier. The image reflected on the ground glass can also be measured for correct size.

Fig. 6-55. Digital readout scaling controls on modern graphic arts camera. Number on the digital readout indicates percentage of enlargement or reduction of original copy. Will image on negative be larger or smaller than original copy? By how much?

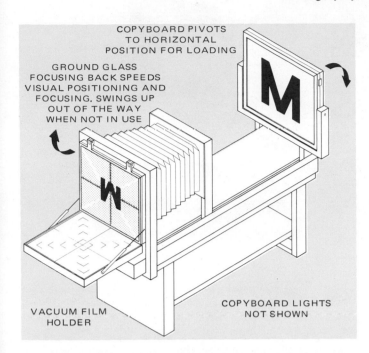

Fig. 6-56. Ground glass screen fitted to most cameras permits sharp focusing of image. Screen image can also be measured to be sure it will be reproduced the correct size.

7. Remove the ground glass screen from the film holder. Close the lens and turn off all lights except the safelight.

8. Remove a sheet of film from storage. Position it on the film holder, Fig. 6-57. Place the emulsion side (light side of film) toward the lens. Film should be slightly larger than the image size reflected on the ground glass.

   Important: Avoid touching the film surfaces. Handle the film by the edges with dry hands.

9. Set the VACUUM SELECTOR VALVE, Fig. 6-58, for the film size. Start the vacuum pump and close the film holder. Vacuum will hold the film tightly against the film holder.

SETTING EXPOSURE

1. Set the lens opening and exposure time as recommended for the film being used. Type of lens and condition of the camera lights can affect exposure time. Your instructor will

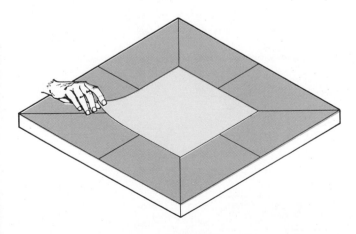

Fig. 6-57. When placing film on film holder, be sure emulsion side (light side) of film is toward lens.

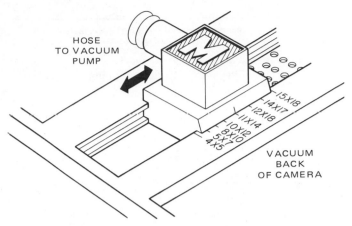

Fig. 6-58. Set vacuum selector valve (if your graphic arts camera is fitted with such a device) for film size being exposed.

Everything takes longer than you think.

Everything takes longer than you think.

Everything takes longer than you think.

Everything takes longer than you think.

Fig. 6-59. Properly exposed and developed negative should look like the original. Examples show problems that may be encountered.

help you determine the correct settings. In general, if the film is fresh; if the camera setting and exposure are correct; if film is properly developed, the resulting negative, Fig. 6-59, should have:

a. Dense black areas and clean, sharp transparent areas.

b. Image edges that are as sharp as the original copy.

c. Few, if any, pin holes in the solid black areas.

d. Line widths the same as the original copy.

   Important: If the image is reduced in size (smaller than full size), a shorter exposure time, or smaller lens opening will be needed. Copy enlargement (more than full size) will require longer exposure time, or a larger lens opening. See table in Fig. 6-60.

Many cameras have a PERCENTAGE CALIBRATED LENS DIAPHRAM CONTROL, Fig. 6-61. This automatically corrects lens setting for enlarging or reducing copy.

2. Turn on the camera lights and make the exposure. The film

WITH A SAME-SIZE (100 PERCENT) EXPOSURE OF 10 SECONDS	
Reproduction Size as a Percentage of Original Size	Adjusted Exposure Time in Seconds
25	4
50	5 1/2
75	8
100 (Same Size)	10
125	12 1/2
150	16
175	19
200	23

Fig. 6-60. Exposure table for copy that is to be enlarged or reduced. The larger the size the greater the exposure. (Eastman Kodak Co.)

Fig. 6-62. A safelight provides enough light for the photographer to see what he or she is doing without exposing the film. Different mounting methods are used. (nuArc Co., Inc.)

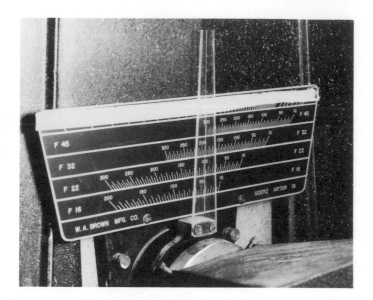

Fig. 6-61. A percentage calibrated lens diaphram control. It automatically compensates for enlarging or reducing copy size.

must be developed and fixed before the lights can be turned on in the darkroom.

DEVELOPING LINE NEGATIVES

The area where film is to be developed must be clean and as free of dust as possible. Dust will cause "pinholes" (small clear spots) in film emulsion. Chemical dust can contaminate and ruin film.

THE DARKROOM

Since film is light-sensitive until it is developed, it must be handled in a darkroom which is sealed against outside light. A SAFELIGHT, Fig. 6-62, can be used with most graphic arts films. The safelight provides just enough light so the photographer can see what he or she is doing. The safelight is usually red. Orthochromatic film does not "see" this color very well. Such a light will not affect film if the film is not exposed to it for too long. Some film is not sensitive to other colors than red. Use only the safelight color specified by the film manufacturer.

Important: For best results when developing film, read carefully the instructions packaged with the film.

PREPARING THE DARKROOM

Arrange the developer, stop bath, fixer and washing trays as shown in Fig. 6-63. Fill each tray about 3/4 in. (20 mm) deep with the appropriate solution.

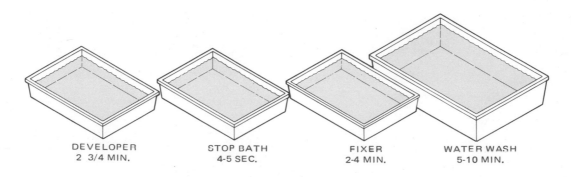

DEVELOPER	STOP BATH	FIXER	WATER WASH
2 3/4 MIN.	4-5 SEC.	2-4 MIN.	5-10 MIN.

Fig. 6-63. Recommended arrangement of developer, stop bath, fixer and washing trays.

Use developers recommended on the instruction sheet. The sheet will also suggest developing times and solution temperatures. *They must be followed very carefully.*

Recommended developer temperature is usually 68 deg. F (20 C). This temperature can be reached by placing the developer tray in a larger tray of either hot or cold water.

Do not add hot or cold water to the developer. It will weaken the solution.

DEVELOPING PROCEDURE

Set the TIMER, Fig. 6-64, for the recommended development time. Start the timer. Then start the development.

1. Drag the exposed film through the developer, light side down. This will wet the emulsion and prevent the formation of air bubbles on the film.
2. Quickly flip the film over so the light side is up. Place it in the developer. Be sure it is completely submerged in the developer. Handle the film by one corner.
3. Gently rock the developer tray, Fig. 6-65. This keeps the solution moving. New developer is continuously furnished to the developing film surface.
4. About 15 seconds before developing time is up, lift the film from the developer and let the solution drain back into the tray.
5. Place the film in a Stop bath for a few seconds. This solution will stop the developing action.

   Stop bath is an acid. Whenever mixing acid with water, always pour the acid into the water.

FIXING AND WASHING FILM

From the stop bath, the film goes into a fixing solution. Fixing removes the remaining unexposed silver particles from the film emulsion. After fixing, the film is no longer light-sensitive.

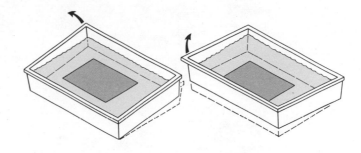
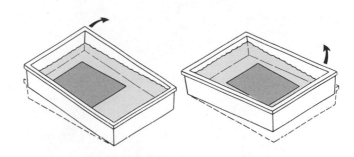

Fig. 6-65. Gently rock trays side to side and end to end while developing film. This keeps fresh developer in contact with negative.

A thorough washing in running water will remove any remaining fixer from the film. The manufacturer will suggest how long a wash is required.

Hang washed film by one corner to dry, Fig. 6-66. *Drying must be done in a dust-free area.*

Important: When your hands have been in various developing solutions, always rinse them in clean water before

Fig. 6-64. Darkroom timer keeps track of time film is in developer, stop bath and fix.

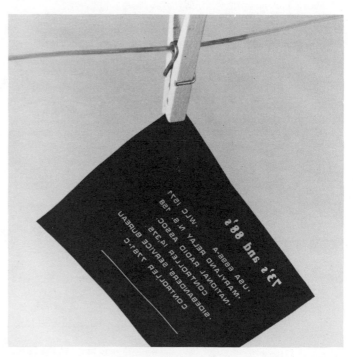

Fig. 6-66. Washed film may be hung by one corner to dry. Drying area should be dust free.

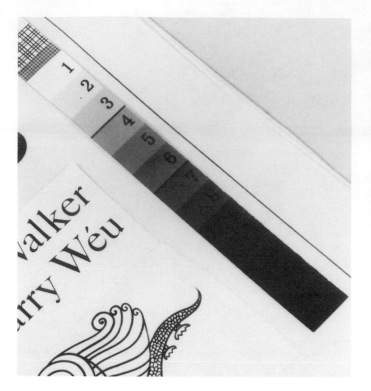

Fig. 6-67. Place a camera operators' sensitivity guide (gray scale) on copy to be photographed. Locate it where it will not cover lines or type.

Fig. 6-68. Solid step 4 of sensitivity guide on negative of normal copy indicates usable negative.

CRITICAL STEP CHART

DENSITY OF COPY	SIZE OF COPY		
	10-40%	41-120%	121-400%
Extra Heavy Copy Black Bold type Etching Proofs Photo Proofs	4 Black	5 Black	6 Black
Normal Copy Good black type proofs with fine serfs Pen and Ink Drawings Printed Forms	3 Black	4 Black	5 Black
Light Copy Gray Copy Ordinary Typewritten Sheets Printed Forms Light Lines Good Pencil Drawings	2 Black	3 Black	4 Black
Extra Light Copy Extra Fine Lines* Pencil Drawings Extra light gray copy	1-2 Black	2 Black	3 Black

*Difficult fine line copy and fine line reductions can usually be improved by fine line development, or still development (not agitated) in regular developer (refer to manufacturer's instructions).

Fig. 6-69. Critical Step Chart shows proper step for various types of copy as well as for reductions and enlargements. (Stouffer Graphic Arts Equip. Co.)

wiping them on the darkroom towel or before touching anything. This will prevent spots on film caused by contamination from dried chemicals.

Chemicals used to process film can cause allergic reactions in some people. Use extreme care when handling them. Wear goggles and protective clothing when mixing and using them.

SENSITIVITY GUIDE (GRAY SCALE)-

Offset plate quality is determined by negative quality. A sensitivity guide, also known as a gray scale, is used to check the many conditions that produce good negatives. Among these conditions are quality of the light source, exposure time, developer temperature and developer exhaustion.

A sensitivity guide is placed on the copy or copyboard next to the material being photographed, Fig. 6-67. It will be recorded on the film along with the copy.

Copy and scale will become visible as the film develops. For normal copy, a solid step 4 on a numbered gray scale indicates a usable negative, Fig. 6-68. Step 5 will appear as a light gray.

If a solid step 4 is not reached in the recommended development time, allow the film to develop a short time longer. However, do not extend development time more than a minute or two. Discard the film if a solid step 4 is not attained with increased developing time. Make a new exposure.

In general, increase exposure time if the gray scale reading is less than step 4. Reduce the time if it is more than step 4. Also see Fig. 6-69.

MAKING A HALFTONE NEGATIVE

Shooting (photographing) a continuous tone illustration calls for a slightly different procedure. (A photograph or artwork that has a full range of grays from black to white is called continuous tone). A HALFTONE SCREEN must be placed between the camera lens and the film as shown in Fig. 6-70. Its purpose is to break the illustration down into a pattern of tiny dots.

All halftone screens fall into one of two basic classifications:
1. Glass screens.
2. Contact screens.
Screens are made in more than one dot pattern. See Fig. 6-71. Contact screens are placed directly on top of the high contrast film. The emulsion side of the screen is against the emulsion side of the film, Fig. 6-72.

Dot size is determined by the amount of light (reflected from the continuous tone copy) striking the film through the halftone screen. When an exposure is made, the whitest areas (highlights) reflect the most light through the screen. This produces a dot on the film that is full size or almost full size. Dark areas (shadows) reflect the least light. Only enough light passes through the screen to make small dots on the film. See Fig. 6-73.

Quite often, continuous tone copy has a DENSITY RANGE that cannot be fully reproduced on the negative by the MAIN EXPOSURE. If you give the film an exposure suitable for the light areas, it may not be enough to make the dots needed in the dark shadows. A second but shorter exposure is usually made to improve shadow detail.

Density range is the measured difference between the lightest and darkest values of a negative. Exposure refers to the quantity of light allowed to act on a light-sensitive material.

The MAIN EXPOSURE is made with the camera lights reflecting the image off the copy. An additional FLASH EXPOSURE improves shadow detail. See Fig. 6-74. This is an

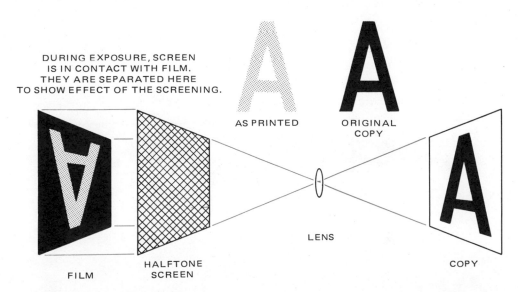

DURING EXPOSURE, SCREEN IS IN CONTACT WITH FILM. THEY ARE SEPARATED HERE TO SHOW EFFECT OF THE SCREENING.

AS PRINTED   ORIGINAL COPY

FILM   HALFTONE SCREEN   LENS   COPY

Fig. 6-70. Halftone screen must be placed between lens and film when photographing continuous tone illustrations.

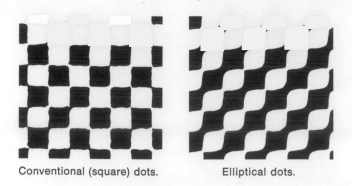
Conventional (square) dots.

Elliptical dots.

Enlarged pattern of a KODAK Gray Contact Screen.

Enlarged pattern of a commercially available screen tint.

Fig. 6-71. Four different halftone screens. Each is greatly enlarged. (©Eastman Kodak Co.)

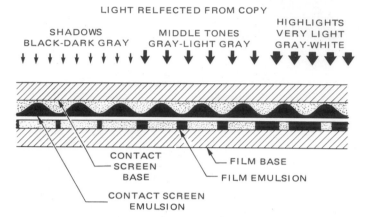

LIGHT RELFECTED FROM COPY

SHADOWS BLACK-DARK GRAY — MIDDLE TONES GRAY-LIGHT GRAY — HIGHLIGHTS VERY LIGHT GRAY-WHITE

CONTACT SCREEN BASE — FILM BASE — FILM EMULSION — CONTACT SCREEN EMULSION

Fig. 6-72. Contact halftone screens must be placed in direct contact with the film.

exposure made by shining a light through the contact screen onto the film. The flash exposure will increase dot size in shadow areas. It will affect dot size in middletones and highlights only slightly, if at all.

When properly made, a flash exposure will improve the quality of the final halftone reproduction. It will be a closer match of the original continuous tone copy.

A special yellow flashing lamp produces the flash exposure, Fig. 6-75. The lamp is about 6 ft. (1.8 m) away. With the film holder open it must shine directly at the film.

The exposure is made with the contact screen in place. Correct exposure (time) is determined by using a KODAK HALFTONE NEGATIVE COMPUTER. See Fig. 6-76.

USING AUTOSCREEN FILM

Halftone negatives can be made using autoscreen film. No halftone screen is needed because a 133-line screen pattern is built into the film.

Either a process camera or a conventional view camera will properly expose autoscreen film. The halftone pattern appears automatically after exposure and development.

Another advantage with autoscreen is that a conventional enlarger and color transparencies will produce halftone negatives. The autoscreen film is placed on the enlarger easel. Then the transparency is projected onto the film. See Fig. 6-77. Use exposure times and developing procedure shown on the information sheet packed with the film.

SPECIAL GRAPHIC ARTS TECHNIQUES

When used properly, special graphic arts techniques add visual impact to the printed page. They may be used to improve reproduction of a flat uninteresting photograph or to center interest.

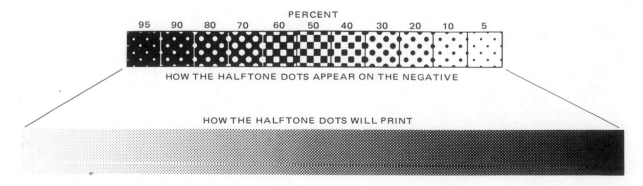

PERCENT

95 90 80 70 60 50 40 30 20 10 5

HOW THE HALFTONE DOTS APPEAR ON THE NEGATIVE

HOW THE HALFTONE DOTS WILL PRINT

Fig. 6-73. Range of dot sizes, given as a percentage, and how they print.

Fig. 6-74. This is how flash exposure affects halftone quality. Left Flash exposure and main exposure. Right. Main exposure only.
(Richard J. Walker)

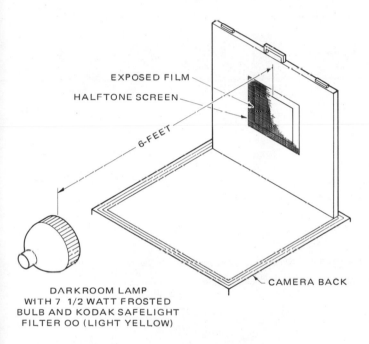

EXPOSED FILM

HALFTONE SCREEN

6-FEET

DARKROOM LAMP
WITH 7 1/2 WATT FROSTED
BULB AND KODAK SAFELIGHT
FILTER OO (LIGHT YELLOW)

CAMERA BACK

Fig. 6-75. Special yellow light is used to make the flash exposure. Film back is opened allowing light to shine directly onto film. Screen is still covering the film.

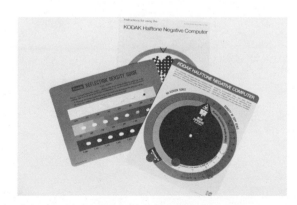

Fig. 6-76. Halftone negative computer works out exposure times.
(©Eastman Kodak Co.)

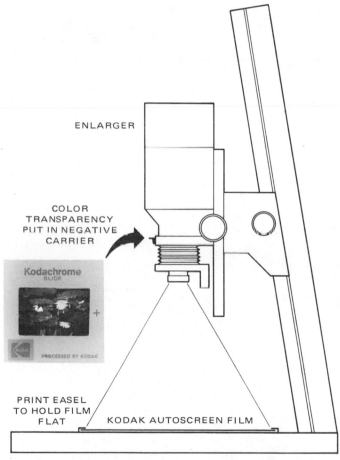

ENLARGER

COLOR
TRANSPARENCY
PUT IN NEGATIVE
CARRIER

PRINT EASEL
TO HOLD FILM
FLAT

KODAK AUTOSCREEN FILM

Fig. 6-77 Making halftone from color transparency (slide). Autoscreen film is mounted on vacuum board under a conventional photographic enlargement. Slide is removed from mount, placed in enlarger and projected onto film.

Fig. 6-78 demonstrates a number of special techniques. Most can be done with a single color. Specialized graphic arts books will explain how they are produced.

To test your knowledge of Photoconversion, refer to Test Questions 20 through 38 at the end of this unit.

65 LINE SCREEN

133 LINE SCREEN

150 LINE SCREEN

MEZZOTINT

DUOTONE

GHOSTED BACKGROUND

HALFTONE — SCREEN TINT

POSTERIZED

Fig. 6-78. These examples show effect of screen coarseness and special screening.

OFFSET IMPOSITION

At this point, all material to be printed (copy) has been converted to film. The operation that assembles the negatives so the images can be transferred to a printing plate is called IMPOSITION or STRIPPING. A person who does this work is called a STRIPPER, Fig. 6-79.

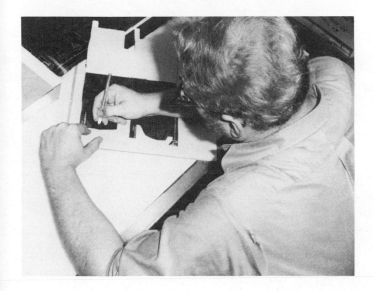

Fig. 6-79. Stripping is assembling, positioning and mounting negatives as they are to be printed.

STRIPPING

Stripping is assembling, positioning and mounting negatives that will be printed on the same plate. The sheet to which the negatives are mounted in called a FLAT, Fig. 6-80.

GOLDENROD PAPER, also known as a MASKING SHEET, is the most common material for flats. Its color (orange-yellow) effectively blocks light that would expose the light-sensitive material on a printing plate. Plastic masking sheets are also available.

Preprinted layout lines make it easy to locate and position negatives on the masking sheet. The GRIPPER MARGIN and MAXIMUM PRINTING AREA is also indicated on them. The gripper margin is the space needed by the press grippers to feed and deliver the paper. It does not receive a printed impression.

STRIPPING TOOLS

Strippers usually prepare flats on a LIGHT TABLE, Fig. 6-81. Layouts are made with stainless steel T-SQUARE, TRIANGLES and RULE, Fig. 6-82.

Pinholes and small imperfections show up as unwanted clear spots on negatives. They are easier to find with a magnifying glass or a LINEN TESTER, Fig. 6-83.

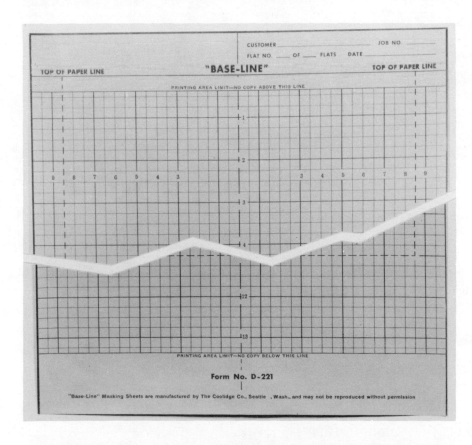

Fig. 6-80. Sheet on which negatives are mounted is called a flat. These preprinted masking sheets (goldenrod) are available for most presses.

Fig. 6-81. Light table makes good work surface for stripping. Light is reflected upward through a frosted glass surface. (nuArc Co. Inc.)

Fig. 6-83. Linen tester magnifies 10X (enlarges 10 times normal size) making it easy to find small imperfections on a negative.

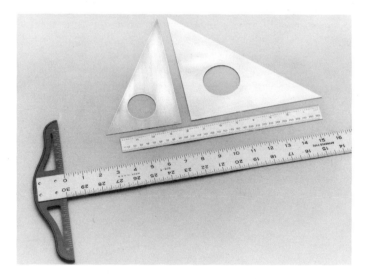

Fig. 6-82. Tools used for stripping in of flats. The steel rule can also be used as a straightedge.

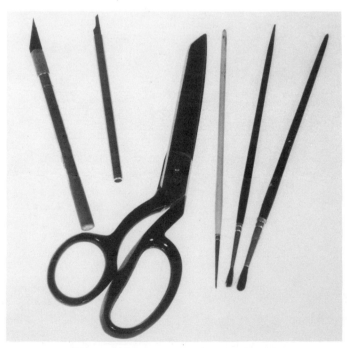

Fig. 6-84. Stripping operations require sharp knives, scissors and several sizes of brushes for opaquing pinholes and scratches in film.

Stripping also requires an assortment of knives, scissors and ARTISTS' BRUSHES. See Fig. 6-84. Negatives and masking material are cut with the knives. The scissors is useful for trimming negatives. *Keep all cutting edges sharp!*

Brushes (very fine to medium widths) are used to OPAQUE film. This is a technique for blocking out film imperfections by painting over them.

A special RUBY RED TRANSPARENT TAPE, Fig. 6-85, secures negatives to flats. The color blocks out the light which affects photosensitive film and plates.

LAYOUT FOR STRIPPING

Negatives must be carefully positioned on the masking sheet (flat). Their location determines how they will appear on the printed page.

Important: The light table's working surface must be clean and free of dust and dirt before stripping can begin.

Fig. 6-85. Negatives are secured to flats with red transparent tape called "lithographers tape." Lighter colored spots on negative are the opaquing solution.

Follow these steps for stripping in a one-page flat:

1. Place the negatives on the light table emulsion side down, Fig. 6-86. Text must be "right reading," that is, you must be able to read the text on the negatives. Negatives having no type on them will have no readable side. In such cases, examine the negative. The emulsion side is the duller of the two sides.

Fig. 6-86. Negative will be readable when emulsion side of film is down.

You can also find the emulsion side by scratching the film (in a non-image area) with a pointed knife, Fig. 6-87. Emulsion will scrape away when scratched.

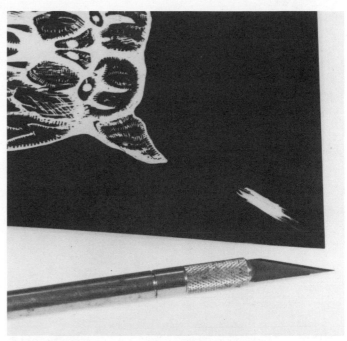

Fig. 6-87. Find emulsion side of film by scraping negative in non-image area. Clear area will appear when emulsion side is scraped. Nothing will happen on the other side.

2. Align the masking sheet with an edge of the light table, Fig. 6-88. Use a T-square. Lightly tape the masking sheet to the light table.

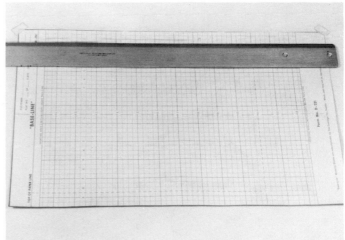

Fig. 6-88. Align masking sheet with edge of light table. Use T-square for the aligning operation.

3. Locate and mark, on the masking sheet, the edges of the paper being printed. See Fig. 6-89. Be sure to allow room at the top for the grippers.
4. Mark the exact position of the negatives within the margins marked on the sheet. See Fig. 6-90.
5. Position the negatives under the marked area or areas on the masking sheet, Fig. 6-91. Align them with the T-square. After they are positioned, hold the negatives and masking sheet in place with pressure from one hand.

Fig. 6-89. Locate and heavily outline margins of sheet to be printed.

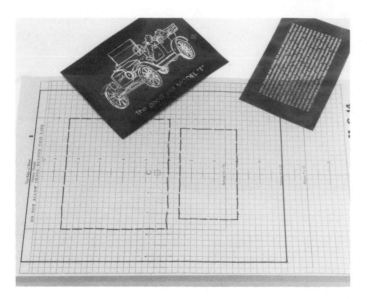

Fig. 6-90. Mark exact location of negatives inside the sheet margins.

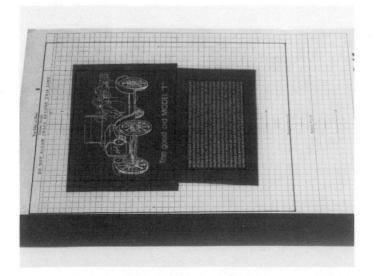

Fig. 6-91. Position negatives under marked area of masking sheet.

6. With the other hand, cut out small triangles or squares from the masking sheet near the corners of each negative, Fig. 6-92.

Cut only through the masking sheet. Do not cut into the negative.

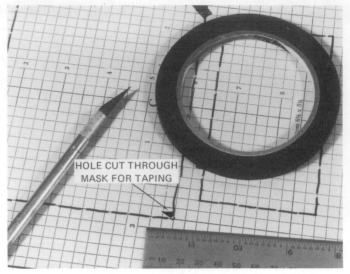

Fig. 6-92. Cut small triangular or square holes through masking sheet near corners of each negative.

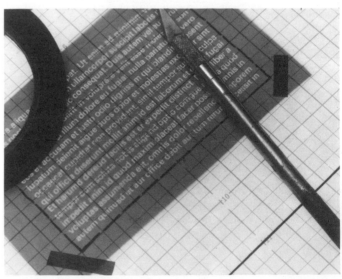

Fig. 6-93. Attach negatives to masking sheet with lithographers' tape laid across each cutout.

7. Cover each cutout with red lithographers' tape, Fig. 6-93. Be sure the tape contacts both film and masking sheet.
8. Turn the masking sheet over. Tape the corners of each negative to the masking sheet, Fig. 6-94.
9. Return the sheet to its original position. The masking sheet will again be on top. With a sharp stencil knife, cut windows in the masking sheet over the negatives, Fig. 6-95. Windows should be 1/8 to 1/4 in. (3 to 6 mm) larger than the image area of each negative.

Important: Do not cut into the negative. Avoid using

Fig. 6-94. Turn marking sheet and negatives over. Tape each corner of negatives to marking sheet.

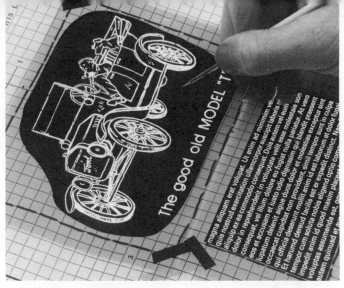

Fig. 6-96. When opaquing pinholes and other flaws, start at the top and work toward the bottom of the negative.

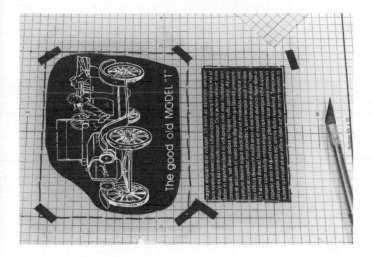

Fig. 6-95. Make "windows" over image areas of negatives by cutting away the mask.

single edge razor blades to cut the windows. Some razor blades are harder than the glass on light tables. They will scratch the glass should you accidently cut through the masking sheet into the top.

10. Carefully check over the flat. Be sure no part of the image remains covered.
11. With the flat still on the light table, examine the image area for pinholes and scratches. Use a small brush and opaquing solution to block them out, Fig. 6-96. Start opaquing at the top of the negative and work towards the bottom. This will prevent smearing wet opaque. Should an error be made, a damp cloth will wipe away the opaque.

COMBINING HALFTONES WITH LINE NEGATIVES

If you recall, halftone negatives and line negatives must be made separately. The area on the pasteup or mechanical to be occupied by the halftone must be covered with red masking film. The red film photographs as a clear window in the negative.

Another method is to use key lines on the layout. These are black lines which mark the edges of the halftone. Fig. 6-97 shows a mechanical masked for a halftone and the negatives.

Fig. 6-97. Halftone's location is indicated by "key lines" or by clear window in main negative.

To strip the halftone into the main negative:

1. Cut the masking sheet away from the area where the halftone will be located.
2. Trim the halftone so it will be slightly larger (1/8 to 1/4 in. or 3 to 6 mm larger on all sides) than the image that is to be printed, Fig. 6-98.
3. Turn the flat over. Then scribe the exact location of the halftone into the emulsion of the main negative. (This step is not necessary if the area was blocked out on the pasteup.)

Fig. 6-98. Trim halftone slightly larger than image to be printed. Halftone trim size is indicated by scribed lines in this example.

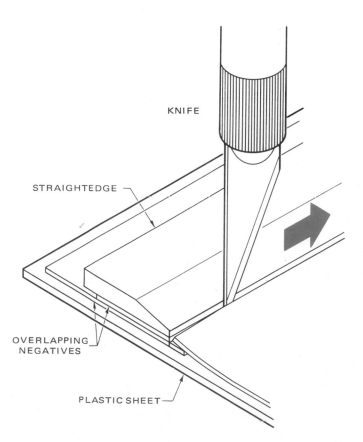

Fig. 6-99. Use straightedge and sharp knife to cut opening for halftone.

4. Turn the flat over so the masking sheet is again on top. Using a straightedge and a sharp masking knife, cut the negatives along the scribed lines, Fig. 6-99.
5. Fit the trimmed negative into the opening. The smaller negative should fit inside the opening in the other negative. See Fig. 6-100. Tape the negatives together.

   Important: Always place the lithographers' tape on the shiny side of the film.

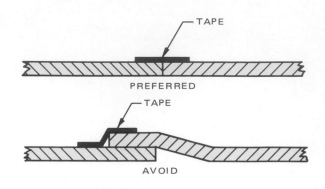

Fig. 6-100. Negatives should butt together, not overlap.

STRIPPING FOR TWO COLOR PRINTING

A separate flat is needed for each color. Registration marks (refer again to Fig. 6-47), placed on the artwork before it is photographed, are used to assure perfect alignment of the colors.

1. Secure the goldenrod masking sheets. One will be needed for each color.
2. Place the masking sheets in perfect register on top of each other, Fig. 6-101.
3. To assure perfect registrations, punch at least two holes

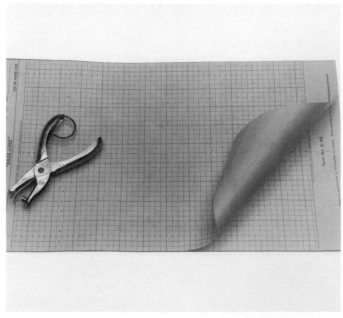

Fig. 6-101. Place masking sheets, one for each color, in perfect register on top of each other.

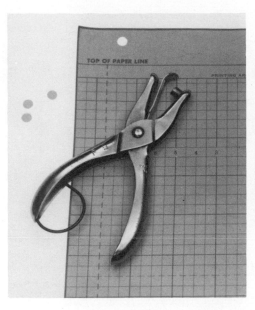

Fig. 6-102. Use holes to assure registration. Left. Hand punched holes will assure perfect alignment. Right. Commercial punches are also available. (Eastman Kodak Co.)

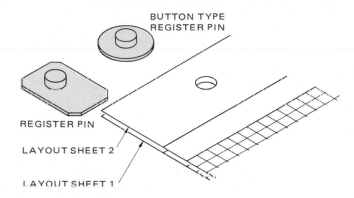

Fig. 6-103. Insert registration pins to keep masking sheets aligned. Tape pins to light table.

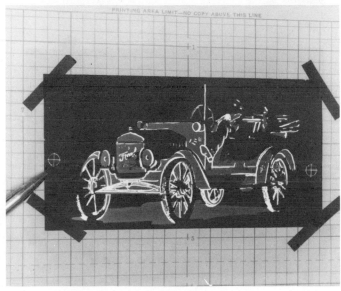

Fig. 6-105. Negatives are properly located when register marks are perfectly aligned.

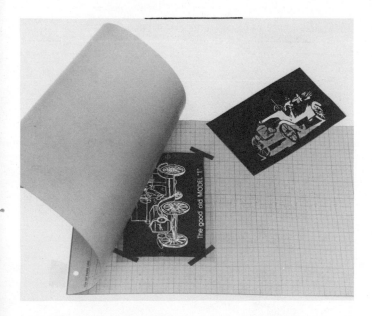

Fig. 6-104. Fold back or remove top masking sheet from the pins. Locate negative on bottom sheet and cut in window.

through the gathered masking sheets. A hole at each end of the gripper margin will be enough, Fig. 6-102.

4. Insert REGISTRATION PINS, Fig. 6-103, into each of the holes. These pins will hold the masking sheets in position when the negatives are stripped in.

5. Fold back the top masking sheet. Then locate and strip in the negative for the first color, Fig. 6-104. Cut out the window.

6. Fold down the top masking sheet. Strip in the negative for the second color. The registration marks on each negative must be perfectly aligned, Fig. 6-105.

To test your knowledge of Offset Imposition, refer to Test Questions 39 through 51 at the end of this unit.

PLATEMAKING

Platemaking is the process of exposing and developing an image on the image carrier. This is accomplished by shining light through the film negative onto the plate; then chemicals prepare the image.

A flat should not be used to make a plate until the film has been cleaned. Wipe both sides of the negatives with a commercial film cleaner. This will remove fingerprints and dirt. An ANTISTATIC BRUSH, Fig. 6-106, will get rid of dust that may have settled on the film after it was cleaned.

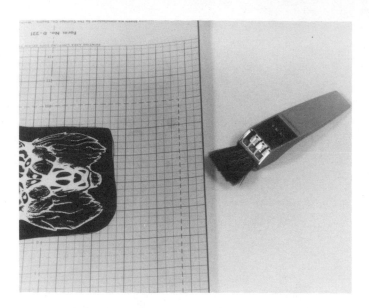

Fig. 6-106. Antistatic brush removes dust from negative before exposing plate. Dust on negative will cause printing problems.

Caution: Clean film with a commercial film cleaner. Never use benzine or carbon tetrachloride. The fumes of both are highly toxic.

MAKING A PROOF

The flat should also be proofed. A proof can be used to check for quality, register and broken images. It will, in addition, provide a means to get the customer's approval for the job.

Make the proofs on light-sensitive materials, either paper or plastic, prepared for that purpose. Existing platemaking equipment can make the exposure. Handle and develop the light-sensitive material as recommended by the manufacturer. The proofs are sometimes called SILVERPRINTS.

OFFSET PLATES

The offset plates you will use are made from aluminum. They will be presensitized, on one or both sides, and cut to press size. Plates are available in four different end styles. See Fig. 6-107. The end style needed depends upon what type of plate clamp the press has.

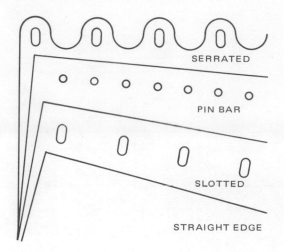

Fig. 6-107. These plate end styles are designed for different presses.

Offset plates are also known as SURFACE PLATES. On a surface plate, the light-sensitive coating becomes the ink receptive image area. There are two kinds of surface plates.
1. ADDITIVE. Ink receptive material is added during processing.
2. SUBTRACTIVE. Ink receptive material (lacquer) is part of the precoating. Processing removes it from nonprinting areas.

PREPARATION FOR EXPOSURE

Plates are exposed on a PLATEMAKER, Fig. 6-108. It provides a high-intensity source of ultraviolet light. It has a vacuum frame that keeps the plate in perfect contact with the flat, Fig. 6-109.

Fig. 6-108. Platemaker exposes sensitized plate. (nuArc Co., Inc.)

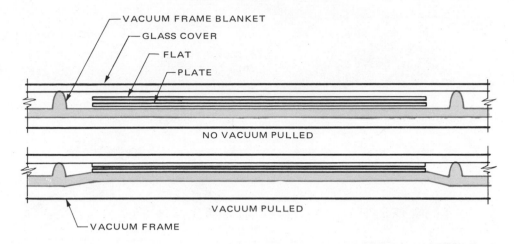

Fig. 6-109. Vacuum frame is needed to keep flat and plate in perfect contact.

To prepare the flat and plate for exposure:

1. Open the vacuum frame. Examine it for dust, dirt and fingerprints. Clean the glass, both sides, if necessary.

2. Position (register) the flat on top of the sensitized side of the plate. Tape flat and plate together at the gripper edge. See Fig. 6-110.

   Caution: Thin metal plates can cause severe cuts. Use care when handling metal plates.

   Important: The emulsion side of the flat must be in contact with the emulsion side of the plate.

Fig. 6-111. Position platemakers' sensitivity guide in a window at lead or tail edge of flat.

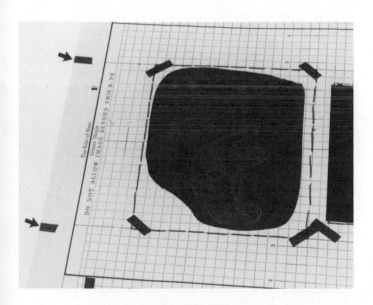

Fig. 6-110. Tape flat and plate together at gripper edge. See arrows.

3. Position a gray scale on the masking sheet at the lead or tail edge of the plate, Fig. 6-111. Cut a window in the masking sheet for it. The scale will help determine whether the plate has been exposed properly. Information furnished with the plates will indicate the gray scale reading recommended for proper exposure for that particular kind of plate.

4. Close the frame and lock it, Fig. 6-112. Turn on the vacuum switch. Pull as high a vacuum as possible (20-22 in. on the indicator.) The metric equivalent is 508-559 mm. See Fig. 6-113.

Fig. 6-112. Close and lock vacuum frame before making exposure.

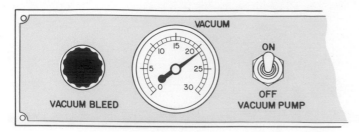

Fig. 6-113. Operator should pull a vacuum of 20-22 in. on indicator before exposing the plate.

5. Flip the frame over so the flat and plate face the light source, Fig. 6-114.

Fig. 6-114. Platemaker frame is flipped over so flat and plate will face light source.

MAKING THE EXPOSURE

Set the timer and turn on the light source, Fig. 6-115. Since many factors control exposure time, your instructor will help you determine the correct exposure time for the plates you are using.

Caution: Avoid looking at the light source of the plate-maker while the plate is being exposed. It can damage your eyesight.

Fig. 6-115. To expose plate, turn on light source. Use manual or automatic control.

PROCESSING PLATES

Either a clean PLATEMAKING SINK, Fig. 6-116, or a PLATE FINISHING TABLE, Fig. 6-117, provides the best conditions for processing offset plates. If a sink or table is not available, a dry, flat surface covered with clean newsprint can be used, Fig. 6-118.

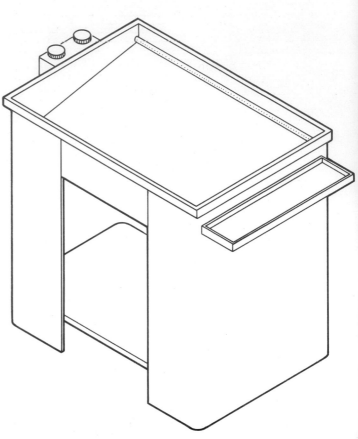

Fig. 6-116. Platemaking sink slopes downward from back to front. Perforated pipe evenly distributes water for flushing plate.

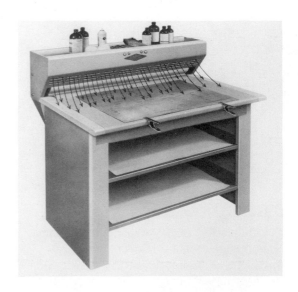

Fig. 6-117. Plate finishing table has heater for rapid drying of plates. Clamps hold paper and plate during developing. (nuArc Co., Inc.)

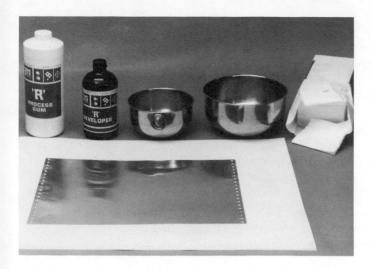

Fig. 6-118. A flat surface, covered with clean newsprint, can be used to process plates if no platemakers' sink or table is available.

Use cellulose sponges for desensitizing and lacquering (developing) plates. Cheese cloth or cotton wiping pads are used for gumming, plate cleaning and plate washing.

When the plate has been exposed it is ready to process. For best results, use the desensitizing and lacquering solutions recommended for the plates being used, Fig. 6-119.

Fig. 6-119. Use processing chemicals specified for the plates being used.

Pour a suitable amount of plate desensitizer on the exposed surface of the plate. The exact quantity will depend upon the plate size. However, about 1/2 oz. per sq. ft. of plate surface is recommended. Spread the solution over the plate with a damp sponge, Fig. 6-120. Use a "figure eight" pattern and medium pressure.

Apply a liberal amount of developer to the plate while it is still moist with desensitizer. (Developer is called plate lacquer by some manufacturers.) Rub the developer over the plate with light pressure until the image is strong and uniform.

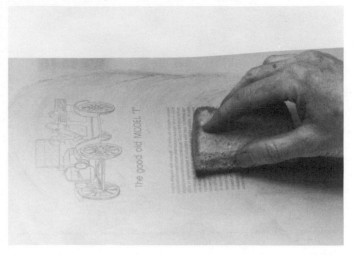

Fig. 6-120. Spread solution over plate with clean, dampened sponge.

A solid 5 or 6 step on the gray scale (check the manufacturers' recommendation for the plate being used) usually indicates the plate has been exposed and developed properly. See Fig. 6-121.

Fig. 6-121. A solid 5 or 6 step on gray scale usually indicates that plate has been properly exposed and developed.

Flush the plate with water and squeegee it. Apply a gum arabic solution with a damp cotton pad, Fig. 6-122. Buff dry with clean cheesecloth. At this point, the plate is ready for the press or for storage. Store plates by hanging, Fig. 6-123, or by stacking, Fig. 6-124. If stacked, slipsheeting will protect the plate against scratching.

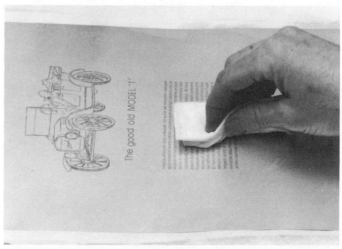

Fig. 6-122. Apply gum arabic solution with a dampened cotton pad. Buff plate dry with cheesecloth.

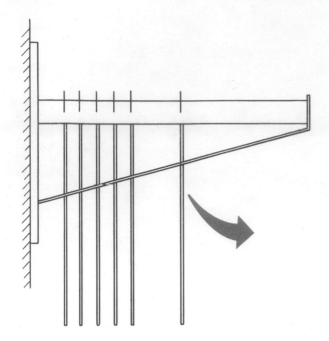

Fig. 6-123. Plates may be stored using special envelopes and racks.

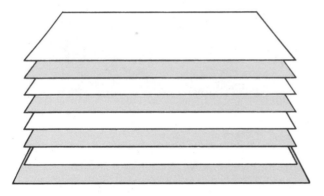

Fig. 6-124. Slipsheet between each stacked plate prevents scratching.

Offset plates can be processed by hand or by automatic platemaking equipment, Fig. 6-125.

Important: The type of plate used will determine how it is to be processed. Follow the manufacturers' recommendations.

MAKING CORRECTIONS

Additions to the plate can be made with a suitable TUSCHE. This is a black liquid used for etching. Be sure the area is dry and free of ink or gum before applying tusche.

Deletions are made with a rubber eraser or hone, Fig. 6-126. An appropriate deletion fluid may also be used if the area being corrected is dry and uninked.

Fig. 6-126. Small deletions can be made on an offset press with a rubber eraser or very fine hone. Deletion fluids are also available.

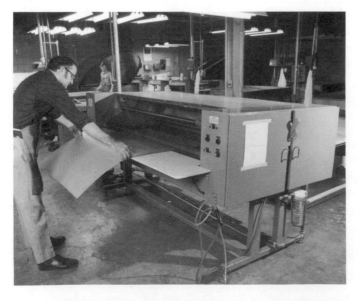

Fig. 6-125. Automatic platemaker receives plate at one end, delivers it developed at the other end. (Veritone Co., Inc.)

OTHER TYPES OF OFFSET PLATES

Paper DIRECT IMAGE offset plates allow the image to be typed or drawn directly on the plate surface. See Fig. 6-127. Special typewriter ribbons, pencils, pens and crayons are needed.

PHOTO DIRECT plates do not require a negative film image. In the platemaking process, the image on the pasteup is made to shine (reflect) onto special presensitized paper plates. A photo direct camera is used, Fig. 6-128. After exposure, the plate is fed automatically through developing and fixing chemicals and processed. See Fig. 6-129. A press-ready plate is delivered by the camera.

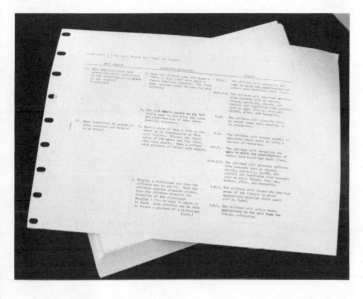

Fig. 6-127. Direct image plate. Copy is typed directly onto plate with special carbon ribbon. Artwork can be done with special grease pencils.

Fig. 6-128. Photo direct camera and plate processor. No film is needed to produce offset plate. (3M Co., Printing Products Div.)

Fig. 6-129. Drawing of the machine for making photo direct offset plates. Exposure, developing and fixing are a continuous operation.

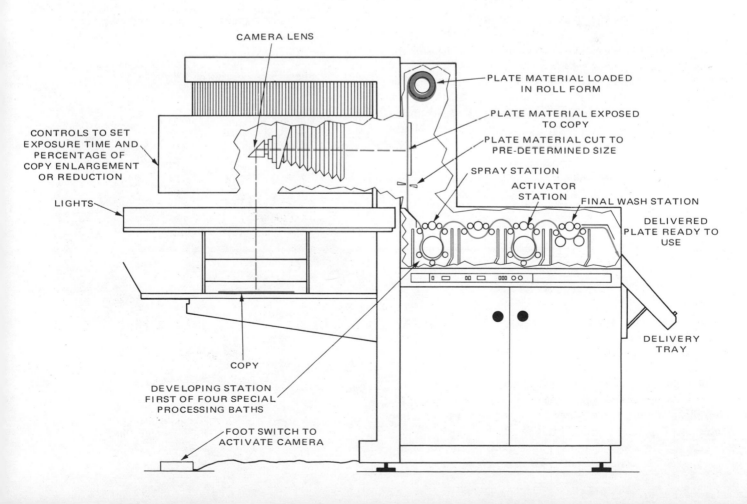

Plates can also be made by the XEROGRAPHIC (electrostatic) process. Most fast printing services, and many offices use this technique. The copier or electrostatic platemaker, Fig. 6-130, exposes the plate automatically and delivers it ready for use. Halftones, large solids and fine line work can be produced on low cost paper plates in as little as 30 seconds.

To test your knowledge of Platemaking, refer to Test Questions 52 through 61 at the end of this unit.

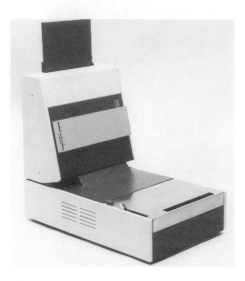

Fig. 6-130. Electrostatic platemaker transfers image from original copy to offset plate and automatically develops it. (Eskofot America, Inc.)

OFFSET PRESSWORK

Modern offset presses are equipped to feed paper automatically. There are two general types of presses: sheet fed and web fed. In a web fed operation the paper moves into the press from a continuous roll as shown in Fig. 6-131. A sheet fed press shown in Fig. 6-132 feeds flat sheets. Offset presses found in most school graphic arts programs are sheet fed like the ones in Fig. 6-133.

Regardless of type, all offset presses have four basic systems, Fig. 6-134.
1. Feeder system.
2. Registration system.
3. Printing system.
4. Delivery system.

FEEDER SYSTEM

Feeder systems are designed to pass one thickness of paper through the press at a time. A web (roll) feeder for a large press was shown in Fig. 6-131. Refer to it again.

The FEEDER TABLE, Fig. 6-135, holds the paper stock to be printed. The table raises as the machine operates so that the top sheet of paper is always at the right height to be fed into the press. Fig. 6-136 illustrates this.

A SHEET SEPARATOR, Fig. 6-137, assures that only a single sheet will be picked up by the SUCTION FOOT (FEET) and moved into the registration unit, Fig. 6-138. The suction foot is hollow and operates on vacuum. Suction can be adjusted for different weights of paper.

Damage may result if several sheets go through the press at the same time. To prevent this, most presses are fitted with a DOUBLE SHEET ELIMINATOR (also called a DOUBLE SHEET DETECTOR), Fig. 6-139. This device will either toss out the multiple sheets or stop the press. When properly adjusted, a press will rarely misfeed multiple sheets.

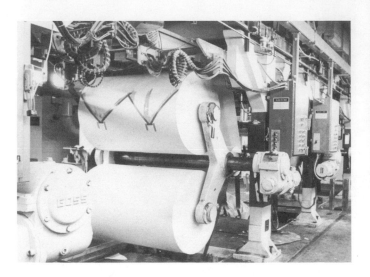

Fig. 6-131. Web fed presses use paper in roll form. Feeder shown holds three rolls. (Today Newspaper, Melbourne, FL)

Fig. 6-132. Sheet fed press. This type is often used for commercial printing. (ATF/Davidson Co., Inc.)

Fig. 6-133. These types of offset presses (duplicators) are found in school graphic arts programs. A—A/M Multigraphic 1250. B—Davidson 500. C—A.B.Dick 310 table top press. D—ATF Chief 115. E—Ditto 217.

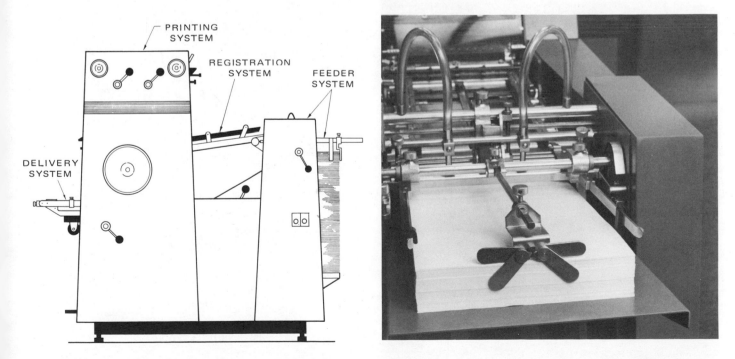

Fig. 6-134. These basic systems are found on all offset presses.

Fig. 6-135. Feeder table. Center bar with adjustable fingers is called backguide. It holds the sheets down.

Fig. 6-136. Feeder table height is maintained automatically as paper is printed. Left. Large stack of paper. Right. Stack, though much smaller, has been raised up to stay in contact with the guides.

REGISTRATION SYSTEM

The registration system positions each sheet exactly where it must be before it enters the printing unit. It makes sure the image will print in the same place on each sheet.

After the paper is picked up in the feeder system, Fig. 6-140, it passes through the multiple sheet detector. Then it moves down CONVEYOR TAPES to the FRONT STOP FINGERS, Fig. 6-141. Each sheet is stopped momentarily and jogged into place for printing, Fig. 6-142. All this occurs in less than a second when the press is printing 5000 sheets per hour.

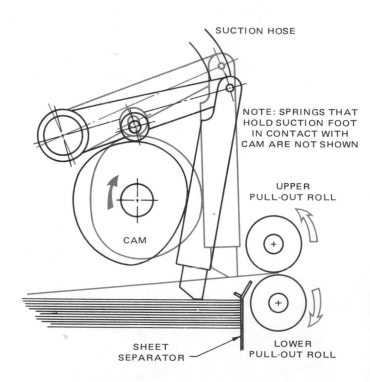

SUCTION HOSE

NOTE: SPRINGS THAT HOLD SUCTION FOOT IN CONTACT WITH CAM ARE NOT SHOWN

CAM

UPPER PULL-OUT ROLL

SHEET SEPARATOR

LOWER PULL-OUT ROLL

Fig. 6-138. Suction foot picks up sheet and feeds it into pullout rollers.

After being jogged into register, the front stop fingers drop. Feed rollers move the sheet into the printing system of the press. See Fig. 6-143.

PRINTING SYSTEM

An offset printing plate is made so the image areas will pick up ink and repel water. Nonprinting areas on the plate pick up

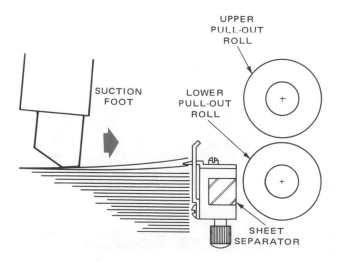

UPPER PULL-OUT ROLL

SUCTION FOOT

LOWER PULL-OUT ROLL

SHEET SEPARATOR

Fig. 6-137. Sheet separator usually assures that only one sheet will be picked up each time by the suction foot or feet.

Lithography or Offset Printing

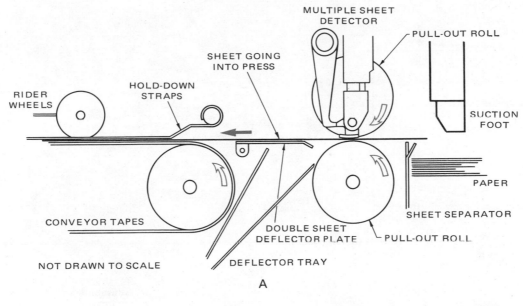

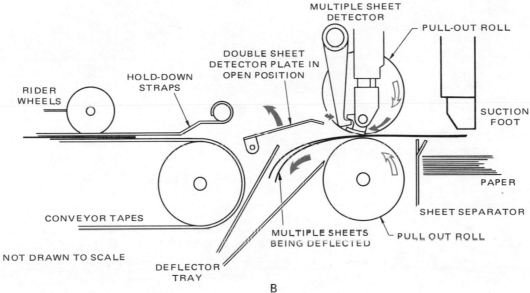

Fig. 6-139. Double sheet eliminator. This device, when properly adjusted, prevents more than one sheet from being fed into the printing unit of the press. A—With single sheet, deflector plate down, single sheet goes into press. B—Deflector trips upward, stops two sheets from entering conveyor.

Fig. 6-140. Suction feet pick up sheet and move it into the conveyor toward the cylinder.

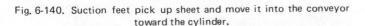

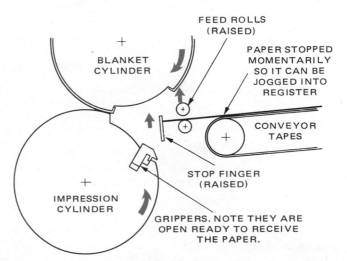

Fig. 6-141. Paper is moved by conveyor tapes to the stop fingers.

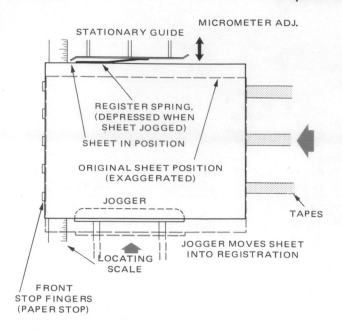

Fig. 6-142. Each sheet is stopped momentarily and jogged into position for printing.

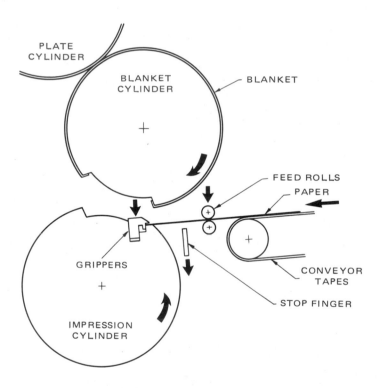

Fig. 6-143. After being jogged into register, feed rollers move sheet into printing system of press.

water and repel ink. The ink and water are transported from storage units on the press itself and are placed on the offset printing plate in carefully measured amounts. This allows the press to produce sharp inked images with clean backgrounds.

The printing system of an offset press is composed of the following units. See Fig. 6-144.

1. Inking system.
2. Dampening system.

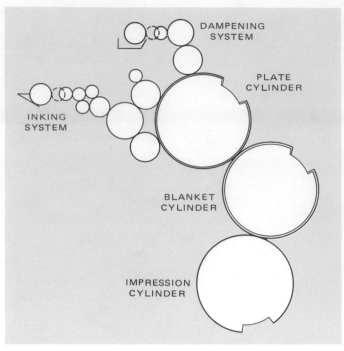

Fig. 6-144. Printing system of a typical offset press. Rollers and cylinders contact each other to apply ink and water to printing plate.

3. Plate cylinder.
4. Blanket cylinder.
5. Impression cylinder.

INKING SYSTEM

An INK FOUNTAIN holds a supply of ink. A blade, which can be adjusted by thumbscrews, controls the amount of ink going to the FOUNTAIN ROLLER. A ratchet lever on one end of the fountain roller governs its speed. Increase its speed for more ink.

A DUCTOR ROLLER picks up ink from the fountain roller and transfers it to the first DISTRIBUTOR ROLLER. The ductor roller oscillates (rocks) back and forth between the two rollers. It is usually fitted with an on—off lever to stop the addition of ink while the press is running.

Distributor rollers spread the ink out into a thin, uniform film. From the distributor rollers, ink goes to FORM ROLLERS that transfer the ink to the printing plate.

Accurate alignment of the form rollers against the plate is essential to assure proper ink coverage. The press must be turned off for the next step. Check alignment by gently bringing the form rollers into contact with the plate cylinder for a moment.

Rotate the handwheel to bring the contact mark around for inspection, Fig. 6-145. If the ink bands are not uniform and parallel (1/8 to 3/16 in. or 3 to 5 mm wide), it will be necessary to adjust or replace the form rollers. The press manual will explain how.

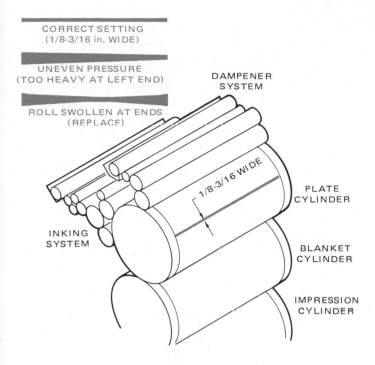

CORRECT SETTING
(1/8-3/16 in. WIDE)

UNEVEN PRESSURE
(TOO HEAVY AT LEFT END)

ROLL SWOLLEN AT ENDS
(REPLACE)

DAMPENER SYSTEM

PLATE CYLINDER

1/8-3/16 WIDE

INKING SYSTEM

BLANKET CYLINDER

IMPRESSION CYLINDER

Fig. 6-145. If form rollers are accurately aligned, ink band should be uniform in weight, and 1/8 to 3/16 in. wide.

DAMPENING SYSTEM

The dampening system, Fig. 6-146, maintains the ink/water balance between printing and nonprinting areas of the plate. It must do this without sacrificing printing quality.

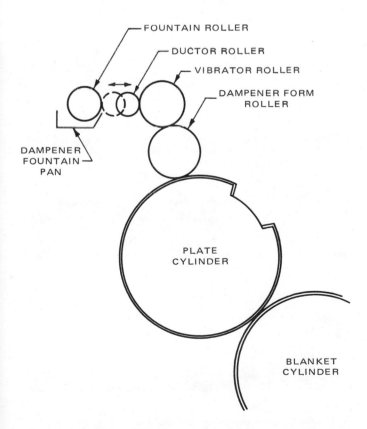

FOUNTAIN ROLLER

DUCTOR ROLLER

VIBRATOR ROLLER

DAMPENER FORM ROLLER

DAMPENER FOUNTAIN PAN

PLATE CYLINDER

BLANKET CYLINDER

Fig. 6-146. Dampener system of a typical offset press. It brings moisture to the non-image areas of the plate.

The FOUNTAIN SOLUTION PAN holds a supply of fountain solution. This solution is a mixture of water, acid and gum arabic. Fountain solution is also known as DAMPENING SOLUTION. A FOUNTAIN SOLUTION BOTTLE maintains fluid level in the pan as solution is used.

Fountain solution is transferred to the ductor roller by the fountain roller. This roller is partially submerged in the liquid. Its finely knurled surface picks up more solution than a smooth surface would. A ratchet system turns the roller a few degrees every revolution of the press.

The ductor roller feeds dampening solution to the OSCILLATING ROLLER.

The oscillating roller insures an even flow of fountain solution to the form rollers. Form rollers coat the non-image area of the plate with a thin layer of moisture. These rollers are usually covered with a sleeve of cloth or paper fiber. The sleeve retains an adequate supply of dampening solution but can respond quickly to adjustments. Cloth sleeves are often referred to as MOLLETON COVERS, Fig. 6-147.

MOLLETON COVERING OVER DUCTOR ROLLER

Fig. 6-147. Dampener ductor and form rollers are often covered with cloth or paper sleeves.

The acidity of fountain solution must be carefully controlled. The symbol pH is used to indicate the strength of an acid solution. The smaller the reading the stronger the acid content of the solution. A pH reading of 4.5 to 5.5 is recommended for most offset plates. Maintain the pH reading recommended for the plates you are using. A paper type pH indicator is suitable for most jobs, Fig. 6-148.

AQUAMATIC SYSTEM

The AQUAMATIC system combines the dampening and inking into one set of form rollers for applying moisture and ink to the printing plate. Fig. 6-149 illustrates the system.

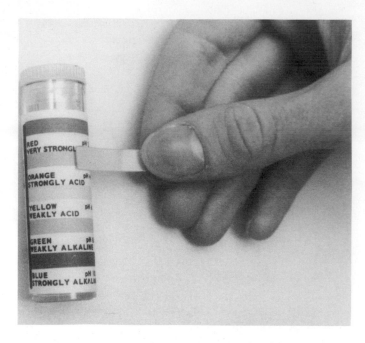

Fig. 6-148. Paper type pH indicator. Paper strip is dipped in solution. It changes color and is compared to sample colors for pH.

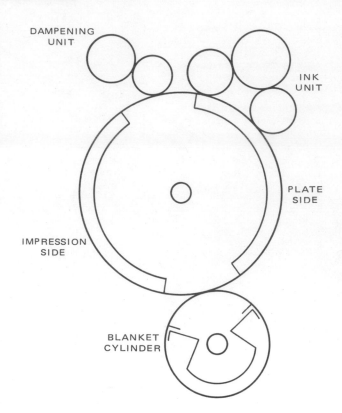

Fig. 6-150. Davidson two cylinder system. One large cylinder does work of impression cylinder and plate cylinder.

The printing plate is attached to the **PLATE CYLINDER** and wrapped around it, Fig. 6-151. Ink applied to the plate transfers to the **BLANKET CYLINDER**, Fig. 6-152, as the press cylinders turn.

The blanket is a rubber surfaced covering on the blanket cylinder. The inked image transfers to the paper when the sheet of paper passes between the blanket cylinder and **IMPRESSION CYLINDER.**

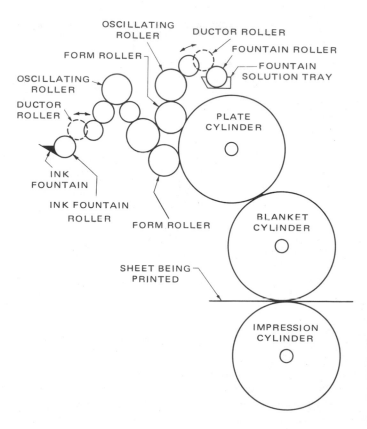

Fig. 6-149. Aquamatic system. Ink and dampener form rollers are combined to put both moisture and ink on the plate.

PRESS CYLINDERS

All offset presses except the Davidson have three main cylinders. The Davidson is a two-cylinder design. Plate and impression cylinder are included on a single large cylinder. See Fig. 6-150.

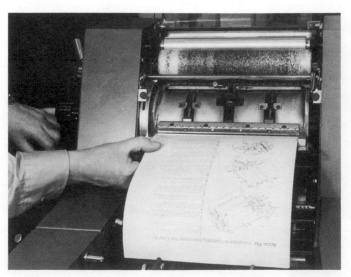

6-151. Offset plate is wrapped around the plate cylinder. Plate must be fastened at both ends and tightened evenly so it will conform snugly to plate cylinder. Overtightening will cause plate tear-out.

Fig. 6-152. Inked image is transferred from plate to blanket and from blanket to paper.

PACKING (sheets placed behind the blanket or plate) may be needed to insure proper pressure between cylinders. Some presses have adjustments to increase the impression.

DELIVERY SYSTEM

The delivery system on an offset press carries the printed sheet away from the printing cylinders and neatly stacks the paper. Either a GRAVITY delivery unit or a CHAIN delivery unit is used.

Gravity or CHUTE delivery is the simpler of the two units, Fig. 6-153. When the impression cylinder gripper opens and releases the printed sheet, EJECTOR ROLLERS propel the paper into a RECEIVING TRAY or chute.

Fig. 6-153. Gravity or chute delivery system is simpler.
(A.M. International, Inc.)

A chain delivery system uses grippers that grasp the printed sheet as it leaves the impression cylinder, Fig. 6-154. The grippers are mounted across two continuous chains that carry the sheet to a receding stacker where it is jogged into a neat pile, Fig. 6-155. After releasing the printed sheet, the grippers continue around to pick up another sheet. The chain is synchronized (operates as one) with the feed system of the press.

To test your knowledge of Offset Presswork, refer to Test Questions 62 through 77 at the end of this unit.

Fig. 6-154. Chain delivery system carries sheets some distance from the impression cylinder and stacks them. Fig. 6-159 shows chain delivery with guard swung out of the way.

Fig. 6-155. Printed sheets are jogged on receding stacker after being dropped by chain delivery grippers.

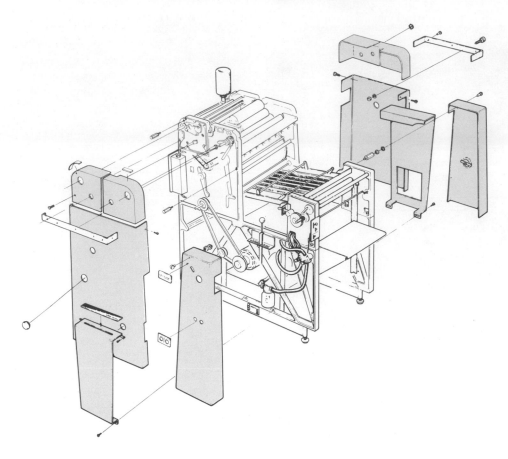

Fig. 6-156. Avoid operating any press that does not have all guards and cover plates in position.   (ATF/Davidson Co., Inc.)

OPERATING THE PRESS

Offset presses of many makes and models can be found in industry and in school graphic arts departments. Space does not permit describing each press in detail.

Regardless of make, all presses have a number of preparatory steps in common. Each step should be completed before attempting to make the first impression. Before use, inspect, clean and lubricate.

INSPECT PRESS

Carefully examine the press. Guards should be in place, Fig. 6-156. Make sure controls and switches are in the OFF position. Turn the press over by hand to check for interference, Fig. 6-157.

Wipe down the blanket, plate cylinder and rollers with a solvent dampened cloth, Fig. 6-158. Take particular care to be sure inking and dampening rollers are clean.

Fig. 6-157. Do not start up a press until you have turned it over by hand to check for interference.

Fig. 6-158. Wipe down blanket cylinder, plate cylinder and rollers with solvent dampened cloth to remove dirt from previous operation of press.

Caution: Discard used solvent and oil soaked wiping cloths into approved type safety containers.

LUBRICATION

Lubricate the press as directed in the operators' manual, Fig. 6-159. Use the correct types and grades of lubricants. Remove excess oil and grease with a cloth wiper.

Never lubricate a press while it is running.

Fig. 6-159. Lubricate press as specified in operators' manual. Guard has been lifted away for better access to chain delivery.

PREPARING FEEDER SYSTEM

1. Lower the feeder table (PAPER MAGAZINE), Fig. 6-160.
2. Establish REGISTER. See Fig. 6-161. This job can be simplified if flats were laid out so the sheet being printed will:

Fig. 6-160. Lower feed table so stock can be placed on it.

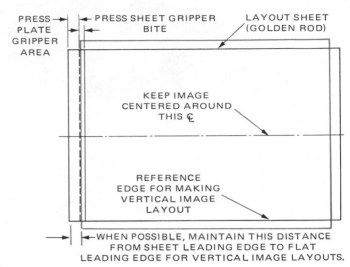

Fig. 6-161. Time is saved establishing register if all flats are laid out so material being printed is centered from right and left edge and if the same distance is maintained from sheet leading edge to flat leading edge.

   a. Be centered from left to right.
   b. Have the same distance from sheet leading edge to flat leading edge.
3. Use the scale on the feeder to position the FRONT and LEFT GUIDES, Fig. 6-162. Lay a sheet of the paper you plan to print on the feeder. Set the RIGHT SIDE GUIDE. It should barely touch the paper without binding.

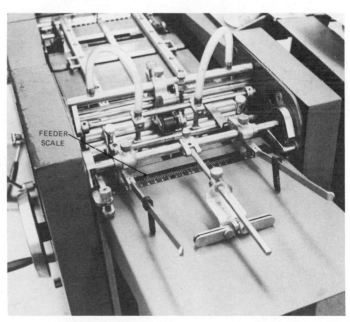

Fig. 6-162. Scale on feeder table helps operator accurately position front and side guides.

4. Place a heavy cardboard or a plywood platform under the paper pile, Fig. 6-163. It will help keep the paper flat in the feeder. The platform should be 1/8 to 1/4 in. (3 to 6 mm) smaller than the paper being printed.
5. Fan the paper pile, Fig. 6-164, and place it in the magazine.

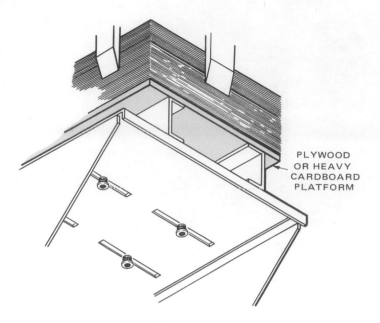

Fig. 6-163. Place heavy cardboard or plywood platform under paper pile. It will keep paper flat in feeder magazine.

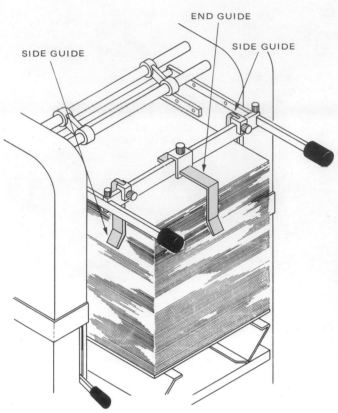

Fig. 6-165. Adjust back guides.

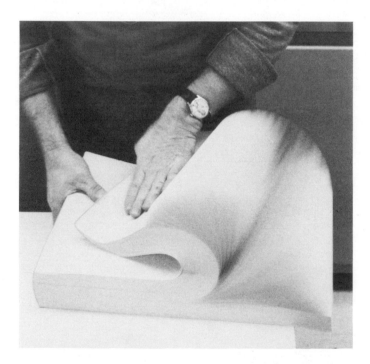

Fig. 6-164. Fan paper pile before placing it on feeder table. It will help remove paper dust and prevent sheets from sticking together.

6. Set the BACK GUIDES in place, Fig. 6-165. The guides hold the paper in place and prevent the stack from shifting during the press run.

7. Rotate the PRESS HANDWHEEL until the suction feet are at their lowest point of travel. Raise the table until the top of the sheet is 1/4 in. (6 mm) below the suction feet, Fig. 6-166.

8. Position the suction feet, sheet separators, BLOWER TUBES AND PULLOUT ROLLS. See Fig. 6-167. Place pullout rolls just outside the suction feet. Adjust the rolls so they exert a light but even pressure on a sheet.

Fig. 6-166. Raise feeder magazine so suction feet or foot is in a position to pick up stock.

9. When only one suction foot is used, locate it in the front center of the paper stack. Pullout rolls should be close to center and at equal distance from each side of the page, Fig. 6-168.

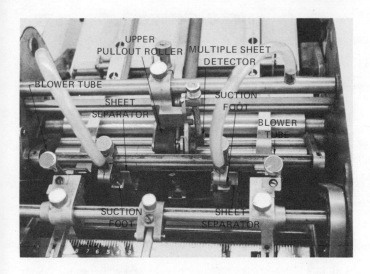

Fig. 6-167. Position suction feet, sheet separators, blower tubes and pullout rolls.

Fig. 6-169. Pile height control is adjusted to suction feet.

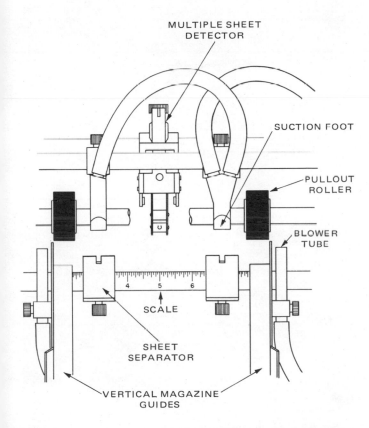

Fig. 6-168. Single pullout roll should be centered over paper pile. Twin pullout rolls should be close to center and equal distance from each side of sheet.

10. Set the **PILE HEIGHT CONTROL** (also called **PILE HEIGHT GOVERNOR**) so it just touches the pile top when the suction feet are at their lowest point, Fig. 6-169. Paper height will be maintained automatically during the press run.

11. Check the setup by turning on the **BLOWER** and **SUCTION VALVES**, Fig. 6-170. Adjust the blowers so the air causes a few of the top sheets to flutter. Vacuum should be strong enough to pick up the top sheet.

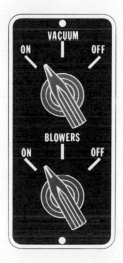

Fig. 6-170. Blower and vacuum control valves on Multigraph 1250 press. Other presses have similar controls.

12. Adjust the double-sheet eliminator, to pass only a single sheet of the paper being printed onto the **CONVEYOR BOARD**. A double sheet should trip the device and be ejected or stop the press. Refer once more to Fig. 6-139.

Your instructor will show you how to make all of these adjustments on the press you will be using. Operation manuals are another source of information.

ADJUSTING THE CONVEYOR SYSTEM

The conveyor system and **REGISTER BOARD** are adjusted for the size of paper being printed. Adjustments must also permit the sheet to enter the printing system straight.

1. Turn the machine by hand until the **JOGGER GUIDE** is at the end of its travel.

2. Position the guide to the same setting as the **LEFT GUIDE** in the paper magazine. Use the register board scale, Fig. 6-171, to make the setting.

Fig. 6-171. Scale on register board is used to adjust press so paper enters printing system at the right spot.   (ATF/Davidson Co., Inc.)

Fig. 6-173. Space conveyor tapes equally across sheet as shown. Center tape only is visible. Outer tapes are concealed by the bars known as "marble guides."

Jogging can be done from either the right or left side, or from both sides. Position of the JOGGER-SELECTOR LEVER, Fig. 6-172, on some machines determines which jogger will be used. When set at the center position, both joggers will operate.

3. Position the STATIONARY GUIDE so the REGISTER SPRING will be slightly depressed when the sheet is against the STOP FINGERS (head stops).

4. Space the conveyor tapes equally across the sheet as it travels down the CONVEYOR BOARD, Fig. 6-173. The two outside tapes must not interfere with the action of the jogger guides and jogger springs.

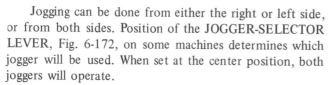

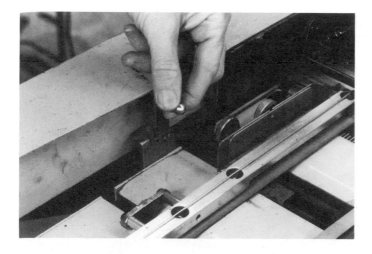

Fig. 6-172. Jogger selection lever on Giant 15 press has three positions. (ATF/Davidson Co., Inc.)

5. Some presses have RIDER WHEELS (also known as skid rolls), Fig. 6-174, or metal HOLD-DOWN STRAPS and MARBLE GUIDES, Fig. 6-175. They should be adjusted to provide enough pressure to move the sheets to the stop fingers.

Set the rider wheels so they are just off the sheet's trailing edge when the paper meets the stop fingers.

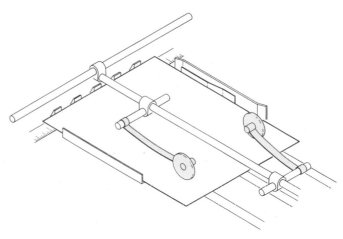

Fig. 6-174. Rider or skid wheels help hold the paper flat as it moves down conveyor.

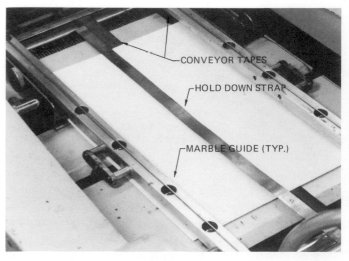

Fig. 6-175. Hold-down strap is permanently fixed over center tape. Marble guides are hollow bars having circular openings which hold steel or nylon balls. These balls press down on the sheet but roll with the conveyor tape.

6. Position the hold-down straps over, and parallel to, the outside conveyor tapes. Place the marble guides over the two outer tapes when only three tapes are used. Use nylon marbles when running average weight stock. Steel marbles may be needed when running heavy or coated papers.

ADJUSTING THE DELIVERY SYSTEM

1. If the press has chute delivery, run a sheet through the press by hand. Stop just after the paper has entered the ejector rollers, Fig. 6-176. Adjust the rolls so they ride in the right and left margins of the printed sheet.

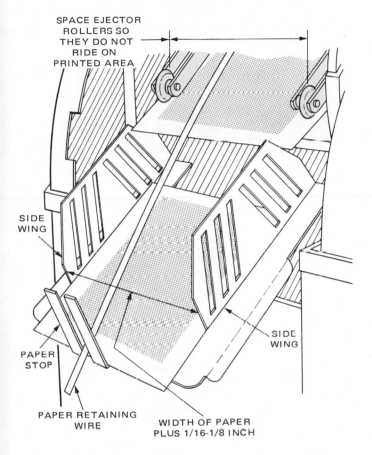

SPACE EJECTOR ROLLERS SO THEY DO NOT RIDE ON PRINTED AREA

SIDE WING

SIDE WING

PAPER STOP

PAPER RETAINING WIRE

WIDTH OF PAPER PLUS 1/16-1/8 INCH

Fig. 6-176. Adjust ejector rolls so they do not ride on image.

2. Continue to turn the press by hand until the sheet is about to be released. Position the SIDE WINGS and PAPER STOP in the DELIVERY TRAY to fit the sheet. Spacing should be about 1/8 in. (3 mm) wider than the width of the sheet. Position the PAPER RETAINING WIRE to deflect the printed sheets into the tray.
3. When a chain delivery is used, run the sheet through until it is about to be released by the DELIVERY GRIPPERS, Fig. 6-177. Move the stationary guide until it lightly touches the side of the sheet. Lock the guide in position.
4. Again, turn the press by hand until the JOGGER has moved as close as it will come to the paper. Position the jogger guide so it barely contacts the sheet.
5. Set the REAR JOGGER. Position it so it pushes the sheet up to the FRONT STOP.

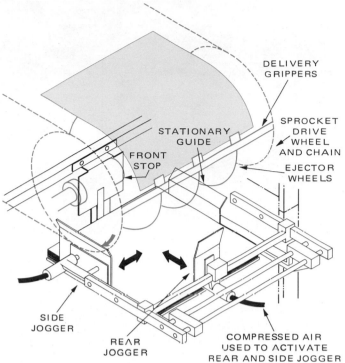

DELIVERY GRIPPERS

STATIONARY GUIDE

FRONT STOP

SPROCKET DRIVE WHEEL AND CHAIN

EJECTOR WHEELS

SIDE JOGGER

REAR JOGGER

COMPRESSED AIR USED TO ACTIVATE REAR AND SIDE JOGGER

Fig. 6-177. Sheet is shown moving through chain delivery unit.

INKING THE PRESS

1. Install the ink fountain and rollers if they have been removed.
2. Turn the HANDWHEEL until the ink ductor roller is not in contact with the fountain roller, Fig. 6-178.
3. Place ink in the fountain, Fig. 6-179. Your instructor will help you estimate how much will be needed.

When using ink from a can, remove and discard any ink skin formed in the can. Scrape an even layer from the surface with an ink knife, Fig. 6-180. Keep the ink surface in the can flat and smooth. Distribute ink across the fountain.

Always remove an even layer from the surface of the canned ink. Never dig down into the ink. The ink skin that forms in these depressions is impossible to remove completely. The can must be discarded.

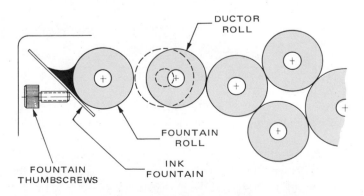

DUCTOR ROLL

FOUNTAIN ROLL

INK FOUNTAIN

FOUNTAIN THUMBSCREWS

Fig. 6-178. Turn handwheel until ink ductor roller is not in contact with fountain roller, then add ink.

141

Fig. 6-179. Adding ink. Spread it evenly across the fountain.

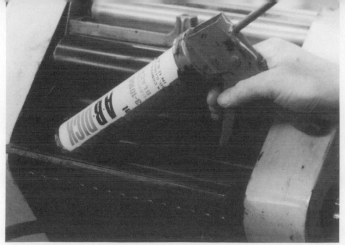

Fig. 6-181. Squeeze an even ink bead across the fountain, then work it in with an ink knife.

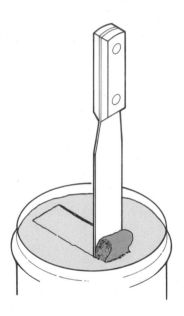

Fig. 6-180. Never dig down into the ink. Rather, scrape an even layer from the top.

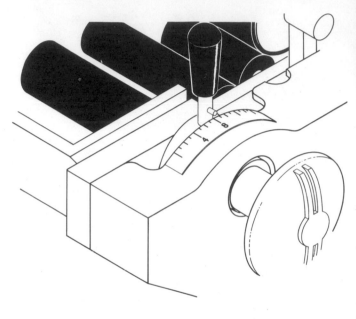

Fig. 6-182. Start with ink control lever set to about midpoint on the scale. Add to or reduce ink coverage as needed.

To use tube ink, squeeze a bead of ink the entire length of the fountain, Fig. 6-181. Work the ink in the fountain with an ink knife.

4. Turn the press on.
5. Move the INK DUCTOR ROLL LEVER to operating position (the ductor roller will contact the fountain roller), Fig. 6-182.
6. Set the INK FOUNTAIN LEVER to the operating position. Your instructor will help you make the correct setting for the job you will be printing.
7. Adjust ink film. INK FOUNTAIN THUMBSCREWS, Fig. 6-183, move the blade toward or away from the fountain roller. Tighten the thumbscrews to reduce the amount of ink going to the plate. Loosen them to increase the ink flow. Adjust the thumbscrews until there is an even transfer of ink from the fountain roller to the ductor roller.
8. Allow the press to run until the rollers are covered with a thin, even film of ink. Turn the machine off.

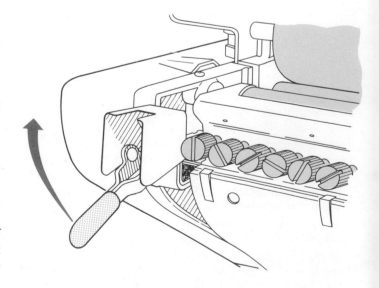

Fig. 6-183. Ink fountain thumbscrews control amount of ink on fountain roller.

PREPARING THE DAMPENER SYSTEM

1. Fill the fountain bottle with the proper mixture of solution concentrate and distilled water. Replace the bottle cap. Insert the bottle into its bracket, Fig. 6-184. Solution will drain from the bottle until it has reached operating level. Solution remaining in the bottle will refill the fountain as solution is used.

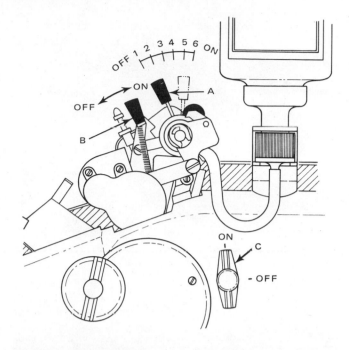

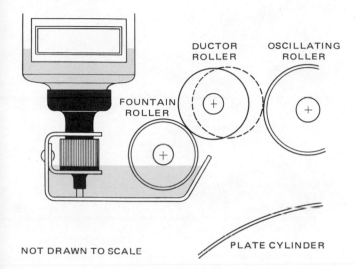

NOT DRAWN TO SCALE

Fig. 6-185. Various roller controls. A—Replex (moisture) control lever. Normal setting is 2 or 3. B—Ductor roller contact lever makes or breaks contact between the ductor roller and fountain roller. C—Disengaging lever or "night latch" disengages ink form rollers to prevent flat spots from developing when machine is idle.

Fig. 6-184. Insert fountain bottle into its fountain bracket. Solution will drain from bottle until fountain reaches operating level.

2. Position the DAMPENER FORM ROLLER to the off position. The roller or rollers will not be in contact with the plate cylinder.
3. Turn the machine over by hand until the ductor roller contacts the fountain roller.
4. Rotate the fountain roller until the ductor roll cover is thoroughly moistened.
5. Turn the press on. Adjust the flow lever to normal operating position, Fig. 6-185. Your instructor will help you with the setting. Allow the press to operate until the form rollers are "run-in." This means that the form rolls have enough moisture to properly dampen the plate. Turn the press off.
6. The press is now ready to operate.

   Caution: Before starting, have your instructor check out your work. Do not start until you have approval.

OPERATING THE PRESS

1. Moisten the plate with a cotton pad dampened with fountain solution, Fig. 6-186.
2. Turn the press on.
3. Lower the dampener form roll. Allow the press to operate for a short time before lowering the ink form rollers, Fig. 6-187. This will permit the non-image areas of the plate to become properly moistened.
4. Lower the ink form rollers.
5. Bring the plate into contact with the blanket.
6. Turn the blowers on.

Fig. 6-186. Moisten the plate with dampener solution before starting up the press.

7. Turn the feeder pump motor on.
8. Print a few test sheets.
9. Examine the test copies for register and for any other adjustments that will have to be made.

   To stop the press, reverse the preceding steps.

IMAGE LOCATION

Examine the trial impressions. Is the image located where it should be on the sheet? Is it sitting square (properly aligned) with the page?

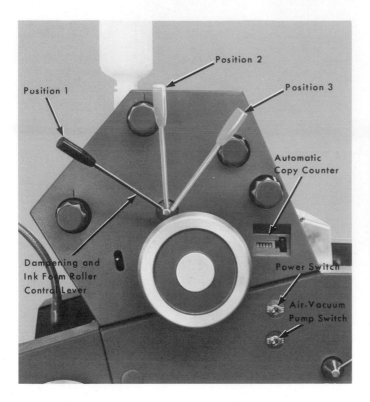

Fig. 6-187. Lower dampener form roller and allow press to run for a short time before lowering ink form rollers. (ATF/Davidson Co., Inc.)

The head margin—this is the space between the top edge and the image—can be increased or decreased. It involves unlocking the plate cylinder from the drive gear and rotating it. There is a scale provided for this operation, Fig. 6-188. It gauges the amount of movement. Be sure to relock the plate cylinder to the drive gear after the adjustment is made.

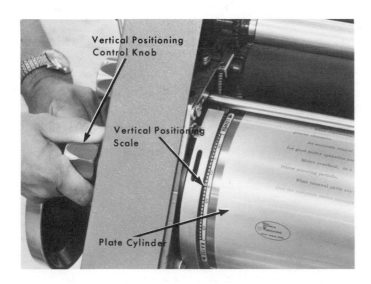

Fig. 6-188. Image can be raised or lowered on sheet being printed by rotating plate cylinder. Measure distance moved on scale at outer edge of cylinder.

Small side adjustments can be made by moving the jogger guide and stationary guide. Too much space on the left means the guides must be moved to the right. Fine adjustments can

be made with the JOGGER MICROMETER, Fig. 6-189. Reposition the paper magazine if necessary.

Clean the blanket each time the image is moved on the printed sheet. Otherwise, you will get a double image.

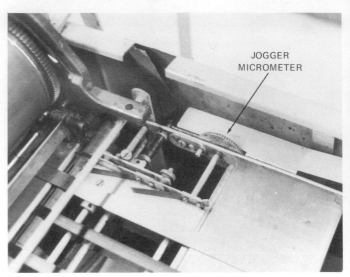

Fig. 6-189. Minor horizontal adjustments can be made of the image with the jogger micrometer.

TROUBLE SHOOTING

Offset printing produces a printed page that has crisp, dark lines. Non-image areas are clean. Registration is excellent. Each sheet dries quickly. There is no offset or smeared ink.

Most problems encountered are caused by:
1. Carelessness.
2. A dirty press.
3. An imbalance between moisture and ink.
   Remaining problems are usually the result of poorly made or improperly processed plates, ink composition and the kind of paper stock used.

SCUMMING

Scumming is ink printing in non-image areas. See Fig. 6-190. The plate does not run clean. Scumming causes and remedies include:
1. Too much ink. Correct by reducing ink flow.
2. Not enough moisture. Increase moisture supply.
3. Dirty dampener roll covers. Clean or replace roll cover.

GRAY COPY

Gray copy is an image that does not print sharp and dark as it should. There are several causes for this condition.
1. Too little ink. Increase ink flow to correct.
2. Too much moisture. Reduce moisture to rectify.
3. Glazed ink rollers. Clean or replace rollers.
4. Glazed blanket. Clean blanket thoroughly.

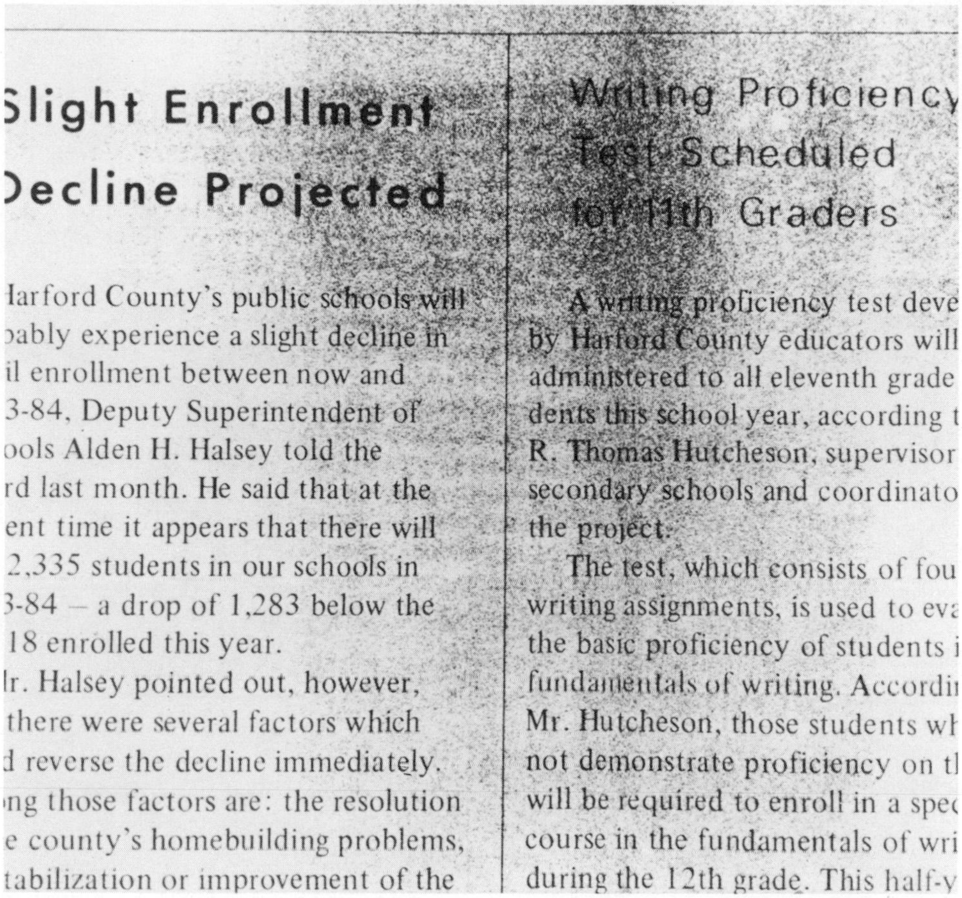

Fig. 6-190. Ink appearing in non-image areas of printed sheet is called scumming.

HICKIES

Hickies, Fig. 6-191, are defects in the printed surface. They are caused by dry ink, dirt or paper dust on the plate and/or blanket. They can usually be eliminated by cleaning the plate and blanket with a lintless cloth moistened with solvent.

Problems caused by dried ink can be avoided by cleaning the ink rollers thoroughly each time the press is used. Replace ink rollers when they become worn or cracked. If hickies still persist, it will be necessary to clean the inking system and use fresh ink.

Paper dust and fibers result when the paper is cut with a dull blade. Fanning the sheets away from the press area will reduce or eliminate most of the dirt.

Fig. 6-191. Hickies are caused by dried ink granules, paper dust or lint on the plate and/or blanket cylinder.

OTHER PROBLEMS

There are many other problems that may be encountered. Space does not permit their discussion. Your instructor will help you correct them as they occur.

CLEANING THE PRESS

The press must be cleaned whenever a different color ink is to be used. It should also be cleaned after the last press run of the day.

Before starting to clean the press, remove the printing plate. Clean, gum and store it if it is to be used again.

Each press manufacturer recommends a way for cleaning its presses. However, if an operator's manual is not available, use the following washup procedures:

DAMPENING SYSTEM CLEANUP

1. Remove the fountain bottle. Discard remaining fountain solution. Rinse clean with clean water.
2. Drain and clean the fountain.
3. Remove and clean the dampening system rollers. Roll the ductor (covered) rollers dry on clean newsprint. If dirty, wash them with a detergent solution. Rinse thoroughly in clean water. Roll dry.

4. Wipe the remaining rollers dry. Replace them in the press or put them on a storage rack.

INKING SYSTEM CLEANUP

1. Remove surplus ink from the fountain with stiff card stock or an ink knife. Discard unused ink. Discard the liner if one was used.

   Caution: Discard solvent moistened cloths in metal safety containers. Do not place them in the regular trash container.

2. Clean the fountain with solvent. Wipe with a solvent moistened cloth.

   Caution: Place unused ink on old newspapers and deposit the paper in a metal safety container. Use care so the ink will not ruin your own or other people's clothing.

3. Clean the fountain roller with a solvent moistened cloth. Ink has a tendency to build up on roller ends. Be sure to clean them thoroughly. Clean the ductor roller the same way. Place the rollers in a storage rack.

4. Put a cleaning sheet in the press. This is a blotter type paper that is attached to the plate cylinder the same way a plate is mounted.

5. Turn the press on. Operate the press at its slowest speed.

6. Place a small amount of solvent evenly across the remaining ink rollers. Use a hand oiler type container, Fig. 6-192. Allow the press to run until the ink has been loosened on the rollers. Lower the ink form rollers. The cleaning blotters will absorb the solvent thinned ink. This sequence may have to be followed several times to remove all of the ink. A new blotter should be used each time.

Fig. 6-192. Apply a small amount of cleaning solvent across ink rollers.

7. Wipe the rollers with a solvent-moistened cloth. Be sure all of the ink is removed, Fig. 6-193.

8. Clean the plate cylinder and blanket with a pad moistened in solvent. This should complete the press cleaning operation.

9. Place the press cover over the machine.

Fig. 6-193. Be sure ink is removed from ends of ink rollers.

To test what you have learned about Operating the Press, refer to Test Questions 78 through 85 at the end of this unit.

TEST YOUR KNOWLEDGE — UNIT 6

1. Lithographic printing is also known by the terms _____ and _____.
2. This type of printing is based on the principle that _____.
3. Describe how the offset printing process works. Use a drawing if necessary.
4. Offset printing is done from thin metal, plastic or paper plates. How is the image usually put on the plate?
5. Printing areas of the plate are processed so they will _____. The nonprinting areas are treated to be _____ to _____. Ink _____ adhere to the non-printing areas of the plate.

Image Generation

6. Image generation is the (record the correct answer or answers):
   a. Preparation of the printing plate.
   b. Preparation of the text, art and photographs that make up the printed message.
   c. Preparation of camera-ready material.
   d. All of the above.
   e. None of the above.
7. There are basically two ways to generate camera-ready copy. What is the difference between hot type and cold type composition?
8. Give examples of hot type composition.
9. List seven examples of cold type composition. Briefly describe each method listed.

Copy Preparation

10. The final assembly of camera-ready art and copy is called _____, _____ or _____.

MATCHING TEST: Match the terms in the first column with the definitions in the second column. Place your answers on a separate sheet of paper. *Do not write in the text.*

11. ____ Pasteup.
12. ____ Velox.
13. ____ Scaling.
14. ____ Cropping.
15. ____ Stat.
16. ____ Waxing.
17. ____ Taping.
18. ____ Oversheet.
19. ____ Register marks.

  a. Tissue or acetate film used to protect the pasteup during handling and storage.
  b. Affixing copy to pasteup with transparent tape.
  c. Halftone positive.
  d. Changing the size of original artwork or illustrations without changing the ratio of their proportions.
  e. All of the art and copy assembled into final form.
  f. Used for alignment purposes.
  g. Print of artwork that has been enlarged or reduced in size photostatically.
  h. Method used to attach art or copy to the pasteup.
  i. Method used to indicate portions of an illustration that are to be eliminated.

Photoconversion

20. A process camera can copy an image (record the correct answer or answers):
  a. The same size.
  b. In reduced size.
  c. In enlarged size.
  d. All of the above.
  e. None of the above.
21. The graphic arts process camera has six basic systems. Name all of them.
22. Line copy is an image made up of _____.
23. Some cameras have a ground glass screen that can be fitted to the camera film board. Of what use is this screen?
24. When placing film in the camera the _____ side of the film must be facing towards the lens.
25. How is film kept absolutely flat on the film holder?
26. In general, if the film is fresh, camera setting and exposure correct and the film properly developed, the resulting negative will have what four qualities?
27. Why must unexposed film be handled in a darkroom?
28. The area where film is developed must be clean and free of dust, otherwise, _____.
29. What are "pinholes"?
30. A safelight cannot be used in a darkroom. True or false?
31. When film is developed, it must be placed in the developing chemicals in a specific order. What is the order?

32. Developing time and developer temperature must be followed very carefully. Why?
33. The sensitivity guide is also known as a _____.
34. Why is a sensitivity guide used?
35. How is the sensitivity guide used?
36. Photographs can be reproduced by the offset process. A halftone screen is placed between the _____ and the _____. It breaks the photograph down into _____.
37. There are two basic types of halftone screens. What are they?
38. What is autoscreen film?

Offset Imposition

39. The operation that assembles negatives so they can be transferred to a printing plate is called _____.
40. The negatives are mounted on a _____.
41. What is the advantage of using goldenrod paper masking sheets with preprinted layout lines?

MATCHING TEST: Match the terms in the first column with the definitions in the second column. Place your answer on a separate sheet of paper. *Do not write in the text.*

42. ____ Light table.
43. ____ Gripper margin.
44. ____ Linen tester.
45. ____ Right reading.
46. ____ Window.
47. ____ Registration pins.

  a. Used to position flats during platemaking.
  b. Unprintable blank edge of paper on which grippers clasp the sheet. Usually 1/2 in. (12.5 mm) or less wide.
  c. Illuminated work surface on which flats are assembled.
  d. Emulsion side of negative is down. Copy is not reversed.
  e. Magnifying device used to check negative quality.
  f. Opening cut in flat for negative.

48. Negatives (and positives) are attached to a masking sheet with _____.
49. How can the emulsion side of a negative be determined?
50. Prepare a sketch showing how two negatives butting together on a flat should be joined.
51. When two colors are printed on the same sheet, perfect register of the colors can be assured if _____ are used.

Platemaking

52. How can dust be eliminated from the film negatives on a flat?
53. Of what use is a proof of the negatives on a flat?
54. Make sketches of the four plate end styles.
55. Plates are exposed on a _____.
56. A gray scale is made when making a plate to (record the correct answer or answers):
  a. Fill in the blank spaces on the plate.
  b. Check on the platemaker.
  c. Help determine when correct plate exposure is made.
  d. None of the above.

57. The plates you use are called surface plates. Why?
58. There are two kinds of surface plates: Additive and subtractive. Briefly describe each type.
59. What safety precautions must be observed when preparing offset plates?
60. Processed plates should be stored by _____ or _____.
61. What kind of an offset plate is a photo direct plate?

Offset Presswork

62. Offset presses are made up of four basic systems. List them.
63. Paper can be fed into an offset press a _____ _____ at a time or continuously from a _____ known as a web.

MATCHING TEST. Match the terms in the first column with the definitions in the second column. Place your answers on a separate sheet of paper. *Do not write in the text.*

64. ____ Feeder table.
65. ____ Sheet separator.
66. ____ Suction foot.
67. ____ Double sheet eliminator.
68. ____ Conveyor tapes.
69. ____ Front stop fingers.
70. ____ Ink fountain.
71. ____ Ink distributor roller.
72. ____ Ink form roller.
73. ____ Dampening system.
74. ____ Ductor roller.
75. ____ Aquamatic system.
76. ____ Blanket cylinder.
77. ____ Plate cylinder.

a. Carries sheet to be printed into registration system.
b. Contains ink supply.
c. Cylinder on which plate is mounted.
d. Holds paper supply.
e. Transports paper from feeder system into registration system.
f. Spreads ink into a thin, uniform film.
g. Assures that only one sheet will be picked up by the suction foot.
h. Prevents more than one sheet from entering printing system.
i. Places ink on the plate.
j. Receives image from the plate.
k. Meters dampening solution into dampening system.
l. Momentarily stops sheet so it can be accurately positioned before it enters the printing system.
m. System where ink and moisture are applied to plate by same form roller.
n. Applies moisture to plate.

Operating the Press

78. Press operation should not be started until what three things are done?
79. Never operate an offset press until all _____ are in place.
80. Identify the parts of the press shown in Fig. 6-194.
81. Most offset printing problems are caused by _____ _____.
82. Scumming is _____. It is most often caused by what three things?

Fig. 6-194. Can you name the parts of the press indicated?

83. Gray copy is an image that is _____.
84. _____ are defects in the printing surface. They are usually caused by _____.
85. List the safety procedures that should be observed when cleaning an offset press.

THINGS TO DO

1. Secure samples of work printed by the offset process. Prepare a bulletin board display with the samples as the theme.
2. Prepare an instructional poster that illustrates how the offset process works.
3. Prepare a litho print from a stone plate.
4. Secure samples of various sizes of used offset plates.
5. Demonstrate how the Variagraph is used.
6. Demonstrate how rub-on materials are used.
7. Demonstrate how dry transfer materials are used.
8. Secure samples of clip art.
9. Demonstrate how Tab type if used.
10. Demonstrate how direct impression plates are made.
11. Demonstrate how to justify text produced on a conventional typewriter.
12. Secure samples of text produced by phototypesetters.
13. Visit a printing plant that uses computer aided composition.
14. Prepare a pasteup with line drawings and text.
15. Secure samples of velox halftone positives.
16. Demonstrate the correct way to use a wax coater.
17. Demonstrate how register marks are used.
18. Clean and organize the school's darkroom.

Lithography or Offset Printing

19. Examine the process camera. Locate the copyboard, lensboard, lens, bellows, camera back, suspension and lighting systems and vacuum system.
20. Prepare the darkroom for processing negatives.
21. Make three negatives of suitable line work. Under develop one sample, over develop the second sample and properly develop the third sample. Prepare a report on how the negative images differ.
22. Make a pasteup of a program for an athletic event.
23. Demonstrate your skill by making negatives for the above and assembling them into a flat.
24. Burn a plate using the above flat.

25. Demonstrate how a gray scale (sensitivity guide) is used.
26. Process the plate.
27. Check out, lubricate and clean an offset press.
28. Prepare the press for operation.
29. Using a plate you have made, or your instructor has furnished, adjust the feed and register systems to print.
30. Adjust ink and dampener systems until the plate prints properly. Have your instructor check samples of your work. When samples have been approved, run the required number of sheets to finish the job.
31. Print a two color job.
32. Clean the press and store the plate you used.

Views of mammoth press room of large daily newspaper. Above. Offset press has many banks (printing units) to handle the many pages of a newspaper. Printing is done at high speed. Right. Closeup view shows how web of paper moves through the press during printing.
(Robert E. Walker)

Unit 7
INTAGLIO PRINTING

Objectives

The technique of printing from an engraved printing plate (the image is cut or etched BELOW the nonprinting surfaces) is explained here.

As you read this unit you will learn that intaglio printing plates are cut or etched by hand. You will learn that gravure printing plates are made mechanically or chemically using photographic techniques. Given the materials and equipment, you will be able to make drypoint engravings and etchings. You will also receive instructions on how to mount the resulting prints for exhibition.

In gravure or intaglio printing, the image area is below the nonprinting areas of a metal or plastic plate. See Fig. 7-1.

Intaglio (pronounced in-tal'-yo) is the term used when the image is incised (cut) by hand. Paper money and some stamps are printed by this process, Fig. 7-2. Prints, Fig. 7-3, made by intaglio are often considered to be a fine arts technique.

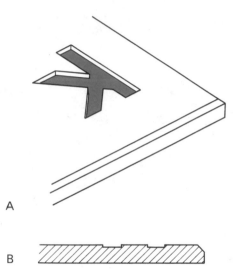

A

B

Fig. 7-1. Intaglio or gravure printing image lies beneath surface of metal or plastic plate. Ink is applied to entire surface of plate; then it is wiped off.

Fig. 7-2. This high speed rotary press prints money.   (Bureau of Engraving and Printing, U.S. Treasury Dept.)

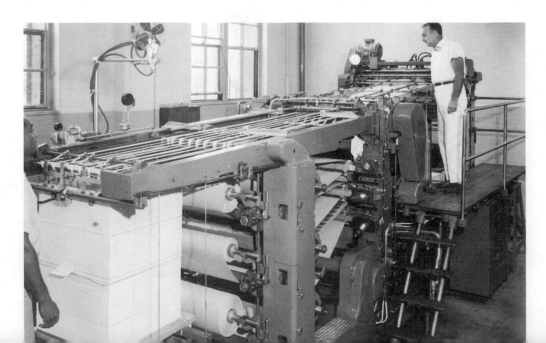

Fig. 7-3. Many prints made by the intaglio process are considered to be in the fine arts category. This is a drypoint print.

Fig. 7-4. Many newspaper inserts, catalogs and greeting cards are printed by the gravure process.

The image is made by engraving, etching or scratching. During printing, ink is applied to the entire surface of the printing plate. Most of the ink is then removed by scraping or wiping. The only ink remaining is in the recessed (sunken) image area.

Paper is placed against the plate while pressure is applied. The paper picks up the ink in the depressions that form the image. In this way the image is reproduced on the paper.

The technique is called gravure when the image is made mechanically or by a photographic and chemical process. Many newspaper inserts, catalogs, greeting cards and packaging materials are printed by gravure. See Fig. 7-4.

INTAGLIO PRINTING TECHNIQUES

Prints produced by the intaglio process are usually hand made. The printing plates can be made by several methods.

DRYPOINT ENGRAVING

Drypoint engraving is a term almost self-explanatory. A clean, scratch-free metal or plastic plate is needed, Fig. 7-5. Copper is preferred. A sharp needle makes the lines that do the printing, Fig. 7-6. The needle, held at about a 60 deg. angle, makes a groove in the plate. The groove has a burr on one side. The burr is removed only when a very fine line is desired. The needle must be drawn across the plate with enough force to turn up the burr.

The burr helps retain the ink for printing. However, it wears rapidly from printing pressure. Only a few sharp impressions can be made.

Drypoint prints can also be made from plastic plates. The plastic should be from .015 to .050 in. (0.38 to 1.3 mm) thick.

1. Draw the image full size on paper. This is necessary because the image will print in reverse.

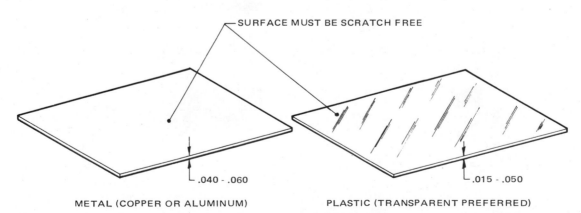

SURFACE MUST BE SCRATCH FREE

.040 - .060

.015 - .050

METAL (COPPER OR ALUMINUM)   PLASTIC (TRANSPARENT PREFERRED)

Fig. 7-5. A clean, scratch-free metal or plastic plate is needed when making intaglio prints by hand.

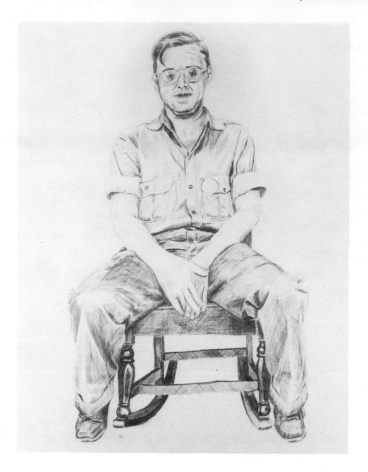 

Fig. 7-6. Intaglio plate and print. Left. Student made this drypoint plate using sharp needle to make lines in plate. Needle, mounted in a wood handle, raises burr on plate. Right. Print made from the drypoint plate. (Bel Air High School)

2. Reverse the image by placing carbon paper under the drawing paper, carbon side up and tracing over the designs. A reverse image will appear on the back of the sheet.

3. Transfer this reversed design to the metal plate with carbon paper.

4. If the design is to be scribed on plastic, tape it under the clear plastic plate.

5. Scribe the lines in the plate. A scribing tool can be made by mounting a steel phonograph needle in a hardwood handle.

The point will need to be sharpened occasionally on a fine oilstone.

6. Line strength (darkness or heaviness) depends upon the width and depth of the drawn line. Make shadows and dark areas by cross-hatching. See Fig. 7-7. The closer together the cross-hatching, the darker the area will print.

Fig. 7-8 shows how a series of drawings is engraved in drypoint on plastic.

 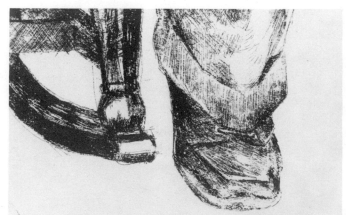

Fig. 7-7. Engraving and print. Left. Note how lines are cut into the plate to make the shadows and dark areas of the print. Right. How the lines in plate print.

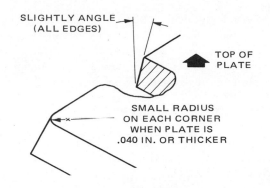

SLIGHTLY ANGLE
(ALL EDGES)

TOP OF
PLATE

SMALL RADIUS
ON EACH CORNER
WHEN PLATE IS
.040 IN. OR THICKER

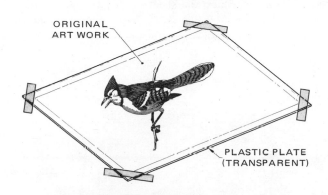

ORIGINAL
ART WORK

PLASTIC PLATE
(TRANSPARENT)

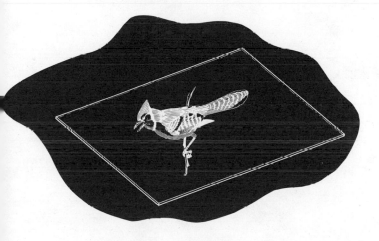

Fig. 7-8. Top. Beveling edges of plate used for drypoint engravings will prevent them from cutting through paper when engraving is printed. Center. Place artwork under transparent plastic plate. Tape to solid surface. Bottom. Drypoint engraving can be checked by sliding sheet of black paper under plastic plate. Engraved lines will appear white against black background.

Fig. 7-9. An etching is made by using acid to cut image into metal plate. Etched plate is shown on press bed. Finished etching is at right.

ETCHING

An etching, Fig. 7-9, requires the action of acid on metal. Cut to size an aluminum, copper or zinc plate of .032 to .060 thickness. Bevel the plate edges and round corners slightly so they will not cut the paper during printing.

Polish the plate to remove scratches. Clean the polished plate to remove all traces of grease and oil. This can be done by rubbing the plate with whiting and water. Chemical cleaning can be done with salt that has been moistened with vinegar or lemon juice. *Avoid touching the face of the plate after it has been cleaned.*

Warm the plate slightly. Cover the polished face with a thin coating of ACID RESIST (wax ground). Paint the back and edges of the plate with asphaltum paint. This protects them from the action of the acid.

Smoke the waxed surface with a candle so you will be able to see the progress of your drawing more easily. Keep the plate moving or the candle flame will melt the wax.

Draw the image. Use a pointed tool to cut through the wax resist. This exposes the metal to the action of the acid.

Preparing the acid bath

A commercially made acid bath (or mordant, as it is called) is preferred. However, a mordant for aluminum and zinc can be made from one part nitric acid and four parts water. Perchloride of iron or a 20-30 percent nitric acid solution is used with copper. Place the acid bath in a glass tray.

Caution: If an acid bath must be mixed, always pour the acid into the water. Wear protective clothing and a face shield. Flush away acid splashed on the skin with copious quantities of cold running water. Then see a doctor.

Planning the etch

The etching operation must be planned carefully. The lightest lines in the image are etched first. Lower the plate into the acid, supporting it with a waxed cord as shown in Fig. 7-10.

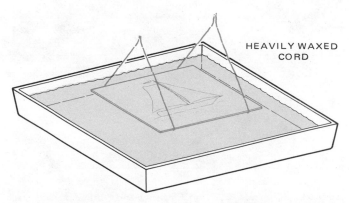

HEAVILY WAXED
CORD

Fig. 7-10. Waxed cord supports plate in acid during etching.

Graphic Arts Fundamentals

The first BITE (acid dip) lasts about a minute. Remove the plate from the acid and wash it thoroughly under running water. When thoroughly dried, STOP OUT (paint) the fine lines with asphaltum paint. This step protects these lines from further etching.

Biting and stopping out continues until all of the desired line weights of the image are properly etched. Then, remove the acid resist (wax and asphaltum) from the plate by dissolving it with a suitable solvent.

Caution: Use solvents in well ventilated areas where there is no danger of fire. Discard soiled rags in suitable safety containers.

The etched plate is ready for printing. See Fig. 7-11.

ENGRAVING

An engraving, Fig. 7-12, is different than either a drypoint or an etching. The lines of an engraving are cut into the metal

plate with a tool called a BURIN or GRAVER, Fig. 7-13. Color gradation (difference) is made by varying the width and depth of the lines that make up the image. Shading and dark areas are made by engraving several lines running close together, or crossing one another. See Fig. 7-14.

PRINTING AN INTAGLIO PLATE

All intaglio plates are printed on an ETCHING PRESS, Fig. 7-15, using ETCHING PAPER. This is a soft and unsized paper. (Unsized means it does not have a coating of clay, glue or plastic.) Prepare paper in advance by dipping alternate sheets in water. Stack the sheets and cover them with wax paper or aluminum foil, Fig. 7-16. The dampened paper can be stacked overnight between glass plates.

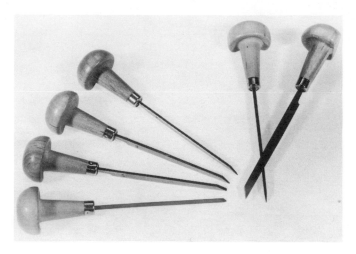
Fig. 7-13. Tools used to make engravings are called burins or gravers.

Fig. 7-11. Etched plate is ready for printing.

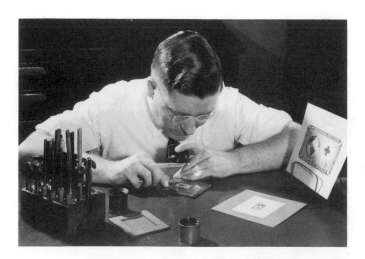
Fig. 7-12. Engraver at Bureau of Engraving and Printing prepares steel master die for postage stamp. He is guided by artist's design at his left.

Fig. 7-14. Money is made from engraved steel plates. Heavy or closely spaced multiple lines are used to make shaded or dark areas of image.

154

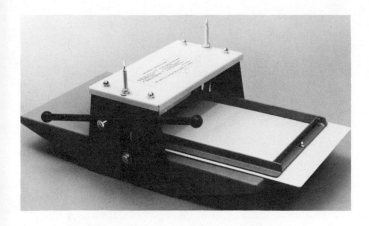

Fig. 7-15. This etching press is hand operated.

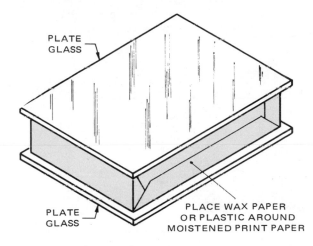

PLATE GLASS

PLATE GLASS

PLACE WAX PAPER OR PLASTIC AROUND MOISTENED PRINT PAPER

Fig. 7-16. Paper used with intaglio plates should be slightly dampened for printing. Alternate sheets are dipped in water.

MIXING VARNISH

Fig. 7-17. Applying etcher's ink to plate. Ink can be thinned with mixing varnish.

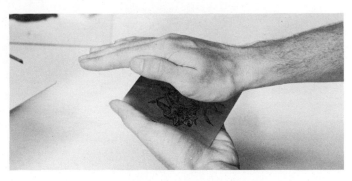

Fig. 7-18. Final cleaning of the printing plate is done with the heel of the hand.

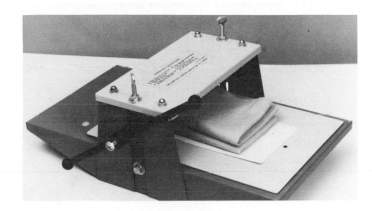

Fig. 7-19. Plate and paper are ready to be run through press. Plate rests on a sheet of heavy paper with image up. A piece of dampened print paper covers plate. Felt blankets have been placed on top.

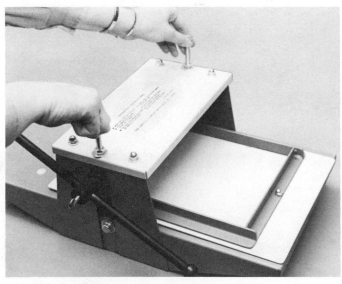

Fig. 7-20. Adjust press to exert sufficient pressure on paper.

Apply ETCHER'S INK, Fig. 7-17, to the engraved plate after it has been warmed. Heat causes the ink to flow better. Wipe off the ink from the entire plate surface. Use a soft cloth. Then clean the plate again with the heel of the hand, Fig. 7-18. The plate and paper are now ready for printing.

Warm the plate again slightly. Place a piece of dampened paper over the plate. Lay the paper and plate on the bed of the etching press as in Fig. 7-19. Place felt blankets over both plate and paper. Adjust the press for pressure, Fig. 7-20. Run the bed through the press, Fig. 7-21.

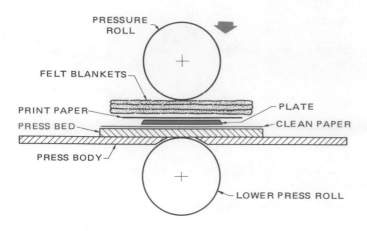

Fig. 7-21. View shows paper and plate going through press.

Place the printed sheet between two white blotters until dry. Repeat the printing operation until you have the right number of good prints. Mount the prints. See Fig. 7-22.

GRAVURE PRINTING TECHNIQUES

Gravure is another term for the intaglio process. It identifies the technique used when the printing plates are made mechanically or photographically. When adapted to the rotary printing press, Fig. 7-23, the process is called ROTO-GRAVURE.

Rotogravure is capable of reproducing black and white and brilliant colors. Printing is rapid and inexpensive.

The rotogravure image is etched or cut into a cylindrical printing plate. Tiny, shallow depressions called CELLS, Fig. 7-24, make up the image. There are 22,500 of these little "ink wells" every square inch. The cells vary in size and depth. The larger and deeper ones transfer more ink to the paper than the smaller, shallower cells. Therefore, they print darker. There are 10 large cells in a period like the one at the end of this sentence.

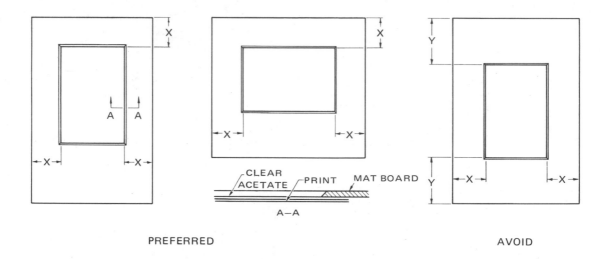

PREFERRED   AVOID

Fig. 7-22. Recommended way to mount plate in heavy paper mat. Mounting prints this way will protect them during handling and framing.

Fig. 7-23. This rotogravure press prints a newspaper supplement. (Diversified Printing Corp.)

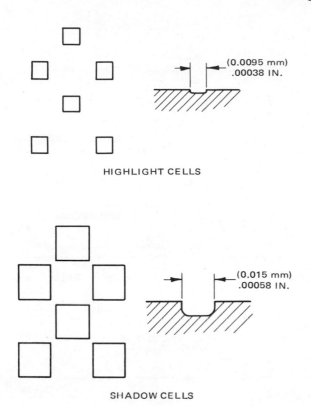

HIGHLIGHT CELLS

(0.0095 mm)
.00038 IN.

SHADOW CELLS

(0.015 mm)
.00058 IN.

Fig. 7-24. Image on rotogravure printing cylinders is made up of tiny cells. The cells vary in size and depth. Larger and deeper cells transfer more ink to paper than do small shallow cells.

The operation of the rotogravure press is shown in Fig. 7-25. The printing cylinder rotates in the ink. This fills the cells that make up the image. A DOCTOR BLADE wipes away all the ink from the surface (nonprinting areas) of the cylinder. Paper is pressed against the printing cylinder by an impression cylinder. The paper draws the ink from the cells to print the image.

The doctor blade is made from a thin strip of high grade steel or nylon. See Fig. 7-26.

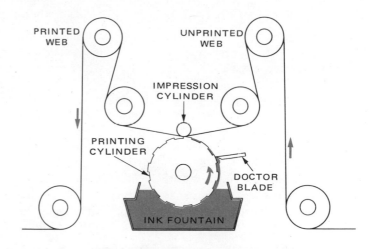

Fig. 7-25. Operation of rotogravure press. Printing cylinder is mounted over the ink well.

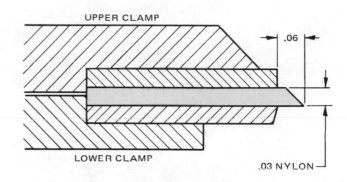

Fig. 7-26. Doctor blade wipes excess ink from cylinder's surface. Only ink in cells remains.

PREPARING A ROTOGRAVURE CYLINDER FOR PRINTING

Rotogravure printing cylinders are expensive to prepare. The operation starts with a copper clad steel cylinder, Fig. 7-27. It is 80 in. (2032 mm) long, has a diameter of exactly 13.685 in. (348 mm) and weighs about a ton (907 kg).

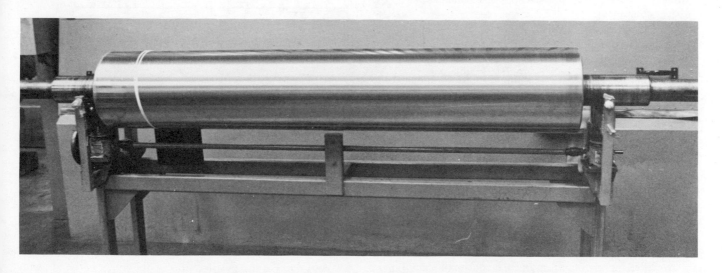

Fig. 7-27. Printing or press cylinder ready to receive image.   (Diversified Printing Corp.)

An electroplating process deposits an additional thin coating of copper on the cylinder. This shell is only .00625 in. (0.16 mm) thick. The cells that do the printing are etched or cut into the copper shell.

After printing, the copper shell is machined away. The cylinder is replated for reuse.

The copper shell is polished with a fine stone to the exact cylinder diameter, Fig. 7-28. Cylinder size must be precise or the printer will have difficulty REGISTERING colors during the printing operation. Register is the term used to describe how one color fits or aligns with other colors that make up the same image.

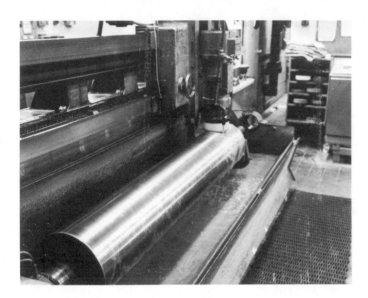

Fig. 7-28. Polishing the press cylinder. It must be machined to exacting dimension. (Diversified Printing Corp.)

The copper press cylinder does not have to be sensitized like printing plates for other printing techniques. There are several ways of placing the image on the cylinder. Two methods, photographic and electronic-mechanical, are the most widely used.

PHOTOGRAPHIC METHOD

When the photographic method is used to prepare the cylinder for printing, a light-sensitive material is employed. Most common of these materials are:
1. A special carbon tissue.
2. ROTOFILM.

Rotofilm is made in three layers, Fig. 7-29. The first layer is acetate plastic. It supports a light-sensitive emulsion. Between these two layers is found a microscopically thin waterproof membrane.

The light-sensitive emulsion records the photographic image. However, it differs from regular photographic film in every other respect.

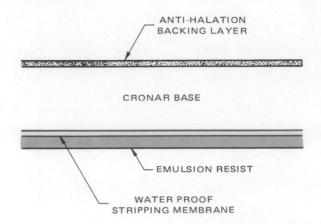

Fig. 7-29. A cross section of rotofilm shows its various layers.

The light-sensitive emulsion hardens in proportion to the amount of light that strikes it, Fig. 7-30. The emulsion also controls the action of the acid etching (eating into) the copper printing cylinder.

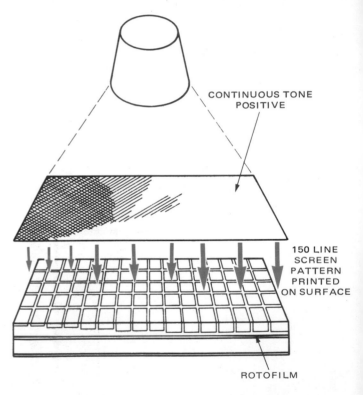

Fig. 7-30. Emulsion on rotofilm hardens in proportion to amount of light that strikes it during exposure.

Preparation of the cylinder for etching starts with exposure of the film through a gravure cross-line screen, Fig. 7-31. Three separate exposures are made following these steps:
1. The screen is carefully aligned over the rotofilm.
2. A yellow light, Fig. 7-32, briefly exposes the film. This step "sets" the nonprinting screen areas between the cells that will print the image.
3. The engraver places over the screen and rotofilm a continuous tone positive film of the image (type, drawings and photographs).

Fig. 7-31. Gravure screen differs from halftone screen used in relief and offset printing. The lines of the grid are transparent.

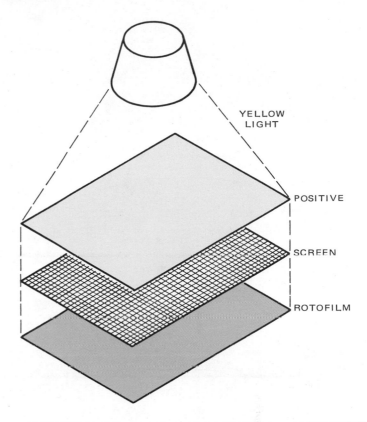

Fig. 7-33. A second exposure is made with yellow light. However, this time a continuous tone positive of the image to be printed is positioned over the screen and film

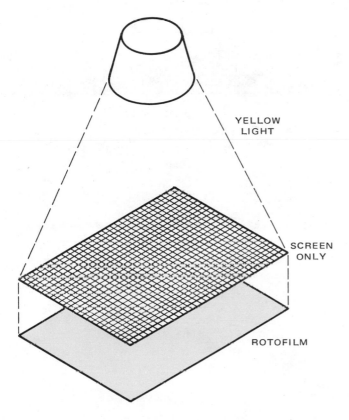

Fig. 7-32. In first step of exposing the film, yellow light is shown through gravure screen onto rotofilm.

4. A second exposure follows, Fig. 7-33. This exposure controls the size of the cells that will be etched into the cylinder.
5. The engraver removes the screen and makes a third exposure. In this one, an ultraviolet light is flashed through the positive, Fig. 7-34. The depth the cells will be etched is determined by this exposure.

An electronically controlled machine develops the exposed rotofilm. As the image develops, the emulsion hardens where it was exposed to light. The degree of hardness is decided by the amount of light that has passed through the positive, Fig. 7-35.

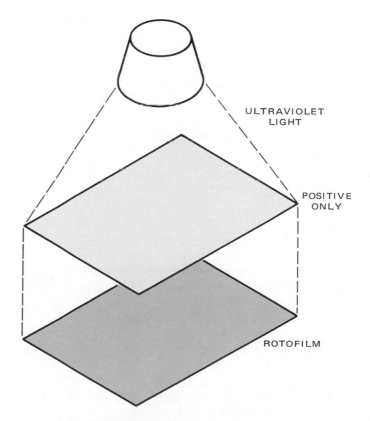

Fig. 7-34. Screen is removed and a third exposure is made by flashing an ultraviolet light through positive. The depth to which cells will be etched is determined by this exposure.

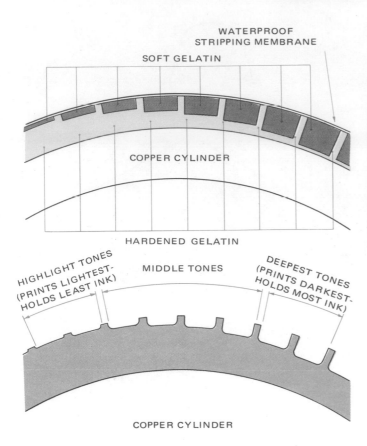

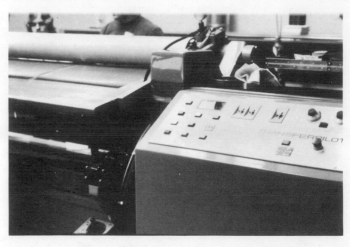

Fig. 7-36. Pressure is used to attach developed film (or carbon tissue) to press cylinder. (Reader's Digest)

Fig. 7-35. During development, the emulsion hardens where it was exposed to light. The degree of hardness is determined by the amount of light that has passed through the positive.

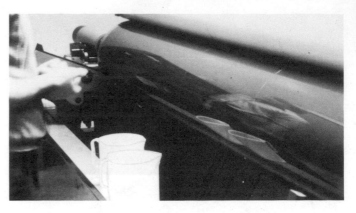

Fig. 7-37. Acetate backing sheet is removed. Only waterproof membrane and emulsion remain on cylinder.

The engraver gives the developed rotofilm (sometimes called RESIST) a final check for quality. It is then sent to the etching department.

TRANSFERRING ROTOFILM TO A PRESS CYLINDER

After being ground to size, the cylinder is placed in a TRANSFER MACHINE. Water flows over the cylinder until a film of moisture covers the entire surface. (Moisture is needed to bond the film to the cylinder.)

Rows of film are carefully placed on the cylinder, emulsion side down. Each row, called a RIBBON, is located according to the order of its appearance in printed form. After the film is in place, a roller applying a pressure of 1300 psi (8963 kPa) bonds the rotofilm to the cylinder, Fig. 7-36. The acetate backing sheet is lifted off, Fig. 7-37. Only the waterproof membrane and emulsion remain on the cylinder.

An acetone bath dissolves the waterproof membrane on the cylinder. A second bath in hot water washes away the unhardened emulsion, Fig. 7-38. Thickness of the hardened emulsion remaining determines how deeply the acid will etch into the copper shell, Fig. 7-39.

Before etching, asphaltum paint is brushed over open spaces on cylinder to protect nonprinting areas from acid. See Fig. 7-40.

Fig. 7-38. After an acetone bath to dissolve waterproof membrane, a bath in hot water washes away unhardened emulsion. (Reader's Digest)

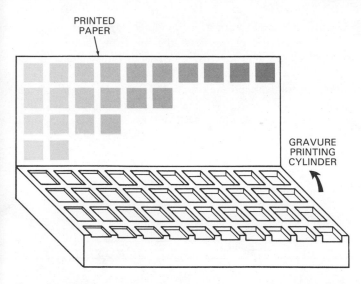

Fig. 7-39. Thickness of the hardened emulsion remaining on cylinder determines how deeply acid will etch into copper shell.

Fig. 7-41. Cylinder is etched on computer controlled etching machine. Cylinder revolves in contact with an acid-bearing roller. Scanner head reads rate of etch and reports to computer. (Reader's Digest)

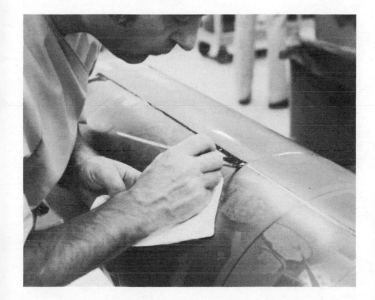

Fig. 7-40. Before etching begins, asphaltum paint is brushed over open spaces on cylinder. This will protect these nonprinting areas from the acid.

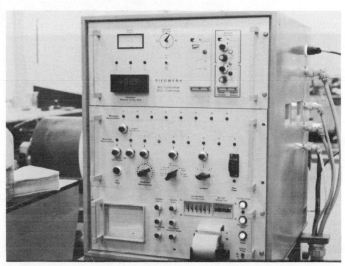

Fig. 7-42. Rate of etch on cylinder is shown on computer panel.

Etching is done on a computer controlled ETCHING MACHINE, Fig. 7-41. The printing cylinder revolves in contact with an acid-bearing roller. A scanner head reads the rate of etch and reports to the computer. Rate of etch is shown on the computer panel shown in Fig. 7-42.

When the scanner reports that the cells are etched throughout the full range of tone scale, the computer halts the etching process. It then causes stop-baths and cleaners to flow over the cylinder. Finally, the cylinder is dried with warm air.

A FINISHER inspects the entire surface of the etched cylinder with a 12-power magnifier, Fig. 7-43. This worker hand etches or burnishes areas needing correction.

Another cylinder is etched for each color to be printed. Cylinders used for long press runs are chromium plated to improve their wearing qualities.

Fig. 7-43. Entire surface of cylinder is inspected.

PRINTING

Fig. 7-44 is a diagram of how a rotogravure press operates. The number of pages on which color will be printed determines the number of printing cylinders used on the press. Each color cylinder rotates in an ink trough of the color it is to print. Surplus ink is removed with a doctor blade.

Paper is pressed against each cylinder by a rubber impression cylinder. The paper draws the ink from the millions of tiny cells etched on the printing surface of the cylinder.

Before full-scale printing is started, several press proofs are made. A rotogravure proof press is used in many plants, Fig. 7-45. Proofs are carefully checked for color accuracy and

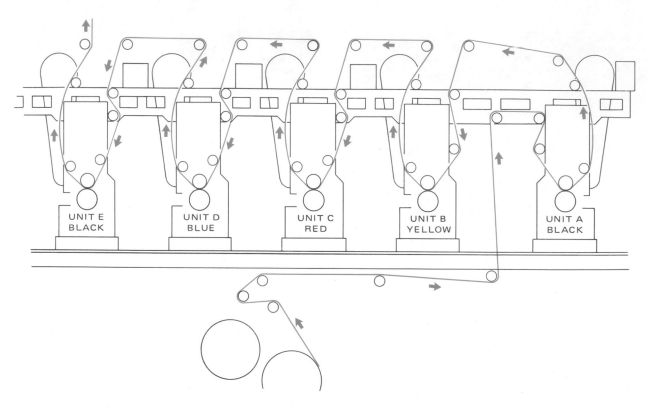

Fig. 7-44. Four-color rotogravure press has five units. (Denver Post)

Fig. 7-45. Four color rotogravure proof press is used by some plants. (Diversified Printing Corp.)

register. Corrections are made, if necessary, to any of the color cylinders.

Color can be intensified (added) by etching ink cells deeper. Color can be made lighter (subtracted) by burnishing to make the cells shallower. They then do not hold as much ink. Burnishing is done by polishing the printing surface to remove a slight bit of metal. Adding to or subtracting from a color is called COLOR CORRECTION.

With corrections made and approved, the press run is started. Paper up to 150 in. (3810 mm) wide is furnished to the press from rolls. The rolls weigh up to 3000 lb. (1361 kg). Just before one roll is completely used up another full roll is spliced into the web. The press does not have to be stopped.

Driers located between printing units speed up drying the ink. For color printing, electronic sensors monitor ink color as it is printed. Color fidelity is maintained by automatic register controls on modern gravure color presses.

It is possible to print more than 40,000 copies an hour of a 48-page magazine or catalog. A typical press run may use as much as 6 tons of ink.

ELECTRONIC-MECHANICAL METHOD

The gravure image can also be engraved into the press cylinder by using electronics. A scanner passes over rotating copy. It generates electrical impulses. The impulses activate a tiny diamond stylus in a cutting head that moves across the press cylinder. Impulse strength depends on tonal values of the copy. This determines how deeply the diamond stylus will engrave the cell in the cylinder, Fig. 7-46.

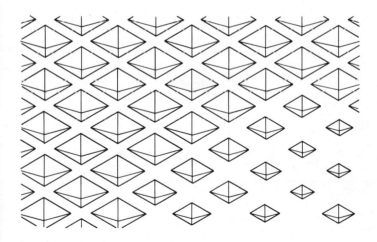

Fig. 7-46. Electronic impulses from a scanner head determine how deeply diamond stylus will engrave cell into cylinder.

TEST YOUR KNOWLEDGE - UNIT 7

1. Prepare a sketch showing how the intaglio process differs from letterpress and offset processes.

2. Describe the intaglio process.
3. What is another term for intaglio? When is this term used?
4. A drypoint engraving is made by (Do not write in the book. Select the correct answer.):
   a. Incising the design into a metal with a graver.
   b. Using acid to cut the design into the metal.
   c. Scratching the design into the metal with a pointed tool.
   d. None of the above.
5. An etching is made by (Do not write in the book. Select the correct answer.):
   a. Incising the design into the metal with a graver.
   b. Using acid to cut the design into the metal.
   c. Scratching the design into the metal with a pointed tool.
   d. None of the above.
6. An engraving is made by:
   a. Incising the design into the metal with a graver.
   b. Using acid to cut the design into the metal.
   c. Scratching the design into the metal with a pointed tool.
   d. None of the above.
7. A mordant is used to _____ _____.
8. A resist is used to _____ _____.
9. Make a sketch showing how the rotogravure press operates. Name the various parts.
10. How are ink cells put on a gravure printing cylinder?
11. Describe how the image is placed on a rotogravure printing cylinder by photographic means.
12. The amount of ink placed on paper by a rotogravure printing cylinder is determined by _____.
13. Work done to a rotogravure printing cylinder to intensify or lighten a color being printed is called _____ _____.

THINGS TO DO

1. Secure samples of material printed by the intaglio process.
2. Prepare an overhead projectual that shows how the intaglio process differs from the letter press and offset processes.
3. Prepare an overhead projectual that shows the operating principle of the gravure press.
4. Visit a printing plant that does gravure printing. Report to the class what you observed.
5. Make and print a drypoint engraving. Mount it.
6. Make and print an engraving. Mount it.
7. Contact the company that engraves and prints the name cards and graduation announcements for your school. Request one of the plates used to print them.
8. Demonstrate how a drypoint engraving is made.
9. Demonstrate how an etching is made.
10. Demonstrate how the etching press is used.
11. Prepare a bulletin board display on the intaglio process.
12. Prepare a term paper on how paper money is printed.

Fig. 8-1. Many well-known things were printed by the screen printing process.

Unit 8
SCREEN PRINTING

Objectives

The basics of screen printing, a form of stencil printing, are discussed in this unit.

After studying it you will understand how screen printing, by both hand and machine techniques, is done. With suitable tools and equipment, you will be able to demonstrate screen printing using cut film stencils, photographically made stencils, tusche stencils, etc. You will also know how to clean and maintain screen printing equipment.

Many well-known products, both flat and three-dimensional, are printed by the screen technique, Fig. 8-1.

Screen printing is a form of stencil printing, Fig. 8-2. A stencil is basically a sheet of material—wax, paper or cloth—through which liquids are not able to pass. Images such as drawings and letters are punched, etched or cut through this material.

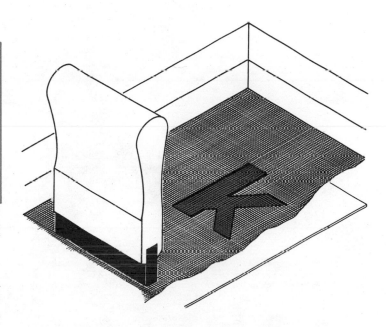

Fig. 8-2. Screen printing is a form of stencil printing.

In screen printing, the stencil is attached to a fine-mesh screen. A squeegee forces a heavy-bodied ink through the image area made in the stencil. The design is transferred directly onto the object.

The procedure is known by many other names: silk screen printing, screen process printing, stencil printing and mitography. It can be done by hand, Fig. 8-3, or mechanically as shown in Fig. 8-4.

MATERIALS AND HAND TOOLS

1. Stencil. A material which carries the design to be printed. The stencil is always adhered to the screen fabric. Materials from which stencils are made include: paper, plastic, wax, gelatin and tusche.
2. Screen fabric. A fine-mesh silk, organdy, nylon, polyester, dacron or wire.

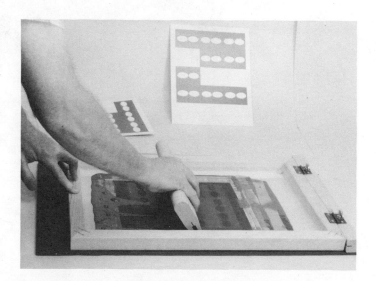

Fig. 8-3. Screen printing by hand requires only a few simple tools.

Fig. 8-4. Automatic screen printing press is used for production work. (American Screen Printing Equipment Co.)

Fig. 8-6. Squeegee. Blade is made of rubber or plastic.

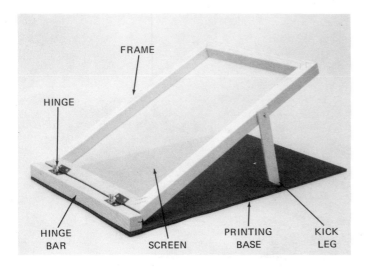

Fig. 8-5. Frame is made of wood or metal. One side is covered with screen made of cloth or wire.

Fig. 8-7. Screen printing ink is available in hundreds of colors.

Fig. 8-8. Poster printed by screen process.

Fig. 8-9. A stencil must be cut for each color.

3. Frame. A wood or metal rectangle which supports the screen fabric, Fig. 8-5. One side is grooved to receive a cord which tightens and holds the screen onto the frame.
4. Printing base. A flat, rectangular board to which the frame is attached with hinges. Object being printed is positioned on the base directly under the stencil.
5. Squeegee. This device forces ink through the screen and image area of the stencil, Fig. 8-6.
6. Ink. A heavy-bodied (thick) fluid which usually has water, lacquer or petroleum as a base. See Fig. 8-7.

MAKING A SCREEN PRINT — HAND CUT STENCIL

High-quality screen reproductions can be made with hand cut film stencils, Fig. 8-8. Multi-colored images can also be printed. However, a stencil must be cut for each color, Fig. 8-9. Some screen prints are considered fine art, Fig. 8-10. Many such prints are on display in art galleries.

FILM CONSTRUCTION

All film used for hand cut stencils has two layers, Fig. 8-11:
1. The film itself.
2. The backing or support sheet.

The layers are held together with a special adhesive. The backing sheet keeps the film stable (holding its size and shape). It prevents shrinking, expanding and tearing. It also holds the cut portions of the film together until it can be adhered to the screen.

TYPES OF FILM

There are two types of hand cut film:
1. Lacquer soluble.
2. Water soluble.

Fig. 8-10. Some screen prints are considered fine art. (Bel Air High School)

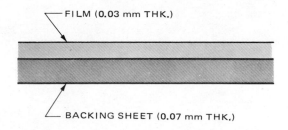

Fig. 8-11. Hand cut stencil film has two layers. Backing sheet is discarded after film has been adhered to screen fabric.

167

In most respect, the films are the same. However, they do require different solvents and different inks.

Lacquer soluble film is adhered to and removed from the screen with lacquer thinner. Therefore, lacquer based inks cannot be used with it. The film would be dissolved.

Water soluble film, of course, uses water for adhering and removal. As you might expect, water based inks cannot be used with it; the film would separate from the screen.

CUTTING THE FILM

1. Prepare the design, both artwork and lettering, Fig. 8-12.
2. Attach the design to a smooth, flat surface. Tape a piece of stencil film over the design, film side up, Fig. 8-13. Cut the film 2 in. (50 mm) larger on all sides.

Fig. 8-12. Both design and lettering should appear on original artwork.

Fig. 8-13. Film is taped over the artwork film side up.

3. Use a sharp knife to make the design in the stencil material, Fig. 8-14. Very little pressure should be needed to cut through the film. Do not cut through the backing sheet.

Avoid using a dull knife. The heavy pressure required to make the cut forces the film down into the backing sheet. This rounds the film edges and creates a groove, Fig. 8-15. Adhering fluid collects in the grooves and attacks the film from both top and bottom. The result is burned (partially dissolved) edges, Fig. 8-16.

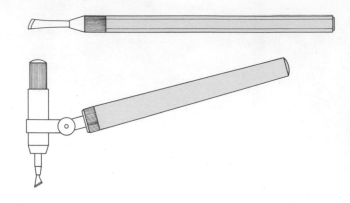

Fig. 8-14. A few of the many type knives that are used to cut image area in film. Blade must be razor sharp.

The rounded edges also cause poor contact between film and screen. Poor contact produces ragged edges even though the film was cut properly.

Use a straightedge to guide the knife when cutting straight lines. Cut curves freehand or with special tools as shown in Fig. 8-17.

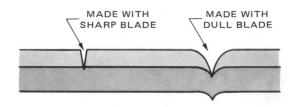

Fig. 8-15. Dull knife forces the film into the backing sheet and creates a troublesome groove. Adhering fluid collects in groove and dissolves film edge.

Fig. 8-16. Difference between properly cut and adhered image and one that has burned (ragged) edges shows up when image is screen printed.

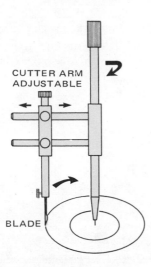

Fig. 8-17. Device used to cut circles in film. Blade can be moved to adjust size of circle.

Fig. 8-19. Small details of the image can be removed with masking tape.

4. Film is removed only from areas that are to print, Fig. 8-18. Remove film from the image area with a knife having a slightly dulled blade. This saves the sharp tip of the cutting knife. A tweezers may be used to peel off the film being removed.

  Small film sections can be removed with tape. Stick a small piece of tape to the film you wish to remove. The film peels away with the tape, Fig. 8-19. This technique assures clean, sharp edges on the stencil.

  Keep the film surface clean and dry when it is being cut. This is especially important when using water soluble film on hot, humid days. A piece of clean scrap paper between film and hand will provide enough protection, Fig. 8-20.

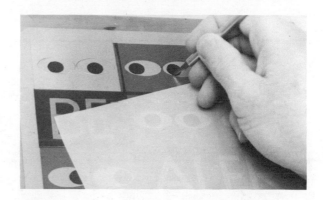

Fig. 8-20. Piece of clean paper between your hand and the film will protect water soluble film from moisture on hand.

ADHERING FILM STENCIL

1. Secure a frame of suitable size. If the screen has been used before, check it for cleanliness. Film cannot be adhered to a dirty screen.
2. Even if the screen looks clean, give it one more washup to be sure. Use the proper solvent to remove hardened ink.

  New screens must also be washed. The fabric has a protective coating called SIZING. Film will not adhere properly until the sizing is removed. Carefully wash the screen fabric with warm water and a good detergent, Fig. 8-21. Rinse with hot water. Let screen dry thoroughly.
3. If lacquer base film is to be used, wash the screen fabric with adhering fluid just before attaching the film.

Fig. 8-21. Wash new screen with warm, soapy water.

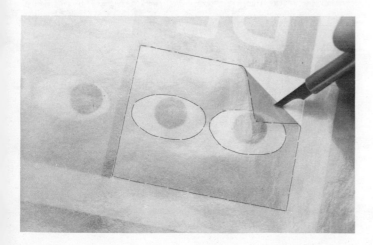

Fig. 8-18. Film is removed only from areas that are to print. Dotted lines show where film has been cut. Ovals in center are non-image area.

5. Examine the film after the image area has been peeled away. Dust, small pieces of film and particles of cement (adhesive which holds film to backing sheet) can be lifted away with a piece of masking tape.

  Modern film has a "stick back" feature. This permits corrections to be made when a non-image area is removed accidently.

4. In addition to being clean, screen fabric must be stretched taut (tight). Screens with even small tears should be replaced.

Adhering water soluble film

1. Lift up screen so you can work on the printing base underneath.
2. Place original design on the base, Fig. 8-22. Bring the screen down and position the original design properly within the screen frame.

Fig. 8-22. Use the original artwork to position the film on the screen. Cardboard guides may be attached at same time.

3. Lift up the screen and wet it thoroughly on both sides. See Fig. 8-23. Use a clean sponge.
4. Lay cut stencil exactly in register atop the original art. Film side should be up.
5. Bring the screen down on top of the stencil. This puts the film side of the stencil against the underside of the screen.
6. Rub a wet sponge over a small portion of the screen (topside) to adhere the stencil at that spot. This will keep the stencil in register during the next step.
7. Lift the screen and turn it over. (Remove the original art from the base board.)

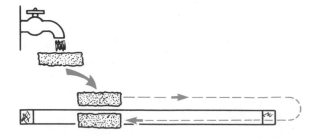

Fig. 8-23. Thoroughly wet both sides of the screen with water. Use a clean sponge.

8. Move a wet sponge over the backing sheet of the stencil, Fig. 8-24. This will adhere the film to the screen.
9. Turn the frame over right side up, again, blot up excess moisture with clean (unprinted) newsprint or a slightly dampened sponge, Fig. 8-25.

Fig. 8-24. With frame flopped bottom up, move wet sponge across backing sheet to adhere film to screen.

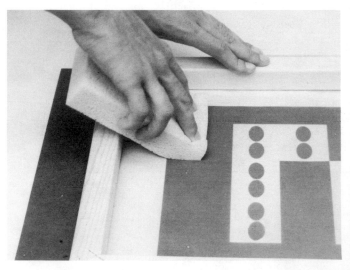

Fig. 8-25. Remove excess water with slightly dampened sponge or clean newsprint.

10. Dry the film with an electric fan, Fig. 8-26.
11. Peel off backing sheet as shown in Fig. 8-27.

Adhering lacquer soluble film

1. Position film stencil on the screen as described for water soluble film.
2. Secure adhering fluid for the film being used. Prepare two clean, absorbent cloth pads, Fig. 8-28.
3. Wet one pad with adhering fluid. Hold it in your right hand. Hold the dry pad in the left hand. Since the fluid evaporates very rapidly, adhere only a small portion of the stencil at a time. Begin at the upper left corner, Fig. 8-29.

Fig. 8-26. Electric fan, directed at top of raised screen will aid drying of film.

Fig. 8-27. Peel away backing sheet. Note that peeling is started at corner of stencil.

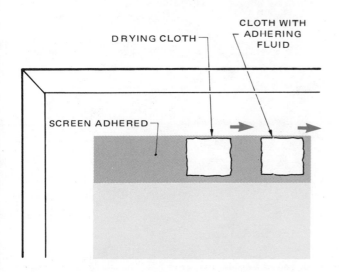

DRYING CLOTH

CLOTH WITH ADHERING FLUID

SCREEN ADHERED

Fig. 8-28. Use two cloth pads for adhering lacquer base film to screen. One is saturated with adhering fluid. The other is left dry to absorb excess adhering fluid. Rapid pickup of fluid helps prevent burning of cut edges.

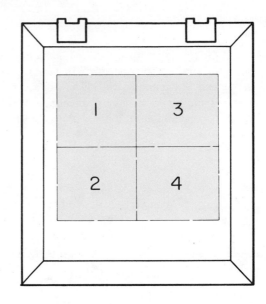

Fig. 8-29. Adhere the film in sections as shown.

Keep hands close together and pass over the first film section, Fig. 8-30. Do not press on, or rub over, the stencil. The rapid moistening and drying will adhere the film. Keep turning the pad in your left hand so a dry portion of cloth will always be against the screen. The faster the adhering film is applied and removed, the sharper the stencil edges will remain.

4. Continue the sequence until the entire film is adhered.
5. Remove the backing sheet when the adhering fluid has evaporated.

Caution: Fumes from adhering fluid for lacquer soluble film are highly volatile and dangerous. Use adhering fluid only in well ventilated areas where there is no possibility of fire. Store solvent-soaked rags in a safety container.

MASKING NONPRINTING AREAS

Nonprinting areas beyond the film must be masked. Proper masking improves print quality and makes cleanup easier. Which of the masking techniques to use will depend on the number of copies to be printed.

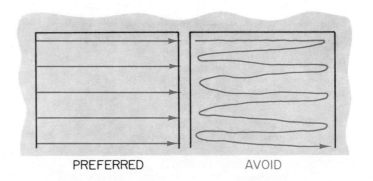

PREFERRED   AVOID

Fig. 8-30. Recommended movement of adhering and drying pads. Dry pad must always follow saturated pad.

PAPER MASKING

If less than 100 copies are to be printed, use a paper mask.

1. Cut a piece of bond or kraft paper to fit inside the frame.
2. Turn the screen bottom side up. Place the paper on the printing frame and mark the area to be cut away as in Fig. 8-31. Make the opening at least 1 in. (25 mm) larger than the image area.

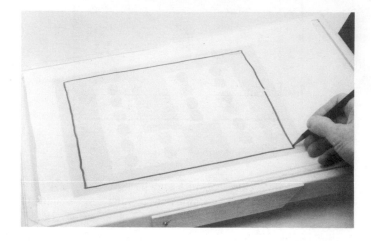

Fig. 8-31. Mark outline to be removed from masking paper. Opening should be at least 1 in. (25 mm) larger than the image area.

3. Remove the sheet from the frame. Cut out the marked area with a knife or single-edge razor blade. *Make the cut on protective cardboard, not on the bare table top.*
4. Tape the paper mask to the screen, Fig. 8-32.

Fig. 8-32. Both inner and outer edges of mask are taped. Tape up inside corners of frame to make cleanup much easier.

LIQUID MASK

Liquid masks are made for both lacquer soluble and water soluble films. Select the liquid suitable for the ink being used. Apply it with a 1 in. brush, Fig. 8-33. Two thin coats will cover better than one thick coat. Liquid mask is also known as BLOCKOUT and FILL-IN.

Liquid mask may also be used to fill pinholes in the film. Hold the frame up to a bright light to locate the pinholes.

Fig. 8-33. Apply liquid mask with a 1 in. brush. Two thin coats will cover better than one thick coat.

TAPE MASKS

Some stencils almost fill the frame. The small open areas that remain can be masked with gummed paper tape, masking tape or blockout material (lacquer or water soluble).

PRINTING

The technique for printing various types of stencils is the same. However, the ink selected must not dissolve the stencil or liquid mask. For example, water base inks cannot be used with a water soluble film stencil.

The printing base may be protected by taping a piece of kraft paper or chipboard (stiff cardboard) to it. See Fig. 8-34. This is needed only if the base is rough or damaged.

Fig. 8-34. Printing base may be protected with a piece of kraft paper or chipboard.

Use original artwork to align the sheet to be printed. Cut guides 3/4 by 1 in. from chipboard. Tape two guides to the long side; one guide to the short side, Fig. 8-35.

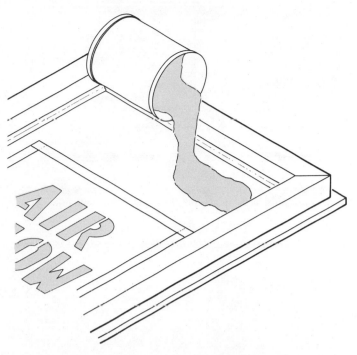

Fig. 8-37. Distribute ink evenly along one end of the frame.

Fig. 8-35. Two aligning guides are used on the long side of the sheet being printed. One guide is taped on the short side.

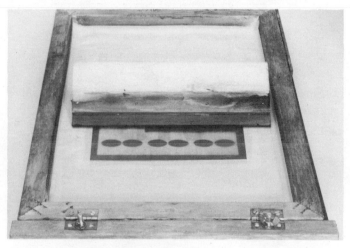

Fig. 8-38. Use a squeegee slightly wider than the design.

You are now ready to print. Use the following procedure:
1. Place first sheet in position against chipboard guides.
2. Lower the screen frame.
3. Tilt the squeegee at about a 30 deg. angle and place it behind the ribbon of ink.
4. Apply downward pressure and pull the squeegee across the stencil, Fig. 8-39. Do not pull the squeegee across the stencil more than once for each sheet of paper printed.
5. If you are working along, place the squeegee against the end of the frame. Raise the frame and support it with the KICK LEG.
6. Remove the printed sheet and insert a new sheet.
7. Place the printed sheets on a DRYING RACK, Fig. 8-40. Start with the bottom shelf. When it becomes filled, lower the next shelf.

Fig. 8-36. Cleanup will be easier if lip of can is protected with tape.

Protect the lip of the ink container as shown in Fig. 8-36. Distribute ink with a spatula or piece of stiff cardboard. Spread the ink evenly across one end of the frame, Fig. 8-37.

Select a squeegee slightly wider than the design, as shown in Fig. 8-38. A square-edged rubber blade, free of nicks, is best for doing flat work.

173

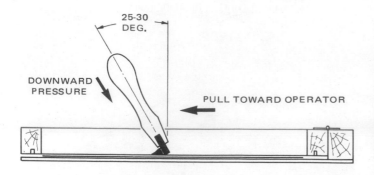

Fig. 8-39. To print, draw squeegee across screen. Ink is drawn across image and small amounts are forced through screen onto print paper.

Fig. 8-41. All these products were printed by the screen process.

Fig. 8-40. Portable drying rack is hinged for easier access. (Advance Process Supply Co.)

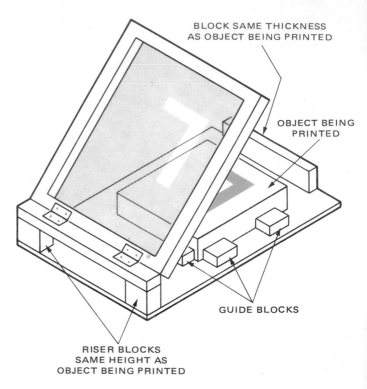

Fig. 8-42. Frame of screen is built up to print thick objects.

PRINTING SPECIAL JOBS

One special advantage of screen printing is its adaptability to all kinds of printing needs. It is possible to screen print on a variety of materials and shapes, Fig. 8-41. Hand printing equipment can be adapted to print on thick, flat objects, Fig. 8-42. Cylindrical objects need a special screen printing unit, Fig. 8-43. The squeegee does not move when a cylindrical object is printed. The screen moves horizontally while the object being printed rotates under the moving screen.

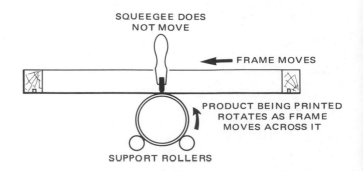

Fig. 8-43. This type of equipment is needed to screen cylindrical objects like drinking glasses, soft drink bottles and novelty items.

CLEANUP

It is important to clean the screen as soon as possible after printing. Dried ink is difficult or impossible to remove and the screen may have to be replaced. This is expensive and creates extra work to fit the new screen in the frame.

To remove ink from the screen:
1. Place sheets of newspaper under the frame.
2. Scrape up surplus ink from the screen. Use a piece of cardboard for this job as shown in Fig. 8-44. Return unused ink to the container.

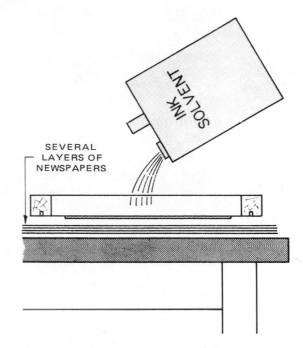

Fig. 8-45. Place newspapers under frame and apply proper ink solvent. Allow it to soak for a few minutes before wiping up. Repeat sequence until all ink is removed.

Fig. 8-44. Use strip of stiff cardboard to remove surplus ink from frame. Avoid using metal spatula. It could damage the screen.

3. Wrap soiled cardboard spatula in newspaper and discard.
4. Remove paper masking, if used. Wrap this in newspaper and discard.
5. Get the proper solvent for the ink used. Use lacquer thinner for lacquer base ink. Use water for water base ink and mineral spirits for oil base ink.
6. Pour the solvent over the screen. Allow it to soak for a few minutes.
    Caution: Work in a well ventilated area. Fumes may be toxic.
7. Wipe solvent-soaked area with an absorbent cloth pad, Fig. 8-45. The newspaper under the stencil will also absorb ink and solvent.
8. Repeat the operation until all ink is removed.
9. Final cleaning requires two cloth pads saturated in solvent. Wipe both sides of screen at same time, Fig. 8-46.
10. Dry screen with cloth pads.
11. Store screen and stencil for future use. Return ink and solvent to storage area.
12. Clean up work area. Discard solvent soaked cloth pads and

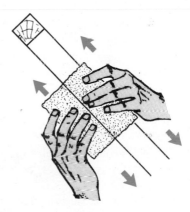

Fig. 8-46. For final cleaning wipe both sides of the screen at the same time. Use cloth pads moistened in ink solvent.

newspaper in closed metal trash container.
13. Wash hands thoroughly.
    Caution: You may be allergic to many of the cleaning solvents used. Wear safety glasses, rubber or plastic gloves and a protective apron when using them.

REMOVING A FILM STENCIL

Water soluble film and mask can be removed from the screen with warm water. Place the frame in a sink. Allow warm water to cover the stencil. The film and mask will dissolve. A soft brush can be used to speed up the job.

If a sink is not available, place newspaper under the screen. Soak a sponge in warm water and rub it over the stencil area, Fig. 8-47. Within a short time the dissolving film will stick to the newspaper. Replace the paper. Repeat the operation until all of the film and mask is removed from the screen.

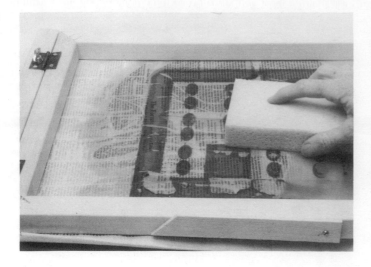

Fig. 8-47. Water soluble film can be removed with warm, soapy water and a soft brush or sponge.

Fig. 8-48. Design for paper stencil must be full size. Note how letters with loose centers are drawn.

A final washing with warm, soapy water and a soft brush will complete the clean-up. Return the frame to storage when it has dried.

Remove lacquer film stencils and mask with lacquer thinner. The method is similar to removing water soluble materials.

Caution: Use lacquer thinner only in a well ventilated area. Place solvent soaked pads and paper in a metal safety container.

Place newspaper under the screen. Pour a quantity of lacquer thinner over the stencil. Rub the stencil area with a cloth pad. The film will dissolve and adhere to the newspaper. Replace the newspaper and repeat the operation. For final cleaning, rub both sides of the screen with cloth pads moistened in lacquer thinner. Return the frame to storage.

MAKING PAPER STENCIL

Simple screen stencils can be made from paper. Tracing paper or mylar drafting film can also be used.

A paper stencil has no backing sheet. Therefore, use care when planning designs with loose centers like an "O." Make the design full size, Fig. 8-48. Study the drawing to see how letters with loose centers are designed with connectors.

Cut the stencil paper to fit inside the frame. Tape the stencil paper over the design, Fig. 8-49. Use a sharp knife to cut away the areas that are to print, Fig. 8-50.

Position the cut stencil on the underside of the frame. Tack it in place with a water soluble glue, Fig. 8-51.

When the glue has dried, tape the loose stencil edges to the frame. Also tape the inside of the frame. Use masking tape or gummed tape.

Fig. 8-49. Tape stencil paper over design. Tracing paper is being used.

There are two other ways for making paper stencils:
1. Coat one side of the stencil paper with lacquer. Apply several coats. After cutting the design, adhere the stencil to the screen. Use a cloth pad moistened with lacquer thinner.
2. Stencil paper can also be coated with shellac. Allow the shellac to dry. Then attach the stencil paper to the original artwork with rubber cement, shellac side up, Fig. 8-52.

   Cut the stencil in the usual way. Then place the stencil, still attached to the original artwork, under the frame. Attach the stencil to the screen with an electric iron. Set the iron to its lowest heat. Do not leave the iron in one place too long.

   An alcohol-moistened cloth pad can also be used to adhere the stencil to the screen.

Letters and designs with loose letters do not need special planning when a paper stencil is attached to a backing sheet.

Regardless of the technique used, original artwork is used to locate the aligning tabs or guides. The paper stencil is now ready for printing, Fig. 8-53.

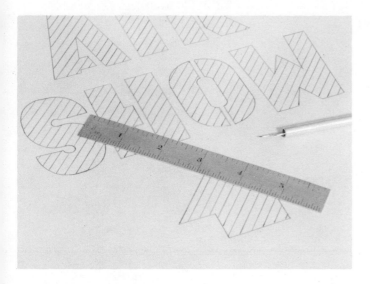

Fig. 8-50. Use a sharp knife to remove the areas that are to print. Straightedge is helpful for cutting straight lines.

Fig. 8-51. Stencil is attached to screen with water soluble glue. It was first positioned over base.

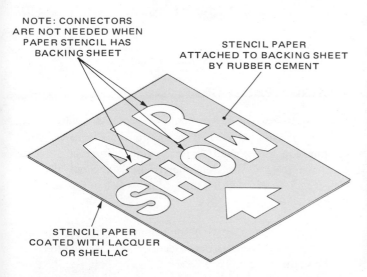

NOTE: CONNECTORS ARE NOT NEEDED WHEN PAPER STENCIL HAS BACKING SHEET

STENCIL PAPER ATTACHED TO BACKING SHEET BY RUBBER CEMENT

STENCIL PAPER COATED WITH LACQUER OR SHELLAC

Fig. 8-52. Stencil is attached to backing sheet with rubber cement.

Fig. 8-53. Printing with paper stencil. This type of stencil is good for simple jobs.

After printing, remove the surplus ink. Then peel the masking tape and stencil paper from the screen. Dissolve the remaining ink with a suitable solvent. Remove the glue spots with warm, soapy water and a soft brush. Return the screen to storage.

MAKING A TUSCHE OR WASHOUT SCREEN STENCIL

The tusche or washout screen stencil is made right on the screen.
1. Draw the design with India ink, Fig. 8-54.

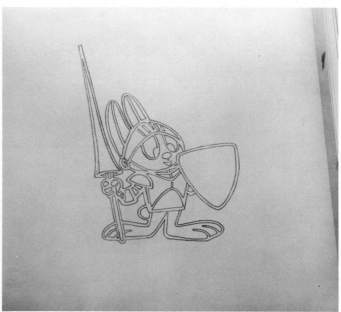

Fig. 8-54. Design is drawn on screen with India ink.

Fig. 8-55. Design is filled in with liquid tusche.

Fig. 8-57. Close-up shows tusche removed from image area.

Fig. 8-56. Coat entire screen with liquid glue.

2. Use a liquid tusche (pronounced like "push ya") or lithographic crayon, Fig. 8-55, to fill in the screen in the areas that are to print, Fig. 8-56.

3. Allow the liquid tusche to dry. This is not necessary if the design is drawn with a litho crayon.

4. Coat the entire screen with a water or lacquer soluble mask. When thoroughly dry, apply a second coat.

5. Tilt the screen upright. Saturate two cloth pads with mineral spirits. Wash the tusche out by rubbing both sides of the design with the pads. The dissolving tusche will carry away the mask over the design. This will leave the screen open where the design was drawn, Fig. 8-57.

6. Mask the inside edges of the frame with tape. Align the guides for printing. Print the copies needed, Fig. 8-58.

7. Scrape excess ink from the screen. Wash remaining ink from the screen with the proper solvent. Remove the mask with water or lacquer thinner. Finish by washing the screen with warm, soapy water.

8. Return the screen to storage.

Always wear some kind of protective clothing when working at your occupation.

Fig. 8-58. Safety poster printed by the tusche stencil method. Lettering was printed on a press.

MAKING A PHOTOGRAPHIC STENCIL

There are two basic methods of making stencils photographically. Both permit halftone prints to be made by screen printing, Fig. 8-59. Materials for making photographic stencils can be purchased from commercial outlets. Since they are light-sensitive, the material must be processed in subdued light until the stencil is developed.

Only general information for making stencils photographically can be given. Each manufacturer has specific directions on how the product is to be used. For best results these directions should be followed.

Fig. 8-59. Illustrations resembling halftones are possible by making the drawing on pebble surface illustrators' board. No halftone screen is required when the drawing is photographed.

Direct photographic stencil technique

The stencil, in this process, is made right on the screen. A light-sensitive emulsion is spread over the entire screen in a smooth, even coat, Fig. 8-60. Avoid using a brush. The emulsion must be applied in an even film or the different thicknesses will require different exposure times. Use a heavy cardboard squeegee.

Clean and degrease the screen. *This must be done or the emulsion will not cover the screen properly.*

Mix the emulsion as directed by the manufacturer. Make only enough to coat the screen.

Caution: Some people may be allergic to the chemicals making up the emulsion. Wear safety glasses, rubber or plastic gloves and protective apron when mixing and using the emulsion material.

Allow the emulsion to dry. Expose the sensitized screen as soon as possible. If necessary, it can be stored for a few days in a light-tight box or cabinet.

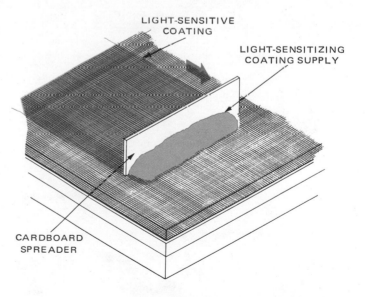

Fig. 8-60. Light-sensitive coating is applied to screen with a squeegee in a uniform film.

Draw the design as it is to appear when printed. Areas that are to print must be opaque, Fig. 8-61. Nonprinting areas should be transparent. Therefore, the design must be placed on

Fig. 8-61. The design is drawn as it will appear in print.

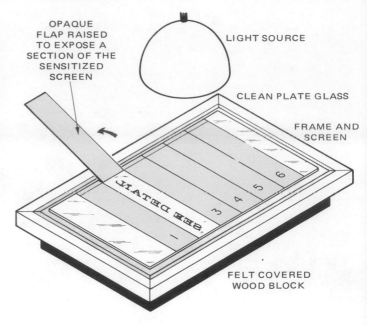

Fig. 8-63. Make a series of trial exposures on a sensitized test screen.

clear glass, tracing paper or clear plastic. Make a separate drawing for each color. The design is now ready for exposure.

Secure a block of wood thicker than the frame but slightly smaller than its inside dimensions. Cover the block with black felt. Put it directly below the light source.

Set the frame over the block, bottom side up. Locate the design on the frame. The right-reading side of the design must be in contact with the screen. Position a piece of clean glass over the design as in Fig. 8-62. This should press the design tightly against the sensitized screen.

Expose the unit to light. Use the light source and exposure time recommended for the emulsion. If they are not known, a series of trial exposures must be made, Fig. 8-63. These tests

will help find the best exposure time for the material being used. It is very difficult to overexpose the screen when the screen and design are properly made.

Washing out the image

The light-sensitive emulsion is hardened when exposed to light. Areas protected by the design are not hardened and can be washed out of the screen with warm water. Follow the developing sequence recommended for the emulsion used.

This is usually done by spraying warm water at 110 to 115 deg. F (43 to 46 C) over the screen. Normal room lighting can be turned on after the entire screen has been wet. Exposure time must be lengthened if nonprinting areas also wash away.

Wash the screen until the printing, or unexposed, areas are free of emulsion. After the water has drained off, blot the screen dry with clear newsprint, Fig. 8-64. Allow the screen to dry thoroughly. Prepare the screen for printing in the usual manner.

Fig. 8-64. Blot the screen dry with clear newsprint.

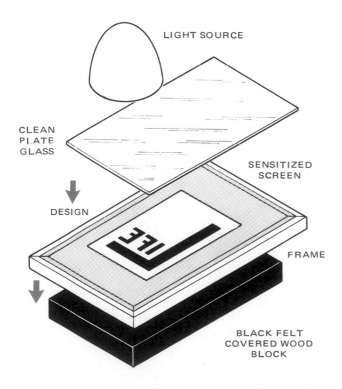

Fig. 8-62. Setup for making stencil by direct photographic technique. Felt covered block supports screen during exposure.

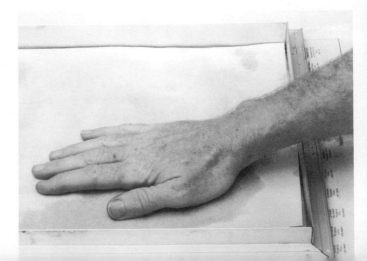

Screen Printing

After the production run, clean the screen. Return surplus ink to the can. Clean the remaining ink from the screen with a suitable solvent.

Each photoemulsion manufacturer recommends a specific way to remove the emulsion from the screen. Be sure to follow these directions.

Caution: Some cleaning processes use a weak lye solution. Wear safety glasses, plastic or rubber gloves and protective apron. Put solution soaked cleaning rags and paper in plastic bags. Place full plastic bags in metal safety cans.

Making indirect photographic stencils

In this process, stencil film is exposed, developed and finally adhered to the screen. This process is faster than the direct photographic stencil process.

There are many types of presensitized screen process photofilm. Carefully read the instructions for the film before you begin.

Stencil film is made up of a light-sensitive emulsion on a plastic backing sheet, Fig. 8-65. Even though the film is light-sensitive, it does not have to be worked in complete darkness. Film should be protected from sunlight and bright fluorescent lights. A yellow "bug lamp" will not affect most of the films and will provide enough light for work.

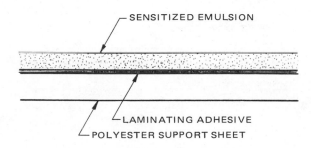

Fig. 8-65. Cross section of a photographic stencil film. Adhesive bonds emulsion to backing.

A photostencil design must be a positive image, Fig. 8-66. It can be drawn or made mechanically and photographed, Fig. 8-67. Areas in the design that are to print (image area) must be opaque. Nonprinting areas should be transparent. Each color in the design will require a stencil.

Clean and degrease the screen after the design has been made. Photostencil film will not adhere properly to a dirty screen. Use a commercial screen degreaser. If none is available, automatic dishwasher powder may be used. Rinse the screen thoroughly. Allow it to drain and dry.

Caution: Cleaning and degreasing chemicals can cause allergic reactions and eye injuries. Some of them are poisonous. Handle them with care. Wear safety glasses, plastic or rubber gloves and protective apron.

POSITIVE

NEGATIVE

Fig. 8-66. Artwork for making a photostencil must be a positive image.

Fig. 8-67. Artwork can be made mechanically and photographed. Lettering may be done with rub-on type.

Most photostencil films are sensitive to light in the blue, violet and near ultraviolet range. Film exposed to a light source rich in this range (called ACTINIC LIGHT) will produce a high-quality stencil.

However, lamps vary greatly in light output. The best exposure time must be found by making a time-step test strip.

181

Time-step test strip

1. Cut a rectangular piece of photostencil film 3 in. by 15 in. (76 by 381 mm).
2. Clean the vacuum frame glass.
3. Place the film and positive in the vacuum frame. Exposure is made through the plastic backing sheet with some photostencil films. See Fig. 8-68. Other films are exposed with the emulsion side towards the positive. *Check the information sheet furnished with the photostencil film.*

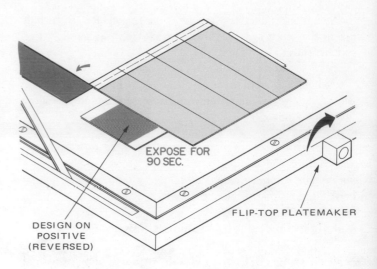

Fig. 8-70. Remove first section and expose film for 90 seconds.

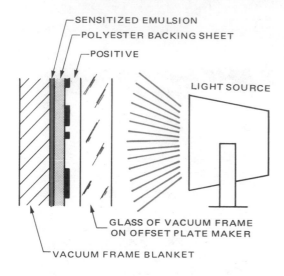

Fig. 8-68. Photostencil film can be placed in vacuum frame for exposure.

4. Cover the film and positive by attaching five sections of thin opaque cardboard to the vacuum frame blanket, Fig. 8-69. Masking films may be used in place of the cardboard.
5. Remove the first section and expose the film for 90 seconds, Fig. 8-70.
6. Reposition the first cardboard section. Remove the second section and expose the film for 135 seconds. See Fig. 8-71.

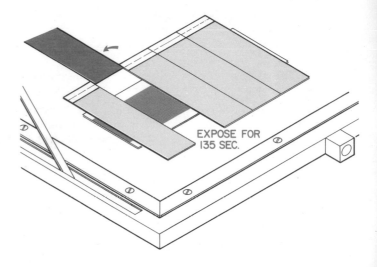

Fig. 8-71. Reposition the first flap. Remove the second section and expose the film for 135 seconds.

7. Continue the exposure sequence. Expose the remaining sections for 180, 225 and 270 seconds.

Develop and wash out the test strip. Adhere it to a clean screen. When the film has dried, peel away the plastic backing sheet. Examine the stencil. Underexposed sections will be thin. In overexposed sections the fine details of the design will be closed or nearly closed, Fig. 8-72.

The final test will be a trial print of the stencil. Check print quality of each exposure strip on the stencil. Best exposure time can now be determined.

Select the best exposure time. Expose your photostencil. Develop photostencils with care. Use only the developer recommended for the film being used. Mix the chemicals in the proper sequence. Stir or shake until the chemicals are dissolved.

Caution: Do not save used developer. Make fresh developer each day.

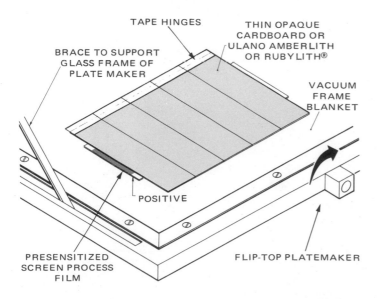

Fig. 8-69. Setup for determining correct exposure time for photostencil film. Flaps will be lifted away one at a time to expose film.

UNDEREXPOSED   PROPERLY EXPOSED   OVEREXPOSED

Fig. 8-72. Results when stencil film is underexposed, correctly exposed and overexposed.

Developing the stencil film

1. Place developer in a clean plastic tray. Be sure chemicals are in the correct temperature range. Protect developer from strong light.
2. Slide exposed film into developer with emulsion side up. Cover the film quickly with developer.
3. Develop film for proper length of time. Rock the tray during developing period, Fig. 8-73.

Remove film from developer. Place it on an inclined flat surface emulsion side up, Fig. 8-74.

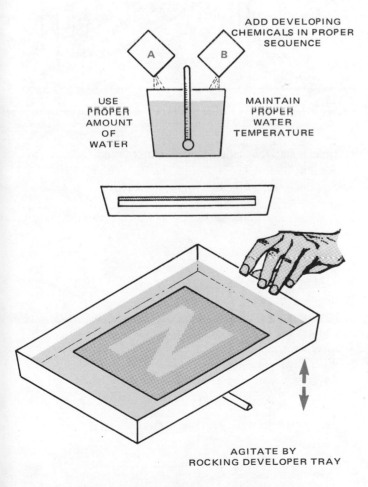

ADD DEVELOPING CHEMICALS IN PROPER SEQUENCE

USE PROPER AMOUNT OF WATER

MAINTAIN PROPER WATER TEMPERATURE

AGITATE BY ROCKING DEVELOPER TRAY

Fig. 8-73. Mix the developer according to directions furnished with the chemicals. Rock the tray while film is developing.

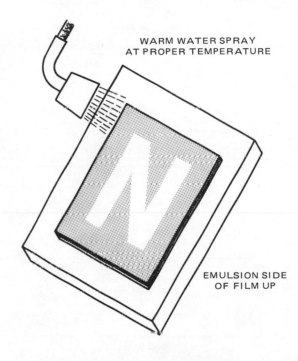

WARM WATER SPRAY AT PROPER TEMPERATURE

EMULSION SIDE OF FILM UP

Fig. 8-74. Place developed film stencil on an inclined flat surface side up. Flood stencil with warm water until all of the emulsion is removed from the unexposed areas.

Flood the stencil with warm water at 90 to 100 deg. F (32 to 38 C). Keep washing the film until the emulsion is removed from the unexposed areas. Finish by rinsing with cold water.

Adhering the film

The chilled film stencil is ready to be adhered. A flat buildup covered with clear newsprint is needed. Place the stencil on the buildup emulsion side up. Carefully lower the cleaned screen onto the stencil, Fig. 8-75.

Avoid excess pressure. The weight of the frame is enough.

Lay clean newsprint over the stencil to remove moisture. Gently wipe over the newsprint with a soft cloth pad. Do this several times. Replace the newsprint each time.

Allow the stencil to dry slowly. Then, peel away the plastic backing sheet. Some adhesive from the backing sheet may remain with the emulsion. Remove it with a soft cloth moistened in naptha or benzine.

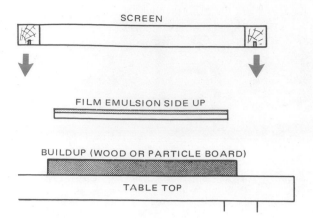

Fig. 8-75. Place moist stencil on buildup with emulsion side up. Carefully lower screen onto it. Buildup should be thicker and slightly smaller than inside of frame.

Block in the open areas around the stencil with masking liquid.

Clean the screen after printing. Wash off ink with the proper solvent, Fig. 8-76. Let the solvent dry.

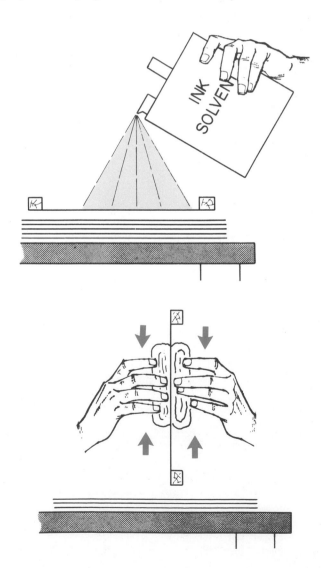

Fig. 8-76. Remove ink with proper solvent.

Removing photostencils

Photostencils are removed from the screen in a different manner than water or lacquer soluble films. A biochemical product known as an enzyme is used. It is a type of protein. Use the following procedure:

1. Wet both sides of the screen.
2. Sprinkle with enzyme and allow to stand for a few minutes.
3. Remove emulsion by washing with hot water and a soft brush, Fig. 8-77.

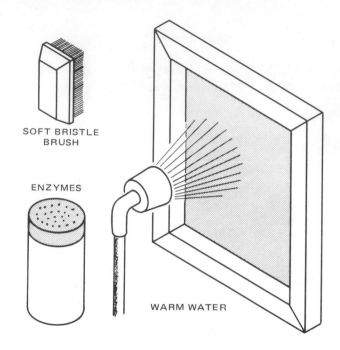

Fig. 8-77. After enzyme has been allowed to soak screen for a few minutes, remove stencil by washing screen with hot water and soft brush.

4. Wipe the screen with white vinegar to stop action of the enzyme solution.
5. Rinse screen thoroughly with cold water. Allow to drain and dry.
6. Return screen to storage.

Most problems that arise when making photostencils are caused by one of the following. Make corrections as recommended by the film manufacturer.

1. Improper handling of the film.
2. Over or underexposure.
3. Using the wrong type of light source.
4. Dirty screen.
5. Wash water too hot or too cold.
6. Applying too much pressure when film is adhered.
7. Removing backing sheet before film has dried.

TEST YOUR KNOWLEDGE — UNIT 8

1. Screen printing is a form of _____ printing.
2. List three other names by which screen printing is known.
3. Screen printing can be done by _____ and by _____.

4. List the names of the equipment and materials used in screen printing. (Place your answers on a separate sheet.)

a. _____ Made of silk, nylon, dacron or wire.

b. _____ Contains the design to be printed.

c. _____ Made of wood or metal and supports screen.

d. _____ "c" (above) is attached to this unit with hinges.

e. _____ Forces ink through "a" and "b" (above) to print design. It has a rubber blade.

5. Make a sketch showing a cross-sectional view of a film stencil. Label the parts.

6. Stencil film is either water or lacquer soluble. True or false?

7. What problem might occur if a dull knife is used to cut a stencil?

8. List safety precautions that should be observed when adhering lacquer base stencil film to a screen.

9. Why must a screen be masked or blocked out?

10. Name five materials of which stencils can be made.

11. The _____ should be slightly wider than the design being printed. It must be free of nicks.

12. Make a sketch showing how a thick object can be screen printed.

13. Make a sketch showing how cylindrical objects are screen printed.

14. List safety precautions that should be observed when removing lacquer base film from a screen.

15. There are two basic methods of making stencils photographically. List them and describe each briefly.

THINGS TO DO

1. Secure examples of products printed by the screen process.

2. Visit a local shop that does screen process work. Report what you have learned there.

3. Design, prepare the stencil and print a single color safety poster. Use a water soluble stencil film.

4. Design, prepare stencils and print a two color greeting card. Use a lacquer base stencil film.

5. Design, prepare the stencils and print a poster advertising a school play or athletic event.

6. Design, prepare and print your school's emblem or mascot on a T-shirt. Use a stencil made photographically.

7. Demonstrate the correct way to adhere lacquer base film to a screen.

8. Demonstrate the correct way to clean a screen for a stencil prepared photographically.

9. Demonstrate how to make a direct photostencil.

10. Demonstrate how to make a photostencil by the indirect method.

11. Construct equipment needed to print cylindrical objects by the screen process technique.

12. Set up a production line to produce felt banners for sale at football and basketball games.

Unit 9
HEAT TRANSFER PRINTING

Objectives

This unit describes the technique of heat transfer printing. The process uses heat and pressure to vaporize the ink and drive the dyes into fabric.

After reading the unit, you will know how heat transfer printing is done commercially. You will also learn how to do heat transfer printing with equipment in the school graphic arts laboratory.

Have you ever printed a novelty design on a piece of clothing using a special transfer and electric iron, Fig. 9-1? If so, you have used a form of heat transfer printing. Another term sometimes used is SUBLIMATION printing.

HEAT TRANSFER PRINTING employs both heat and pressure to move an inked design from a specially printed paper to cloth, Fig. 9-2. The paper can be in roll or sheet form. The design may be line work in solid colors or four-color process. In either case, original artwork is exactly reproduced.

In commercial heat transfer printing, the design or pattern is first printed on a special thermoprinting paper. This printing is usually done by the gravure process. Inks formulated specifically for heat transfer printing must be used.

Fig. 9-1. T-shirt decals are a form of heat transfer printing.

Printing directly on cloth with other printing processes can be difficult. Cloth has a tendency to stretch and is often highly absorbent. These factors make exact color registration impossible or costly. Heat transfer printing eliminates these problems. The printed paper is brought into direct contact with the cloth on a HEAT TRANSFER PRINTING MACHINE like the one shown in Fig. 9-3.

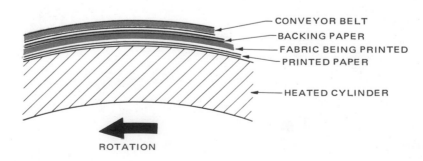

CONVEYOR BELT
BACKING PAPER
FABRIC BEING PRINTED
PRINTED PAPER

HEATED CYLINDER

ROTATION

Fig. 9-2. Heat transfer printing employs heat and pressure to move design from specially printed paper to cloth.

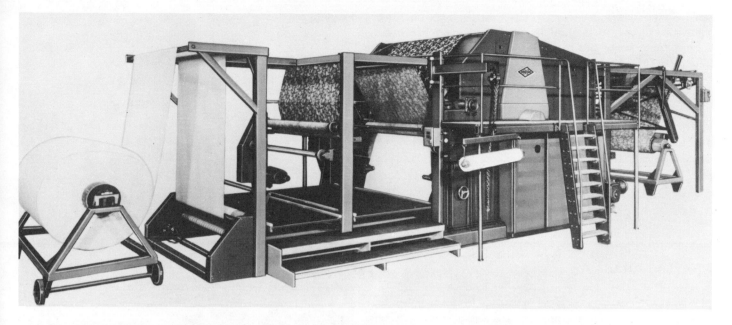

Fig. 9-3. Heat transfer printing machine. Cloth rolls can be printed at speeds in excess of 3000 metres (10,000 ft.) an hour. (Herbert Kannegiesser Corp.)

Printing can be done on individual cloth products, Fig. 9-4, or continuously. With the latter, printing is carried on at speeds in excess of 3000 metres (nearly 10,000 ft.) an hour, 24 hours a day.

PRINTING BY HEAT TRANSFER

In a commercial heat transfer printing operation, Fig. 9-5, fabric is taken from the CLOTH STORAGE TROLLEY to the feeding system of the transfer printing unit. Driven rollers and edge guides carry the fabric to an OVERFEED DEVICE. This device insures that the cloth is not stretched before being fed into the printing unit.

Unprinted fabric, printing paper and protection paper come together at the NIP to form a sandwich. The sandwich is held against and driven around the heated cylinder by the endless apron.

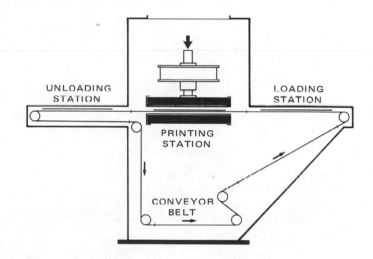

Fig. 9-4. Schematic shows type of equipment used to print individual cloth products.

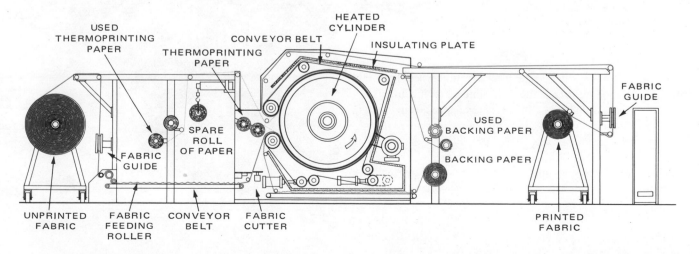

Fig. 9-5. The heat transfer printing operation. Fabric and inked image are sandwiched over a heated drum. (Herbert Kannegiesser Corp.)

After the design has been transferred to the cloth, the sandwich is taken off the heated cylinder at a point just above the nip. Here, fabric and papers are separated. Printed cloth is carried over the machine by a conveyor belt to the back of the machine where it can be rerolled or pleated. The cloth cools on the way to the back of the machine.

The used printing paper is taken up at the front of the machine. Backing paper is taken up at the back of the machine close to the FABRIC TAKE-UP device.

A wide range of colors and patterns can be printed by the heat transfer printing process. At present, apparel fabric, sheets and upholstery cloth are being printed in quantity.

HEAT TRANSFER PRINTING IN THE SCHOOL GRAPHIC ARTS LAB

It is possible to print student designs that can be applied to cloth by the heat transfer process. The design must first be printed on a transfer sheet by the offset method. Artwork must be prepared in reverse, Fig. 9-6, but is made press ready in the same way as regular copy.

Fig. 9-6. Student designed artwork for heat transfer printing. Note that it is printed on transfer sheet in reverse.

A special SUBLIMATION INK is required. This is an ink that changes from a solid state into a vapor when heat is applied. The vapor returns to the solid state when it contacts a cooler surface. Sublimation inks are available from most graphic arts supply houses. They are more expensive than regular offset inks.

Caution: Some people may be allergic to the fumes given off when sublimation inked designs are heated during the transfer process. Work in a well ventilated area.

Commercially prepared work is printed on a special transfer paper, Fig. 9-7. However, a good grade of offset or book paper will produce satisfactory results.

Fig. 9-7. Hundreds of commercially prepared heat transfer sheets are available. Most are designed to be applied to T-shirts.

If a design requires several colors, all of the colors are printed on the same transfer sheet. Allow the inks to dry thoroughly. Inks used for heat transfer printing are not usually as bright on the transfer sheet as regular offset would be. Nevertheless, they become more colorful when transferred to cloth.

Most heat transfer designs prepared in school are applied to pennants and T-shirts. While the inks will print well enough on a polyester and cotton blend of cloth, they work best on 100 percent polyester cloth.

The cloth must be washed to remove all traces of the sizing used in manufacture. Allow the garment or cloth to dry.

First print the design on the transfer sheet. When dry it is ready to be applied to cloth.
1. Set the heat control on the iron to "cotton," Fig. 9-8.

Fig. 9-8. Set thermostat to "cotton" when using an electric iron to apply heat transfer printing to cloth.

Allow it to heat up. Do not use the steam unit. If a press designed for heat applied transfers, Fig. 9-9, is used, set the thermostat to 390 deg. F (199 C) and allow the platen to come to temperature.

Caution: The heat used to apply your design can cause severe and painful burns. Work with care.

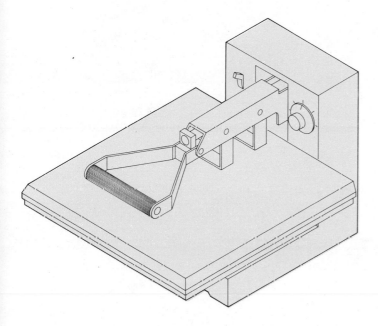

Fig. 9-9. Press designed to apply heat transfer printing to T-shirts.

2. Place a piece of clean cardboard between the two layers of cloth, Fig. 9-10. This will prevent the design from "bleeding" through.
3. Position the design face down on the cloth.
4. Place a clean sheet of paper over the design. The heat source should never be allowed to come into direct contact with the transfer sheet.

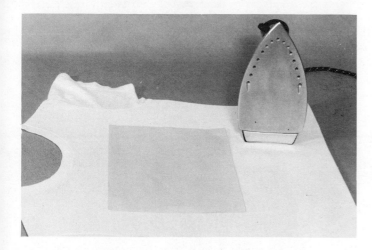

Fig. 9-10. A piece of cardboard should be placed between the two layers of cloth. This prevents design from "bleeding" through to second layer of cloth. Cardboard also keeps cloth taut and prevents creases from forming under transfer sheet. Heat transfer sheet is placed face down on cloth. A piece of clean paper is then placed over transfer sheet. Iron should not come into contact with transfer sheet.

Fig. 9-11. After cooling, transfer sheet is peeled from the design. The T-shirt is ready to wear.

5. Apply heat for 20-30 seconds or as recommended by the ink manufacturer. Use care to prevent the transfer sheet from shifting. Remove the heat source. Allow the work to cool.
6. Carefully peel back a corner of the transfer sheet. If the design is not completely transferred, replace the top sheet and apply heat for another 10-15 seconds.
7. When the design has transferred, allow the transfer sheet to cool. Carefully remove the sheet from the transferred design. The product is now ready for use, Fig. 9-11.

TEST YOUR KNOWLEDGE — UNIT 9

1. To put it simply, heat transfer printing is done by using ___
___.
2. Sublimation printing is the same as heat transfer printing. True or false?
3. Give an example of heat transfer printing.
4. Heat transfer printing is usually done on _____.
5. _____ _____ or _____ _____ can be used as transfer paper.
6. Why is printing directly on cloth difficult?
7. The heat transfer printing machine operates by bringing _____, _____ and _____ together to form a sandwich. The design is transferred when the sandwich is _____ and _____ the heated cylinder by the endless apron.

THINGS TO DO

1. Secure examples of heat transfer printing.
2. Demonstrate a simple heat transfer printing techique to your fellow classmates.
3. Secure information on the heat transfer printing process. Organize and bind the material and file it in the graphic arts lab's technical library.

Fig. 10-1. Ink jet printing head. This unit prints up to 48,000 characters a second or 45,000 lines a minute.   (Mead Digital Systems, Inc.)

Unit 10
INK JET PRINTING

Objectives

This unit has to do with the newest word and illustration reproduction technique — ink jet printing.

You will learn in this unit how a computer is used to control the placement of tiny ink droplets on a rapidly moving web of paper to form the required words and illustrations. You will understand how this printing technique is used to advantage in advertising and for rapid addressing of mail.

Fig. 10-2. At present, ink jet printing can reproduce only line art. However, halftone illustrations are being produced with experimental ink jet printing units.

Ink jet printing is the most recent of the printing processes. A noncontact method of printing, it uses no type, printing plates or film. Nothing touches the print paper but tiny drops of ink.

TYPES OF INK JET PRINTING SYSTEMS

At present, there are two basic types of ink jet printing systems. They are products of the Mead Corporation and A.B. Dick Company.

DIJIT SYSTEM

The DIJIT® system was developed by Mead Digital Systems, a Division of the Mead Corporation. DIJIT is an acronym for Direct Image by Jet Ink Transfer. (An acronym is a word formed by combining the initial letter of a series of words.)

HOW IT WORKS

A minicomputer controls jets in the printing head that form characters. Extremely fast, it provides up to 48,000 characters per second. This makes it possible to print up to 45,000 lines of type every minute. See Fig. 10-1. Thus, an ink jet printer, when properly programmed, could print one copy of a 350 page book every 37.5 seconds.

At present the process can print only line art graphics (illustrations), Fig. 10-2. Halftones are being produced experimentally. Full color reproduction is in the research stages. The technique is only a few years old. Its potential, when fully developed, will have printing speeds many times faster than present equipment.

The DIJIT printing head, Fig. 10-3, is made up of ink jets spaced 100 to the inch. There may be as many as 1280 jets on a printing head. An individual ink jet is used for each dot in a row of many dots across the printing surface.

Ink is forced through the jet where ultrasonic vibrations break it into tiny drops, Fig. 10-4. Each jet and each drop of ink is controlled by a minicomputer. The computer makes 25 million decisions every second.

The ink drops pass through a CHARGE PLATE. The computer "reads" the information fed into it and charges some of the drops. The falling ink drops pass through a very strong electrostatic field. The charged ink drops are deflected into a reservoir and the ink is reused. The ink drops that did

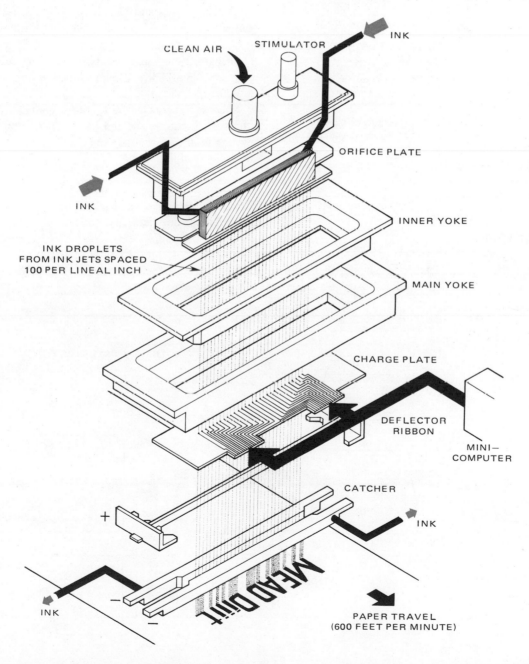

Fig. 10-3. A generalized diagram of the ink jet printing head. Ink jets are spaced 100 to the inch. (Mead Digital Systems, Inc.)

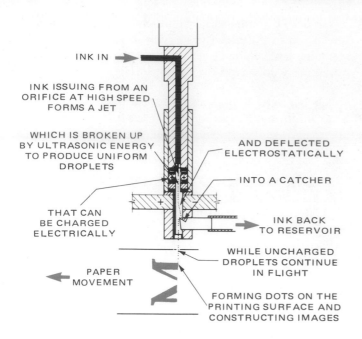

INK IN

INK ISSUING FROM AN
ORIFICE AT HIGH SPEED
FORMS A JET

WHICH IS BROKEN UP
BY ULTRASONIC ENERGY
TO PRODUCE UNIFORM
DROPLETS

THAT CAN
BE CHARGED
ELECTRICALLY

AND DEFLECTED
ELECTROSTATICALLY

INTO A CATCHER

INK BACK
TO RESERVOIR

PAPER
MOVEMENT

WHILE UNCHARGED
DROPLETS CONTINUE
IN FLIGHT

FORMING DOTS ON THE
PRINTING SURFACE AND
CONSTRUCTING IMAGES

Fig. 10-4. A typical ink jet used on the DIJIT system. Some ink drops are deflected and recycled. Others form patterns on the paper.

not receive a charge are not affected by the electrostatic field and fall onto the paper where they create the wanted pattern.

Instead of generating a single character at a time, the ink jets print the entire line simultaneously. However, neither plates nor type touch the paper. Tiny particles of ink drop onto the paper surface. The DIJIT printer is shown in Fig. 10-5.

VIDEOJET SYSTEM

The VIDEOJET SYSTEM®, developed by A.B. Dick, also depends upon the behavior of a fluid ink to form alpha-

numeric characters, Fig. 10-6. (Alphanumeric means letters and numbers.) The ink is under the influence of ultrasonic vibration, electrostatic and hydraulic pressure.

HOW IT WORKS

The pressurized ink stream from a single nozzle assembly is broken into tiny drops by ultrasonic vibration. As the ink passes through a CHARGING TUNNEL, each drop receives a proportional negative charge just before the drop breaks off.

The ink drops proceed through a pair of DEFLECTION PLATES. The negatively charged ink drops are deflected up toward the POSITIVE DEFLECTION PLATE. The degree of charge determines the degree of deflection. That is, drops with a larger negative charge will be deflected more than drops receiving a lesser negative charge. The degree of deflection controls where the drops will strike the printing surface.

Uncharged drops are not deflected. They are picked up by an INK SENSOR and returned to the ink supply.

A computer or magnetic tapes contain the material or information to be printed, Fig. 10-7. Coupled with the printing head they generate the electrical impulses which guide the droplets of ink.

Videojet units currently use a 5 by 7 dot matrix character font, Fig. 10-8. That is, each character is constructed from seven vertical dots and five horizontal dots.

A 40 by 24 dot matrix is in the experimental stages of development. The more dots used to form a character, the better the character looks.

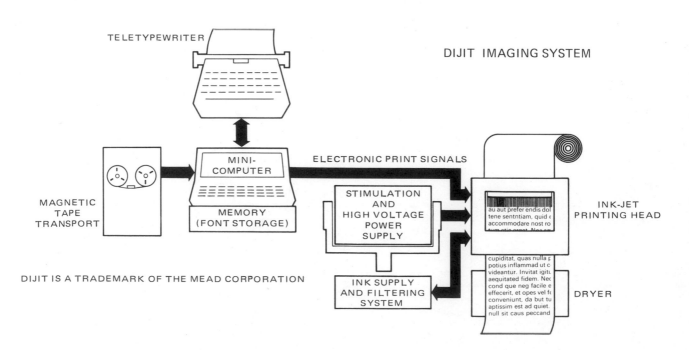

TELETYPEWRITER

DIJIT IMAGING SYSTEM

MINI-COMPUTER

ELECTRONIC PRINT SIGNALS

MAGNETIC
TAPE
TRANSPORT

MEMORY
(FONT STORAGE)

STIMULATION
AND
HIGH VOLTAGE
POWER
SUPPLY

INK-JET
PRINTING HEAD

DIJIT IS A TRADEMARK OF THE MEAD CORPORATION

INK SUPPLY
AND FILTERING
SYSTEM

DRYER

Fig. 10-5. A schematic shows how various units of DIJIT ink jet printer are coupled. (Mead Digital Systems, Inc.)

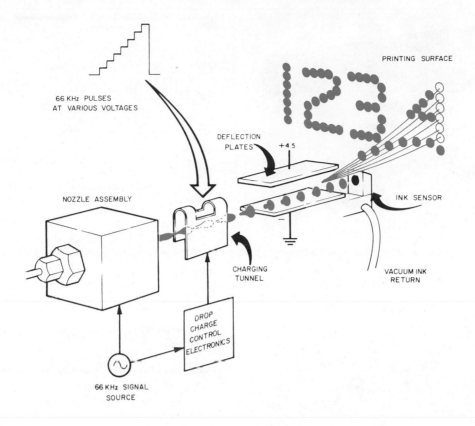

Fig. 10-6. A diagram of the VIDEOJET system showing how the deflected ink drops form a character. (A.B. Dick Information Products Div.)

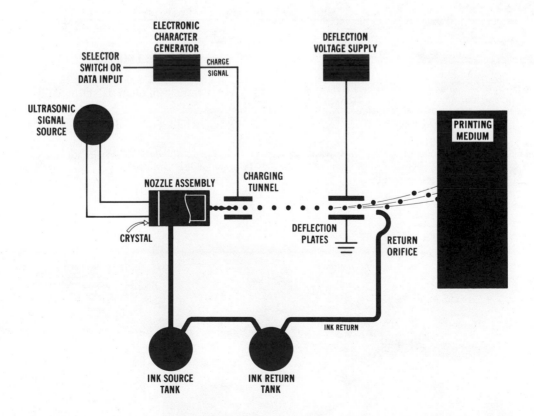

Fig. 10-7. Operation of the Videojet printer. Data input may be from coded computer or magnetic tapes.

Fig. 10-8. Each character is formed from a five dot vertical and a seven dot horizontal pattern. (A.B. Dick Information Products Div.)

Fig. 10-9. The Videojet printer can address newspapers and magazines at high speeds. It eliminates use of expensive labels and label-affixing machinery. Bold face feature allows selective emphasis of one or more lines in the address to speed postal handling.

every service call. . . even if you just run out of gas in your driveway(1). If you have an accident that disables your car more than 50 miles away from **Main Street**, we'll reimburse you up to $100 cash for the expenses you incur within 3 days after the accident. Or, if you're planning to buy a new car, the Club has an optional new service that could save you up to $1,000 or more(2).

Fig. 10-10. Sample of individualized advertisements produced by the ink jet process. (Mead Digital Systems, Inc.)

USES FOR INK JET PRINTING

The most important uses of ink jet printing are in periodical addressing, Fig. 10-9, and in direct mail applications, Fig. 10-10. However, since the ink jet process is capable of printing on almost any type of surface — rough, smooth and, in some cases, three dimensional, Fig. 10-11, many new uses are under development.

TEST YOUR KNOWLEDGE - UNIT 10

1. Ink jet printing is very unusual because: (Place correct answer on a separate sheet.)
   a. It is a noncontact method of printing.
   b. No type, printing plates or film are used.
   c. Nothing touches the paper but tiny drops of ink.
   d. All of the above.
   e. None of the above.
2. List the two ink jet systems now in use.
3. What do the above systems have in common?
4. How do the two systems differ?
5. Describe how the two systems operate.

THINGS TO DO

1. Secure sample of material printed by the ink jet printing process.
2. Prepare a bulletin board display on ink jet printing.

Fig. 10-11. Videojet printer being used to bottom code plastic containers. It was fitted to conveyor system. Coding is done at rate of 180 containers per minute. (A.B. Dick Information Products Div.)

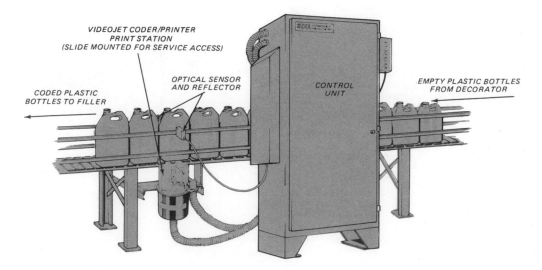

Unit 11
AUXILIARY GRAPHIC ARTS OPERATIONS

Objectives

This unit describes several operations often used for finishing and improving the appearance of graphic arts products.
By studying the unit you will learn how many auxiliary graphic arts operations are performed. These operations include corner rounding, jogging, numbering, perforating, laminating, embossing, die cutting, thermography and rubber stamp making.

Most auxiliary graphic arts operations are intended to improve the appearance of the finished product. They often create effects that add an interesting quality to a printed piece when used separately or in combination.

CORNER ROUNDING

Rounding of corners, Fig. 11-1, is a die-cutting operation that usually takes place after the job is printed. Often, such jobs are printed two or more "up" on a single sheet of paper. When cut apart the corners are square and must be rounded.

Rounding is done on a CORNERING MACHINE, Fig. 11-2. Replaceable DIES permit a range of corner radii to be cut, Fig. 11-3. Some machines can be adjusted to round two corners at a time.

Fig. 11-2. Foot operated corner rounding machine. Sheets are stacked on table and many are trimmed at one cut. (Challenge Machinery Co.)

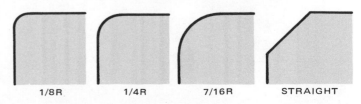

| 1/8R | 1/4R | 7/16R | STRAIGHT |

Fig. 11-3. A few of the types and sizes of corners that can be cut.

Fig. 11-1. Many printed items we see every day have had their corners rounded. The rounding was done for better appearance and wear. Moreover, cards with rounded corners are easier to fit into electronic scanning devices.

JOGGING

After paper has been printed, cut, collated or rounded, it often does not lie evenly in a pile, Fig. 11-4. Paper in this condition will not properly fit into other machines for further processing. Jogging will even up the sheets. The JOGGER, Fig. 11-5, vibrates the sheets into a neat pile or stack. However, avoid jogging work while the ink is wet.

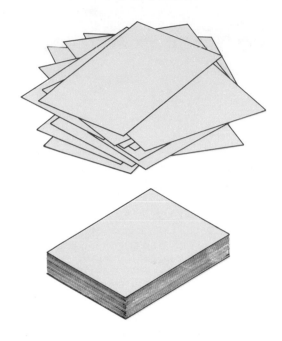

Fig. 11-4. Jogging vibrates paper sheets into even piles or stacks.

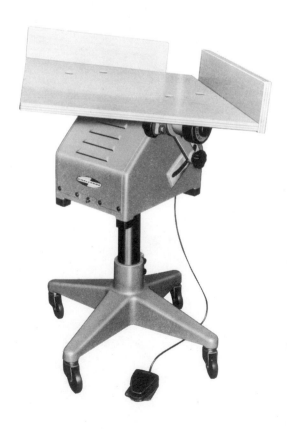

Fig. 11-5. Jogging machine has vibrating top. (Challenge Machinery Co.)

NUMBERING

Tickets, invoices, certificates and similar printed work must be numbered for security and control purposes, Fig. 11-6. Numbering is done on the press with one or more numbering machines. See Fig. 11-7.

A raised section on the device is depressed each time the numbers imprint on the paper. The next number in the sequence is rotated into place when the depressed section returns to its original position.

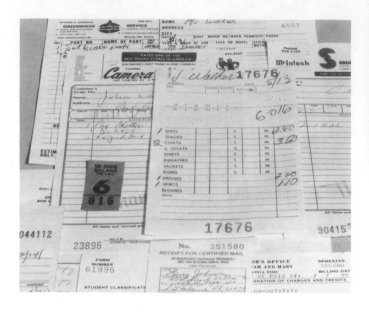

Fig. 11-6. Numbering is done for security and control purposes.

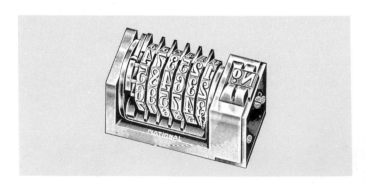

Fig. 11-7. This numbering machine is designed for platen presses.

PERFORATING

Perforating cuts rows of slots and dots across a sheet, Fig. 11-8. The cuts make the paper easier to fold or tear. A steel PERFORATING RULE, Fig. 11-9, is used for this task. It will work only on letterpress. The rule is locked in the chase. Ink rolls must be removed to avoid damage if a type-high perforating rule is used. Perforating rule lower than type high which will not touch the ink rolls can also be used during the printing operation. However, the tympan (bed supporting sheet being printed) must be built up where the perforating rule strikes.

Fig. 11-8. Perforating makes paper easier to fold or to tear apart.

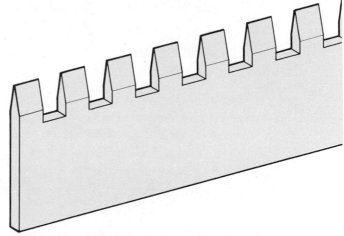

Fig. 11-9. Steel perforating rule is used in relief printing.

PERFORATING WHEELS are used on many offset presses. The wheels perforate the paper as it delivers from the press. FORM ROLLS are added to provide a suitable cutting surface. Perforations made with such a wheel must be made parallel to sheet travel.

STRIP PERFORATING RULE, Fig. 11-10, can also be used on an offset press. It has teeth in the middle of the strip and is attached to the impression cylinder by special pressure sensitive tape. Printing and perforating can be done in one operation. Perforating with strip perforating rule can be done across, parallel to and/or at any angle to paper travel through the press.

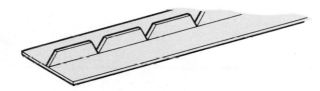

Fig. 11-10. Perforating rule is attached to impression cylinder of offset presses.

LAMINATING

Laminating applies a plastic film to printed material, Fig. 11-11. The film prevents tampering with the printed surface. It

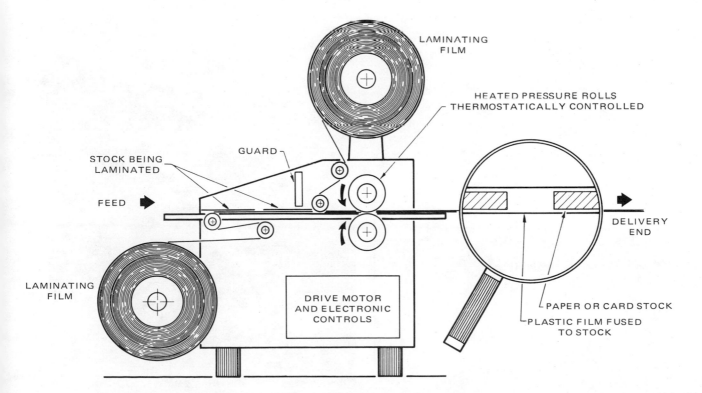

Fig. 11-11. Laminating applies a protective plastic film to both sides of a printed piece. Laminating protects the printed surface from tampering and damage.

also protects the printed surface from water, dirt, grease, oil or wear and tear.

EMBOSSING

Embossing is a three-dimensional printing technique, Fig. 11-12. Male and female dies, Fig. 11-13, are pressed one into the other with the stock between them. This raises the surface of the paper, leaving in it the design worked into the dies.

For most jobs, the female die is cut by hand in brass. The male die is made from fiberglass and epoxy. It is formed the first time the female die strikes it on the press.

Embossing can be done hot or cold. The paper and type of die determine the method. A heavy-duty press with heating facilities, Fig. 11-14, is required to furnish the heat and pressure needed.

Fig. 11-12. Embossing is a three-dimensional printing technique.

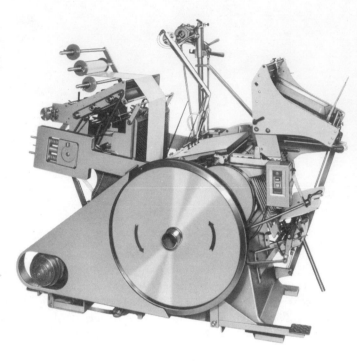

Fig. 11-14. This automatic press does embossing and foil stamping. (Brandtjen & Kluge, Inc.)

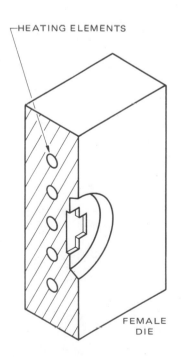

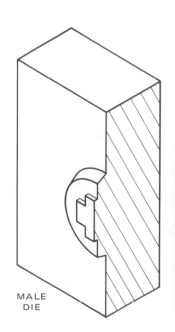

Fig. 11-13. Male and female dies raise stock surface using heat and pressure.

SCORCHING is a variation of embossing. Higher than normal embossing temperature is used to singe the paper slightly. A brown tint is produced on the raised surface.

GLAZING, Fig. 11-15, is a smooth, "ironed" effect. It is used on heavy, textured paper. Proper glazing requires carefully controlled temperature and pressure.

FOIL STAMPING

All roll-leaf hot stamping materials are generally included in the term FOIL. The types include metallic, gloss or matte finished, textured or patterned stock, Fig. 11-16.

Almost all foils are opaque (cannot be seen through) and can be used to overprint dark colored papers, Fig. 11-17.

COMBINATION EMBOSSING AND FOIL STAMPING

The embossing and foil stamping technique produces a special effect on the printed page, Fig. 11-18. Both operations are done at the same time. Special brass dies are needed for this type of work.

Fig. 11-15. Embossing and glazing produces an "ironed" appearance on textured paper. (Apex Die)

Fig. 11-17. Gold foil was used to overprint dark cover on this promotion piece. (Brandtjen & Kluge, Inc.)

Fig. 11-16. Foil is hot stamped on paper. The foil used for this design has a wood-grained finish.

Fig. 11-18. Embossing and foil stamping were combined to produce effect shown here.

Fig. 11-19. Some die-cutting trims paper stock so it can be folded into three-dimensional shapes.

DIE-CUTTING

Die-cutting trims paper stock into irregular special contours. Sometimes the dies produce cuts so that the stock can be folded into three-dimensional shapes, Fig. 11-19. Steel knives for cutting, and rounded rule for scoring are mounted in a base, Fig. 11-20. They must fit tightly into the outline cut into the base.

Laser beam cutting, controlled by a computer, is the latest development in shaping the outline in the base plate. See Fig. 1-32 through Fig. 1-35 in Unit 1 for information on this new technique.

Rubber blocks, cemented alongside the knives, push the stock off the die after it has been cut. The hobby industry uses die-cutting to cut sheets of wood parts to shape, Fig. 11-21.

THERMOGRAPHY

Thermography, Fig. 11-22, is a printing technique for producing a raised printed surface. Even though it is a specialized production process, it can be done by hand.

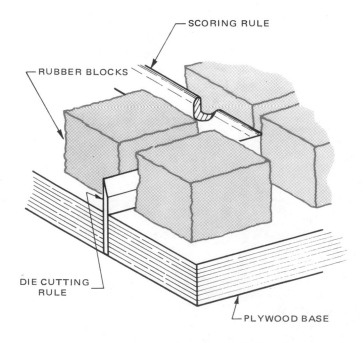

Fig. 11-20. Steel knives for cutting and rounded rule for scoring are mounted on a nine ply, 5/8 in. plywood base. The rubber blocks push the die-cut stock off of the knives.

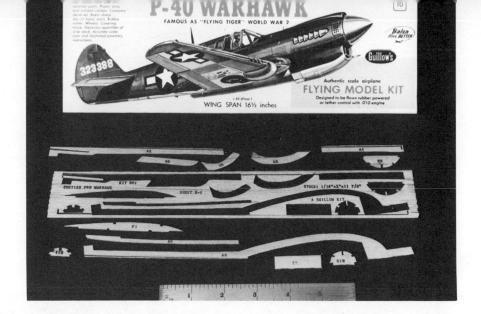

Fig. 11-21. Hobby industry uses die-cutting to cut wood model parts to shape.

Fig. 11-22. Thermography produced a three-dimensional effect on this printed sheet. (Virkotype, Inc.)

Fig. 11-23. Putting rosin powder on a printed card by hand. Excess is removed before heat is applied.

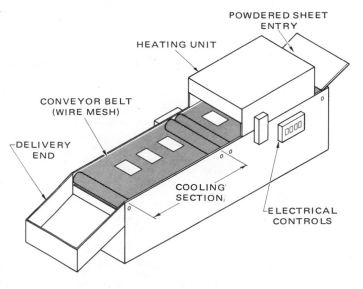

Fig. 11-24. Typical small thermograph machine will handle printing pieces like calling cards or greeting cards.

While the ink is still wet, the printed area receives a dusting of special rosin powder. See Fig. 11-23. Some powder adheres to the moist ink. The excess is removed. Heat is applied to melt the rosin powder, Fig. 11-24, causing the ink and powder to fuse, expand and harden. The result is a raised surface.

Powders in neutral colors permit the ink color to show through. Opaque powders hide the base ink color and add a color of their own. Metallic powders are also available.

201

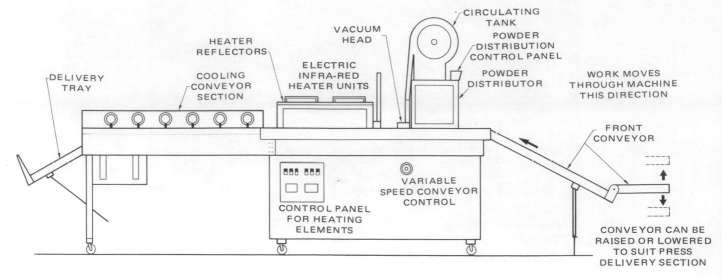

Fig. 11-25. An automatic high speed thermograph machine can be fitted to the delivery end of most presses.

Fig. 11-26. Rubber stamp is simplest example of flexographic printing.

Avoid using type smaller than 8 point for thermography. Small type has a tendency to fill in when the powder is heated. Fig. 11-25 shows how thermography is used on high speed presses.

FLEXOGRAPHIC PRINTING

As its name suggests, flexographic printing or flexography is done with flexible rubber plates. A type of relief printing, the image area is raised above the surrounding surface.

The rubber stamp illustrates flexographic printing in its simplest form. The printing plate is made in the same way when high speed commercial presses are used. For more on flexography and its uses, turn to Unit 5, Fig. 5-144.

MAKING A RUBBER STAMP

Rubber stamps are simple to make, Fig. 11-26. The process takes about 20 minutes. The technique is basically the same one used by commercial printers working on large presses.

Safety

Because high temperatures must be used in making rubber stamps, certain precautions must be taken.
1. Use care in working around stamp-making equipment and materials. Severe burns may result from accidental contact with them.
2. Wear insulated gloves if it becomes necessary to handle anything before it cools.
3. Use the stamp press only in areas cleared of scrap paper, rags and solvents.
4. Make certain the stamp press is turned off and the plug pulled before you leave the stamp making area.
5. Have burns treated promptly.

Preparing the mold

1. Compose, proof, correct and clean the letterpress typeform you plan to use. Several stamps can be made at one time.

   Regular foundry type may be used. However, brass type made for stamp making and embossing is preferred. Letters on brass type are cut deeper. Also, brass type is not greatly affected by the high temperatures needed to make rubber stamps. *Do not use stamp-making type for other printing purposes.*
2. Lock the typeform in the center of the special chase, Fig. 11-27. Metal furniture is best. Heat will dry out wood furniture and cause it to shrink. The typeform might then fall from the chase as it is withdrawn from the press.
3. Turn on the stamp press, Fig. 11-28. Allow it to heat up to operating temperature.

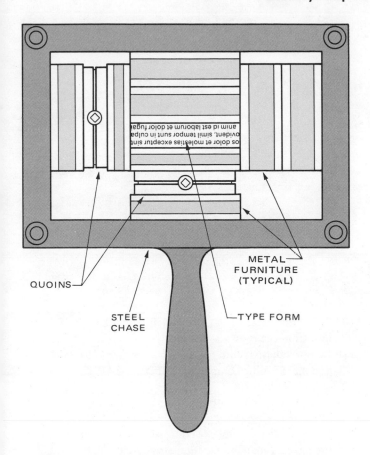

Fig. 11-27. Chase with type in place for making rubber stamp mold or matrix. Special brass or bronze type and metal furniture should be used.

QUOINS

STEEL CHASE

METAL FURNITURE (TYPICAL)

TYPE FORM

Fig. 11-29. Bakelite mold material should be cut large enough to cover the type. Allow a small margin on all sides.

5. Place the typeform and chase in the press, Fig. 11-30. Allow it to preheat for two minutes.

6. While the chase and type are heating, dust the red side of the bakelite with soapstone. Remove excess powder by lightly tapping an edge of the bakelite on a hard surface.

Fig. 11-28. Rubber stamp press. Heat is thermostatically controlled. (Sanders Machinery Inc.)

4. While the press is heating, cut a piece of bakelite mold material large enough to cover the type, Fig. 11-29. Bakelite is a plastic that softens when it is first heated. When heated to about 300 deg. F (149 C), it hardens permanently.

Fig. 11-30. Place chase into press for preheating.

7. Withdraw the chase from the stamp press. Carefully center the bakelite over the typeform. Red side must be down, Fig. 11-31. Place a piece of paper over the bakelite. This will prevent the plastic from sticking to the press platen.

8. Insert the unit in the press. Be sure the plastic does not shift from its position.

Fig. 11-31. Remove preheated chase and position bakelite mold material over type.

9. Raise the press bed until the first resistance is felt, Fig. 11-32. Wait one minute for the plastic to soften. Raise the bed until the limits on the chase, Fig. 11-33, are against the press platen. This action forces the type into the softened plastic.

Fig. 11-32. Put chase and mold material into press. Raise press bed until the first resistance is felt. After plastic has softened raise the press bed until the chase limits are against press platen.

Fig. 11-33. Pen indicates stop limits on chase.

Fig. 11-34. Remove the mold from the type after the chase and type have been allowed to cool.   (Sanders Machinery Inc.)

10. Allow the mold to bake for 10 minutes. Then remove the unit from the press. Let it cool.
11. Remove the bakelite mold or matrix from the typeform. The mold is now complete. See Fig. 11-34.

Making the rubber stamp

12. Cut a section of rubber stamp gum large enough to cover the mold or matrix.
13. Lightly dust the mold and gum with soapstone, Fig. 11-35. Remove excess powder.
14. Place the rubber gum, dusted face down, on the mold. Place paper on top of the gum and under the bakelite matrix.
15. Place the matrix and gum on the vulcanizing tray, Fig. 11-36. Insert the unit into the stamp press.
16. Tighten the press handwheel until the limits on the vulcanizing tray, Fig. 11-37, are against the platen. Heat for six minutes to vulcanize the rubber gum.

Fig. 11-35. Lightly dust mold and gum with soapstone.

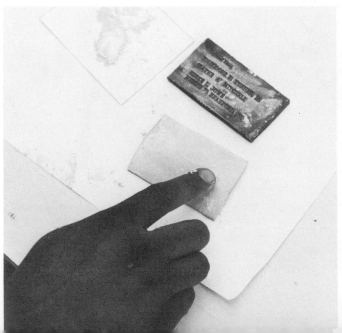

Fig. 11-36. Place matrix or mold and rubber gum on the vulcanizing tray and insert in the press.

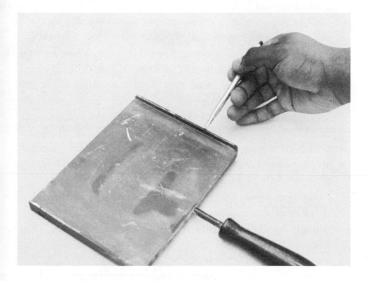

Fig. 11-37. Tighten press handwheel until limits on tray are against press platen. Limits are indicated by pencil.

17. Release the pressure and remove the tray from the press. Allow the mold and vulcanized rubber stamp to cool.
18. Check the rubber stamp for proper vulcanization. Press a thumb nail into the rubber. If no permanent mark is made in it, the rubber is properly vulcanized.
19. Separate the rubber stamp from the matrix or mold as shown in Fig. 11-38.

Fig. 11-38. Allow to cool until it can be handled safely, then remove rubber stamp from mold.   (Sanders Machinery Inc.)

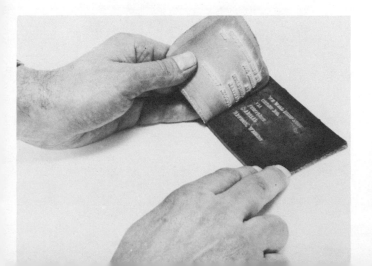

Fig. 11-39. Trim away edges leaving only image area of stamp.

20. Cut the stamp from the rubber section, Fig. 11-39.
21. Secure a section of mounting strip and cut it to length. Use a fine tooth dovetail saw.
22. Apply rubber cement to both the mounting strip and the back of the rubber stamp. Allow to dry briefly.
23. Press the two pieces together, Fig. 11-40.
24. Make a print of the stamp.
25. Insert it under the clear plastic strip, Fig. 11-41.

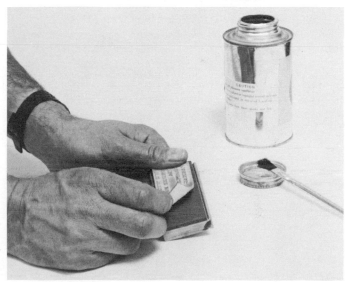

Fig. 11-40. Attach stamp to mounting strip with rubber cement.

Fig. 11-41. Make a print of the stamp. Cut it to size and fit it under the clear plastic strip on top of the handle strip.

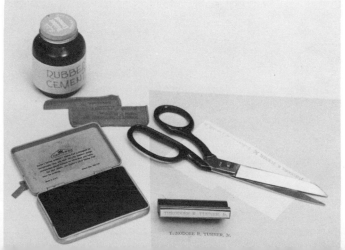

TEST YOUR KNOWLEDGE – UNIT 11

MATCHING TEST. Match terms in the first column with phrases in the second column. Place the question number on your answer sheet and, immediately after the number, the letter of the phrase best describing the term.

1. _____ Corner Rounding.
2. _____ Jogging.
3. _____ Numbering.
4. _____ Perforating.
5. _____ Laminating.
6. _____ Embossing.
7. _____ Scorching.
8. _____ Glazing.
9. _____ Foil Stamping.
10. _____ Die-Cutting.
11. _____ Thermography.

a. Cuts paper stock so it can be folded into three-dimensional shapes.
b. Can be metallic, gloss or matte finished, textured or patterned stock. Heat and pressure are used to impress the design onto the paper.
c. Produces a two-toned image on heavy textured stock.
d. Area being impressed is given a very smooth finish. Heat and pressure must be carefully controlled.
e. Technique that produces a raised printed surface.
f. Evens up printed sheets after they have been printed.
g. Used for security and control purposes.
h. Cuts rows of slots or dots across a sheet so it will fold or tear easier.
i. Cuts radii on corners of paper.
j. Sandwiches printed sheets between two plastic films.
k. A three-dimensional printing technique. Dies are used to raise the stock surface.

THINGS TO DO

1. Secure examples of printed work that has had the corners rounded or angled.
2. Collect examples of numbered printing.
3. Get several examples of printed work that has been perforated.
4. Gather samples of laminated printed materials.
5. Collect examples of embossed, scorched and glazed printed stock.
6. Secure printed materials that are examples of foil stamping.
7. Prepare a bulletin board display of die-cut work.
8. Find examples of work that uses thermography to produce the raised printed surface.
9. Demonstrate how thermography is used in printing.
10. Make a rubber stamp with your name and address on it. After you have completed the stamp prepare a report for your instructor. List the steps of the procedure as you remember them. Describe injuries which could occur during the process and safety rules which must be followed.
11. Using the rubber stamp prepared in the previous project, prepare a half dozen sheets of stationery. Experiment with different positions for the lettering and stamp the sheets with your name and address. Select and display those you think are best.
12. Collect greeting cards—Christmas, birthday, "get well"—and examine them for special finishing processes. Identify the processes. Discuss unidentified processes with your instructor.
13. Develop a finishing processes chart. In the first column, list the finishing processes you have studied in this unit. In the second column, describe the process in your own words. In the third column, as well as you can, prepare simple diagrams to illustrate the finishing method. Refer to the illustrations in the textbook.

Unit 12
BINDING AND FINISHING

Objectives

The binding and finishing of printed products are explained in this unit.

You will learn how printed material is assembled into book form, and study the techniques used to bind them. With the proper tools and equipment at your disposal, you will be able to demonstrate many binding and finishing operations.

Most printed material must go through various BINDING and FINISHING operations. Binding means collecting and joining single sheets or groups of sheets (called signatures) together into books, magazines or pamphlets. Other operations such as embossing and die-cutting may be considered either as auxiliary operations, printing operations or as finishing operations. In commercial plants with many departments, they may be a part of either operation. Another operation considered a part of finishing is packaging.

BINDING OPERATIONS

Many kinds of bindings are used to hold sheets together. Some are designed for a short life or low cost. Other bindings are intended for long and hard usage. Many of the common bindings are shown in Fig. 12-1. How many of them have you seen in use?

PAMPHLET OR WIRE BINDING

The term, pamphlet or wire binding, is used when brochures, booklets and some magazines are bound, Fig. 12-2. There are five steps or operations in pamphlet binding.
1. Scoring.
2. Folding.
3. Gathering.
4. Stitching (or stapling).
5. Trimming.

Fig. 12-1. Binding is any mechanical method for holding pages together.

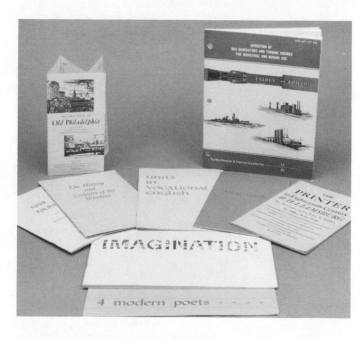

Fig. 12-2. Examples of pamphlet binding. This term is used when folders, booklets and some magazines are bound by stitching.

Some binding jobs will require all five operations. But most will not need that many.

Scoring

Scoring is the process of putting a crease in paper to make it easier to fold. This is usually necessary only on heavier stock.

Scoring is often done with a round face steel rule, Fig. 12-3. It is mounted in a folder or in a platen press. Sometimes a rotary (roller) creaser is mounted on the machine to score the paper as it moves through the folder.

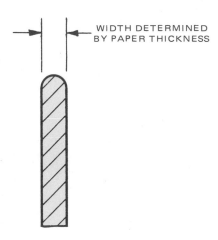

WIDTH DETERMINED BY PAPER THICKNESS

Fig. 12-3. Scoring is usually done with round face steel rule. It can be used on a platen press or in a folding machine.

Folding

When a larger printed sheet is made up of several smaller sheets, it must be reduced to the single page size by folding. Folders usually make two types of folds, Fig. 12-4:

1. Parallel—two or more folds run in the same directions.

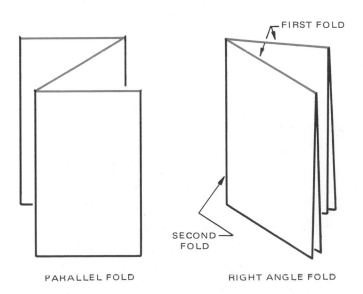

FIRST FOLD

SECOND FOLD

PARALLEL FOLD

RIGHT ANGLE FOLD

Fig. 12-4. Folds are either parallel or at right angles.

2. Right angle—each succeeding fold is made at right angles to the previous fold. Some of the common folds are shown in Fig. 12-5.

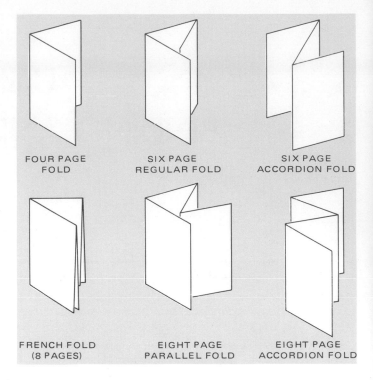

FOUR PAGE FOLD

SIX PAGE REGULAR FOLD

SIX PAGE ACCORDION FOLD

FRENCH FOLD (8 PAGES)

EIGHT PAGE PARALLEL FOLD

EIGHT PAGE ACCORDION FOLD

Fig. 12-5. Some of the more common types of fold. Not all of them can be used for pamphlet binding.

High speed folding is done automatically on machines that can be adjusted for the desired fold or folds. See Fig. 12-6. These folders operate on either the BUCKLE or KNIFE principle, Fig. 12-7.

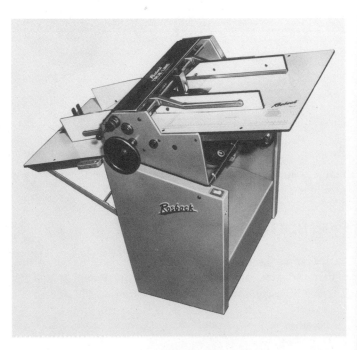

Fig. 12-6. This automatic folding machine is designed to handle small sheet sizes.

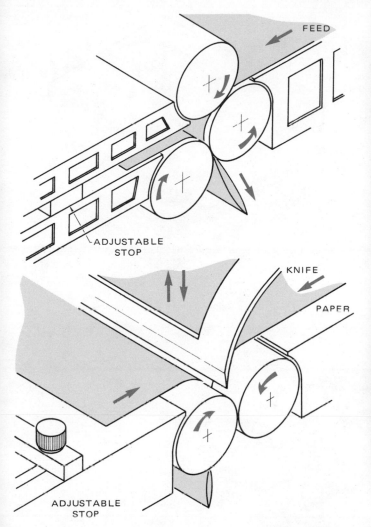

Fig. 12-8. Collating marks (black bars) are printed at different positions on fold of each signature. Do you see the one that is out of order?

Fig. 12-7. Two types of high speed folders. Top. In buckle type folding operation, sheet is fed into machine until it buckles and is pulled through two lower rollers. Bottom. Knife type folding operation. Knife pushes sheet into rollers.

Gathering

Gathering means assembling printed sheets in page order. This operation is often incorrectly called COLLATING. Collating means to examine the gathered sheets or signatures to make sure that they are in the proper sequence (order) before they are bound. COLLATING MARKS are printed at different positions on each signature fold, Fig. 12-8.

HAND GATHERING is practical when a limited number of single sheets must be assembled into complete sets. Stacks of printed sheets are arranged in sequential (numerical) order on a table, Fig. 12-9. Workers gather the material by walking around or along the table, removing a sheet from each paper stack.

SEMIAUTOMATIC GATHERING is done on machines that can deliver up to 20 printed pages at a time. See Fig. 12-10. This type of assembly is used for loose-leaf and mechanical binding.

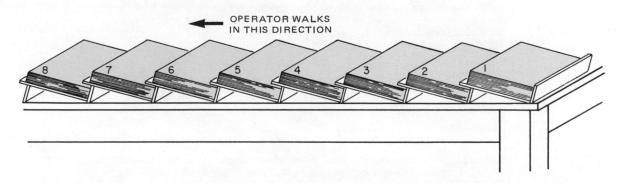

Fig. 12-9. Stacks of printed sheets are arranged in sequential order on a table for hand gathering.

Fig. 12-10. Semiautomatic gathering machine. Fingers within each slot push top sheet of each pile out far enough so they can be gathered as a group. (The Challenge Machinery Co.)

Fig. 12-11. Collated sheets are cross stacked.

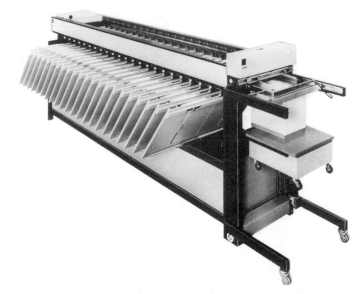

Fig. 12-12. Automatic machines like these gather rapidly. Top. High speed, automatic collator. (Standard Duplicating Machines Corp.) Bottom. Sheridan 20-box gathering unit feeding into binder. Machine operates at 120 books a minute. (Rand-McNally & Co.)

Printed sheets are placed in bins on the machine in order. The top sheet of each pile is pushed forward when the feed switch is activated. The gathered sheets are removed by the operator and cross stacked as in Fig. 12-11.

AUTOMATIC GATHERING is done at high speed with large machines like the one shown in Fig. 12-12. A bin or box at each of many stations on the machine holds single sheets or folder signatures.

As a conveyor belt advances from one station to the next, swinging pickup arms, located at each station, place a sheet or signature on top of previously gathered material. See Fig. 12-13. A full set of signatures in proper sequence comes off the end of the belt. Fig. 12-14 pictures a machine that gathers, binds and trims.

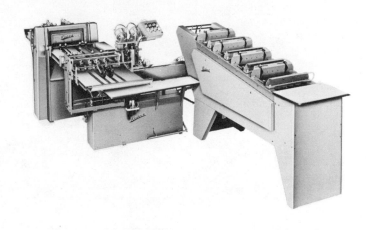

Fig. 12-14. This unit automatically collates, stitches and trims all three sides of signature in a single pass through the machine. It is very fast. (F.P. Rosback Co.)

Stitching

Stitching or stapling is the next binding operation after gathering has been completed. There are two methods of attaching the staple:
1. Saddle stitching.
2. Side stitching.

Both methods are illustrated in Fig. 12-15. As you can see, a saddle stitch is made by driving the staple through the fold and clinching (closing) it inside the fold. The side stitching staple is driven through the signatures from top to bottom. Closure is on the back cover.

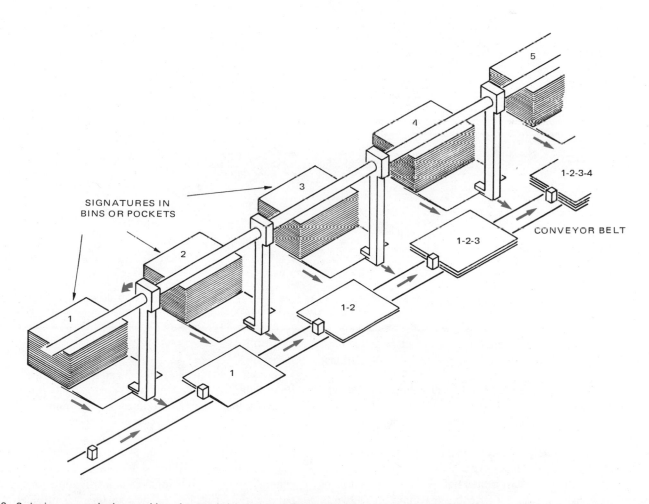

Fig. 12-13. Swinging arm gathering machine. An arm is located at each station. As conveyor belt advances from one station to next, the swinging arm places sheet or signature on top of previously gathered signatures.

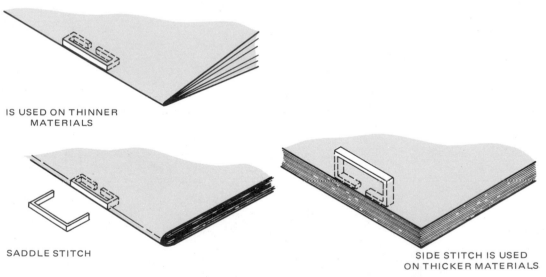

IS USED ON THINNER
MATERIALS

SADDLE STITCH

SIDE STITCH IS USED
ON THICKER MATERIALS

Fig. 12-15. Gathered materials are bound by stitching. Top. Examples of work that has been stitched. Bottom. Thickness of the sheets determines how signatures are bound.

Saddle stitching is used when the pamphlet or magazine is thinner. Side stitching is used with larger, thicker publications.

Perhaps you have also noticed a difference in the way saddle stitched signatures are assembled. Unlike side stitched materials, where signatures are stacked one on top of the other, saddle stitched signatures are placed astraddle a V shaped conveyor. Each successive signature is placed astraddle the previous signature. The cover finally is added in the same fashion. Then the staples are added before the assembled piece leaves the conveyor. Typical stitching machines are shown in Fig. 12-16.

Trimming

Booklets, pamphlets, folders and magazines are trimmed on three sides (top, bottom and right). This is necessary to remove folded edges and to improve appearance.

Small jobs are trimmed on hand or power operated guillotine paper cutters. See Fig. 12-17. Large production runs can be trimmed on three sides at one time with three-knife trimmers, Fig. 12-18. Some trimming is done on programmed paper cutters, Fig. 12-19. These cutters will automatically shift to preset sizes after each cut.

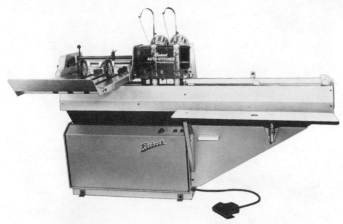

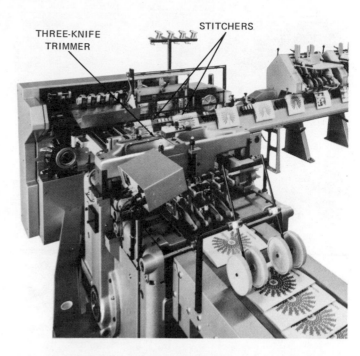

Fig. 12-18. Automatic collating, stitching and three-knife trimming unit. Three sides of the work are trimmed to size automatically. (Muller-Martini Corp.)

Fig. 12-16. Stitching machines come in many sizes and shapes. Top. Semiautomated saddle stitcher. Bottom left. Foot operated stitcher. (Acme Staple Co., Inc.) Bottom right. Hand operated saddle stitcher. (The Swingline Co.)

Fig. 12-19. Programmed paper cutter. It adjusts automatically to a predetermined series of cutting sizes. (MBM Graphics)

OTHER KINDS OF BINDINGS

Printed material can be bound in many ways besides wire. Cost and use determine the type of binding that will be used. Some are designed to allow addition of new material; some allow pages to lie flat. Durability under hard use is also a factor. In some instances the binding must be inexpensive but flexible.

LOOSE-LEAF BINDING

There are three commonly used types of loose-leaf bindings:
1. Ring binder.
2. Binding post.
3. Binding post tongue cover.

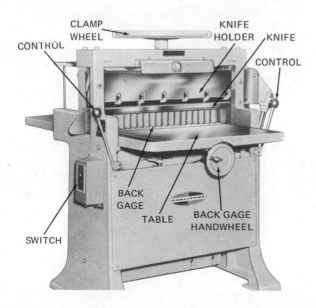

Fig. 12-17. Power operated guillotine type paper cutter. Knife descends under great pressure to trim stacked materials. (The Challenge Machinery Co.)

Fig. 12-20. Types of loose-leaf bindings. Top. Binding post. Middle. Binding post, tongue cover. Bottom. Ring binder.

Fig. 12-20 shows all three types. This method of binding permits sheets to be added and removed easily. Pages may be removed without spoiling the binding or releasing other pages.

Ring binder

Ring binding allows pages to lie flat when open. No large margins are necessary at the binding edge. The printed area can be larger. Binder rings are exposed when the book is open. This is the best binding for quick addition or removal of sheets.

Binding post

Post bound pages do not lie flat. The book must be held open while one is reading. A larger margin is needed on the binding edge. Binding posts are exposed. New sheets are not easy to add.

Binding post, tongue cover

Like the post bound book, pages do not lie flat. The book must be held open when read. A larger margin is needed on the binding edge. Binding posts are hidden. New sheets are not easy to add.

Mounting holes for loose-leaf bound materials are made with a PAPER DRILL, Fig. 12-21. The drill tool is a hollow steel tube that has been sharpened. PAPER STOPS for locating the holes on the edge of the paper are adjustable. See Fig. 12-22. The BACK GUIDE or FENCE is also movable. Stacks of paper up to 1 in. (25 mm) thick can be drilled on most machines if a wax stick is touched to the rotating drill. The wax acts as a lubricant preventing the drill from turning the paper that is being drilled.

Fig. 12-21. Using a paper drill. Note that all guards are in place. (Cheney State College)

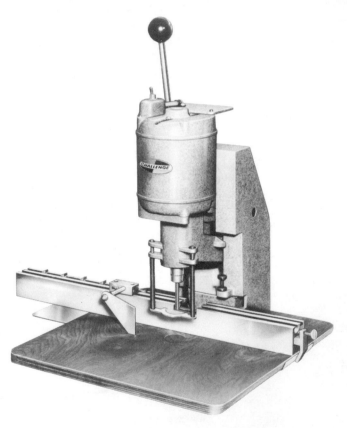

Fig. 12-22. Single unit paper drill makes one hold at a time. Projections on left side of guide are dogs for adjustable stop. (The Challenge Machinery Co.)

Gang paper drills (several drills on one machine controlled as one) make several holes at one time. See Fig. 12-23.

ADHESIVE (PERFECT) BINDING

Adhesive or Perfect Binding is inexpensive. The book is held together by a flexible adhesive applied to the edges of the sheets. Paperback books, telephone directories and many catalogs are bound this way, Fig. 12-24.

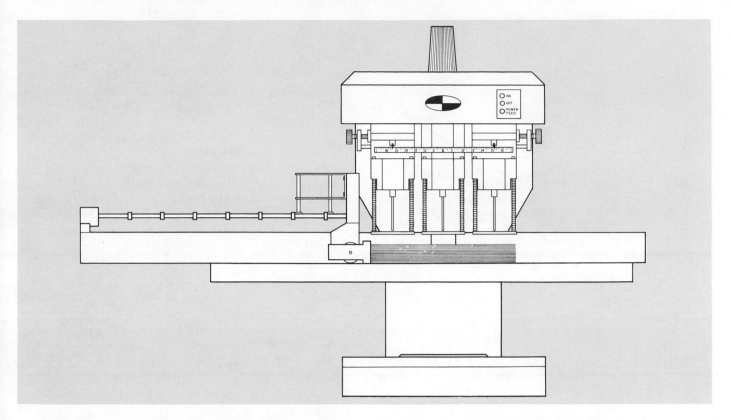

Fig. 12-23. Gang paper drill. Several holes can be drilled at one time. Drills can also be repositioned for different sheet sizes.

Fig. 12-24. Perfect type bindings. Flexible glue holds pages together.

Fig. 12-25. Rotary machine applies glue for perfect binding and attaches covering. (Muller-Martini Corp.)

The graphic arts industry uses automatic machines, Fig. 12-25, to do perfect binding. The machines gather, collate, clamp and glue. The backs of the signatures are ground off to leave a rough surface and to expose edges of all sheets. A flexible plastic base adhesive is applied and the cover is attached. After trimming, the books are packaged.

PERFECT BINDING BY HAND

Perfect binding done by hand is known as PADDING, Fig. 12-26. Gathered sheets are JOGGED until they are neatly stacked. Next, the sheets are weighted down or put in a PADDING PRESS.

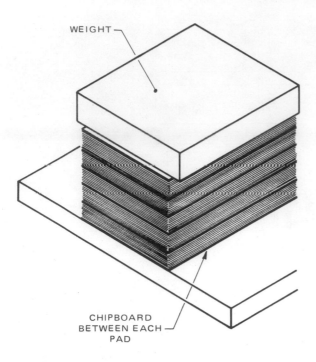

Fig. 12-26. Perfect binding by hand is known as padding. A special adhesive is brushed on one edge of a pile of sheets.

Padding adhesive is brushed on and allowed to dry. If additional binding strength is needed, a piece of SUPER is placed on the adhesive. Super is a coarse, open-weave reinforcing cloth. It is also known as CRASH and MULL. A second coat of adhesive may then be applied.

MECHANICAL BINDINGS

There are two basic types of mechanical binders:
1. PLASTIC COIL.
2. SPIRAL WIRE.

Both types are shown in Fig. 12-27. Mechanical binders work well on books that must open flat. They run through a series of round or slotted holes punched along the binding edge of the sheets.

Mechanical bindings make it possible to bind pages of different size in the same book. Most of the bindings are rugged and will take hard abuse. It is possible to imprint plastic bindings or give them attractive color schemes. Pages can be torn out without affecting other pages in the book. Extra margin must be allowed along the left hand edge of the page for the binder.

Using plastic coil binding

1. Gather, jog and trim sheets to the desired sizes.
2. Adjust the multiple punch, Fig. 12-28, for sheet size. Punch the holes for the binder coil. The holes may be rectangular or T-slotted. See Fig. 12-29. Avoid trying to punch too many sheets at one time. A plate on the machine will indicate the maximum paper thickness that can be punched at one time.
3. To bind, lay the correct size and length binder in place on the machine, Fig. 12-30.
4. Pull the handle down to open the plastic fingers.
5. Place the book on the plastic fingers.
6. Return the handle to its original position to close the fingers.
7. Remove the bound book from the binder.

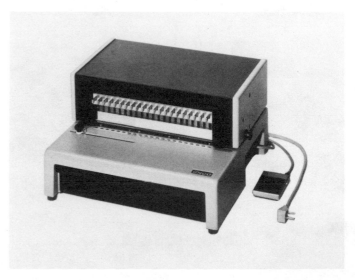

Fig. 12-28. This machine is used to punch holes for plastic coil binding. (IBICO)

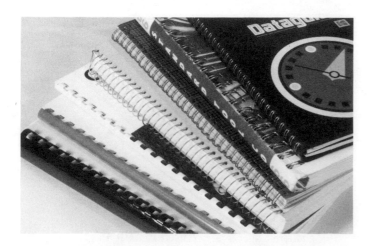

Fig. 12-27. These mechanical bindings are durable and make the books easy to use.

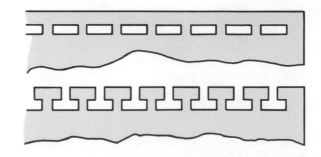

Fig. 12-29. Types of holes that can be made with multiple punch machine. Machine can be hand or power operated.

Using spiral wire binding

1. Gather and jog the sheets and trim them to size.
2. Punch holes. Thread a wire spiral through the holes and lock it in place.

CASE OR CONVENTIONAL BINDING

A CASE BOUND book, Fig. 12-31, is one having a hard (rigid) cover as distinguished from a soft (flexible) cover

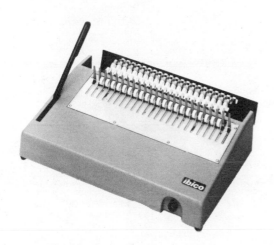

Fig. 12-30. When binding with plastic coil binder, sheets are placed in correct sequence on an expanded plastic coil in this machine. Then coil is closed. (IBICO)

pamphlet. The book you are reading is case bound. It is fitted with a good quality hard cover. Case binding, the most expensive type, has been in use since before the invention of printing.

Case binding is best used on thick, heavy books. However, any size book can be case bound. The hard covers protect the signatures and will withstand hard usage. This type of binding can be colorfully and attactively finished.

Phases of binding

There are 12 basic phases in case binding. These are shown in Fig. 12-32. When done on a production basis it is known as EDITION BINDING.

The phases are:
1. Printing.
2. Folding.
3. Gathering.
4. Sewing.
5. Smashing and trimming.
6. Gluing
7. Rounding.
8. Lining.
9. Covering.
10. Stamping.
11. Casing in.
12. Pressure and drying.

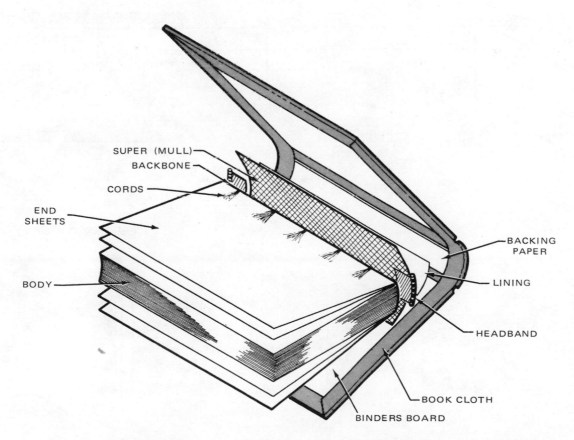

Fig. 12-31. Parts of a case bound book. Good bindings have many parts.

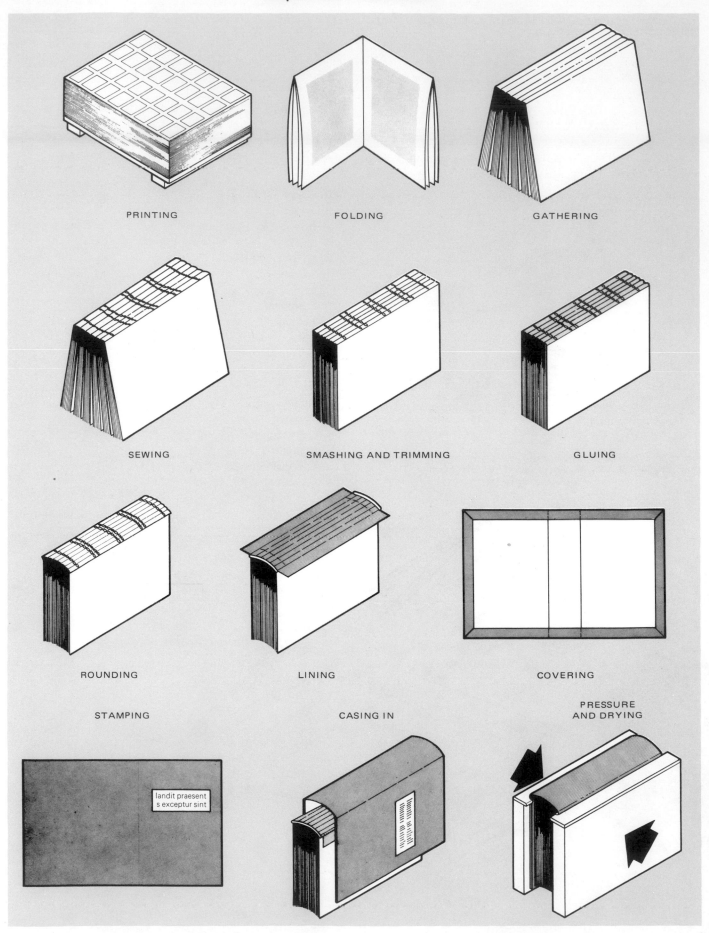

PRINTING

FOLDING

GATHERING

SEWING

SMASHING AND TRIMMING

GLUING

ROUNDING

LINING

COVERING

STAMPING

CASING IN

PRESSURE AND DRYING

landit praesent
s exceptur sint

Fig. 12-32. There are 12 phases or steps in the production of a case bound book.

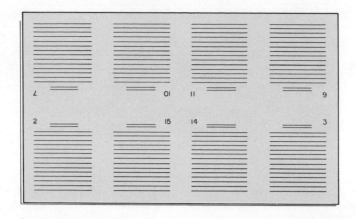

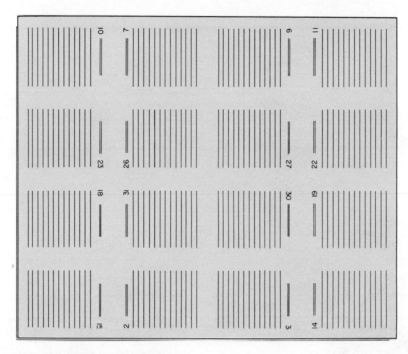

Fig. 12-33. Book size and weight of paper (thickness) determine the number of pages that will be printed on each signature. Top. An 8 page signature. Bottom. Signature of 16 pages.

Printing. All the pages of a book cannot be printed at one time. They are grouped in even numbers of pages known as signatures. This term is already familiar. Standard signatures consist of 8, 16, 32, or 64 pages. The book size and weight of paper used determines the number of pages to be printed in each signature, Fig. 12-33.

Folding. The signatures—large flat sheets, at this point—must be folded to page size. A typical folding sequence is shown in Fig. 12-34. These folds must be made in the correct order so that the pages will be in correct numerical order.

Gathering. All of the signatures necessary for the book must be gathered in the right order. The first and last signatures will have ENDSHEETS attached to them. These sheets, also called ENDPAPERS, are made of heavy paper and are folded over once just like a four-page signature. They are glued to the signatures in an operation called TIPPING. Purpose of the endsheets is to attach the signatures to the cover.

Sewing. Stout thread holds the case bound book together. The sewing is done by machine. First, the pages of each signature are bound together; then, the signatures are sewn to one another. No cords are used.

Smashing and trimming. During the sewing operation, the bound edge of the book has gotten thicker. Great pressure and heat is used to flatten it. This operation is called SMASHING. TRIMMING cuts away a small portion of the top, bottom and fore edge (outside edge) of the signatures. This removes the unwanted folded edges found on some pages and makes the edges even. Trimming is done on a three-knife trimmer, Fig. 12-35.

Gluing. An adhesive is applied to the backs of the signatures. This will hold them together as one solid unit.

Rounding. With the signatures firmly clamped, a concave roller is run over the back of the book to round it. This causes the

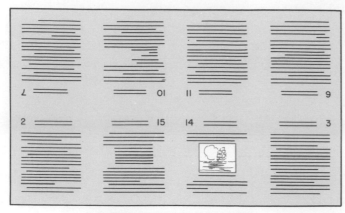

1. SHEET READY FOR FOLDING

2. FIRST FOLD

← SLIT →

3. SECOND FOLD AND SLIP HEAD

4. THIRD OR BACK FOLD

Fig. 12-34. An example of a folding sequence. Do you see how pages fold into the right order?

Fig. 12-35. Three-knife trimmer trims fore edge and ends of a signature in a single operation. (Muller-Martini Corp.)

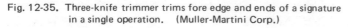

fore edge to take the same concave shape as the roller. This step also rounds the back and forms the hinge.

Lining. Super (a gauze-like cloth) and head bands are glued to the back. See Fig. 12-36. They are then covered with a section of heavy paper or cloth.

Fig. 12-36. Lining and headbanding is done by machine. Top. View of entire machine. Bottom. Closeup shows liner section. Sensors prevent feeding of liner material if no book is in position to receive them. (Smyth Manufacturing Co.)

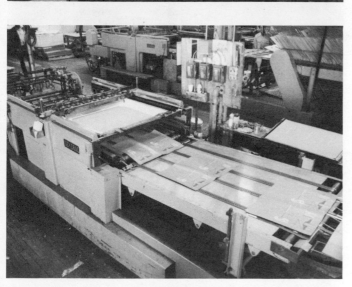

Fig. 12-37. Silkscreening book cover. Top. Stencil used to print cover of drafting book. Center. Feed end of silkscreen printing machine. Bottom. Delivery end of slikscreen printing machine. (Superior Silk Screen Industries, Inc.)

Covering. While the body of the book is being assembled, the cover or case is being made. The case is made up of two boards (heavy cardboard), a protective cover of cloth or plastic and a strip of heavy paper or cloth for the backbone.

The cover material is glued to the outside of the boards. Heavy paper or cloth is attached to the inside of the cover.

A cover design is often silkscreened or printed by offset on the cloth before it is fitted to the case. Fig. 12-37 shows a cover being silkscreened.

Stamping. This operation is performed only if the cover is to receive decoration after it is made. Heat, pressure and foil are used to apply the title, author's name, publisher and any line art, Fig. 12-38.

Fig. 12-38. Gold foil stamping a book cover. Foil is fed in ribbon width that matches cover area receiving the impression. Foil is released from its carrier backing by heat and pressure from dies on the machine. (Rand McNally & Co.)

Casing in. Case and book are joined by an operation called casing in. This is done automatically on a CASING-IN MA-CHINE, Fig. 12-39. Rollers apply glue to the endsheets. The bound signatures are then inserted in the covers.

Pressure and drying. The assembled books are placed between boards which shape the case hinge line. Pressure and heat are applied to speed the drying process. After final inspection, the books are stacked for packaging and shipment.

BINDING A BOOK BY HAND

Few school graphic arts programs are able to print a book large enough to need case binding. However, it is easy enough to hand bind a book of blank pages, Fig. 12-40.

Fig. 12-39. Casing-in machine has capacity of 1500 books an hour. (Smyth Manufacturing Co.)

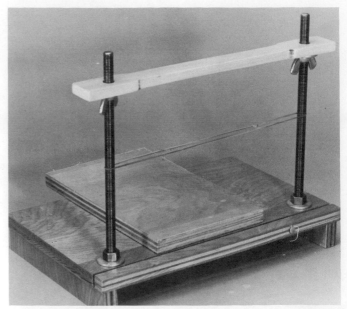

Fig. 12-40. School graphic arts project. Blank pages are bound for an autograph book.

Books have been hand bound this way for hundreds of years. Today, however, few are capable of doing this work with the same skill as the early bookbinders.

EQUIPMENT NEEDED

Tools and equipment needed for hand binding are simple, Fig. 12-41. Suitable binding equipment can be made in the graphic arts and woods program, Fig. 12-42. Many of the hand tools, Fig. 12-43, are already in the shop.

Fig. 12-41. A few simple pieces of equipment can be purchased for book binding. Top. Sewing frame. Middle. Backing clamp. Bottom. Standing press.

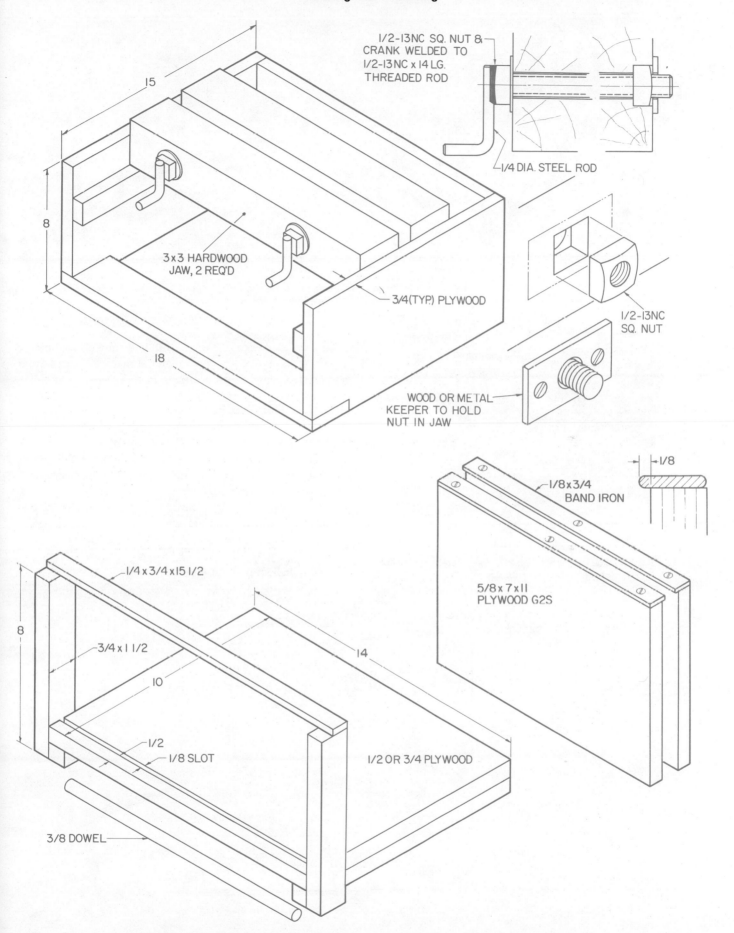

1/2-13NC SQ. NUT &
CRANK WELDED TO
1/2-13NC x 14 LG.
THREADED ROD

1/4 DIA. STEEL ROD

15

8

3x3 HARDWOOD
JAW, 2 REQ'D

3/4 (TYP.) PLYWOOD

18

1/2-13NC
SQ. NUT

WOOD OR METAL
KEEPER TO HOLD
NUT IN JAW

1/8

1/8 x 3/4
BAND IRON

5/8 x 7 x 11
PLYWOOD G2S

1/4 x 3/4 x 15 1/2

8

3/4 x 1 1/2

10

14

1/2

1/8 SLOT

1/2 OR 3/4 PLYWOOD

3/8 DOWEL

Fig. 12-42. This bookbinding equipment can be made in the woodshop and graphic arts lab.

223

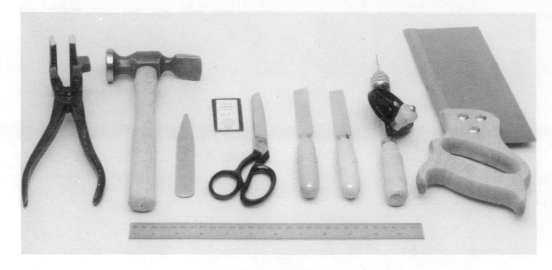

Fig. 12-43. These hand tools are needed in bookbinding. Left to right. Nipper, backing hammer, bone folder, packet of needles, hand shears, corner knives, hand drill, backsaw and steel rule.

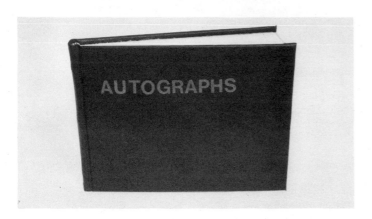

Fig. 12-44. Student-made autograph book is constructed from blank sheets folded down to size.

An autograph book, Fig. 12-44, is a simple case-binding project. It has 96 pages. Cover material may be secured from an upholstery shop. Cloth, plastic or leather can be used.

BINDING THE SHEETS

1. Secure six sheets of 17 in. by 22 in. bond paper.
2. Fold each sheet as shown in Fig. 12-45. Folding will produce a signature 4 1/4 in. by 5 1/2 in. Each signature will have 16 pages.

   The last fold will be easier to make if the signature is slit as shown. (If you are working in metric sizes, select the A2 sheet in the ISO "A" series. It measures 420 mm by 594 mm. It will fold to a 16-page signature 105 mm by 148 mm. This is about 4 by 5 4/5 in.)

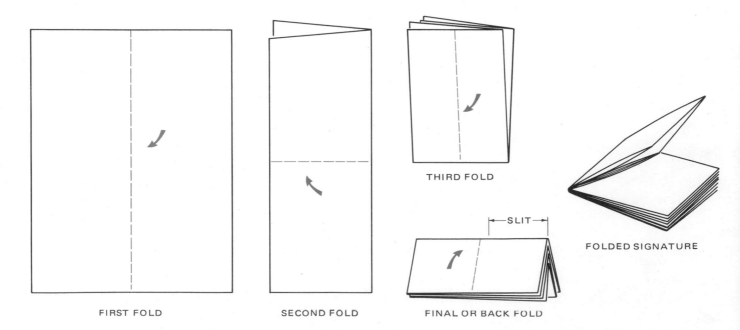

FIRST FOLD

SECOND FOLD

THIRD FOLD

SLIT

FINAL OR BACK FOLD

FOLDED SIGNATURE

Fig. 12-45. Folding sequence for signatures used to make autograph book.

3. Cut two decorated endpapers 4 1/2 by 11 in. or 105 mm by 297 mm if you are working in metric. They may be hand marbled or purchased already decorated, Fig. 12-46. (Refer to Fig. 12-75 through Fig. 12-82 and related text for instructions on how to make marbled paper.) End-papers give a finished appearance to the book. They also help secure the book in the case.

4. String the SEWING FRAME with heavy cord, Fig. 12-47. Three cords are ample for a book of the size being made. Tapes may be used in place of the cords, Fig. 12-48.

5. Wax the binders' thread as shown in Fig. 12-49. Thread it onto a heavy needle.

6. Place the signatures and endpapers in the backing clamp, Fig. 12-50. Mark the back for the location of the cords and kettle stitch locations. Cut through the folds with a backsaw.

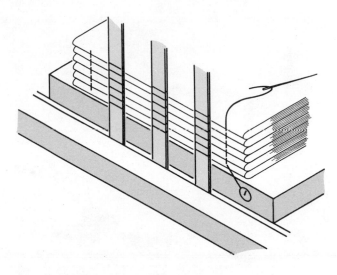

Fig. 12-48. Cotton tapes may be used in place of the heavy cord.

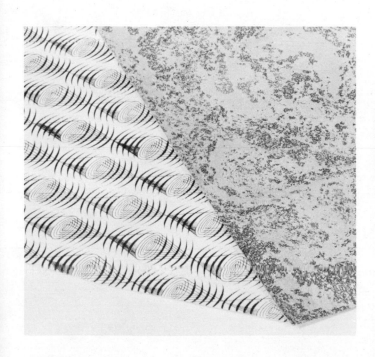

Fig. 12-46. Endpapers are usually decorated. They may be commercially made, like the one on the left, or marbled in the graphic arts lab like the sample on the right.

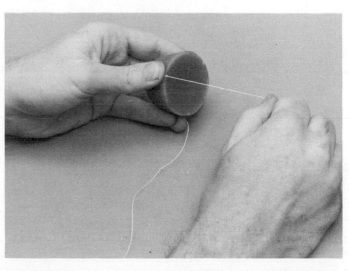

Fig. 12-49. Wax binders' thread with bees wax to make thread easier to pull through paper.

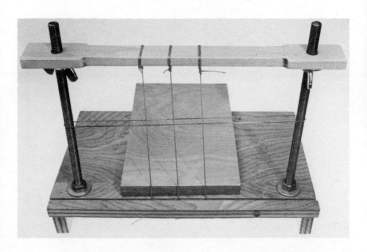

Fig. 12-47. String sewing frame with heavy cord as shown.

Fig. 12-50. Place signatures in backing clamp and mark off locations of cords and kettle stitches.

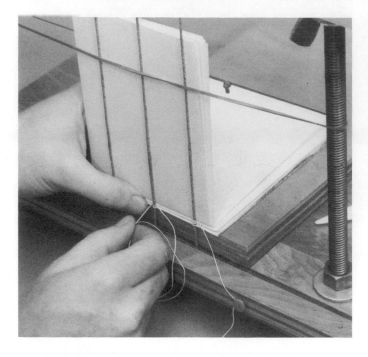

Fig. 12-51. Sewing signatures to cords. Rubber band holds signature open while it is being sewn.

7. Lay one of the endpapers in the sewing frame. Tack the binders' thread to the right of the front edge of the frame.

8. Sew the first endpaper and the signatures onto the cords, Fig. 12-51. Sew back and forth, first moving across through one signature and then back through the next. Start the needle from the back. Push it through the first saw kerf. Follow the fold to the first cord. Wrap the waxed thread around the cord. Move along the fold to the next cord, wrap, and proceed to the end kerf. Bring the needle out through the kerf. Tie the signatures together at each end with a kettle stitch, Fig. 12-52.

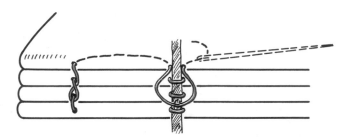

Fig. 12-52. Kettle stitch, left, holds signatures together.

9. Complete the sewing operation by stitching the top endpaper into place.

10. Return the sewn signatures to the backing clamp. Apply glue to the backs of the signatures, Fig. 12-53.

11. When glue has dried, remove the signatures from the clamp. Trim signatures to 3 3/4 by 5 1/4 in. (Metric dimensions may be trimmed by 6 mm.) Plan the cuts carefully. The edges of the glued signatures will have a tendency to tear if not clamped properly in the paper cutter. See Fig. 12-54.

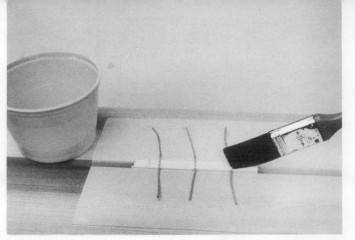

Fig. 12-53. Glue backs of signatures to reinforce sewing.

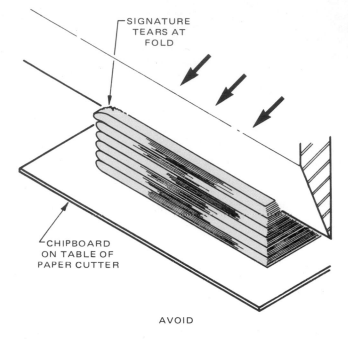

SIGNATURE TEARS AT FOLD

CHIPBOARD ON TABLE OF PAPER CUTTER

AVOID

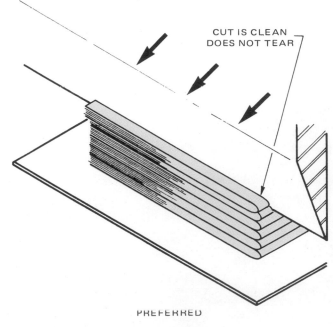

CUT IS CLEAN DOES NOT TEAR

PREFERRED

Fig. 12-54. Use care when trimming glued signatures to size.

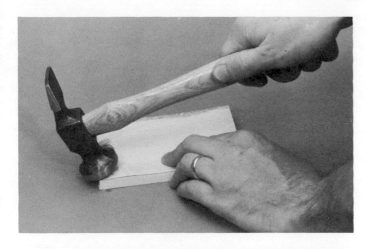

Fig. 12-55. Use backing hammer to round back of book.

12. Place the sewn and glued signatures on a smooth, flat surface. Round the back as in Fig. 12-55.
13. Mount the book firmly in the clamp. Finish rounding the back with glancing blows, Fig. 12-56. A properly rounded back is shown in Fig. 12-57.

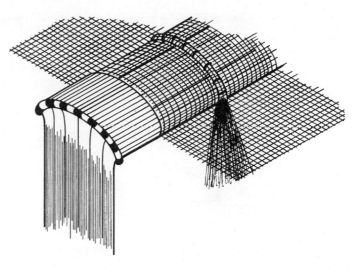

Fig. 12-58. Headbands and super are glued in place. Headbands protect the binding when the book is pulled from a book case.

14. Glue the headbands and super into place, Fig. 12-58.
15. Unravel the cords as shown in Fig. 12-59. This permits them to lay flatter and provides greater holding power when glued to the case, Fig. 12-60.

Fig. 12-56. Finish rounding book in backing clamp. Use glancing blows of hammer.

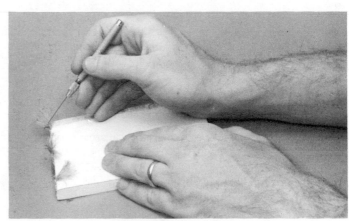

Fig. 12-59. Ends of binding cords are unraveled or frayed with needle held in pin vise.

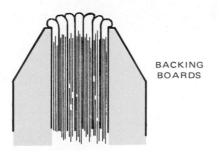

BACKING BOARDS

Fig. 12-57. Properly rounded back deforms folds of signatures slightly.

Fig. 12-60. Unraveled cord ends are fanned to lie flat and cover more surface when they are glued to the case.

Fig. 12-61. Use straightedge and knife to cut backing boards to size.

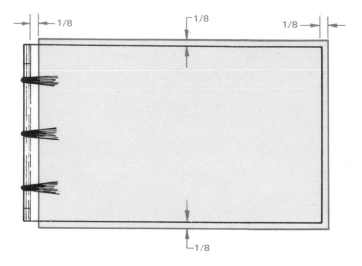

Fig. 12-62. Determining backing board size. Subtract space for the hinge and add space for overhang at head, foot and fore edge.

Fig. 12-63. Use tape to temporarily mount cover boards. Check for proper fit.

PREPARING THE COVER

16. Cut the backing boards, Fig. 12-61. Allow for the hinge and overhang at head, foot and fore edge, Fig. 12-62.
17. Temporarily mount the cover boards. Attach tape across the back of the book as shown in Fig. 12-63.
18. Remove the cover boards and lay them out flat on the cover material. The tape will maintain the proper spacing across the back and hinges.
19. Mark the material as shown in Fig. 12-64. Cut it to size. Allow for gluing. See Fig. 12-65.

Fig. 12-64. Covering material is marked for cutting.

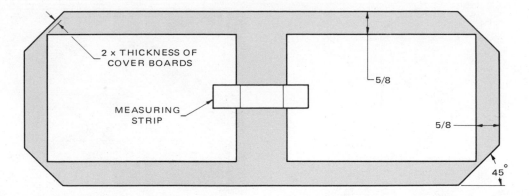

Fig. 12-65. Make allowances necessary to have cover material fit backing boards properly.

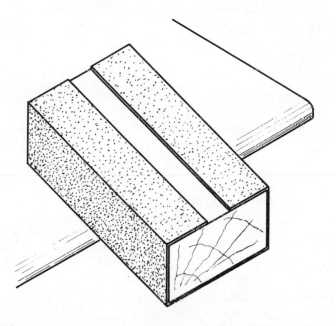

Fig. 12-66. Round edges of backing board slightly with medium grit sandpaper. Use a sanding block.

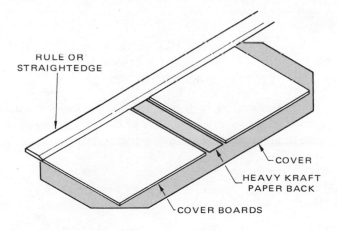

Fig. 12-67. Use a steel rule or straightedge to align cover boards when they are being glued to covering material.

20. Round the edges of the backing boards with medium sandpaper, Fig. 12-66.
21. Glue the backing boards and heavy kraft paper backbone

to the cover, Fig. 12-67. Use a steel straightedge to assure proper alignment.
22. The corners are folded for gluing as shown in Fig. 12-68.
23. Place the freshly glued case (cover) between waxed paper and place in the press until the glue has dried.
24. Prepare the book for gluing to the case. Place a section of waxed paper between the first signature and the end-papers. Apply glue by brushing away from the back, Fig. 12-69. Be sure there is ample glue on the super and cords.
25. Position glued side of the book on the case. See Fig. 12-70.
26. Turn the book over, repeat step 24 and attach the remaining half to the case, Fig. 12-71.
27. Clamp the freshly glued book between pressing boards and place in the backing clamp, Fig. 12-72. Apply clamping pressure. Leave the book in the clamps until the glue has dried.
28. After final inspection, the book is ready for finishing.

FINISHING A HAND BOUND BOOK

To the bookbinder, finishing means stamping, printing and decorating the cover. If the cover is to be finished by silkscreening or letterpress, the printing must be done before the case is attached to the book.

The book title can also be HOT STAMPED onto the cover. Foils that resemble gold and silver are used. In addition, foils are available in a range of colors.

The simplest way to hot stamp makes use of a hand PALLET, Fig. 12-73. Special brass type (foundry type would be ruined in a short time) is mounted in the pallet. The type is heated to about 300 deg. F (149 C). Foil is placed into position on the book cover. The type, held in the pallet, is pressed against the foil. Heat and pressure causes the foil to adhere to the cover material. Since only the type is in contact with the cover the type image is left on it. Practice hand stamping on scrap material before hot stamping your completed book.

Fig. 12-74 shows a hot stamping press. A guide on the press bed assures accurate alignment of the lettering. Pallet heat is controlled by a thermostat.

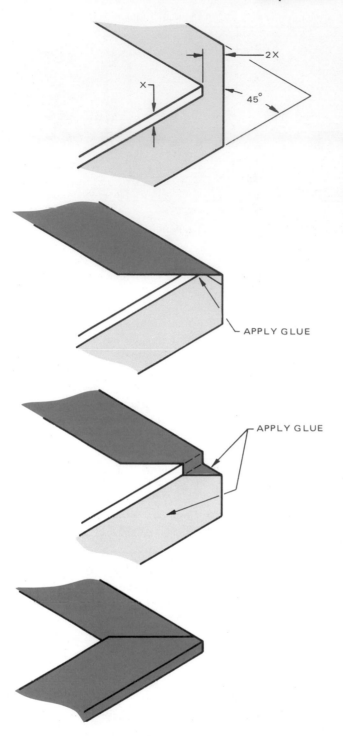

2 X

X

45°

APPLY GLUE

APPLY GLUE

Fig. 12-68. Follow above corner folding sequence.

Fig. 12-69. Place waxed paper between endpapers and cover boards before applying glue. Apply glue by brushing away from back. Be sure there is ample glue on super and cords.

After hot stamping, allow the type to cool. Wipe it clean with a soft cloth and return it to its case.

Caution: Type, when ready to use, is very hot. Use care when stamping the book cover. Treat burns immediately, no matter how slight.

HOW TO MAKE MARBLED ENDPAPERS

True marbling, Fig. 12-75, is becoming a lost art. The materials needed are too hard to obtain for the average school graphic arts program. The process also creates disagreeable odors.

However, simpler marbling techniques are available. They produce a colorful but random design on the paper. Only inexpensive equipment is needed.

The easiest method is to float thinned printing inks on a water size. Paper placed on the water picks up the pattern. The design cannot be controlled as it is in true marbling.

Fig. 12-70. Carefully position glued side of book on one side of case.

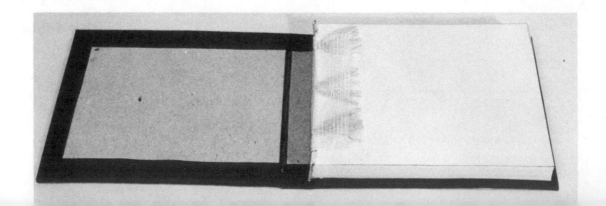

Fig. 12-71. Glue remaining half to case. Remove surplus glue along edges with a damp cloth.

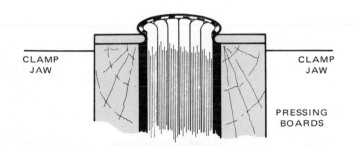

CLAMP JAW

CLAMP JAW

PRESSING BOARDS

Fig. 12-72. Put freshly glued book between pressing boards and place in backing clamp.

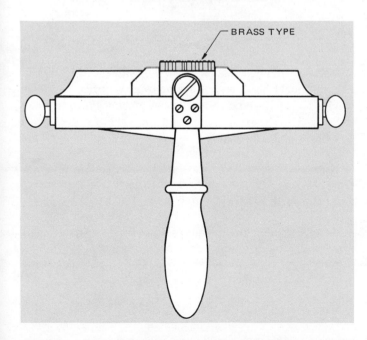

BRASS TYPE

Fig. 12-73. Hand pallet holds type for applying gold or silver foil lettering to book covers.

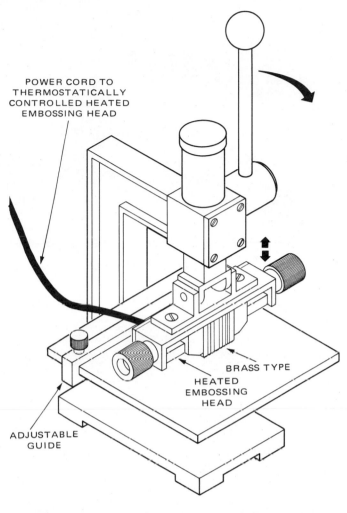

POWER CORD TO THERMOSTATICALLY CONTROLLED HEATED EMBOSSING HEAD

BRASS TYPE

HEATED EMBOSSING HEAD

ADJUSTABLE GUIDE

Fig. 12-74. Hot stamping presses are found in many graphic arts labs.

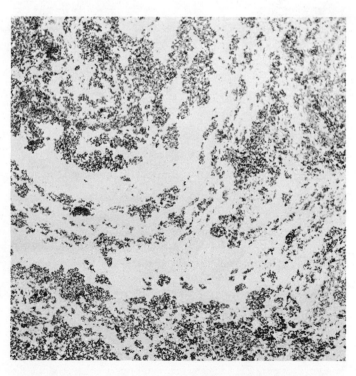

Fig. 12-75. Marbled sheet makes attractive endsheets.

Fig. 12-76. Tray should be slightly larger than largest sheet that is to be marbled.

The printing inks are thinned with rectified turpentine or kerosene. The amount of thinner added depends upon the marbling technique developed by the individual.

Equipment

Select the following pieces of equipment:
1. A shallow tray, Fig. 12-76, slightly larger than the paper to be marbled. Fill about three-fourths full of water.

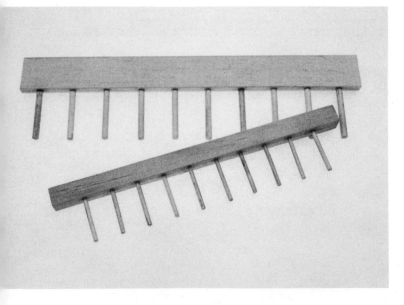

Fig. 12-77. Wood combs are used to move the ink pattern on the water.

2. Wood combs, Fig. 12-77, to break up and move the ink pattern on the water. Combs can be handmade using finishing nails or doweling for the teeth. On one comb, space the teeth on 1/2 in. centers. On the other, allow 3/4 in. between centers.
3. Eye dropper, Fig. 12-78, for dropping ink into the water. One is needed for each color.

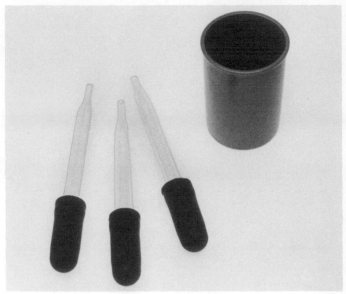

Fig. 12-78. Eye droppers are needed to drop the thinned printers ink on the water. There should be an eye dropper for each ink color.

Fig. 12-79. Marble effect is created as ink film spreads over water.

Place the thinned ink on the water with the eye dropper. The ink should break up and spread over the surface as shown in Fig. 12-79. Run the comb through the ink film and water size, Fig. 12-80. Float the paper on the water. Avoid trapping air bubbles under the paper.

Remove the marbled paper from the water. Allow it to dry. Place the marbled sheet between two pieces of clean newsprint. Press with a warm iron to remove wrinkles.

Another marbling technique is to float the ink on a glue based size. This has advantages over a water size. The ink pattern is partially controllable, Fig. 12-81. Also, colors are more brilliant even though the same inks are employed.

Make the glue size by dissolving 6 oz. of a good hide glue and 6 oz. of glycerine in a small amount of warm water. When thoroughly dissolved and mixed, add two quarts of warm water. The size is now ready to use.

When the glue size is fresh, partially controllable effects are possible. The size will hold the pattern for about 30 seconds after the comb is run through the ink film.

Size more than a week old produces an entirely different pattern, Fig. 12-82. For best results, strain the size after making six to eight marbled sheets.

When the sheet has dried, wash it to remove excess glue size that may have adhered to the paper. *Caution: Paper must be dry or the ink will be washed off before it has a chance to set.*

Protect the marbled sheet by placing it between two sheets of clean newsprint. Press the dried sheets with a slightly warm iron to remove wrinkles.

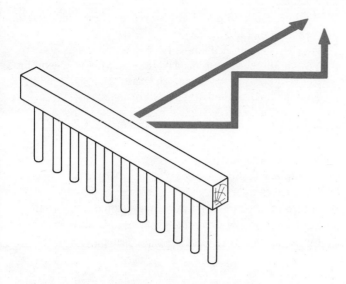

Fig. 12-80. Run comb through ink film on surface of pan. Move in a straight or zigzag pattern.

Fig. 12-81. These marble patterns were made using a glue size instead of a water size. Marble effect is more pronounced when glue size is used.

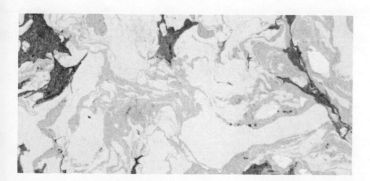

Fig. 12-82. Effect produced when size was more than a week old.

TEST YOUR KNOWLEDGE — UNIT 12

1. After printing, most jobs go through various _____ and _____ operations.

MATCHING QUESTIONS. Each phrase on the right describes a word in the left column. Place the letter of the phrase that best describes a word in the appropriate blank space. (Place answers on separate sheet.)

2. ____ Binding.
3. ____ Scoring.
4. ____ Folding.
5. ____ Gathering.
6. ____ Stitching.
7. ____ Trimming.
8. ____ Padding.
9. ____ Signature.
10. ____ Jogged.
11. ____ Collating.
12. ____ Super.
13. ____ Loose-leaf binding.
14. ____ Perfect binding.
15. ____ Mechanical binding.
16. ____ Case binding.
17. ____ Smashing.
18. ____ Rounding.
19. ____ Stamping.
20. ____ Covering.

a. Groups of sheets making up a book.
b. Type of perfect binding.
c. Assembling sheets in predetermined order.
d. Creasing paper for easier folding.
e. Collecting sheets or signatures and joining them into a book or pamphlet.
f. Laying one part of a sheet over another part.
g. Coarse, open-weave reinforcing cloth.
h. Padding is an example of this type of binding.
i. Pressing a curve in the fore edge of a case bound book.
j. A ring binder is this type of binding.
k. Assembling a pamphlet with staples.
l. Sheets of paper uniformly "edged-up" and neatly stacked.
m. The plastic coil and spiral coil binding fit into this category.
n. Placing title on book cover.
o. Cutting sheets or signatures to size.
p. Gluing cloth to cover boards.
q. Compacting book's folded edge.
r. When a book is given a hard cover.
s. Examining gathered sheets or signatures to be sure they are in the proper sequence.

21. To the bookbinder, finishing operations mean _____
_____ .
22. Marbling is a technique for _____ the endpapers of a book being bound.

THINGS TO DO

1. Design, assemble and case bind a book to hold samples of the work you have printed.
2. Design, assemble and case bind an autograph book.
3. Construct a sewing frame.
4. Design, assemble and plastic coil bind a book to hold samples of the work done in your school's graphic arts lab.
5. Design, assemble and plastic coil bind a photograph album.

6. Prepare a bulletin board display on the tools and materials used in book binding.
7. Prepare a paper on the history of book binding.
8. Visit a museum that displays books with fine bindings. Report your observations to the class.
9. To your class, demonstrate the proper way to:
   a. Case bind a book.
   b. Operate a paper drill.
   c. Do padding.
   d. Bind with plastic coils.
   e. Stamp a rebound book's title on the case. Use gold foil.
10. Secure examples of the various ways books are bound.
11. Demonstrate how to marble paper using a water size.
12. Demonstrate how to marble paper using a glue based size.

Unit 13
DESIGN

Objectives

This unit provides the fundamentals needed to design and lay out attractive printed materials.
After reviewing it, you will be aware of the many things that must be kept in mind when designing. You will have the basic information needed to prepare acceptable printed materials.

Graphic design is the art of planning the layout of printed work, Fig. 13-1. Well designed printed material should:

1. Attract the reader's attention.
2. Be easy to read and understand.
3. Have a lasting effect on the reader.

Printed matter is worthless if no one is attracted to it or reads it. It is wasted if no one remembers its message.

FACTORS IN GRAPHIC DESIGN

Many factors must be kept in mind when designing printed work. These factors are guidelines that will help you produce good graphic designs that will be acceptable to a customer. *They are not to be considered a strict set of design rules that will guarantee good results.*

UNITY WITH TYPE

Unity is a quality in all graphic design that ties parts of a whole together. Using one family or style of type helps unite elements (parts) of a design. See Fig. 13-2. Unlike parts destroy the unity in a design. Unrelated typefaces create a

JAMES JOYCE

U LYSSES

Fig. 13-1. Graphic design is the art of planning the layout of printed material. It should be simple and attract the reader's attention. This is the title page of a book.

Industrial Education

Bel Air High School
Bel Air, Maryland

Industrial Education

Bel Air High School
Bel Air, Maryland

Fig. 13-2. Carefully thought out design at top uses one family or style of type. This serves to bring the design together. At bottom, two type styles seem to separate elements into two messages.

Industrial
Education
IN THE
BEL AIR HIGH SCHOOL
BEL AIR, MARYLAND

Fig. 13-3. Avoid using several different typefaces in the same design. A design employing a hodgepodge of typefaces, like this one, tends to be distracting and uninteresting.

hodgepodge such as the one in Fig. 13-3. Hard-to-read typefaces, however attractive, should be avoided. They prevent the reader from getting the message, Fig. 13-4.

The best...
FLANAGAN'S
MOUSTACHE WAX

Fig. 13-5. Select a typeface that fits the job. Type used in this advertisement is masculine like the figure and the product. Note how the gentleman's eyes direct attention to the message.

CAR WASH
FRIDAY
$1.50

Mark Twain on the Mississippi

CAR WASH
FRIDAY
$1.50

Fig. 13-4. Type used in a design should be easy to read. Without sign at bottom could you read the one at top?

Fig. 13-6. Use contrast to create interest and attract attention. Top. The book jacket showing Mark Twain is simple and indicates the book concerns him. Bottom. You can tell immediately that the business using this sign is open 24 hours a day.

Select a typeface that suits the job. If the message is about strength, then the type should suggest strength. If delicacy is wanted, type should be delicate. See Fig. 13-5.

EMPHASIS

Another quality of good design is emphasis or contrast. Used in a design it makes one of the elements stand out. It creates interest and attracts attention. See Fig. 13-6. Try to keep designs simple, Fig. 13-7.

Lines are sometimes used to guide the reader's eye to the message, Fig. 13-8. They can be thin, wide, straight, curved or angular.

Larger type can be employed to make important parts of the message stand out (emphasis). See Fig. 13-9. Important elements of the design can also be emphasized with color as in Fig. 13-10.

Repetition is another way to create interest and accent the printed message. Fig. 13-11 shows a style of drawing being repeated.

BIG BAD BART'S
RANCH
DRY BONES, ARIZONA

ALL STAR RODEO

JULY 23, 19XX
2:00 P.M.

Fig. 13-9. Use larger type to make important parts of the printed message stand out.

Fig. 13-7. Keep the design as simple as possible. The simple geometric figures in this design are arranged to look like the front of a bank.

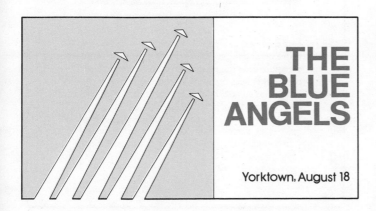

Fig. 13-8. Lines, whether they are straight, curved or angular can often be used to guide the reader's eyes to the message.

DANGER

RADIATION FROM RADIOACTIVE
MATERIALS *CANNOT* BE. . . .

SEEN
HEARD
FELT
TASTED
SMELLED

PROTECT YOURSELF. WEAR
YOUR RADIATION MONITOR.

Fig. 13-10. Color can be used to emphasize important ideas or elements.

Fig. 13-11. Repetition of the basic theme of the design can be used to create interest and accent the printed message.

Many graphic designers use a paper's texture or textured background, Fig. 13-12, to make the design more eye catching and interesting. Rub-on or patterned film background designs are available commercially.

BALANCE

When a design is in formal balance (or symmetrical), use familiar shapes, Fig. 13-13. Symmetrical or formal balance means that the design balances equally on each side of an imaginary center line. See Fig. 13-14.

Fig. 13-12. In addition to using the paper's texture, a wide range of patterned films are available to help produce an endless combination of effects for graphic design applications. Many graphic designers utilize patterned films to add "extra punch" to their work.
(chartpak, Times Mirror Co.)

Fig. 13-13. Use simple geometric shapes when designing symmetrical layouts. The simple and familiar rectangle makes the text more pleasing in this layout. Notice the use of ornamentation.
(Schneidereith & Sons, Baltimore)

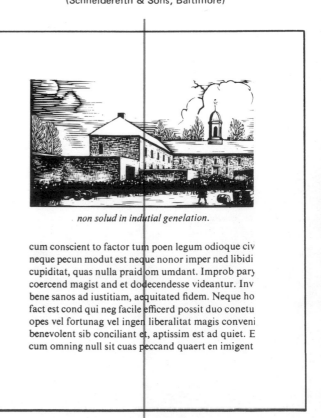

non solud in indutial genelation.

cum conscient to factor tum poen legum odioque civ
neque pecun modut est neque nonor imper ned libidi
cupiditat, quas nulla praid om umdant. Improb pary
coercend magist and et dodecendesse videantur. Inv
bene sanos ad iustitiam, aequitated fidem. Neque ho
fact est cond qui neg facile efficerd possit duo conetu
opes vel fortunag vel ingen liberalitat magis conveni
benevolent sib conciliant et, aptissim est ad quiet. E
cum omning null sit cuas peccand quaert en imigent

Fig. 13-14. Symmetrical design has elements balancing equally on both sides of an imaginary center line.

tempor cum soluta nobis
impedit anim id quod ma
voluptas assumenda est,
autem quinusd et aur of
atib saepe eveniet ut er r
recusand. Itaque earud re
au aut prefer endis dolori
tene sentntiam, quid est
accommodare nost ros q
tum etia ergat. Nos amic
fier ad augendas cum cc
odioque civiuda. Et tamc
est neque nonor imper n

Eveniunt, da but tutung benevolent sib conciliant et, al
ssim est ad quiet. Endium caritat praesert cum omning
null sit caus peccand quaeret en imigent cupidat a natura
proficis facile explent sine julla inura autend unanc sunt isti
Lorem ipsum dolor sit amet, consectetur adipscing elit, sed
diam nonnumy eiusmod tempor incidunt ut labore et dolore

AVOID

Eedit anim id quod maxim placeat face
ptas assumenda est, omnis dolor rep
autem quinusd et aur office debit aut tun
atib saepe eveniet ut er repudiand sint et
recusand. Itaque earud rerum hic tenetury
au aut prefer endis dolorib asperiore repel
tene sentntiam, quid est cur verear ne ad
accommodare nost ros quos tu paulo ant
tum etia ergat. Nos amice et nebevol, ole:

AVOID

Ead augendas cum conscient to facto
que civiuda. Et tamen in busda tane
est neque nonor imper ned libiding gen e
cupiditat, quas nulla praid om umdant. In
potius inflammad ut coercend magist anc
videantur. Invitat igitur vera ratio bene sa
aequitated fidem. Neque hominy infant a
cond que neg facile efficerd possit duo (
effecerit, et opes vel fortunag vel ingen lil

PREFERRED

Fig. 13-15. Asymmetrical means the design has elements of unequal weight on either side of an imaginary center line. But informal balance is achieved by moving the smaller element further from the center of the layout.

Fig. 13-16. Well designed printed pages are properly proportioned. Proportion, in this case, refers to the ratio of length to width of the printed sheet.

An ASYMMETRICAL or INFORMALLY BALANCED layout is often used in graphic design, Fig. 13-15. The graphic elements are shifted so that an equal amount is no longer placed on either side of the imaginary center line shown in Fig. 13-14. Still, they are placed in such a way that they appear to be balanced. Informal balance is used often in advertising. It allows the designer more flexibility than does formal balance.

PROPORTION

The printed page must also be properly PROPORTIONED, Fig. 13-16. Proportion refers to the ratio of length to width of the sheet being printed. Sheet size is determined by the message and size of type and illustrations being printed. However, economy must also be considered. Slight changes in sizes often permit more usable sheets to be cut from standard stock sizes. There will be less waste. Paper is expensive and must, therefore, be used to best advantage. A well proportioned page, and how it was attained, is shown in Fig. 13-17.

MARGINS tend to give stability to the printed page. These are the nonprinted areas surrounding the printed material. Side margins should be equal in width. The top margin is the same size or slightly larger. The base margin is the widest. See Fig.

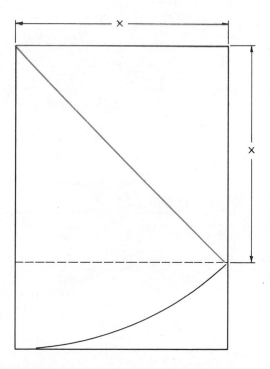

Fig. 13-17. This mechanical method is a simple way to get a well proportioned page. Simply extend one side of a square the length of its diagonal.

Fig. 13-18. Margins are the nonprinted (blank) areas surrounding the printed material. Margins anchor the message to the page.

13-18 for an example. For additional information on design refer to page 310.

ORNAMENTS AND BORDERS

The designer may want to use an ORNAMENT, Fig. 13-19, for decorative purposes, or to set a mood. Ornaments used in relief printing are cast as one piece of type, Fig. 13-20.

Fig. 13-20. Typical of ornaments used in letterpress, these are cast in metal and are type high.

Ornaments can refer directly to the contents of the page or may be symbolic in nature. If not properly selected and used, however, ornaments add meaningless clutter which can only detract from the appearance of the job.

DECORATIVE BORDERS can also be used to add interest to a design, Fig. 13-21. Border material must be carefully selected to go with the type being used, Fig. 13-22.

COPYFITTING

Determining how much type will fit in a certain space or how much space a manuscript will take is called COPY-FITTING. There are two basic steps:

1. Find out the number of characters (letters, spaces and punctuation) in the manuscript copy.
2. Select a size of type and line length. Then determine how many characters will fit on each line. Divide this number into total characters to find number of lines.

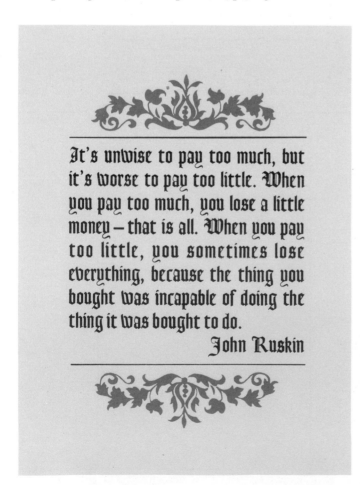

It's unwise to pay too much, but it's worse to pay too little. When you pay too much, you lose a little money — that is all. When you pay too little, you sometimes lose everything, because the thing you bought was incapable of doing the thing it was bought to do.

John Ruskin

Fig. 13-19. Ornaments are often used for decorative purposes or to establish the mood of the message. (Champion International Corp., Paper Div.)

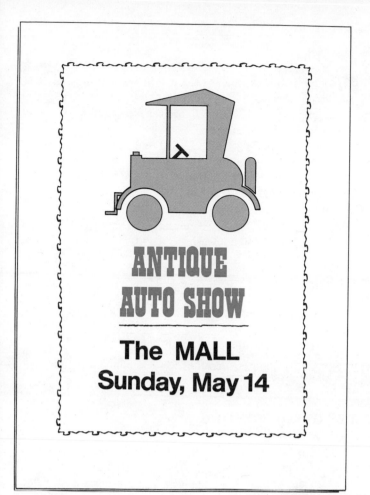

Fig. 13-21. Decorative border is used to improve appearance of poster designed to advertise antique auto show.

CHARACTER COUNTING

The amount of copy is usually determined by taking a character count. This can be done with a special gage or ruler, Fig. 13-23, or by making an actual count.

If copy is short, the gage can be used to accurately count each individual line. If there is a great deal of copy, it is more practical to make an average line count. This method is illustrated in Fig. 13-24.

PREFERRED   AVOID

Fig. 13-22. Select border that will complement, rather than detract, from type used in design.

To count characters without a gage:

1. With a ruler, draw a light line straight up and down the page of copy just to the right of the last character in the first line.
2. Count the number of characters in the first line.
3. Multiply the number of characters by the number of lines in the copy.
4. To this total, add the number of extra characters to the right of the vertical line drawn in Step 1. The new total is the actual number of characters in the copy.

FINDING NUMBER OF PRINTED LINES

To find the number of lines of space your copy will fill:

5. Compute how many type characters will fit in one line.
   a. Consult a type manufacturer's chart to see how many of

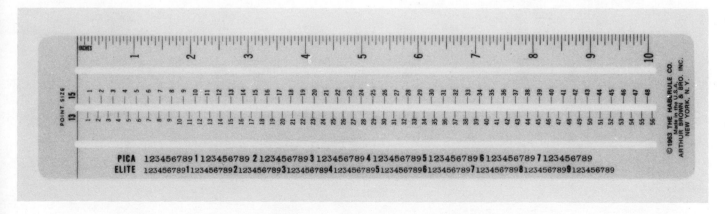

Fig. 13-23. Plastic type gage is used for rapid calculation of number of characters in a piece of copy. Two rows of numbers (marked "pica" and "elite") measure number of characters in line for each size of typewriter type.

In many ways the "second-rough" is the most critical and most diff[icult] stage. As pipes and fittings are located the plumber must be constantly aware of the requirements for the fixtures to be installed later and mai[ntain] allowances for finished wall and flooring materials yet to be installed [by] other craftsmen. If both of these factors are properly accounted for, [...]

regardless of the stage of the plumbing installation in which the work [...]

on "how-to" information about the installation of the various types of [...] accomplished during the various stages of the plumbing installation. [It is] hoped that this brief description of the total process will provide the reader with a frame of reference from which to relate the specifics of [in-] stalling pipe and fittings.

Fig. 13-24. Using the type gage. Lay gage across line of type. Align first character with first number on gage. Read down from last character in line to number on gage. This gives character count for line. To quickly count whole page of copy, take average between shortest and longest line. Then, multiply by number of lines.

the typeface chosen will fit in one pica of space. Multiply by the number of picas in your line. (If your column width is in inches, consult Unit 5, Fig. 5-6 and convert.)

b. If no manufacturers' charts are available, but you have lines of the type, count the characters in several lines of the width selected and take an average.

6. Divide the number of characters that will fit on one line into total characters from Step 4. The answer is the number of lines of printed material.

FINDING THE DEPTH OF COPY

While you now know the number of lines you will have, you still must find out how much vertical space the lines will take up on the page or layout.

7. Determine how much space one line will occupy (depth). In most cases, type is specified as a double figure. For example, 9/10 or 9 on 10 means a 9 pt. type with 1 point of leading between lines.

8. On the type gage, Fig. 13-25, find the column or gage corresponding to the point size of the type plus leading. For example, 9/10 would require use of the 10 point gage.

9. Find the number on the gage corresponding to the number of lines of type.

10. Read across to the inch rule. This will be approximately the depth of the copy when set in type and placed in the layout or form.

Another method may be used in the absence of a gage:

11. Multiply the depth of each line in points by the number of lines.

12. Divide by 72 (number of points in an inch).

$$\text{Inches of depth} = \frac{\text{depth of 1 line} \times \text{number of lines}}{72}$$

DESIGNING PRINTING

The first thing to do before planning a layout is to study good examples of printing. You can study the work of experienced designers to appreciate the principles of good design.

Next, make many freehand sketches, Fig. 13-26. Each should show a different way of presenting the message. Draw them in small scale. At this point you are interested only in ideas. Quarter size is usually large enough. Their purpose is merely to help you develop a number of ideas. You will refine them later. Such sketches are called ROUGHS. Finally, select from all of the roughs the designs you like best. Draw full size the ones you have picked. From these select one which will be prepared for printing.

Work with a T-square, angles, templates and instruments. Use full size type and illustrations, Fig. 13-27. Make the

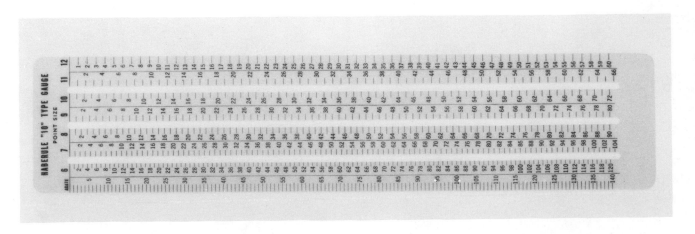

Fig. 13-25. Depth gage shows how much space any number of lines will take up on page. Point size is given at top of each column on gage.

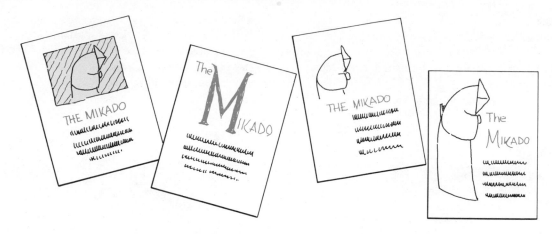

Fig. 13-26. Start your own design by making many freehand sketches.

Fig. 13-27. Use instruments, full size type and illustrations when making final design.

drawings on tracing paper. Changes will be easier to make on tracing paper. Lettering, decorations and illustrations used in the design can be traced quickly and accurately.

TEST YOUR KNOWLEDGE — Unit 13

1. Graphic design is the _____
_____
_____.
2. Name three qualities that all well designed printed
material should have.
3. Check which of the following contribute to good design:
   a. Simplicity.
   b. Using one family or style of type.
   c. Emphasizing important ideas with color.
   d. None of the above.
   e. All of the above.
4. _____ is a principle of design which has to do with the size of one element as it relates to another element.
5. When selecting typefaces for a printed job, use type _____ . Avoid using a _____ of _____ or _____ typefaces.
6. Prepare a rough sketch showing a symmetrical layout.
7. A symmetrical design is also known as a formally balanced layout. True or false?
8. Margins on a printed page are the (List the correct answer or answers on your answer sheet):
   a. Spaces between lines of type.
   b. Nonprinted areas around the printed matter.
   c. Ideas used to keep the design simple.
   d. All of the above.
   e. None of the above.
9. Ornaments are used in graphic design to _____
_____.
10. In copyfitting, the first basic step is to find out the _____ in the manuscript copy.
11. What does "10/12" mean in type size and leading?
12. Why should many freehand sketches be made when starting to design a printed job?

THINGS TO DO

1. Design a cover for a notebook to hold examples of the work you design and print.
2. Make a collection of printed material. Classify it according to use — tickets, programs, posters, forms, etc. Prepare a bulletin board display showing the best designs.
3. Design a poster for a graphic arts display.
4. Design a calendar of games for the football, basketball, baseball, track or hockey teams.
5. Design a letterhead for yourself.

6. Design a name card for your father.

7. Design a "Things Needed" book for your use when you go shopping.

8. Design a tool loan form for the Industrial Arts Department in your school.

9. Design a poster, tickets and program for a play that your school will stage.

10. Design the poster and tickets for a dance to be sponsored by your school. The dance is to be called "The Clod Hop."

11. Design a ticket for a card party.

12. Design and make a full size, four-color layout for a record album.

Unit 14
COLOR

Objectives

This unit will explain the nature of color and how color can be used in graphic arts design.
After studying the unit you will understand more readily why and how color is used in graphic arts design. In addition, you will learn how full color images are prepared and printed.

Color is an important part of our lives. It surrounds us in nature. It is in the things we make and buy.

Can you imagine a world where everything looks like the pictures on a black and white television screen? Such a world would be indeed drab, Fig. 14-1.

Color can set moods and create impressions. Reds and yellows are warm, advancing colors. They come right at you. Blues and greens are cool, receding colors. They have a relaxing effect on us.

Color can change how things appear. Dark colors make objects appear smaller. Light colors make things look larger.

There are even colors the eye cannot see. These are the infrareds and ultraviolets, Fig. 14-2.

Fig. 14-1. Color makes things attractive. Without it, things like toy figures would look very drab.

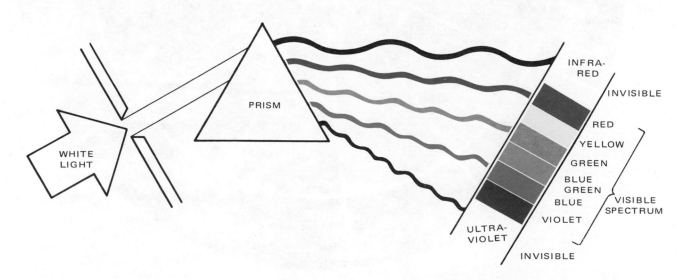

Fig. 14-2. There are two colors the human eye cannot see — infrared and ultraviolet.

245

WHAT IS COLOR?

Fig. 14-3. Color cannot be seen without light. Can you see the black cat in this coal mine?

Color is a visual sensation. It is seen but it cannot be heard or felt. It cannot be seen unless there is light, Fig. 14-3. Color can be described by three basic qualities:

1. HUE usually means the basic name of the color. For example, red, yellow, blue or green. See Fig. 14-4.
2. INTENSITY is the amount of the color in a hue. For example, a vivid red is almost pure red, but a dark red has been subdued (partly neutralized) by adding black to it. The intensity of a color can be lessened also by adding white or a complementary color (from the opposite side of the color wheel). The colors in the center of the color chart, Fig. 14-4, have had white added to them. They are known as tints of the regular colors. The outer ring is made up of shades of the same colors. Fig. 14-5 shows what happens

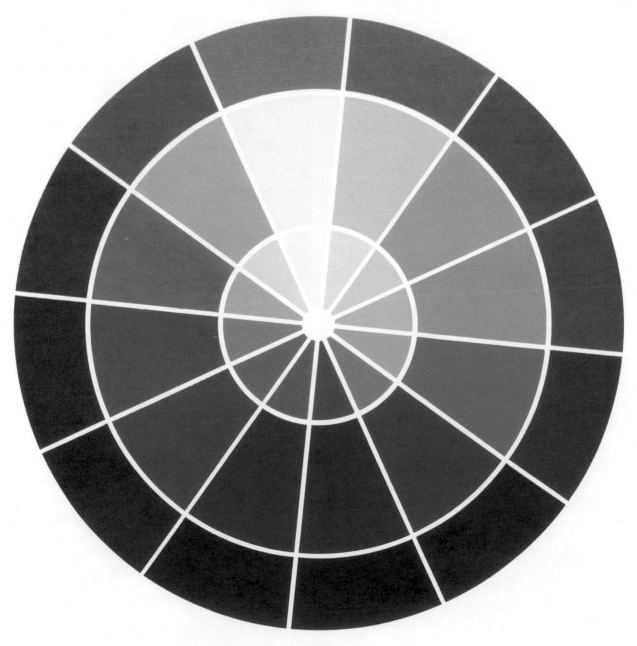

Fig. 14-4. Each color on this color wheel is a hue. A hue is the name of a color.

Fig. 14-5. Intensity of the orange sample at top was reduced by adding blue to it in other two samples.

when a complementary color is used to reduce intensity. Other words sometimes used in place of intensity are SATURATION, PURITY OF COLOR and CHROMA. They all mean the same thing.

3. VALUE (lightness) refers to how light or dark a color is. It is the quality by which the similarity of a series of grays, ranging from black to white is expressed. See Fig. 14-6. It also describes the difference between any strong color and

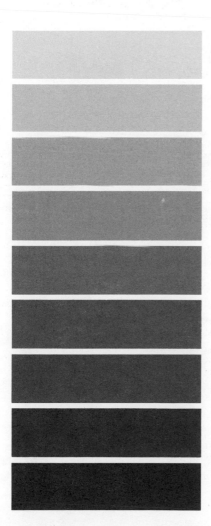

Fig. 14-6. Value describes the lightness or darkness of a color. Tints are light colors. Shades are the darker colors.

a tint or shade of the same color. For example, red can become pink, if lightened, or maroon, if darkened.

PRIMARY COLORS

White light is a mixture of all colors in the rainbow. For practical purposes, this array of colors may be described as combinations of red, green and blue light. You can prove this with three similar flashlights and some filters purchased at a photo supply house. Cover the lens of one flashlight with a red filter, another with a green filter and the third with a blue filter. See Fig. 14-7.

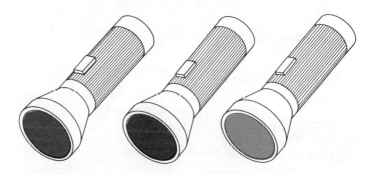

Fig. 14-7. Flashlights with lenses covered by filters can be used to prove that white light is a mixture of all colors.

Turn the flashlights on and arrange the lights on a screen made of white cardboard. Room lighting should be subdued. Adjust the lights until the color circles just overlap as in Fig. 14-8. New colors are formed where the lights overlap.

The three colors, red, green and blue, are called ADDITIVE PRIMARY COLORS. When lights of the three colors are added together, white light is formed.

Fig. 14-8. The three colors — red, green and blue — form white light when added together. For this reason, they are called additive primary colors. Note how other new colors are formed where two lights overlap.

Note: White light will not be seen and colors will not be exact unless the filters are of exact color.

The pigment (coloring agent) in an object determines its color. Opaque (cannot see through) objects REFLECT and ABSORB light. See Fig. 14-9. Transparent objects TRANSMIT and ABSORB light, Fig. 14-10. The light reflected and transmitted is the color seen.

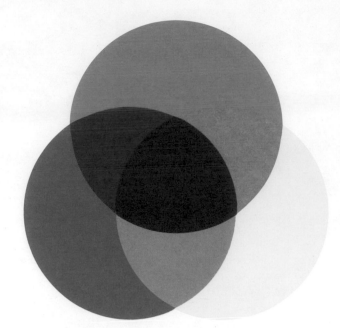

Fig. 14-11. While most ink colors can be made by blending red, blue and yellow, this is not entirely true. If these colors were used for full color printing, the resulting image would be "muddy" in appearance. The colors would not be true.

Fig. 14-9. Pigments in opaque objects like these trees, reflect and absorb light.

Fig. 14-12. In the graphic arts, ink and paper color blend differently from the colors in light. Full color printing can be produced using three colors, cyan, magenta and yellow. (Black is added for tone control.)

Fig. 14-10. Pigments in transparent objects transmit and absorb light.

COLOR USE IN THE GRAPHIC ARTS

In the graphic arts, paper and ink are used to control reflected light (the color we see). Colors in the paper and ink blend differently than the colors in white light, Fig. 14-11.

Three colors of ink, CYAN, MAGENTA and YELLOW, Fig. 14-12, produce the rainbow of printed colors. (They must be printed on white paper.) These three colors are called

SUBTRACTIVE PRIMARY COLORS. Cyan, magenta and yellow each represent two additive colors after one primary color (blue, red or green) has been subtracted from white light. See Fig. 14-13.

Color is used in the graphic arts for many reasons:
1. EMPHASIS, Fig. 14-14. This quality makes words, parts of words or other elements stand out.
2. CONTRAST, Fig. 14-15. A background of different color makes printed matter easier to read.
3. IDENTIFICATION, Fig. 14-16. Organizations which adopt a certain color as their own soon become associated with that color. An example is the colors representing your school.
4. APPEARANCE, Fig. 14-17. Colorful printed pages are more attractive to the reader.
5. IMPACT, Fig.14-18. The visual effect of one object to another object is heightened with color.

The next time you are in a supermarket, look at the displays of detergents and breakfast cereals. See how manufacturers have used color on their products. This has been done to draw your attention.

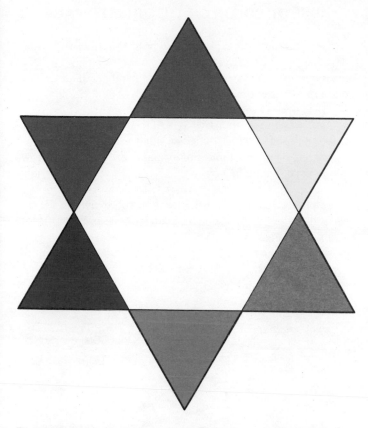

Fig. 14-13. The colors, cyan, magenta and yellow are called subtractive primary colors. Each of these colors is made up of two additive colors after one primary color has been subtracted from white light.

CHOCOLATE

Fig. 14-14. Color can be used for emphasis. See how the letters, "h," "o" and "t" stand out.

CONTRAST

Fig. 14-15. Color can be used for contrast to make the printed message easier to read.

Fig. 14-16. Color is often used for identification purposes. The Red Cross is known around the world by the color of their symbol.

GOLDEN DRAGONS

By John Richard Walker
Illustrated by Larry Wéu

GOODHEART - WILLCOX COMPANY, INCORPORATED

CHICAGO, MONTREAL AND AMSTERDAM   MCMLXXXVIII

Fig. 14-17. Color can make the printed page more attractive.

Fig. 14-18. Color can create impact.

PUBLIC
BROADCASTING
SYSTEM

Fig. 14-19. A logotype (usually called a logo) is a symbol or letter(s) representing words, a name or product. Companies often use them in advertising to build brand recognition.

LETTERHEADS
THAT "tell it
like it is"

A collection of actual letterheads
in use today on Hammermill Bond

Fig. 14-20 The easiest way to add color to a printed page is with colored paper and/or ink. (Hammermill Paper Co.)

USE OF COLOR ON THE PRINTED PAGE

Color use in the graphic arts can be as simple as a single line or type or LOGOTYPE printed in color, Fig. 14-19. A logotype (usually called a "logo") is a symbol, shape or letter that represents entire words or a name.

Another simple approach is to use colored stock (paper) and/or colored ink, Fig. 14-20. Be sure to select a pleasing, but legible, color combination. For example, consider using brown ink on paper with a brown tint.

Color is often used to call attention to key words, ideas or parts of illustrations. Sometimes it is used simply to create variety. See Fig. 14-21. Avoid using dark colors such as green or blue. A tint of these colors will usually produce the necessary contrast.

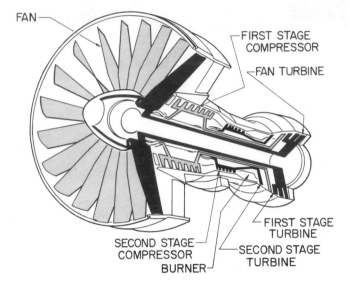

Fig. 14-21. Color can be used to emphasize key ideas.

FOUR COLOR PROCESS PRINTING

To produce printing in four colors, four printing plates are needed. A plate is made for each of the three process ink colors, cyan, magenta and yellow. A fourth plate is made for black ink. While you may not be aware of the black in a color photograph, it is there. It helps produce the shadows and is useful in controlling the other colors.

Reproducing a color photograph, Fig. 14-22, is similar to printing a black and white photograph. But, of course, the process is more complex. In the unit on *Offset Printing* you learned how to make a halftone negative of a photograph. You will recall that the halftone had a dot pattern.

DOT PATTERNS

If you examine a magnified section of a color reproduction, Fig. 14-23, you will see a similar dot pattern made up of different colors. Note also that only the three colors and black

Dot sizes are given as a percentage of the area each one covers. A 50 percent dot will cover half of the space alloted to it. A small dot pattern, such as 10 percent, would print the color as a light tint. A large dot pattern, such as 90 percent, would print the color near its full intensity.

COLOR SEPARATIONS

The four halftone plates used in four color process printing are made by photographing the original full color photograph or drawing through FILTERS of different color. Four separate exposures are made, each time with a different filter in front of the lens. The filter is a colored piece of gelatin or glass.

Photographing through a blue filter will record on the film negative all of the blue in the original photograph or illustration. (This negative is screened also so that it has the necessary dot pattern to make a printing plate.) A separate negative is needed for each color.

When the negative image becomes a positive (after the printing plate is exposed under the negative and developed) it will have only the image of the colors that produce yellow. (The red and green remaining in white light, after blue is removed, produce yellow.) The halftone plate made from the negative is called the YELLOW PRINTER.

The halftone plate made through a green filter will print the red and blue of the original illustration. Blended visually, blue and red appear as magenta. This is the MAGENTA PRINTER.

The CYAN PRINTER is made by photographing the original art through a red filter. Fig. 14-25 shows the color printers and demonstrates how they produce color. The BLACK PRINTER is needed because the yellow, magenta and cyan inks used are not "pure" in color. Perfect colors are impossible to make. When printed, the three colors are "muddy" in the shadow areas. Black compensates for the color impurities and makes the shadows black.

Halftone plates made by this technique are called COLOR SEPARATIONS. Such separations can also be made electronically. See Fig. 14-26.

Fig. 14-22. This illustration was produced by four-color process printing. A plate was needed for each of the colors.

Fig. 14-23. The dots of cyan, magenta and yellow blend together to fool the eye into seeing a rainbow of colors.

were needed to produce the full range of colors. The dots vary in size, as shown in Fig. 14-24, to give a full range of tones for any color.

CYAN

MAGENTA

YELLOW

90 PERCENT   10 PERCENT

Fig. 14-24. A full range of tones of a given hue can be printed by varying halftone dot size.

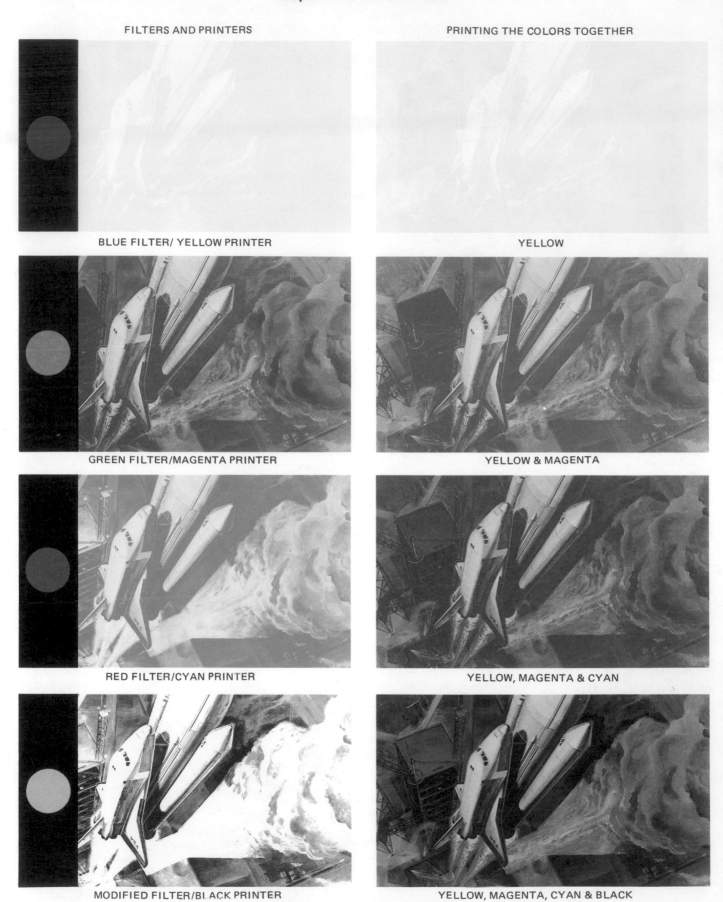

FILTERS AND PRINTERS

PRINTING THE COLORS TOGETHER

BLUE FILTER/ YELLOW PRINTER

YELLOW

GREEN FILTER/MAGENTA PRINTER

YELLOW & MAGENTA

RED FILTER/CYAN PRINTER

YELLOW, MAGENTA & CYAN

MODIFIED FILTER/BLACK PRINTER

YELLOW, MAGENTA, CYAN & BLACK

Fig. 14-25. Color halftone plates are made by photographing the full color original through filters of different colors. Sometimes the black plate is made by partial exposures from the first three filters.

Color in the Graphic Arts

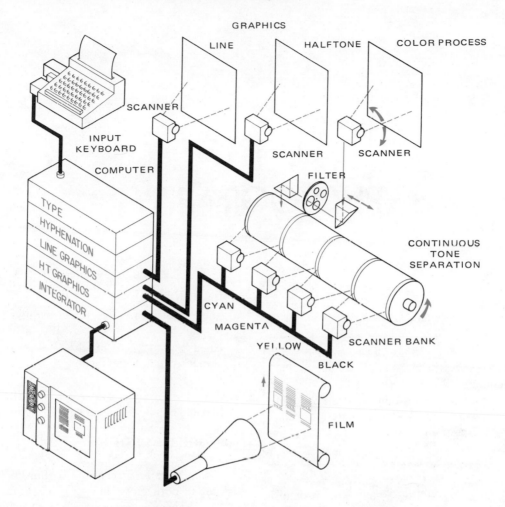

Fig. 14-26. Four color process plates can also be made electronically.

TEST YOUR KNOWLEDGE — UNIT 14

1. Why does color play such an important part in our life?

MATCHING TEST. Select from the right-hand column the statement which best defines each word in the left-hand column. Do not write in the book. Write the question numbers on a separate sheet. After each number, place the letter of the correct description.

2. ____	Hue.	a.	The amount of the color.
3. ____	Intensity or saturation.	b.	Symbol or letter that represents an entire word or name.
4. ____	Value or lightness.	c.	Made of gelatin or glass and fits over camera lens.
5. ____	White light.	d.	Base name of the color.
6. ____	Additive primary colors.	e.	Combination of red, blue and green light.
7. ____	Subtractive primary colors.	f.	Red, green and blue.
		g.	How light or dark a color is.
8. ____	Logo.	h.	Cyan, magenta and yellow.
9. ____	Filter.	i.	Negative used to make halftone color printing plate.
10. ____	Four color process printing.	j.	Full color artwork printed from yellow printing, cyan printing, magenta printing and black printing halftone plates.
11. ____	Color separation.		

THINGS TO DO

1. Make a collection of the different ways color is used in the graphic arts.
2. Visit a printing plant that does four color process printing. Request samples of a job at different stages of printing. Prepare a report on your observations. Explain the stages of the samples, if you can.
3. Prepare a poster showing examples of how color is defined. Use examples of hue, intensity (or saturation) and value (or lightness).
4. Using three flashlights, demonstrate to the class that red, green and blue light will produce white light when they are blended together.
5. Design a bulletin board display that shows examples of color being used in the graphic arts for emphasis, contrast, identification, appearance and impact.
6. Bring to class empty cereal and detergent containers. Examine them carefully and explain how the manufacturers used color to attract the buyer's attention.
7. Demonstrate how different colors and tints can be mixed by using only red, blue, yellow and white inks.
8. Using a bright color of ink, show how it can be subdued by the addition of small amounts of black ink.
9. Invite a camera operator from a local printing plant to explain how color separations are made.

Unit 15
PHOTOGRAPHY

Objectives

This unit provides an introduction to photography as a hobby and as a process which produces illustration material for graphic arts.

Through the unit, you will be introduced to the basics of photography. You will learn how to operate a camera, develop film, make a print and how to use an enlarger to make an enlarged print.

Photography is a big part of the graphic arts. Without it, most modern printing techniques would not be possible. Photography is also a very popular hobby.

PHOTOGRAPHS

A photograph, Fig. 15-1, is a picture that has been made by light striking a light-sensitive material. Photographs can be made in black and white or in full color.

Several things are essential to start the picture that will end up as a finished photograph:
1. There must be enough light to record the subject or scene being photographed.

2. There must be a piece of light-sensitive film to receive and record the light rays. (Actually, light-sensitive materials could be attached to cloth, glass or other materials. However, film, being flexible and rugged, has proven to be the most practical.)
3. A portable container must be used which will protect the film and expose it to light when a picture is taken.

NATURE OF LIGHT

If you were to open a roll of film in darkness and then develop it, nothing would appear on the film. There would be no image. Why? Because there was no light to affect the light-sensitive crystals in the film.

Again, if film is exposed to light coming at it from all directions, it would not record an image. When developed the film would be an overall gray or black. Light must be carefully directed so that the rays are not scattered.

FILM

Film, Fig. 15-2, is a strip of flexible plastic. It has a dried and toughened gelatin coating on one side. Suspended in the

Fig. 15-1. A photograph is a picture that has been made by light striking light-sensitive film.

Fig. 15-2. Film is made in a great number of sizes, types and "speeds." A film's speed indicates its sensitivity to light.

gelatin coating are millions of light-sensitive crystals made from silver compounds. The light-sensitive crystals undergo a chemical change when exposed to light. This light-sensitive coating is called the EMULSION. See Fig. 15-3.

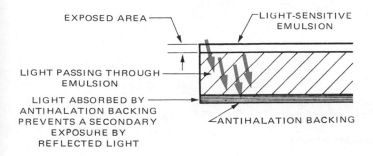

Fig. 15-3. Greatly enlarged cross section of typical black and white film. Film for color photography is much more complex.

CAMERA

It is the CAMERA which controls the light. See Fig. 15-4. Several parts are necessary for proper control. See Fig. 15-5.

There must be a light-tight box which holds the film and protects it from unwanted light. There must be an opening at the front. This opening is fitted with a plastic or glass LENS whose purpose is to direct the light rays in an orderly fashion so they will make a sharp picture on the film. In other words, it focuses light entering the camera so that it falls on the film as a sharp image.

Fig. 15-4. Camera and film are required to start process that results in finished photograph. Two popular modern cameras are shown. One uses two lenses — one for viewing, one for exposing film.

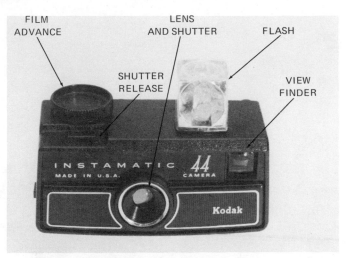

Fig. 15-5. A camera holds the film and protects it from light until photograph is to be taken. Top. Lens and shutter control light which exposes film. Bottom. Camera back provides access to load and unload film. Some display exposure information.

A SHUTTER is located in the same opening with the lens. Its job is to control the amount of light coming through the lens and striking the film. When it is closed, no light can enter the camera. When opened, it will keep track of time and close within seconds or even a fraction of a second.

A SHUTTER RELEASE controls the shutter, When pressed, it causes the shutter to snap open. A timer in the shutter measures the time elapse and closes the shutter again.

A FILM ADVANCE lever or knob is fitted to the camera to advance the film after each exposure to light. It simply rolls up the exposed section on a spool and draws an unexposed section into place to take the next picture.

A VIEWFINDER on the top or back of the camera helps the photographer to COMPOSE the picture. Composing is making sure all of the subject will appear on the film. After the scene has been composed, the shutter release is tripped. The shutter opens to expose the film. Fig. 15-5 shows a front and back view of a camera.

Fig. 15-6. Many types of cameras are manufactured. From left. Single lens reflex, twin lens reflex, inexpensive Instamatic, pocket size Instamatic.

TYPES OF CAMERAS

Many types of cameras are made, Fig. 15-6. Popular units intended for general use include:

1. Single lens reflex camera (commonly called as SLR). The scene to be photographed is viewed through the same lens used to expose the film.

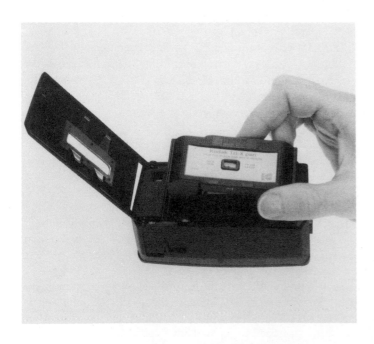

Fig. 15-7. Dropping film into an Instamatic camera. Film cartridge automatically programs camera for type of film being used.

2. Twin lens reflex camera. The scene is viewed through the top lens while the film is exposed through the bottom lens.
3. Simple box-type camera with fixed focus (lens does not move for distance settings). An example of these is the Instamatic series made by Kodak.

Cameras intended for professional and special use include:

1. Press camera. This type is used by newspaper photographers who want a larger negative size for maximum detail. Many use 4 x 5 in. film. However, the press camera is not as popular as it once was. Many photographers now prefer more compact units which will use 120 (2 1/4 x 2 1/4 in.) or 35 mm film.
2. View camera. This type gets its name from the fact that it is focused by viewing the subject in a ground glass. It is used in studios or on location when correction of distortion is important.

The novice (new) photographer should start with a simple camera like the one shown in Fig. 15-5. This camera has fixed controls. The photographer need only be concerned with composing and taking the picture.

The film for this camera comes in a preloaded cartridge. It is just dropped into the camera, Fig. 15-7. The camera takes satisfactory photographs under general light conditions.

When the camera is loaded, it is ready to take the first picture. Space does not permit going into all photo-taking aspects. It is suggested that you read one of the many good photography handbooks.

TAKING THE PHOTOGRAPH

To make an exposure, the shutter is opened briefly (usually 1/60 or 1/125 sec.). Light, which is a form of energy, strikes and changes the light-sensitive crystals in the emulsion. The degree of change depends upon the amount of light striking the film. The more light striking the emulsion, the greater the effect.

There is no immediate change in the emulsion where it has been struck by the light. However, there has been a CHEMICAL change. The chemical change can be made visible. This is done by processing the film in a solution called a DEVELOPER. The developer alters the tiny crystals in the film emulsion. It changes them to pure silver which is black. The image is formed by these blackened crystals.

The resulting film image is called a NEGATIVE, Fig. 15-8. As the name suggests, it is a reversal of the tones of the image photographed.

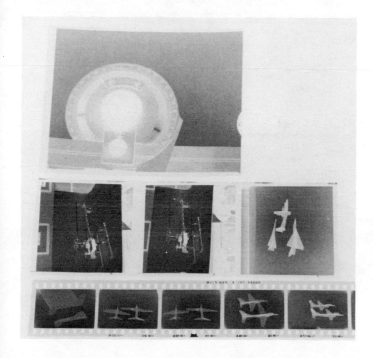

Fig. 15-8. Camera produces negative from which photograph is made. Light portions of the negative are the dark areas of the subject.

DEVELOPING FILM

Film must be developed in complete darkness. The film is placed into the developer for a period of time. The exact time is determined by:
1. The kind of film.
2. Type of film.
3. Temperature of the developer.

Some of the developer remains on the film when it is removed from the solution. If not neutralized, the film will become OVERDEVELOPED. The exposed areas will become too dark.

Developing action can be halted by putting the film in a STOP BATH. Developer can also be neutralized with water if used as specified by the film manufacturer.

The developer brings out the latent (hidden) image on the film. But the image is not permanent. All of the crystals in the emulsion were not fully affected by the light when the picture was taken. They are still light-sensitive. The light-sensitive crystals will become black metallic silver if exposed to light. They must be removed from the emulsion. If not removed, the negative will become completely black. No image will appear.

A FIXING SOLUTION or FIXER will prevent this from occurring. The film must be placed in the fixing solution right after it is removed from the stop bath. The fixing solution converts the underexposed light-sensitive crystals into a water soluble compound. This compound can be removed by washing the film in running water.

Technically, developing film is a complex chemical process. It has been greatly simplified for amateur photographers. They can produce quality negatives by carefully following the film manufacturer's directions. The negative is the first step in making a finished photograph.

HOW TO DEVELOP BLACK AND WHITE PHOTOGRAPHIC FILM

Start by carefully studying the information sheet that comes with each roll of film. It includes development times for several different types of developing solutions. The sheet also shows how developer temperature can affect the development time. Fixing and washing times are also specified.

SETTING UP TO DEVELOP FILM

Secure the required developing chemicals, Fig. 15-9. Prepare them in the amounts you will need. Caution: Always pour acid into water to avoid danger of violent reactions. The chemicals and water must be measured carefully, Fig. 15-10. Place enough chemicals for your developing job in suitable plastic containers, Fig. 15-11.

Fig. 15-9. Secure chemicals listed on the information sheet supplied with the film. If chemicals are in powder form, carefully mix them according to the instructions on the chemical packet.

Fig. 15-10. Measure chemicals and water carefully using graduates such as shown. Scales are marked in both metric and conventional measure.

Fig. 15-11. Have the correct amount of each developing chemical in easy-to-handle plastic bottles.

Processing chemicals that are too warm or too cold can be brought to correct developing temperatures by placing them in a water bath as shown in Fig. 15-12.

Arrange the film, developing reel, film tank, tank top, device for opening the film and a pair of scissors on the work area, Fig. 15-13. Place them so you can easily find them since you will be working in the dark.

Fig. 15-12. Bring developing chemicals to temperature recommended on film information sheet. Use warm water if chemicals are below the desired temperature, ice cubes if chemicals are too warm.

Fig. 15-13. Arrange tools and equipment on work area so you can easily find them in the dark.

Fig. 15-14. If this is your first experience in developing film, practice loading developing reel in the light. Use scrap film.

Note: You may have some trouble the first time you load the developing reel. To prevent this, use scrap film and practice load the reel several times in the light, Fig. 15-14. Then try loading the reel in the dark. When loading can be done without difficulty, continue with the following steps:

1. Turn out the light. Film must be removed from the spool and loaded in the developing tank in complete darkness.
2. Open the film magazine, Fig. 15-15. Remove the film. Trim both ends of the film with scissors.
3. Load the film on the developing reel. *Hold the film by the edges. The film emulsion can be scratched or marked with finger prints if you do not.*
4. Place the loaded reel in the developing tank. Put on the tank lid. Lights may now be turned on.

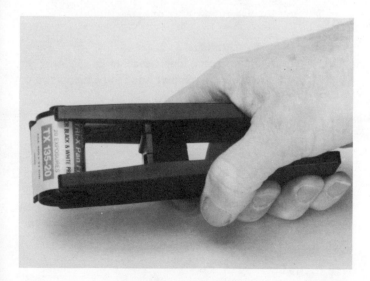

Fig. 15-15. Open film casette in complete darkness using special tool. After film has been placed in developing tank, remaining operations can be done with room lights on.

Fig. 15-16. Pour premeasured developer into tank.

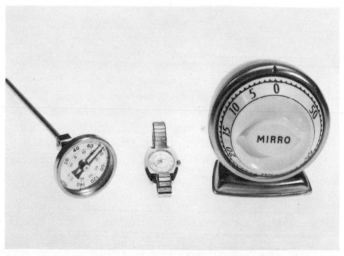

Fig. 15-17. Length of developing time is determined by developer temperature. Use accurate thermometer and timing device.

5. Pour the premeasured developer into the tank, Fig. 15-16. Start the TIMER, Fig. 15-17. Developing time depends upon developer temperature. Check sheet furnished with film for this information.
6. Start agitating the developer immediately, Fig. 15-18. This is done as recommended for the tank being used. Agitate for the first 30 seconds. Then agitate for 5 seconds every 30 seconds.
   Agitation is very important. If too little is done, spots and streaks will appear on the film.
7. When about 45 seconds remain of the developing time, pour out the developer. It is not necessary to discard the developing chemical after each use. Follow instructions from the manufacturer.
8. Fill the tank with the stop bath right away. Agitate the solution. Return the stop bath to its container for reuse. Use a funnel to prevent spilling. If water was used as a stop bath, discard it.
9. Pour the fixer into the tank without delay. Fixing time for the film being developed is included on the film information sheet. Agitate the solution every 30 seconds.

Fig. 15-18. Agitate the film as recommended on information sheet.

Fig. 15-19. Cut developed film into lengths of several frames and store them in plastic or glassine envelopes.

Fig. 15-20. Negative, top, reverses tones in scene below. Light areas appear dark on the negative while dark areas appear light.

10. Return the fixer to the proper container for reuse.

Caution: These chemicals can cause severe skin irritation. They will also damage your clothing. HANDLE THEM WITH CARE. Wash your hands after the developing process is finished. Wear safety glasses when working with chemicals.

11. Open the developing tank.

12. Wash the film in running water for at least 30 minutes. Washing time can be shortened by washing the film in Permawash or a similar solution.

13. Treat the film with a WETTING AGENT. This prevents water spots from forming on the film. Hang the film in a dust-free area to dry. If you have no wetting agent, wipe the film with a sponge specifically designed for photo work. *Avoid using cloth, paper towels, squeegee or other types of sponges.* They will scratch the film.

14. When the film is dry, cut it into lengths of several frames, Fig. 15-19. Store them in plastic or glassine envelopes until you are ready to make prints. Do not cut the film into single frames. This makes the film hard to handle while printing.

15. Clean up the developing area. Wash all equipment with clean water. Let it dry in a dust free area.

PRINTING PHOTOGRAPHS

Producing a suitable negative is only part of photography. Look at a negative and you will see that the tones of the original scene are reversed, Fig. 15-20.

The next part of the photographic process is called PRINTING. It transfers an image, using light, from the negative to light-sensitized paper. Light-sensitive papers are manufactured in many sizes and thicknesses. They are also available with different surface finishes and contrasts (inten-

sity of tones in the picture). All papers of this type must be put through developing baths to produce an image. Another type of paper requires no developing and can be used without darkroom conditions.

HOW PRINTING WORKS

When light passes through the negative, it falls on light-sensitive paper. The light chemically changes particles in the paper. When placed in developer, those light-struck particles turn dark. Other particles not exposed to light are not affected. Thus, the light causes the paper to reproduce the image on the negative.

THE PRINT

When the exposed paper is developed, fixed and washed it becomes a PRINT. (Fixing is done with a chemical bath that takes away the light sensitivity and makes the image permanent.) Prints can be made by either of two methods: Contact printing and projection printing.

CONTACT PRINTING

No expensive equipment is required for contact printing. The negative is placed atop a piece of printing paper and this "sandwich" is exposed to light.

Two types of paper are used for contact printing. One type must be handled in darkness or under approved safelights both before and after exposure. Development must take place under the same dark conditions.

The second type of paper may be used under normal room light and needs no chemicals for developing. Known as PRINTING OUT paper, it is found under the trade name, Kodak Studio Proof F. To use printing out paper:

1. Place the negative on a sheet of Studio Proof F paper emulsion-to-emulsion. (On the paper, the emulsion side is shiny; on the film it is the dull side.)
2. Place negative and paper between two pieces of glass that are hinged along one side. The negative must be on top as shown in Fig. 15-21. Use tape for the hinge.

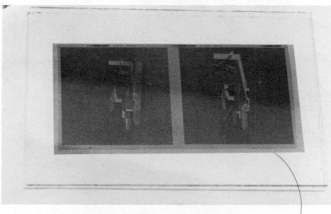

Fig. 15-21. Top. Place negative, emulsion (dull side) down, on top of print paper. Bottom. Place film and print paper between two pieces of glass so that paper and film are held tightly together.

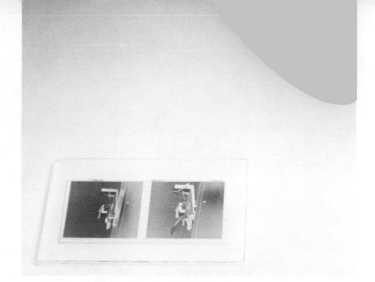

Fig. 15-22. Expose film and print paper to direct sunlight or to a bright light.

3. Expose the print to direct sunlight or to a bright light. See Fig. 15-22. Be sure the negative is toward the light. Determine exposure time by watching the border around each negative. When the borders are very dark the exposure is complete. If you wish the image to be permanent, continue through the remaining steps.
4. Immediately after exposure, immerse the print paper in a rapid fixer. This is important to make the image permanent. Fixing solution should be at room temperature. Leave the print in the rapid fixer for 5 minutes, Fig. 15-23.

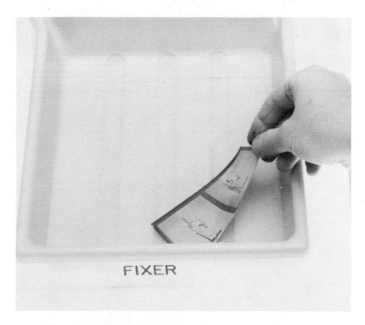

Fig. 15-23. Place exposed print paper in rapid fixer for at least 5 minutes. This will make image permanent on print paper. If not fixed, image will gradually fade away.

5. After fixing, wash the print for 10 minutes in clean, running water at room temperature.
6. Sponge off excess water. Allow the finished print to dry face up on clean white paper, Fig. 15-24.
Note: Since the fixing solution tends to bleach the image, exposure time may need to be increased. Trial and error will help you decide the best exposure time.

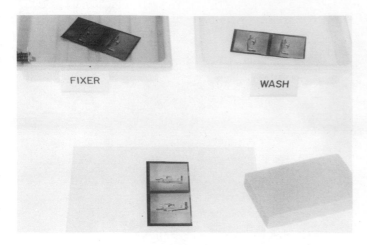

Fig. 15-24. After washing print in water, sponge away excess moisture. Allow prints to dry face up on clean white paper.

PROJECTION PRINTING

Projection printing is usually called ENLARGING. It has several advantages:

1. The photographer has a great deal of print control. Minor errors often can be controlled or removed. Under-exposed areas on a negative can be lightened by DODGING. Over-exposed areas can be darkened by BURNING-IN.
2. The photographer can improve the composition of a print by CROPPING or MASKING, Fig. 15-25.
3. The print can be made larger than the negative.

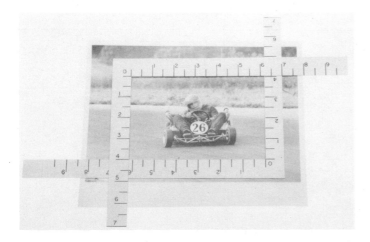

Fig. 15-25. Scene can be made more interesting by cropping which excludes unwanted areas.

HOW TO MAKE AN ENLARGEMENT

Print enlarging requires an ENLARGER, Fig. 15-26. The enlarger has:

1. A light source.
2. A lens that can focus.
3. A way to hold the negative (NEGATIVE CARRIER).
4. A device to hold the print paper (HOLDER or EASEL).
5. A method for adjusting the distance between the lens and the print paper.

Fig. 15-26. An enlarger. Light is projected through negative and lens produces enlargement below on easel.

An enlarger does not have a shutter like a camera. A timer may be employed to control exposure time. The timer turns the enlarger light on, measures the time in seconds and then turns the light off. See Fig. 11-27.

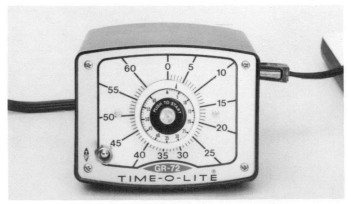

Fig. 15-27. Timer turns light source on and off to control exposure time.

HOW TO USE THE ENLARGER

Making an enlargement is not difficult. However, good prints require cleanliness, care and patience.

To make an enlargement:

1. Check over the enlarger. If it has a glass negative carrier, remove dust and fingerprints from the glass.
2. Clean the negative. Remove dust from both sides. Use a brush designed for the job or dry, compressed air. Refer to Fig. 15-28.

Fig. 15-28. Clean dust from both sides of negative with a clean, soft brush, a burst of dry, compressed air or with an electrically charged brush designed for cleaning negatives.

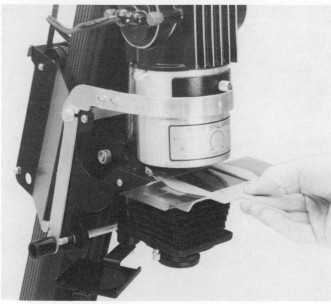

Fig. 15-29. Loading negative in enlarger. Top. Place negative in negative carrier with emulsion (dull) side of film towards lens. Bottom. Slip negative carrier into enlarger. Avoid touching negative surfaces with your fingers.

Fig. 15-30. Safe light produces illumination that does not expose print paper. Information sheet packed with print paper will indicate proper color safelight and how far away it must be from print paper.

3. Place the negative in the negative carrier, Fig. 15-29, with the emulsion side towards the lens. The image should be upside down. If this is done, the subject will be upright when viewed on the easel.
4. Lay a piece of white paper in the paper holder (easel). Place the holder on the baseboard of the enlarger.
5. Turn off the darkroom light. a SAFE LIGHT, Fig. 15-30, may be turned on. Be sure the safe light is recommended for the print paper being used.
6. Turn on the enlarger light source. Raise or lower the enlarger head until the image is the desired size. The lens should be wide open. See Fig. 15-31. This makes the image brighter and easier to see. Focus the lens until the image is at maximum sharpness. There are tools to help you in focusing, Fig. 15-32.

No lens performs best wide open. Stop the enlarger lens down to f/8 or smaller to make the exposure.

Switch off the enlarger light source. Replace the paper in the paper holder with a strip or sheet of sensitized print paper. You are now ready to make a test for proper exposure. (Exposure time will depend on many things, paper sensitivity, lens opening being used, negative density and how large the image is to be made.)

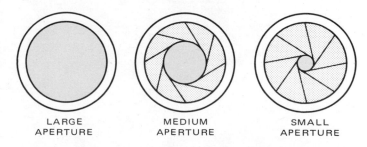

LARGE APERTURE   MEDIUM APERTURE   SMALL APERTURE

Fig. 15-31. Enlarger lenses, like more expensive camera lenses, have diaphragms which can change the size of the opening from wide open to a pinpoint hole. Size of this opening is given in f-stops.

Fig. 15-32. Magnifying device is used to aid in focusing enlarger for maximum image sharpness.

Turn on the enlarger light source. Expose the test strip as follows:

1. Expose the entire strip for 2 seconds.
2. Cover one fourth of the strip with cardboard. Expose for 4 more seconds.
3. Cover half of the strip. Expose for 8 more seconds.
4. Cover three quarters of the strip. Expose the remainder for an additional 16 seconds.

Each exposure doubles the previous exposure — 2, 4, 8 and 16 seconds. See Fig. 15-33.

Develop the test strip. Examine it closely. Select the exposure time that will give the best print. If none of the exposures is suitable, run another test strip. This time use longer or shorter exposure times. Exposure times will vary according to how fast (sensitive to light) the paper is. When satisfied with an exposure time, make your enlargement.

PRINT PAPERS

Print paper is made by many manufacturers. For best print results, develop each kind of paper as recommended by its manufacturer.

Print papers come in different weights (thickness), surface textures and contrasts.

1. Weight. Print paper weights include LIGHT, MEDIUM and HEAVY. Lightweight paper is used for economy. Heavy-

15-33. Test strip showing various exposure times to help determine the best exposure time for negative being enlarged.

Fig. 15-34. Extreme tonal values (very light and very dark areas) indicate that a contrasty negative was used to produce this print.

weight paper is the best choice if the finished print is to be handled a great deal.

2. Surface texture. GLOSSY print paper has a shiny surface. SEMI-MATTE print paper has a slightly glossy surface. MATTE finish paper has no gloss or sheen. Some print papers are made with finishes that resemble silk, canvas, burlap, etc.

3. Contrast. Printing papers can control the contrast on prints. A HARD (high contrast) paper will add contrast to the print tones. It is used when there is not much contrast (little difference between dark and light areas) on a negative. A CONTRASTY negative has extreme differences between the light and dark areas. It should be printed on SOFT (low contrast) paper, Fig. 15-34. The degree of contrast is shown on the print paper package. It will be S (soft), M (medium), H (hard), EH (extra hard) or UH (ultra hard). S is the highest contrast while UH offers extremely low contrast. Most negatives will produce satisfactory prints on M paper.

Note: Some print paper makers use numbers to indicate the degree of contrast. The paper is labeled "No. 1" (least contrast) to "No. 6" (most contrast). Most negatives will produce satisfactory prints on No. 2 or No. 3 paper.

MULTIPLE or VARIABLE contrast paper has different ranges of contrast built into the sensitized surface. However, FILTERS must be used between the lens and the print paper to control the degree of contrast, Fig. 15-35.

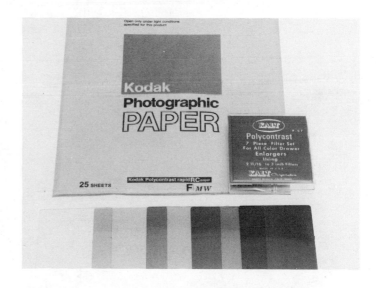

Fig. 15-35. Filters (plastic sheets of varying degrees of value are used to control print contrast on multiple or variable contrast print papers.

HOW TO DEVELOP PRINT PAPER

There are many kinds of print paper. Space does not permit explaining how to use all of them. The following instructions are for using KODABROME RC paper, Fig. 15-36.

Read the information sheet that comes with the print paper. Kodabrome RC paper is resin (Plastic) coated. The coating is water resistant. It has a shorter processing and drying time than other papers.

Fig. 15-36. Carefully read information sheet that comes with the print paper. Following these instructions will help you produce better prints.

A safe light with an OC (light amber) filter and a 15 watt bulb can be used with this paper. Locate the light at least 4 ft. from the work area.

Three trays are needed: one for DEVELOPER, one for STOP BATH and one for FIXER, Fig. 15-37. Two pairs of print tongs are needed. Since developer can be ruined if contaminated by the stop bath or fixer, use one pair of tongs in nothing but the developer. The second pair can be used in both the stop bath and fixer.

Dektol and D-72 developers are suitable for this paper if mixed 1:2. That means one part developer and two parts water. Expose the print paper. Slide the paper quickly into the developer so the entire sheet becomes wet at the same time. Keep the developer at 68 deg. F (20 °C). Recommended developing time is one minute with constant agitation. Observe the print carefully as it is developing. Do not allow it to become too dark.

Remove the print from the developer. Holding it above the developer tray, let it drain briefly. Transfer it to the stop bath for five seconds. *Do not allow the tongs to come into contact with the stop bath.* Maintain stop bath temperature at 65—75 deg. F (18 — 24 °C).

Transfer the print to the fixer. *Use the second pair of tongs.* The print should remain in the fixer bath for 2 minutes. *Agitate the prints by interleafing them frequently during fixing.* Maintain fixer bath at 65 — 75 deg. F (18 — 24 °C). See Fig. 15-38.

Resin coated (RC) paper needs only 4 minutes of washing in running water. Prolonged washing is not recommended.

For fast drying, remove surface water with a soft, wet viscous sponge, cloth, blotter or squeegee, Fig. 15-39. Prints are dried at room temperature.

Note: Other types of print paper may need longer fixing and washing times. Some need to be washed for up to an hour. Drying may have to be done on a PRINT DRYER, Fig. 15-40. *Never try to dry resin coated papers on a dryer. The heat will melt the coating and the print will stick to the dryer surface. Also, RC prints need not be ferrotyped.*

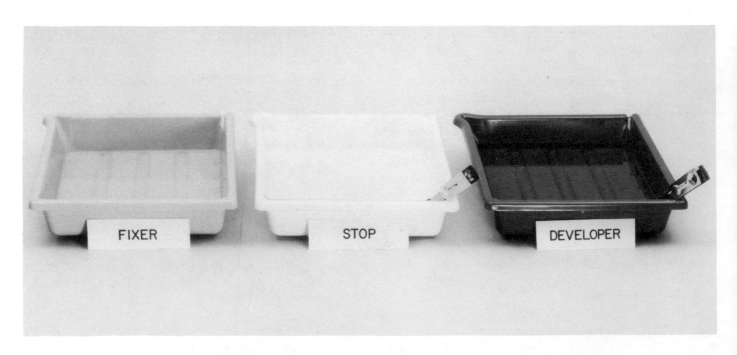

Fig. 15-37. Three trays are needed for developing prints. Two print tongs are required to avoid contaminating developer. Some photographers use a third tongs to remove prints from fixer.

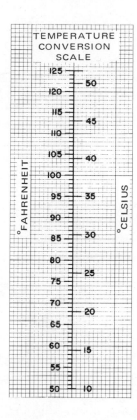

Fig. 15-38. Temperature conversion scale compares Celsius and Fahrenheit temperatures.

Fig. 15-40. A print dryer. In normal operation the canvas is stretched across the dryer surface to hold prints flat during drying.

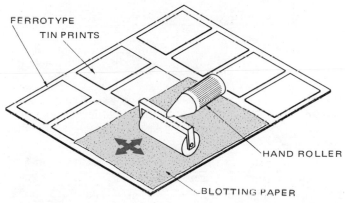

Fig. 15-41. Glossy prints are placed on the tin print side down. Blotter is placed over them and hand roller is run lightly over blotter to absorb excess moisture. Prints must be pressed against polished metal surface to remove bubbles of air between print and plate surface.

Fig. 15-39. Remove surface water from prints with sponge designed for photographic purposes.

Prints that are to have a glossy surface can be rolled onto a FERROTYPE PLATE, Fig. 15-41. The ferrotype plate, also called a ferrotype tin, is a piece of sheet metal (brass or steel) with a polished chromium plated surface on only one side.

To process these prints, place them face down on the polished face of the ferrotype plate. Lay a blotter over the prints and run a hand roller lightly over the blotter. This removes the excess moisture. Roll the prints again applying some additional pressure. This will remove the air bubble trapped between the print surface and the tin. The better the contact between the face of the paper and the polished surface, the better the gloss finish will be.

Glossy prints placed on a ferrotype plate can be dried in a dryer or stood on edge to dry naturally. When dry, the prints will lift away from the ferrotype.

After prints are made, it is good practice to discard the developer. However, if it is not exhausted or has not been used to develop many prints it can be saved for future use. *Do not return it to the same bottle with fresh, unused developer.* Return stop bath and fixer to storage bottles. Be careful not to spill or splash the chemicals around the darkroom.

Wash trays, tongs and ferrotype tin (if used) with clean water to remove traces of chemicals or dirt. Dry them and return to storage. Wash your hands thoroughly with soap and water to remove chemicals.

To avoid contamination of printing paper, never handle the dry paper with darkroom chemicals on the hands. Carefully wipe up all spills and wash with clean water to avoid chemical contamination of the darkroom.

TEST YOUR KNOWLEDGE — UNIT 15

1. A photograph is a picture that has been made by _____.

MATCHING TEST. Match the terms in the first column with the definitions in the second column. Place the letter of the definition in the appropriate blank. *Do not write in the text.*

2. ____ Camera.
3. ____ Lens.
4. ____ Shutter.
5. ____ Shutter release.
6. ____ Film advance lever.
7. ____ Viewfinder.

a. Advances a section of unexposed film into place to take the next picture.
b. Located in the same opening as the lens.
c. Controls the shutter.
d. Lets the photographer see what will be in the photograph.
e. A light-tight box.
f. Focuses light as it comes into the camera so that it will form a sharp image on the film.

8. What is film?
9. Film must be processed in complete darkness. True or false?
10. The film image brought out during processing is called a _____ because it is a _____ of the _____ photographed.
11. After film has been exposed, it is processed in a solution called a _____. From this solution it goes into a _____ to stop developing action. Finally, the film is placed in _____.
12. The next step in the photographic process is to make a positive from the processed film called a _____.
13. Prints can be made by _____ and _____ printing methods.
14. Why must dust be removed from film when it is used to make prints?
15. What is a safe light?
16. A test strip is made to determine proper _____.
17. What three properties must you look for in print paper?
18. A ferrotype tin is (record the correct answer):
    a. A light-tight container for holding print paper.
    b. A polished flat sheet used for drying glossy prints.
    c. A tray for developing solutions.
    d. A polished surface for drying resin-coated printing paper.
    e. Used in place of a print dryer.

THINGS TO DO

1. Secure a simple camera. Before inserting film, examine the camera. Locate the shutter, lens, shutter release, film advance lever and viewfinder. *Caution: Do not touch the lens or shutter. Should the lens be touched accidentally, clean it with tissue and cleaner especially made for this purpose. Do not use your handkerchief, paper towel or facial tissues. They will scratch and ruin the lens.*
2. Expose a roll of film (black and white). Develop the exposed film.
3. Make contact prints from your exposed film.
4. Examine the contact prints carefully. Select one or two of the best and make 8 by 10 in. enlargements.
5. Experiment by using different types of black and white film in your camera. Prepare a report on how they differ.
6. Make a series of enlargements using different types and grades of print papers. Arrange a display of the prints. Discuss the differences in paper with your instructor. Arrange to have the display exhibited at school.
7. Make a simple pinhole camera. Use the plans in the workbook for this text. Expose and develop the film. NOTE: you may have to take several photographs to determine the proper exposure time.
8. Plan a photo contest for your class. Make a list of at least three print categories. For example: people, scenes in your school, familiar things, crazy things, home, etc.
9. Display the prints. Judging should be done by outside professional photographers. Awards can be ribbons and/or certificates made in the graphic arts laboratory.
10. Visit the studio of a professional photographer. Report the trip to the class.
11. Have a professional photographer talk to your class on career opportunities.
12. Give a report on light meters.
13. Give a demonstration on lighting for photographic purposes.
14. Demonstrate the various artificial light sources used for photographic work.
15. Demonstrate how some color films are developed.
16. Demonstrate how color prints are made from color negatives.
17. Demonstrate how color prints are made from color transparencies.
18. Have a newspaper photographer talk to your class about his or her work.

Unit 16
PAPERS AND PAPERMAKING

Objectives

This unit explains how paper is made and how to identify different kinds of paper.

After reading the text and studying the illustrations in this unit you will understand how machine made papers are manufactured. You will also learn how to make paper by employing hand operations.

Thousands of different kinds of printing paper are manufactured, Fig. 16-1. The range of thicknesses (weights), finishes and colors is great. By the year 2000 it is estimated we will be using 100 million tons of paper each year.

HOW PAPER IS MADE

Although some papers are made from rags, most papermaking material comes from trees, Fig. 16-2. Many types of trees are used in papermaking. If we manage our forests properly and do not waste paper, we should have a ready supply.

Fig. 16-1. A few of the many thousands of different kinds of printing paper that are available to the graphic arts industry.

Fig. 16-2. Most papers begin as trees.   (Hammermill Paper Co.)

At the tree farm, loggers fell the trees and cut them into 8-ft. logs. The logs are hauled to the paper mill by truck, rail or ship, Fig. 16-3.

Workers weigh and grade the logs at the receiving station. Other workers feed them into a rotating DRUM DEBARKER, Fig. 16-4. The tumbling action of the drum removes the bark. In some mills high pressure water jets do this job.

Cleaned and debarked logs are ready to be made into pulp. The wood is converted into pulp in two ways:
1. MECHANICALLY.
2. CHEMICALLY.

Fig. 16-3. Logs for papermaking are received at this paper manufacturer by boat, rail and truck.

Fig. 16-4. This debarking machine is 67 ft. long and 12 ft. in diameter. It strips the bark from the logs by friction.   (Hammermill Paper Co.)

MECHANICALLY MADE PAPER PULP

Pulp made mechanically is called GROUNDWOOD. Huge grinding wheels, Fig. 16-5, chew up the logs into small pieces. Groundwood is the least expensive pulp. Paper made from it soon yellows and deteriorates (falls apart). For this reason it is used for disposable products such as newspapers, cheap magazines and paper towels. These articles do not need to have a long life.

CHEMICALLY MADE PAPER PULP

To make pulp chemically, cleaned and debarked logs go through a CHIPPER, Fig. 16-6. Here they are reduced to 3/4 in. square chips.

Screening removes splinters and sawdust before the clean and uniform chips are blown onto huge outdoor storage piles. Hardwood chips and softwood chips are stored separately.

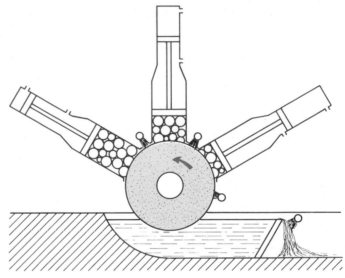

Fig. 16-5. Groundwood pulp, used in making inexpensive papers is prepared by feeding logs against large grinding wheels.

The long fibers of soft wood such as pine and spruce, give paper strength and tear resistance. Short fibers from hardwoods (oak, maple and beech) are added in varying quantities. They provide bulk, smoothness and opacity to the paper.

Long CONVEYORS, Fig. 16-7, carry the chips back to the plant to be made into pulp. Chips are steam heated and mixed with WHITE LIQUOR, a chemical solution of caustic soda and sodium sulfide.

REMOVING LIGNIN

This mixture is pumped to the top of a 23 story DIGESTER, Fig. 16-8. Here it passes through several cooking stages. LIGNIN is dissolved and removed from the wood

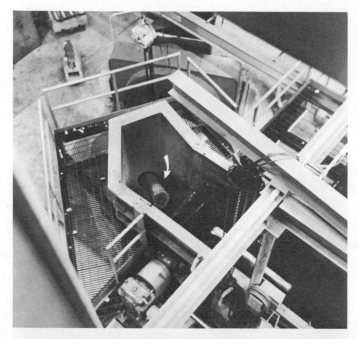

Fig. 16-6. Several steps in preparation of chemically made pulp. Top. Chipper chews logs (arrow) into chips. Bottom. Logs are cut into 3/4 in. square chips. (Hammermill Paper Co.)

Fig. 16-7. Wood chips on a conveyor are on their way into the paper mill. (Westvaco Corp.)

Fig. 16-8. Continuous digester can produce 600 tons of wood pulp daily. (Westvaco Corp.)

during the three hour cook. (Lignin is the natural adhesive that holds wood fibers together.)

The cooked chips are washed just before they leave the digester. The spent chemicals, now called BLACK LIQUOR, return to a chemical recovery plant. There, certain processes clean and restore them to full strength for reuse.

Chips feed into the digester and pulp is withdrawn continuously. The pulp comes from the digester in a light shade of brown. It is about the same color as the familiar grocery bag.

But, to make printing papers, the pulp must be bleached white. This takes place in a series of stages, Fig. 16-9.

When the pulp has been bleached to a snowy white, it is ready for the paper mill. Each stage in converting logs to pulp requires great amounts of clean water.

Refining the pulp

The pulp is not quite ready to be made into paper. Bleached wood fibers are like miniature drinking straws. Smooth, hollow and fairly rigid, the fibers cannot lock together to form a strong paper. They must be cut and shredded to break them down further.

Fig. 16-9. Wood pulp is being bleached to a snowy white before it goes to the paper mill. (Hammermill Paper Co.)

Fig. 16-10. Refining is the last step in preparing pulp so it can be made into paper. Coloring matter, sizing and fillers are added to the pulp during the refining operation. (Hammermill Paper Co.)

This operation is done in a REFINER, Fig. 16-10. At the same time coloring matter, sizing and fillers are added to the bleached pulp. The kind and amount of these materials determines the type of paper that will be made.

The prepared stock (called FURNISH) is now ready to be made into paper. It contains about 99.5 percent water. Papermaking machines are huge. Some are longer than a football field, Fig. 16-11. A large section of the machine is designed to dry the paper.

Furnish is flowed from a headbox onto a moving fine mesh FOURDRINIER wire screen, Fig. 16-12. The endless wire screen, moving at speeds up to 30 mph, shakes back and forth to weave and mat the fibers together as the water drains off.

The mat of paper (called a WEB) is dried by traveling it up and down over as many as 50 steam heated DRYING ROLLS, Fig. 16-13. But its surface remains rough. Many papers must be given a smooth, glossy finish. This can be done by passing the web between polished steel CALENDAR ROLLS, Fig. 16-14. A smooth finish can also be applied by coating the paper with a thin film of clay or plastic, Fig. 16-15. Some grades of paper receive as many as five separate coating applications.

Papermaking is a complex operation that uses the skills of many highly trained craftspeople. The complete operation is shown in Fig. 16-16.

Fig. 16-11. Papermaking machine may be 450 ft. long.

Fig. 16-12. Wet end of a paper machine. At this stage the pulp (called FURNISH) contains about 99.5 percent water. The layer of pulp is supported by a fine screen which moves along toward rollers. (Westvaco Corp.)

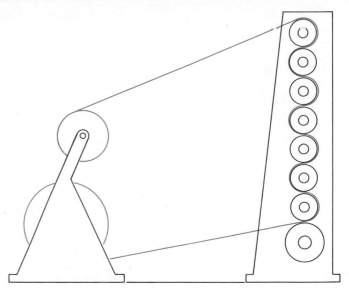

Fig. 16-14. Many papers are given a smooth, glossy finish by passing the web of paper between polished steel calendar rolls.

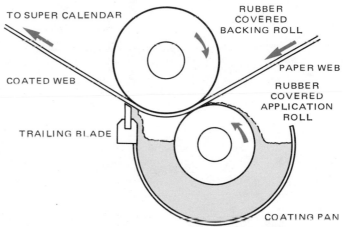

Fig. 16-15. Some papers are coated with a thin film of clay or plastic.

Fig. 16-13. Another view of a papermaking machine. Paper has been dried and surface polished. (Westvaco Corp.)

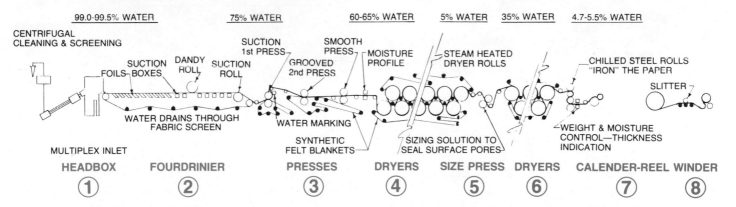

Fig. 16-16. Drawing represents complete papermaking operation. (Hammermill Paper Co.)

1. Headbox spreads pulp and water mix evenly over moving wire.
2. Fine woven screen lets water drain away; pulp is retained; becomes a thin mat.
3. Mat enters wet rollers carried by felt blankets. More water is removed. Smoothing roller flattens mat some more.
4. Steam heated cylinders dry paper to 5 percent moisture.
5. Size press applies 10 percent starch solution to both sides of paper.
6. Second dryer removes moisture applied to sheet in size press.
7. Polished rollers "iron" and control thickness of sheet. Reel winds paper on mandrel.
8. Winder unwinds paper from mandrel, passes sheet across slitter to trim edges and cut paper to final width.

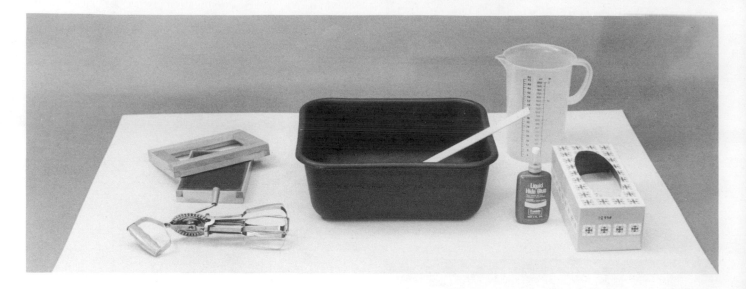

Fig. 16-17. Paper can be handmade in the school's graphic arts lab. Items include hand beater, mold, plastic tub, pitcher of warm water, box of tissues and some glue. A small amount of starch (not shown) is also needed.

Fig. 16-18. Shred 30-40 facial tissues into tub.

Fig. 16-19. Fill tub about three-fourths full of warm water.

MAKING PAPER BY HAND

You can make paper in your school's graphic arts lab. Only simple equipment is needed.

1. Gather the equipment and material. See Fig. 16-17.
2. Make the pulp.
   a. Shred 30 to 40 facial tissues, Fig. 16-18. *Do not use wet strength tissues.*
   b. Place the tissues in a plastic tub that will hold at least 10 qt. of water. Fill the tub about three-fourths full of warm water, Fig. 16-19.
   c. Mix 1 tablespoon of instant starch in 1 cup of water.

Add to the shredded paper and water.
   d. Small amounts of liquid fabric dye may be added to color the paper.
   e. Stir the mixture with an egg beater, Fig. 16-20, or an electric mixer until the mixture is smoothly blended. This forms the pulp.
3. Make the paper. This will require use of the MOLD AND DECKLE. See Fig. 16-21. The deckle has a fine-mesh screen stretched over a light wooden frame. It fits inside the mold.
   a. Dip the mold and deckle into the pulp edge down, as in Fig. 16-22. When it is fully submerged, turn the unit

Fig. 16-20. Stir tissue and water mixture with egg beater until all of tissue has broken down into smooth pulp.

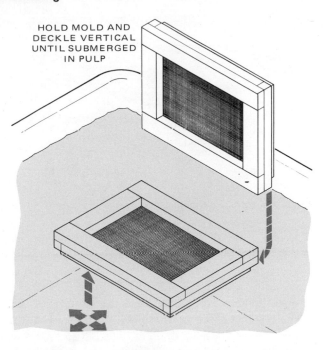

HOLD MOLD AND
DECKLE VERTICAL
UNTIL SUBMERGED
IN PULP

Fig. 16-22. Dip mold and deckle into pulp with a scooping action. Agitate mold so that it will be leveled and solidly packed with pulp as it is lifted from the tub.

Fig. 16-21. Mold and deckle are designed for making paper by hand. They are a "scoop" for gathering up pulp from tub.

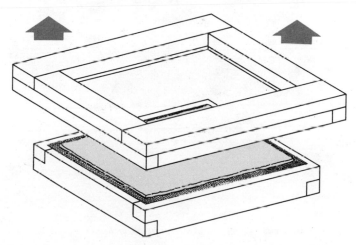

Fig. 16-23. Remove deckle from mold by lifting it straight up.

until the screen in horizontal. Agitate the unit as it is being lifted from the pulp. This distributes the pulp evenly over the wire screen. Continue to hold the mold in a horizontal position as it is lifted from the pulp.

b. Remove the deckle from the mold, Fig. 16-23. Lift straight up.

c. Gently place the mold face down on a piece of damp blotting paper, Fig. 16-24. This operation is called COUCHING (pronounced "kooching").

Fig. 16-24. Mold with deckle removed. It is ready to be placed on a piece of damp blotting paper (see sheet in background) for removal.

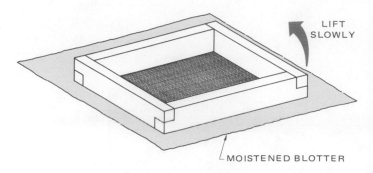

Fig. 16-25. Gently raise the mold. Wet pulp will stick to blotting paper.

d. Gently raise the mold, Fig. 16-25. The newly made sheet will adhere to the blotting paper.

e. Place another damp blotter on top of the newly made paper. Make several additional sheets of paper by repeating the operations. Place the pile of wet sheets and blotting paper on newsprint. Put a board on top of the pile and weight it down, Fig. 16-26, for several minutes. This will help to remove excess moisture.

Fig. 16-26. Weight down pile of wet sheets to remove excess moisture.

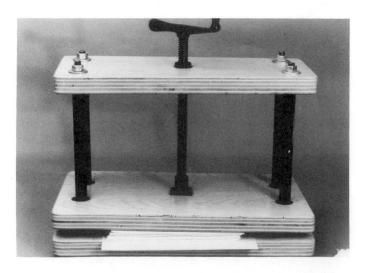

Fig. 16-27. A simple press is also good for removing excess moisture.

Fig. 16-28. Place damp sheet between two sheets of smooth blotting paper and press dry with warm iron.

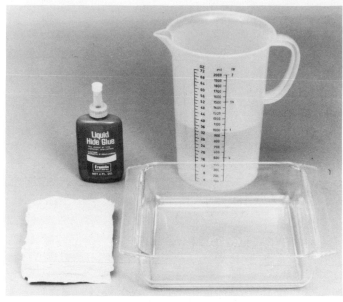

Fig. 16-29. Sizing for paper is made by dissolving liquid hide glue in warm water. Coating is done by dipping paper in the solution.

f. A small press may also be used to remove the moisture. See Fig. 16-27.

g. Place the first damp, newly made sheet between dry blotting paper and press it dry with a warm iron, as in Fig. 16-28.

4. Handmade paper can be used for letterpress and intaglio printing. The sheet must be SIZED if it is to be used for writing purposes. Sizing is a liquid coating that fills the tiny pores of the paper. It stops the pores from soaking up too much ink.

To size the new paper:

a. Dissolve 1 to 2 oz. of liquid hide glue in about 48 oz. of warm water. Pour this glue and water mixture into a clean tray, Fig. 16-29.

b. Quickly dip the sheet into the size.

c. Place the sized sheet on a dry blotter. Cover with a sheet of ledger paper and roll the excess size from the new sheet, Fig. 16-30.

d. Put the size dampened sheet between two pieces of smooth, uncoated paper and press it dry with a hot iron.

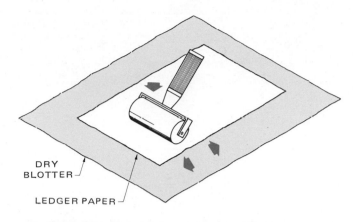

Fig. 16-30. Remove excess sizing by rolling sheet between a dry blotter and a sheet of ledger paper.

Fig. 16-31. Trim edges of paper with scissors or paper cutter.

ISO "A" AND "B" SERIES

SIZE DESIGNATION	TRIMMED SIZE	
	mm	Inches
A0	841 x 1189	33.11 x 46.81
A1	594 x 841	23.39 x 33.11
A2	420 x 594	16.54 x 23.39
A3	297 x 420	11.69 x 16.54
A4	210 x 297	8.27 x 11.69
A5	148 x 210	5.83 x 8.27
A6	105 x 148	4.13 x 5.83
A7	74 x 105	2.91 x 4.13
A8	52 x 74	2.05 x 2.91
A9	37 x 52	1.46 x 2.05
A10	26 x 37	1.02 x 1.46
B0	1000 x 1414	39.37 x 55.67
B1	707 x 1000	27.83 x 39.37
B2	500 x 707	19.68 x 27.83
B3	353 x 500	13.90 x 19.68
B4	250 x 353	9.84 x 13.90
B5	176 x 250	6.93 x 9.84
B6	125 x 176	4.92 x 6.93
B7	88 x 125	3.46 x 4.92
B8	62 x 88	2.44 x 3.46

Fig. 16-32. Table of metric paper sizes. The A series will be used for general printing and stationery. The B series will be used mostly for posters and wall charts.

If preferred, the dampened sheet may be hung up to air dry.

e. Trim the edges of the paper with scissors or paper cutter, Fig. 16-31.

PAPER GRADES

Determining what paper to use for a printing job is not a simple task. Paper mills produce many hundreds of different grades, weights and kinds of papers for printing. The kind of paper used will depend on the intended use of the product. If you examine the paper used in a newspaper, a textbook, a paperback novel and a bible you will note that each is different.

A newspaper, for example is rough looking and the paper tears easily. Pages of a textbook are made of thicker, whiter and glossier paper. The paper must be made to suit the usage. Newspapers are read once and thrown away. Books are reused time after time and the paper must hold up under repeated usage.

To understand paper we must realize that it is classified (separated into groups) in different ways:

1. By size of sheets or width of rolls.
2. By weight which really refers to the thickness. (This is called BASIS WEIGHT.)
3. By kind or grade.

BASIC PAPER SIZES

Each type of printing paper is made (cut) to more than one size. However, one size is known as the standard or BASIC SIZE. In conventional U.S. measure (our inch-pound system) there is a relationship between the basic size and the weight (thickness) designation of paper. This will be seen later.

Paper sizes are given in inches. Some popular standard sizes are: 17 x 22, 17 x 28, 25 x 38, 19 x 24 and 24 x 38.

But the graphic arts industry is slowly shifting to metric sizes. See Fig. 16-32. Paper is being cut to ISO (International Organization for Standardization) sizes. There is an A and B series in metric to fit the needs of all kinds of printing from posters to labels and calling cards.

The main advantage of metric size paper is that all sheets have the same proportion as shown in Fig. 16-33. Small sheets can be cut from larger ones without waste. Also, camera-ready material will fit any size of sheet by simple photographic enlargement or reduction.

BASIS WEIGHT

In conventional measurement, weight (thickness) of paper is based on what a whole ream (500 sheet) will weigh in one certain standard basic size. This is known as the BASIS WEIGHT.

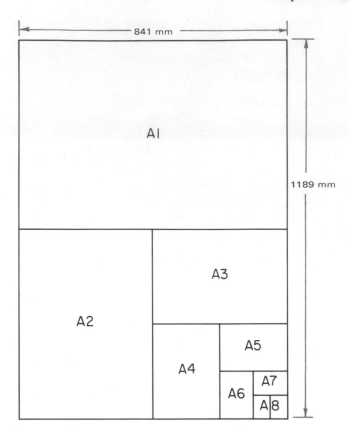

Fig. 16-33. The main advantage of metric sized paper is that all sheets have the same proportions. Each sheet size is double the next smaller size. A 10, not shown, is the smallest metric sheet in the A series.

TYPE OF PAPER	CAN BE USED FOR	BASIC SIZE IN INCHES
Bond	Letterheads, business forms, direct-mail advertising	17 x 22
Book	Books, brochures, pamphlets, direct-mail advertising	25 x 38
Newsprint	Direct-mail advertising, newspapers	24 x 36
Duplicator	Spirit-duplicated materials	17 x 22
Mimeograph	Mimeographed materials	17 x 22

Fig. 16-34. Basic size is a standard size for each kind of paper. This size is not the same for all paper.

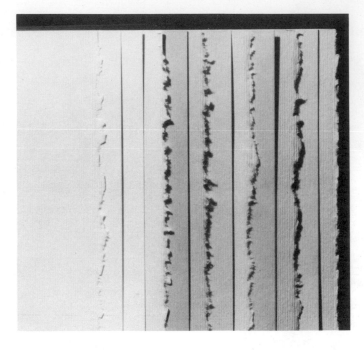

Fig. 16-35. Deckled edge is found on some cover papers.

For example, 500 sheets of 17 x 22 in. BOND paper weigh 20 lb. It is called 20-pound paper because that is its basis weight.

The basis weight is always the weight of the basic sized ream. However, the basic size of different papers is not always the same. See Fig. 16-34. Paper manufacturers provide charts showing basic sizes and basis weights of their papers.

The term basis weight is not used in the metric system. Thickness of sheets is given in GRAMMAGE. This is the weight, in grams, of a square metre of the paper. (The symbol for square metre is m² and the symbol for grams per square metre is g/m².) Grammage does not depend on paper size.

KINDS OF PAPER

Many of the papers you will be using are listed here. The basic size of each paper is shown in parentheses.
1. BOND (17 x 22). Used for stationery and business forms. Has a hard surface and takes ink well. Bond paper has good erasing qualities. Made in many weights and colors.
2. BOOK (25 x 38). Comes in many weights and bulks. Used for books, magazines, catalogs and programs. Made with ANTIQUE (natural rough finish) and smooth finishes.
3. COATED (25 x 38). Has a smooth, glossy coating. Used in quality color process printing. Sharp, clean halftones are produced on coated stock.

4. TEXT (25 x 38). Used for printing announcements, booklets and brochures. Available with interesting textures and in many colors. Often used with DECKLED EDGE, Fig. 16-35.
5. COVER (20 x 26). Term applied to papers used for outside covers of booklets, catalogs, manuals and brochures. Made in many attractive colors. Finishes that simulate leather, cloth and linen are available.
6. OFFSET (25 x 38). Similar to coated and uncoated papers made for letterpress. However, sizing has been added to resist the moisture present in offset printing.
7. INDEX (22 1/2 x 35 and 25 1/2 x 30 1/2). Used where inexpensive stiff paper is needed. Takes ink well. Made with antique and smooth finishes and in many colors.
8. RAILROAD BOARD (22 x 28). Heavy stock used for tickets and posters. Made with an inexpensive cardboard core sandwiched between two sheets of coated paper. Made in a wide range of bright colors.
9. CHIPBOARD (22 1/2 x 34 1/2 and 26 x 39). An inexpensive gray colored board. Backs of padded material are made from chipboard. Also used to protect paper when it is being trimmed in a paper cutter.

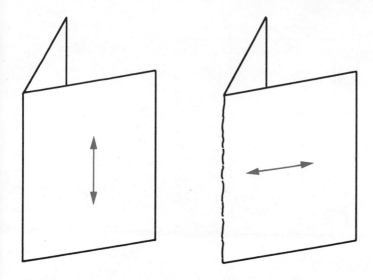

Fig. 16-36. Paper should be cut so a fold will be parallel with the paper grain. A ragged fold will result from a cross-grain fold.

CUTTING PAPER

Usually paper must be cut to size before it can be printed. Plan carefully when cutting. Keep waste to a minimum. Paper is expensive.

Several factors must be considered when cutting paper:
1. Type of job to be printed. Jobs such as programs must be folded. The paper, therefore, must be cut so the fold will be parallel to the grain of the paper, Fig. 16-36.

    Grain direction may be printed on the paper package label, Fig. 16-37. If this information is not available, there are ways to test for grain direction. One way is the wet test. Cut a small section from the paper. Moisten one side with water. The sheet will curl toward the dry side. The axis of the curl will always be parallel to (go the same way as) grain direction, Fig. 16-38.
2. Size of stock sheet.
3. Number of press sheets needed. It is customary to allow 10 percent spoilage on the average press run.
4. Best way to cut the stock sheets. To hold down waste, the craftsperson must figure how to cut the most smaller press sheets from a stock sheet. This can be done mathematically by dividing the dimensions of the smaller sheet into the

Fig. 16-37. Sometimes grain direction information is shown by underlining one dimension of the size marked on the package label. The grain runs parallel to the underlined dimension. Sometimes the label will be marked "grain long" or "grain short."

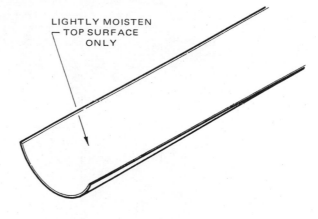

Fig. 16-38. Grain direction can also be found by lightly moistening one side of the sheet. The sheet will curl. The axis (hub) of the curl will be parallel with the grain direction.

larger sheet dimensions. Some typical problems will show how this is done.

PROBLEM ONE: How many stock sheets 17 x 22 in. will be needed for 500 letterheads 8 1/2 x 11 in.?
1. Add 10 percent to total number of letterheads needed. This will make up for spoilage during printing:

Number of press sheets needed = 500
10 percent added for waste = 50
Total press sheets needed = 550

2. Find out how many press sheets (letterheads) can be cut from the 17 x 22 in. stock sheet.
a. Divide the press sheet size into the stock sheet size. Use both the vertical method the the diagonal dividing method.

Basic formula: $\frac{\text{Dimensions of the stock sheet}}{\text{Dimensions of the press sheet}}$

2 x 2 = 4   Vertical method:
17 x 22   (Divide 8 1/2 into 17 = 2)
8 1/2 x 11   (Divide 11 into 22 = 2)
     (2 x 2 = 4 sheets)

1 x 2 = 2   Diagonal method:
17 x 22   (Divide 8 1/2 into 22 = 2)
8 1/2 x 11   (Divide 11 into 17 = 1)
     (1 x 2 = 2 sheets)

The vertical method will provide the most sheets with the least waste.
b. There is a drawing method of calculating the number of sheets needed. It is shown in Fig. 16-39. View A shows how the stock would lay out for the vertical method of figuring stock. View B corresponds to the diagonal dividing method.
3. Calculate the number of stock sheets needed for 550 letterheads. Use the formula:

$\frac{\text{Total number needed}}{\text{number which can be cut from each sheet}}$

$\frac{550}{4}$ = 137 1/2 (round off to 138)

279

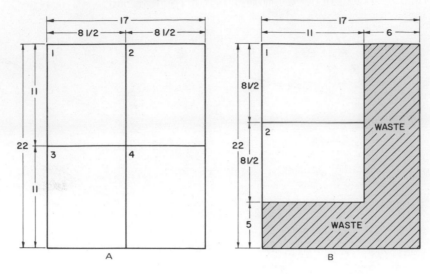

Fig. 16-39. A drawing should be made before cutting paper. This will be a double check on your calculations.

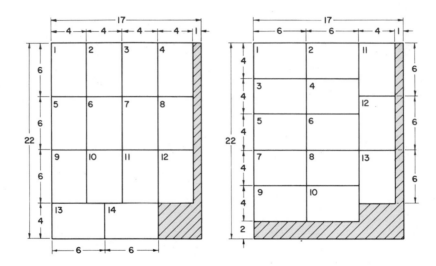

Fig. 16-40. More complicated drawing. Note how it is possible to cut more press sheets from a piece of stock than was indicated mathematically.

PROBLEM TWO: How many stock sheets will be needed for 1000 forms 4 in. x 6 in.? Stock sheet size is 17 in. x 22 in.

Calculate number of sheets that can be cut from the stock sheet:

$$\frac{4}{17} \quad \frac{3}{x \quad 22} = 12 \qquad \frac{2}{17} \quad \frac{5}{x \quad 22} = 10$$
$$4 \quad x \quad 6 \qquad \qquad 6 \quad x \quad 4$$

Again, before cutting paper make a drawing like those shown in Fig. 16-40. By careful planning we can cut 14 press sheets from a stock sheet size instead of either 10 or 12 as computed by the division method.

Add wastage and find total press sheets needed.

Number of press sheets needed = 1000
10 percent waste = 100
Total press sheets needed = 1100

Number of press sheets that can be cut from each stock sheet = 14

To calculate the number of stock sheets needed divide 1100 by 14 = 78 4/7 (round off to next whole sheet = 79 stock sheets needed).

CUTTING CHART

The cutting chart, shown in Fig. 16-41, is like the drawing made to check on the number of press sheets that can be made from a stock sheet. It is used by the printer to avoid making wrong cuts. Prepare the chart in such a way that the least number of paper cutter settings are made.

HOW TO USE A PAPER CUTTER

Caution: The paper cutter has a razor sharp blade. Use extreme care when operating the machine:

1. Only one person is to operate a paper cutter at a time.
2. Do not operate a paper cutter unless all guards and safety devices are in place and operating properly.
3. Use care when handling paper. It can cause bad cuts.

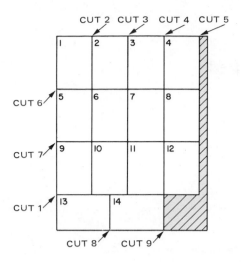

Fig. 16-41. Cutting chart gives printer order of cuts to be made on stock sheet. See how the sequence is arranged to avoid frequent changes in cutter settings?

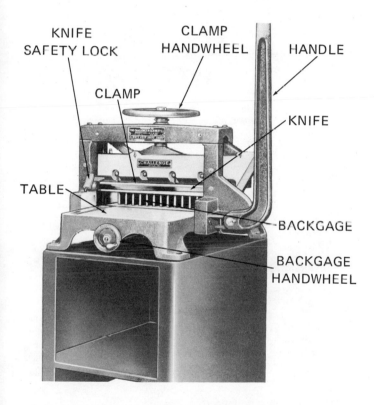

Fig. 16-42. Hand operated paper cutter. Lever controls cutting. (The Challenge Machinery Co.)

The paper cutter may be hand operated, Fig. 16-42, or power operated, Fig. 16-43. Check the machine over carefully. Clear the BED of paper scraps and tools.

Depth of cut is set with the BACKGAGE HANDWHEEL, Fig. 16-44, located on the front of the machine. This adjusts the distance between the BLADE and the BACKGAGE. A MEASURING TAPE on some cutters moves with the back fence and shows the depth of cut, Fig. 16-45. Other cutters have a scale stamped into the bed. It can be used to set the back fence, Fig. 16-46.

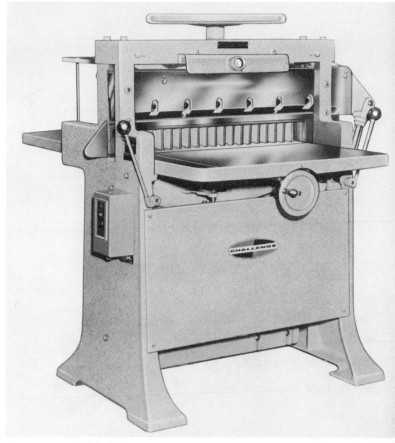

Fig. 16-43. Power operated paper cutter. Electric motor provides power for the blade.

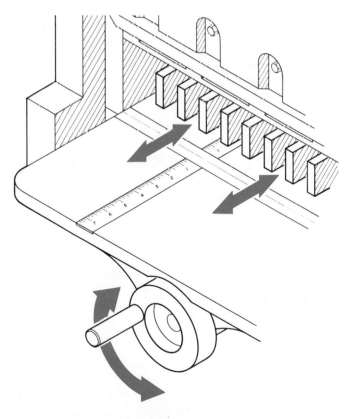

Fig. 16-44. Use the backgage handwheel to set depth of cut.

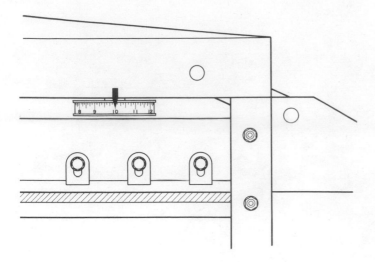

Fig. 16-45. Some machines are fitted with a measuring tape that indicates the depth of cut. However, it is recommended that you always check the setting with an accurate wood rule. Measure twice — cut only once.

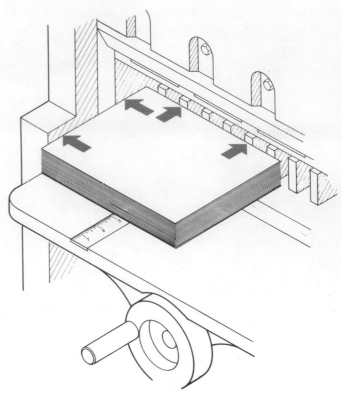

Fig. 16-47. Jog paper against back fence and left side of cutter. This will assure that all of sheets are in contact with these parts of machine.

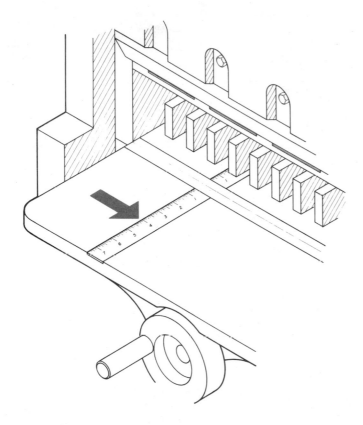

Fig. 16-46. Most cutters have rule engraved into cutter bed. It can be used to set depth of cut.

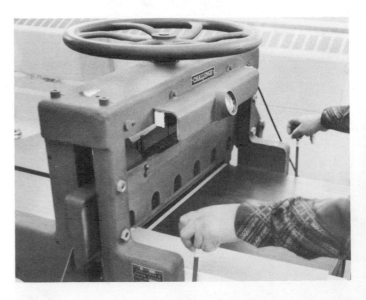

Fig. 16-48. Do not operate a paper cutter unless all of the safety devices fitted to the machine are operating properly. Note that two hands must be used to operate the cutter. (Cheney State College)

Use a **WOOD MEASURING STICK** on paper cutters not fitted with measuring devices.

Jog the paper against the back fence and left side, Fig. 16-47. A piece of chipboard placed on top of the paper stack will protect the top sheets from damage.

Lock the paper in place by lowering the **PAPER CLAMP**. Turn the **PAPER CLAMP WHEEL** clockwise.

Lower the blade in one continuous motion. Most cutters have built-in safety devices. They require the operator to use both hands to operate the cutter, Fig. 16-48. Do not use the cutter if the safety device does not function properly.

After making the cut, raise the **HAND LEVER** until it locks in place. Loosen the paper clamp wheel. Remove the paper. Adjust the cutter and make the second cut.

Clean the bed of scraps. Turn power off on power cutter before walking away from the machine.

TEST YOUR KNOWLEDGE – UNIT 16

1. Most paper is made from _____.
2. What is a debarker?
3. The _____ are converted into pulp _____ or _____.
4. How is groundwood pulp made?
5. Papermaking requires great amounts of _____.
6. Make a sketch of the mold and deckle used in making paper by hand.
7. Why is paper coated or sized?
8. Each type of paper is made to a _____.
9. There are _____ sheets of paper in a ream.
10. What is the meaning of the term basis weight?
11. Paper used for most stationery is called _____ paper.
12. Books and magazines are usually printed on _____ paper.
13. _____ is made in many attractive colors. Finishes that simulate leather and cloth are also available.
14. Jobs that require an inexpensive, stiff paper are printed on _____.
15. Railroad board is a heavy stock that is made with an inexpensive _____.
16. How many stock sheets of paper will be required to print 100 letterheads 8 1/2 in. x 11 in.? Stock sheet size is 17 in. x 22 in. Allow 10 percent for waste. Include all of your work on the answer sheet.
17. How many stock sheets of paper will be needed to print 500 report cards 5 in. x 7 in.? Stock sheet size is 25 in. x 38 in. Allow 10 percent for waste. Include all of your work on the answer sheet.
18. List three precautions that should be observed when using a paper cutter.
19. Paper cutters may be _____ operated or _____ operated.
20. The built-in safety devices on modern paper cutters require the operator to use _____ when cutting paper.

THINGS TO DO

1. Secure paper samples. Mount them on index cards and catalog them for your school's graphic arts technical library.
2. Prepare a bulletin board display on paper and paper-making.
3. Demonstrate how to make paper by hand.
4. Secure and show a film on papermaking.
5. Get samples of the materials that go into the manufacture of paper. Place them on display in the graphic arts lab.
6. Organize and set up a company to manufacture greeting cards on handmade paper.
7. Clean, repair and lubricate the paper cutter in your graphic arts lab. Use caution when handling the cutter blade.
8. Demonstrate the correct way to use a paper cutter.
9. Make a poster on the safe and correct way to use a paper cutter.
10. Visit a paper supply warehouse. Tell your class what you observed. How is paper sold? How is it received by the warehouse? How is paper shipped to printers?
11. Visit a paper mill. Prepare a report on what you saw, smelled and heard.
12. Prepare a report on conservation programs used by the papermaking industry.

Fig. 17-1. This is the mixing room of an ink manufacturer, pigments are usually ground here and blended with different liquids. (National Assoc. of Printing Ink Mfgs., Inc.)

Unit 17

PRINTING INKS

Objectives

This unit describes the qualities of printing inks and how they are manufactured.
You will learn about the different kinds of printing inks, why they are needed, how they are formulated and the correct way to mix colored inks.

The printing ink industry is small. However, it is one of the most complex and advanced industries in the United States. Nearly a million new ink formulas are developed each year, Fig. 17-1.

KINDS OF PRINTING INKS

Each printing process needs its own type of ink. Surface finish and absorbency of the SUBSTRATE must also be considered. (SUBSTRATE is the surface on which the printing is done. It can be paper, fabric, metal, plastic, glass or wood, Fig. 17-2.) For these reasons, printing inks are usually custom made for a specific job.

Some inks CURE (dry) by absorption into the paper. Other inks cure when they come into contact with oxygen in the air. This is called OXIDATION. Still other inks dry by solvent evaporation.

Lithographic inks must be designed to print in the presence of water. They are very strong in color. This compensates for the small amount of ink that is applied to the paper.

Metal decorating inks are made to dry on metal surfaces by high temperature baking, Fig. 17-3. Gravure inks dry by solvent evaporation.

Metallic inks have fine metal flakes in their composition. Magnetic inks are used to print bank checks and business

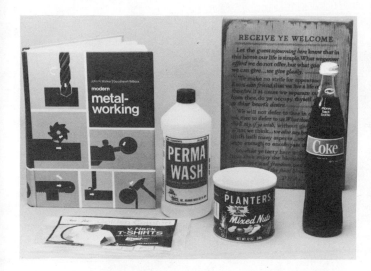

Fig. 17-2. Ink must be specially prepared to print on various substrates. A substrate is the base material on which the ink is coated or printed.

Fig. 17-5. Newspaper inks dry by absorption. The paper "blots up" the ink. (Brevard TODAY — Florida)

INGREDIENTS IN PRINTING INKS

Printing ink is usually formulated for a specific application, Fig. 17-6. In manufacturing inks, three types of ingredients are used, Fig. 17-7:

1. VEHICLE, the liquid part of ink. Made from varnishes, oils and resins, the vehicle holds and carries the pigment. It also aids in binding ink to the substrate. The vehicle determines how the ink will dry (by absorption, oxidation or evaporation.)

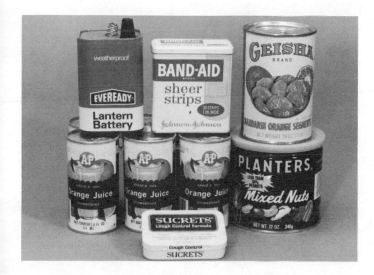

Fig. 17-3. Inks for printing on metal surfaces dry by being baked at high temperatures.

forms, Fig. 17-4. They are made with pigments that can be magnetized after printing. The printed characters can then be recognized by special electronic reading equipment.

Inks for printing wallpapers, some greeting cards and novelties are water soluble. The presses can be cleaned with water.

Letterpress inks would give poor results if used on an offset press. Inks for printing newspapers (they dry by absorption), Fig. 17-5, are very different from inks for printing on plastic films (they dry by solvent evaporation).

Fig. 17-4. Magnetic inks are used to print these special characters. The printed characters are recognized and instantly read by electronic reading equipment.

Fig. 17-6. A densitometer is being used to measure the light reflected from a printed surface. It is a control instrument for checking the uniformity of print color. (NAPIM)

Fig. 17-7. Ingredients for making ink when received by an ink manufacturer. The ingredients — pigments, vehicles and additives, are in powder, liquid, solid paste and gum forms. (NAPIM)

2. PIGMENT, the fine particles that give color to printing inks, Fig. 17-8. Pigments are OPAQUE or TRANSPARENT. Transparent inks do not have great hiding power. (This means ability to cover up the color of the substrate. The color of the previous printing or substrate shows through the ink.) This "show-through" is desirable for some jobs.

3. ADDITIVES, special ingredients to impart special characteristics to ink. They determine drying ability of ink, ink gloss, scuff-resistance (Fig. 17-9), fade resistance, etc. Additives include driers, waxes, lubricants, solvents, binders, wetting agents, antioxidants, antiskinning agents and body gum.

Fig. 17-8. This three roller mill is grinding pigment. (NAPIM)

USING PRINTING INKS

Printing problems caused by ink can be kept to a minimum by:

1. Using the correct ink for the printing process and paper being printed.
2. Keeping inks clean. Remove ink from a can by scraping, Fig. 17-10. *Do not dig down into the ink.* Some inks develop a "skin" of semi-hardened ink on exposed surfaces after a can has been opened. Remove and discard the skin before taking ink for the press.
3. Keeping the inking system of the press clean. Wash the press with recommended solvents. Be sure all solvent is wiped away with a lint free cloth before applying ink.
4. Using ink rollers that are in good condition and which are made for the kind of ink being used.

MIXING PRINTING INKS

Almost any color on ink can be mixed, Fig. 17-11. Just use white and black and inks of the three primary colors. Metallic silver inks are made by mixing aluminum flakes in a varnish to which driers have been added. Gold tone inks are made using copper-zinc flakes.

Before attempting to mix inks be sure they have the same characteristics and come from the same manufacturer.

Color inks should be purchased ready mixed for long press runs. The ink manufacturer must be furnished with a color sample of the ink, a paper sample and information on the type of press that will be used.

When mixing tints for a short press run, add small amounts of colored ink to mixing white until the desired tint is obtained. *Never add white ink to colored ink to make a tint.*

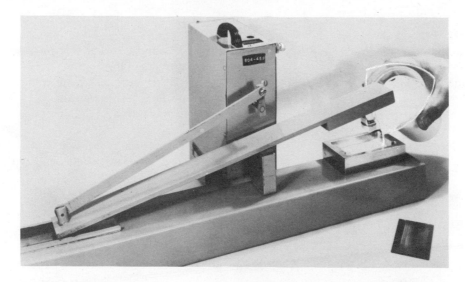

Fig. 17-9. An abrasion tester. The test is designed to determine the ability of the ink to withstand the effects of rubbing and scuffing.

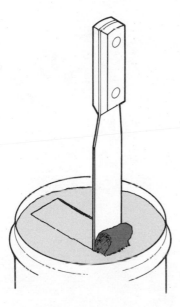

Fig. 17-10. Remove ink from containers by scraping the surface of the ink. Do not dig down into the ink.

Fig. 17-11. Checking the color of a newly mixed ink against a color standard. Light box provides a uniform, color corrected light source. (NAPIM)

Do the mixing on a smooth clean surface. Many printers use heavy plate glass. For safety, edges of the glass should be ground smooth. Thoroughly clean the mixing surface and ink knife before mixing colored inks or tints.

Wash the press inking system several times before using colored inks or tints. A very small amount of another color can change the hue being printed.

INK SAFETY

1. Wash your hands thoroughly after mixing or using inks.
2. Stop the press to remove any hicky or foreign particles from the ink system or plates.
3. Return all solvents to proper storage.
4. Place solvent soaked rags in metal safety cans. Do not leave them in your locker.

TEST YOUR KNOWLEDGE — UNIT 17

1. Printing inks are usually _____ for a specific job.
2. What is a substrate?
3. List the three ways inks cure.
4. What is unusual about the ink used to print identifying characters on bank checks and business forms?
5. Name and briefly describe the three ingredients found in printing inks.
6. List three ways to keep ink problems to a minimum when printing.
7. Almost any color or tint of ink can be mixed if five basic ink colors are available. What colors are they?

8. What precautions should be observed when mixing inks?
9. When mixing color tints (check the correct answer):
   a. Mix the white ink into the color ink until the desired tint is mixed.
   b. Mix color ink into white ink to mix the tint.
   c. Mix small amounts of color ink into white ink until the desired tint is mixed.
   d. None of the above.
10. What is the difference between a transparent ink and an opaque ink?

THINGS TO DO

1. Gather samples of printed materials that illustrate the various types of inks.
2. Sort out the inks available in your school's graphic arts lab. Discard those that have oxidized (dried out). Inventory the usable inks according to color, weight and type (letterpress, offset, silkscreen, etc).
3. Demonstrate the proper way to mix a color tint.
4. Prepare a term paper on the history of printing inks.

Unit 18
OFFICE GRAPHIC ARTS EQUIPMENT

Objectives

This unit is a survey of the graphic arts tools and equipment adapted to business office use.

Reviewing the unit, you will learn how the following office oriented graphic arts equipment is used: spirit duplicator, mimeograph duplicator, xerographic (electrostatic) copiers, thermographic copiers, collators, paper cutters, folders and binding devices. You will be able to make spirit duplicator masters and mimeograph stencils.

Business offices handle immense quantities of printed and illustrated matter. Much of the material must be reproduced rapidly and at low cost. This is done on simple graphic arts equipment made just for office use.

Those who operate these machines do not have to be highly skilled in printing. Print quality is often not as important as getting rapid and low-cost reproduction of the information. Paper cutters, collating and binding equipment, folders, etc., are made just for office use.

SPIRIT DUPLICATING MACHINES

The SPIRIT DUPLICATOR, Fig. 18-1, uses a process which is basically planographic. Printing is done from a carbon image on a smooth, flat piece of paper, Fig. 18-2. The machine is simple to use. Almost anyone can operate it.

The image carrier is a paper master that is part of a spirit duplicator master unit. The master unit, Fig. 18-3, has two parts:
1. A paper master sheet.
2. A carbon sheet.
A tissue paper insert often separates the two sheets until they are ready to be used.

The image is typed or drawn on the front of the paper master sheet, Fig. 18-4. In the process, carbon is transferred to

Fig. 18-1. Spirit duplicator is used when less than 200 copies are required. (Standard Duplicating Machine Corp.)

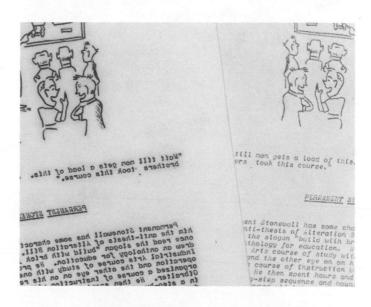

Fig. 18-2. Spirit duplication printing is done from a carbon image area on a smooth, flat piece of paper. The carbon image area is shown to the left. The printed sheet is at the right.

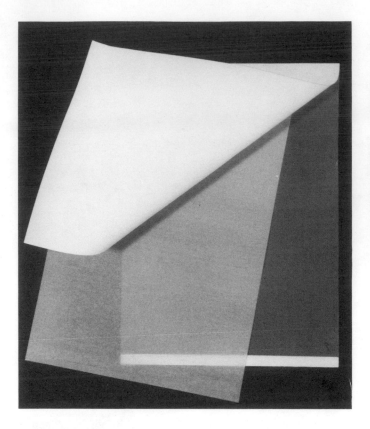

Fig. 18-3. The spirit duplicator master unit has two parts. The paper master sheet and the carbon sheet. The carbon sheet is discarded after the image is made. A tissue paper separator prevents carbon being transferred to the paper master until the unit is to be used.

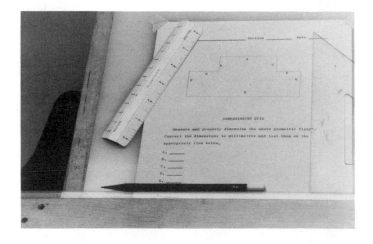

Fig. 18-4. The image is typed or drawn on the front of the paper master sheet.

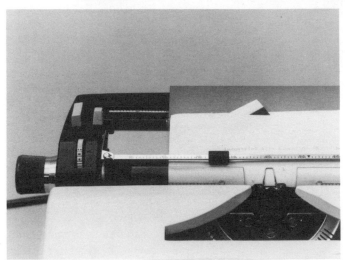

Fig. 18-5. Errors can be removed from the spirit master. Top. Scrape or erase the carbon image area from the back of the master sheet. Bottom. Make corrections by placing piece of unused carbon sheet in place. Then retype or redraw correct information.

the back of the master sheet. Discard the carbon sheet after the image is made.

Make corrections by scraping or erasing the carbon image from the back of the paper master. After removing the carbon, place a piece of fresh carbon paper in place and make the correction, Fig. 18-5.

Draw or write on the master sheet with a fine tip ballpoint pen. Heavier lines are made with a 2H lead pencil. Work on a

hard, smooth surface like plate glass or Formica. Caution: If a plate glass work area is used, remove sharp edges from the glass with fine emery cloth.

Place the paper master sheet on the machine's master cylinder carbon side up. See Fig. 18-6.

HOW THE SPIRIT DUPLICATOR WORKS

Print paper is moistened with duplicating fluid as it is fed into the machine, Fig. 18-7. Fluid dissolves the carbon in the image area. The pressure cylinder presses the print paper against the master cylinder. A small amount of carbon is transferred when the moistened paper comes into contact with the master sheet.

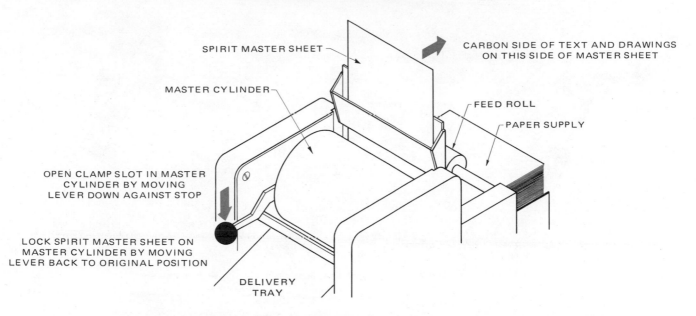

18-6. Mount paper master sheet in the duplicator's master cylinder carbon side up.

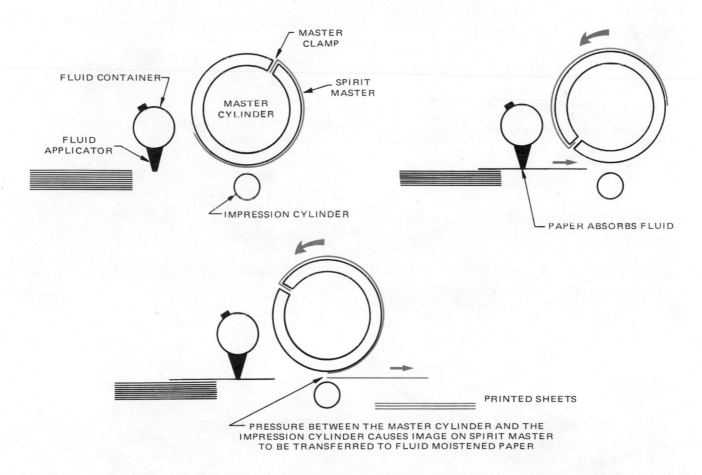

Fig. 18-7. How the spirit duplicator works. Paper is moistened with duplicating fluid as it is fed into the machine. Fluid dissolves the carbon that makes up the image area. The pressure cylinder presses the print paper against the master cylinder and master sheet. A small amount of carbon is transferred when the moistened paper comes into contact with the carbon image.

Up to five colors (red, green, blue, purple and black) can be printed at one time on a spirit duplicator. For example, suppose a portion of the image is to be printed in red. A red carbon sheet is placed under the paper master when the red portion of the image is made, Fig. 18-8. Other color carbons can be placed under the paper master in the same way.

MIMEOGRAPH DUPLICATOR

Mimeograph duplication is a form of stencil printing. Ink passes through the image area which has been drawn or typed on a stencil. Stencils are made from a porous tissue paper that is coated on both sides with a waxlike material, Fig. 18-9.

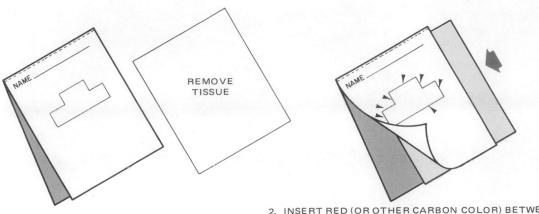

1. DO ALL TEXT AND DRAWINGS THAT ARE TO PRINT PURPLE (BASE COLOR OR MASTER CARBON).

2. INSERT RED (OR OTHER CARBON COLOR) BETWEEN PAPER MASTER AND CARBON. DO WORK THAT IS TO PRINT RED.

Fig. 18-8. How color is added to the master sheet. Separate carbon is used for each color.

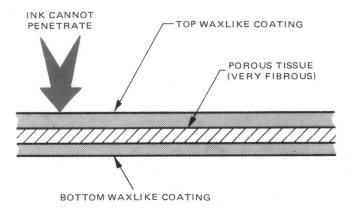

Fig. 18-9. Mimeograph stencil is made from a porous tissue paper that is coated on both sides with a waxlike material.

Fig. 18-11. Mimeograph duplicator will fit on a table top. (Heyer, Inc.)

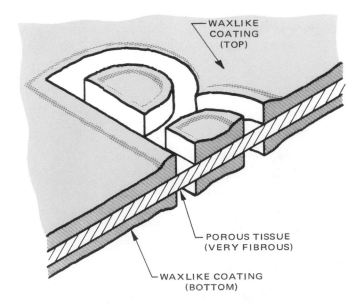

Fig. 18-10. Pressure from the typewriter printing key or stylus push aside the coating where they strike or draw on the stencil. Ink can penetrate the stencil in this area and will print.

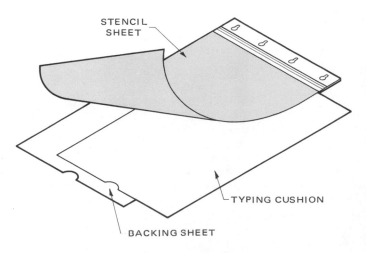

Fig. 18-12. Basic stencil unit is made up of stencil sheet, backing sheet and typing cushion. The backing sheet and typing cushion are discarded after the stencil is made or "cut."

Pressure from the tools or machines used to prepare the image area push aside the coating, Fig. 18-10. The porous tissue is exposed and will permit ink to pass through the stencil and print on the paper. Only one color can be printed at a time.

Printing is done on a MIMEOGRAPH DUPLICATOR. See Fig. 18-11.

Mimeograph stencils are made as a three or four-part "sandwich." A basic unit consists of a stencil sheet, a backing sheet and a typing cushion, Fig. 18-12. Four-part units have a plastic film top sheet, Fig. 18-13. The plastic top sheet prevents the typewriter keys from cutting out the centers of closed letters (like "o") from the stencil.

Fig. 18-13. Four-part stencil units have film top sheet. This film sheet prevents typewriter keys from cutting out the centers of closed letters.

PREPARING A MIMEOGRAPH STENCIL

A mimeograph stencil can be "cut" with a typewriter or drawn by hand with a round-pointed stylus, Fig. 18-14. When typing a stencil, an electric typewriter is preferred, Fig. 18-15. It produces a better image because the letters strike the stencil with uniform pressure. Some typewriters can change the type being used, Fig. 18-16.

Fig. 18-15. Most stencils are "cut" on a typewriter. Top. Conventional electric typewriter. Bottom. Modern single element electric typewriter. Element is simple to replace and many different typefaces can be printed by same machine. (Royal Typewriter Co.)

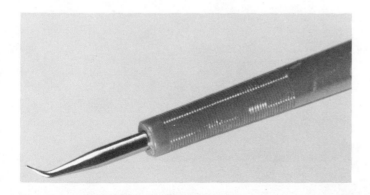

Fig. 18-14. Round-pointed stylus for cutting lines in the stencil. Many different sizes and shapes are available.

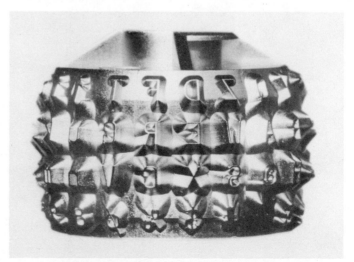

Fig. 18-16. Typewriter element. A different element is needed for each type style. (Royal Typewriter Co.)

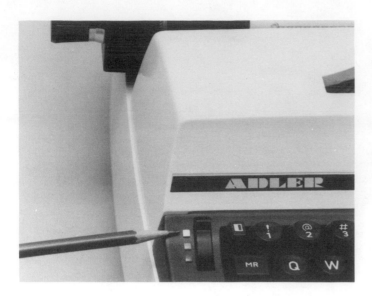

Fig. 18-17. Cutting a stencil or typing a spirit duplicator master sheet works best if ribbon selector lever is on "white" or "stencil" position.

For best results, clean the type on the machine before typing the stencil. The ribbon selector lever should be set to the white or stencil position, Fig. 18-17. The type will then make direct contact with the stencil. They will not strike the typewriter ribbon. Typing mistakes can be removed with CORRECTION FLUID.

When using a manual typewriter, strike the keys with uniform pressure. Use the guide lines printed on most stencils to position the image.

Drawing and writing is done with a stylus having a rounded point. Width of the point and pressure applied will determine image line width.

An ILLUMINATED DRAWING BOARD, Fig. 18-18, may be used for convenience. Artwork can be placed below the stencil and traced.

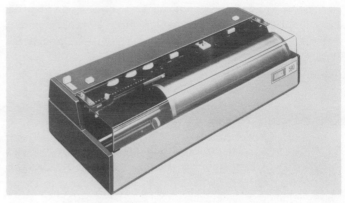

Fig. 18-19. Electronic photo stencil maker will reproduce halftones and illustrations of all kinds.

Stencils can be made electronically. PHOTO STENCIL MAKERS, Fig. 18-19, reproduce line drawings, photographs, newspaper clippings and screened pictures on a stencil. Typewritten pages can also be put on the stencil. This saves retyping.

Fig. 18-20. Top. This automated offset duplicator and platemaker are designed for office use. Bottom. Closeup of press control panel. (American Type Founders Co.)

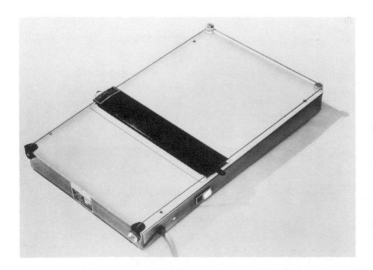

Fig. 18-18. Illuminated drawing board. Artwork is placed below stencil for easy tracing. (Porta Trace, Div. of Gagne Assoc., Inc.)

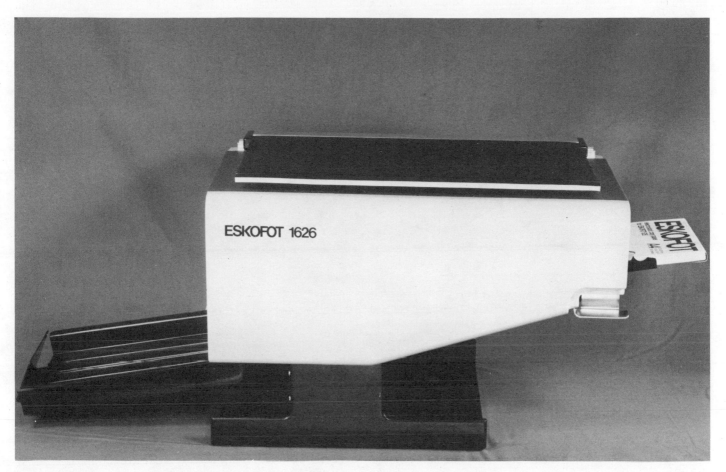

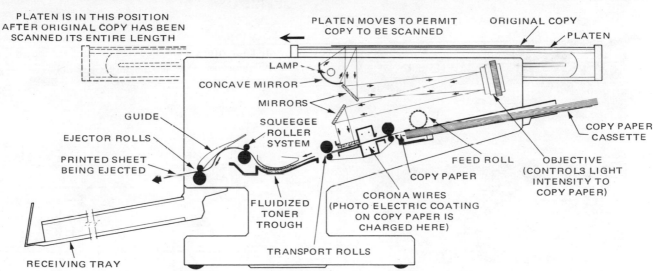

Fig. 18-21. Top. This electrostatic copying machine makes use of liquid toner. (ESKOFOT American Inc.) Bottom. Diagram of operation.

Material to be reproduced on the stencil is attached to one cylinder of the machine. A stencil is mounted on the other cylinder. A scanner moves over the copy and controls a stylus that "cuts" the image into the stencil. Work printed from the stencil will be an exact copy of the original.

OFFSET DUPLICATORS

Small OFFSET DUPLICATORS, Fig. 18-20, operate on exactly the same principle as the larger offset presses. Offset printing is described in Unit 6. Also, see Fig. 4-6, Fig. 4-7 and Fig. 4-8.

LIMITED NUMBER COPYING MACHINES

When only a few copies of an original are needed one of the following reproduction methods are used:
1. ELECTROSTATIC COPYING, Fig. 18-21. This process is better known as xerographic printing. Unit 4 describes how the process works. Also refer to Fig. 4-24.

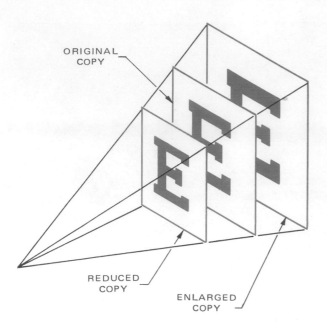

Fig. 18-22. Some copying machines can enlarge or reduce the size of the original copy.

Some machines is this group can enlarge or reduce the size of the original document, Fig. 18-22. A recent development permits full color reproductions of artwork, slides and color photographs, Fig. 18-23. Although originally designed for single-copy reproductions, many new machines are capable of printing several thousand copies an hour.

Fig. 18-23. This electrostatic copier can reproduce original copy in full color enlarging or reducing the size of the original color copy, as needed. (Xerox Corp.)

2. THERMOGRAPHIC COPYING, FIg. 18-24. Process uses infrared radiation to develop a heat sensitive paper. Ink in copy being reproduced must contain carbon black or metallic compounds. The specially treated paper is placed on top of the original, Fig. 18-25. When the two sheets are fed into the copier:
   a. Infrared radiation passes through the treated paper.
   b. Radiation generates heat as it is absorbed by the ink on the original.

Fig. 18-24. Thermographic copying machine produces image on heat-sensitive paper.

   c. Heat is transferred to the treated paper. It develops heat-sensitive chemicals in the paper to form the image area.
   d. A reproduction of the original is made from the top sheet; then the top sheet is thrown away.

OTHER GRAPHIC ARTS EQUIPMENT FOR OFFICE USE

Many other types of graphic arts equipment have been adapted for office use. Most are smaller versions but operate on the same principle as the larger machines. See Fig. 18-26 through Fig. 18-31.

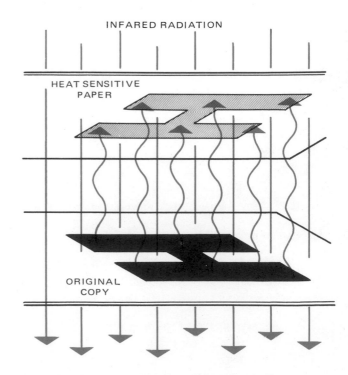

Fig. 18-25. How a thermographic copier works.

Fig. 18-26. Table top, electrically operated paper cutter was designed especially for office use. (Michael Business Machines Corp.)

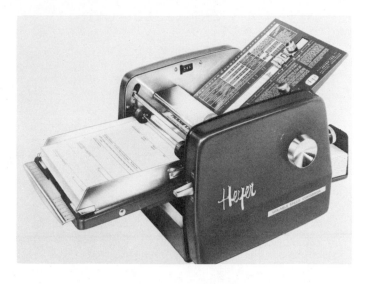

Fig. 18-29. Small paper folder makes simple parallel folds. (Heyer, Inc.)

Fig. 18-27. Collator aids office worker in gathering printed sheets in sequence for binding. The Swingline Co.)

Fig. 18-30. Combination punch and plastic binding machine cuts holes and slots and installs the binding strip. (Ibico, Inc.)

Fig. 18-28. Offset platemaking unit. No film or darkroom facilities are needed. (Gavaert)

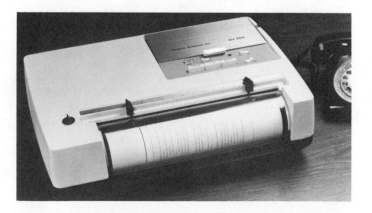

Fig. 18-31. Facsimile transceiver permits copy, both text and illustrations, to be transmitted and received through ordinary telephone lines. (Graphic Sciences, Inc. Burroughs Corp.)

TEST YOUR KNOWLEDGE – UNIT 18

1. Why has graphic arts equipment been developed for business office use?
2. This equipment has been designed (record the correct answer or answers):
   a. To be easy to use.
   b. To reproduce printed matter rapidly and economically.
   c. So operators do not have to be skilled workers.
   d. All of the above.
   e. None of the above.
3. The spirit duplicator is basically a _____ process.
4. Describe how the spirit duplicator works.
5. Corrections can be made on a spirit duplicator master sheet by _____ and _____.
6. Describe how the mimeograph duplicator works.
7. List the various ways a mimeograph stencil can be made.
8. Describe the thermographic copying process.

THINGS TO DO

1. Visit the business education department of your high school. What equipment do they have that is similar to equipment found in the graphic arts lab? (If your school does not have a business education department, make a similar survey of office equipment used by the school secretaries.)
2. Design and produce a multicolor spirit duplicator master sheet on some area of the graphic arts. Duplicate enough copies for each member of the class.
3. Design and make a mimeograph stencil. Reproduce enough copies for each member of the class. Explain what happens to the image when correction fluid is used on a mimeograph stencil.
4. Secure samples of the various types of printed matter duplicated in a business office. Prepare a bulletin board display with the material.

ACKNOWLEDGEMENTS

While it would, indeed, be a pleasant task, it would be impossible for one person to develop the material included in a text of this nature by visiting the various graphic arts areas and observing, studying and taking the photographs firsthand.

My sincere thanks to those who helped in the gathering of the necessary material, information and photographs. Their cooperation was heartwarming.

A special thanks to William Securro, principal, and Donald Bates, graphic arts instructor, of the Harford County (Maryland) Vocational-Technical High School; Don Truitt, chief, printing dept., Board of Education of Harford Co.; Robert Garbacik, principal, and Stephen Marcin, graphic arts instructor, Bel Air Senior High School; Dr. John Stamboolian, visual communications, Cheyney State College; William Baron, ATF/Davidson Co.; Michael Green, manager of educational services, Advance Process Supply Co.; and Barry Neal, corporate technical director, Diversified Corp.

We have endeavored to give credit where due. Any omission was purely accidental.

GRAPHIC ARTS TERMS

ABSOLUTE HUMIDITY: Actual weight of water vapor contained in a unit weight of air.

ACCORDION FOLD: A term used to describe two or more parallel folds which open like an accordion.

ACTINIC LIGHT: The part of the light spectrum that activates or hardens a light-sensitive coating.

AD COPY: Copy used to produce an advertisement.

ADDITIVE PLATE: Offset plate that requires an application of lacquer or developer after exposure to reinforce or intensify the image.

ADDITIVE PRIMARY COLORS: Combination of red, green and blue light which, together, produce white light.

AGAINST THE GRAIN: Folding or feeding stock at right angles to the grain of the material.

AGATE LINE: A standard measurement for depth of columns of advertising space. Fourteen agate lines are considered to be one column inch.

ALKALINE: Solution having a pH of more than seven.

ALTERATIONS: Changes made in copy after it has been set in type.

AMPERSAND: Name given to the character "&."

ANTIOXIDANTS: Agents which slow down the action of oxygen in drying oils used in inks that are subject to oxidation.

ANTIQUE FINISH: A term describing the surface texture, usually on book and cover papers, having a natural rough finish.

APPRENTICE: A person in training who has not completed the program of study to become a journeyman.

ARTIST: The person who prepares "artwork" in any of its forms.

ARTWORK: All original art copy (illustration), whether prepared by an artist, camera or other mechanical means.

ASCENDER: The portion of a type character that extends above the common body height of the lower case characters, for example, b, d, f, h, k, l and t.

ASPHALTUM PAINT: An acid proof paint made from petroleum, coal tar or mineral pitch.

AUTOSCREEN FILM: Graphic arts film with a built-in screen image to produce a halftone.

BACKBONE: The back of a bound book connecting the two covers; sometimes called the Spine.

BACK CYLINDER: Another term for the impression cylinder.

BACKING AWAY FROM FOUNTAIN: A condition caused by thick ink. Unable to flow, it loses contact with the fountain roller. Little or no ink is transferred to the ductor roller. Eventually the printed image becomes uneven, streaked and weak.

BACK GAGE: A movable fence on a paper cutter which governs dimension of paper or manufactured product being cut or trimmed.

BACKING UP: Printing the reverse side of a sheet already printed on one side. In electrotyping it means backing the copper sheet with metal to make the plate the right thickness.

BAIL: The metal band on a platen press that holds the tympan sheets on the platen.

BASE: The wood, metal or plastic block on which the printing plate is mounted; in ink manufacture, the substance (vehicle) in which the pigment or dye is mixed.

BASIS WEIGHT: The weight in pounds of a ream of paper (500 sheets) at a given standard size for that grade of paper: 25 x 38 for book paper, 20 x 26 for cover paper, etc. For example, a ream of 80-lb. cover paper will weigh 80 lb.

BAS RELIEF: Sculpture in which some details are slightly raised above a flat surface and no details are below the flat surface.

BEARERS: Bands on each end of printing cylinders that roll in contact with one another to maintain exact separation between the cylinders.

BED: The flat surface to which the form is clamped on a flat bed relief printing press.

BIMETAL PLATE: In lithography, a printing plate in which the image area is copper or brass and the nonimage area is aluminum, stainless steel or chromium.

BIND: To join sheets together by means of thread, wire, adhesives or other means. Also: to enclose the sheets by attaching a cover.

BINDER: The components in an ink film that hold the pigment to the printed surface.

BINDER BOARD: A smooth heavy fiber board used as book covers.

BINDING VARNISH: A viscous varnish in the ink that is used to toughen the dried ink film.

BLACK LIQUOR: Spent chemicals used to break down wood chips into pulp for making paper. Solution is made up of caustic soda and sodium sulfide.

BLACK-AND-WHITE or B&W: Copy, photo or printing produced by black on a white background.

BLANKET: Rubber surfaced covering used on the blanket

cylinder to transfer the inked image from the plate to the sheet being printed.

BLEED: A printed area that extends to the edge of a page, usually done by printing beyond the actual work size and then trimming the paper. Also: the spreading of ink into an unwanted area.

BLIND: Term used to describe an offset plate that will not accept ink.

BLIND EMBOSSING: A design that is stamped without using foil or ink, giving a bas-relief effect.

BLINDING: The term used when a plate image has lost its ink receptivity.

BLOWUP: An enlargement of copy element.

BOARD: A heavy-weight, thick sheet of paper or other fibrous material, usually thicker than 6 mil (0.006 in.).

BODYING AGENT: A material added to an ink to increase its viscosity (resistance to flow).

BODY TYPE: Type used for the main part or text of a printed piece, as distinguished from headings.

BOILERPLATE: Stereotype mats supplied to newspapers on a variety of subjects such as comics, syndicated columns, publicity and filler material.

BOLD: In type design, a typeface whose lines have been thickened to produce a heavier or blacker printed character.

BONDING: Attaching materials together by adhesives.

BOND PAPER: Grade of writing or printing paper where strength, durability and permanence are essential requirements. Used for letterheads, business forms, etc.

BONE FOLDER: Piece of flat, smooth bone or plastic used to fold sheets by hand.

BOOK CLOTH: A cloth or clothlike material used to bind and protect books.

BORDER: A printed line or design surrounding an illustration or other printed matter.

BRAYER: A hand roller for distributing ink.

BROADSIDE: Any printed advertising circular.

BROCHURE: A pamphlet bound in booklet form.

BROKEN IMAGE: An incomplete image on an offset plate.

BRONZING: Printing with a sizing ink, then applying bronze powder to the wet ink to produce a metallic lustre.

BUCKLE FOLDING: A method of folding paper which forces the sheet against a stop until the paper buckles and goes through folding rolls.

BURNING-IN: In offset printing, shining ultraviolet light through negatives contacted to a plate for purpose of exposing the plate.

BY-LINE: Line at the head of a newspaper or magazine column or article indicating the writer.

CAKING: The collection or buildup of pigment on the plate, rollers or blanket. Caking is usually caused by the inability of the ink vehicle to hold the pigment in suspension; also known as piling.

CALENDAR: A set or stack of horizontal cast-iron rollers at the end of a papermaking machine. The paper is passed between the rollers to increase the smoothness and gloss of its surface.

CALIFORNIA JOB CASE: Compartmented drawer designed to hold a font (caps, lower case and figures) of type.

CALIPER: The thickness of a paper sheet measured under specific conditions and usually expressed in thousandths of an inch.

CAMERA: Device used to make the negative for a photograph. In the graphic arts: the device used to photographically enlarge, reduce, color separate and screen materials for reproduction by printing.

CAP: Printer's term for capital or capitalize.

CARBON ARC: A high intensity ultraviolet source using carbon rods to produce the light.

CARBON BLACK: An intensely black, finely divided pigment obtained by burning gas or oil with a restricted air supply.

CARCINOGEN: A substance which causes cancerous growths in living tissue.

CARDBOARD: A heavy paperboard made in many densities and thicknesses.

CASE: The covers of a hardbound book.

CASE BOUND: Book bound between stiff covers.

CATCHING UP: Term indicating that nonimage areas of an offset plate are taking ink or are scumming.

CELL: A small etched or engraved depression in a gravure cylinder that carries the ink.

CENTERLINE: A short line applied to copy, negative or flat to indicate center of the trim margins of a form, or of all the forms on a press sheet. Centerlines are also used for registration purposes.

CHALKING: A condition which causes poor bonding between the pigment in the ink and the paper. Pigment is easily rubbed off as a powder.

CHASE: Rectangular metal frame in which type and plates are locked up for letterpress printing.

CHIPPER: Machine with many rotating knives or cutters that reduces pulpwood logs to chips about 1 in. square and 1/8 to 3/16 in. thick.

CHROMA: See intensity.

CIRCULAR SCREEN: A circular shaped halftone screen.

COLD COLOR: A color on the blue side of the color wheel.

COLD TYPE: Type generated by other methods than casting in metal.

COLLATE: Gather together in proper sequence the signature or pages of a book.

COLLATING MARKS: A mark or bar printed on the outside fold of each signature of a book to aid in keeping signatures in proper sequence for binding.

COLORANT: The color portion of an ink. It may be a pigment, a dye or a combination of the two.

COLOR SEPARATION: Separating color illustration into three or four process colors for purpose of producing printing plates.

COMBINATION PLATE: Term used when halftone and line copy are combined on one plate.

COMPOSING ROOM: The area in a printing plant or typesetting shop where the type is set.

COMPOSING STICK: A small tray where hand set type is assembled and justified.

COMPOSITOR: One who sets type in preparation for printing.

COMPREHENSIVE: A detailed sketch that shows the position and appearance of copy elements for the job to be printed.

COMPUTERIZED COMPOSITION: Unjustified tapes are produced on a keyboard and then run through a computer programmed to hyphenate, justify lines of type and make other typographic decisions to produce body text ready for pasteup. Sometimes a computer produced second tape is used as input for phototypesetting or line casting equipment.

CONDENSED TYPE: A narrow or slender typeface.

CONTACT: Photographic image made by direct contact of negative with print paper during exposure.

CONTACT POSITIVE: A positive print made by placing a film negative into contact with undeveloped film and exposing to light.

CONTINUOUS TONE: A photographic image that contains tones ranging from black to white.

CONTRAST: Difference between light and dark areas.

COPY: All material (art, text and photos) furnished for the production of printed work.

COPYBOARD: A frame that holds original copy while it is being photographed on the camera.

COPYFITTING: Determining the amount of manuscript copy that can be fitted into an area of specified size using a particular size and style type.

COUCH: In papermaking, pressing the newly made paper onto felt or blotting material to extract the water.

COVER: The outer sheet(s) of a bound or stitched book, booklet or magazine.

COVER PAPER: A general term applied to a great variety of papers used for the outside covers of catalogs, booklets, brochures and similar pieces.

CRASH: See super.

CREEP: Term used when packing sheets on the plate or blanket cylinder of an offset press move.

CROP: To eliminate portions of a photograph or other type illustration to be used on a plate. Portions to be eliminated are indicated with "crop marks."

CROP MARKS: Marks used on illustrations, artwork and photographs to show or denote the area to be used.

CRT (cathode ray tube): Part of electronic typesetting system which displays the type as the operator is setting it.

CURL: Distortion of a sheet of paper caused by moisture. Curl side is the concave side of the sheet.

CURVED PLATE: An electrotype or stereotype which is precurved to fit the cylinder of a rotary press.

CUT: A relief printing plate. Also: to dilute or thin a printing ink with solvents or with a clear base.

DAMPENERS: Rollers that carry the dampener solution from the vibrator roller to the offset plate.

DAMPENING SOLUTION: Solution used to keep the non-image areas of an offset plate moist.

DANDY ROLL: A wire cylinder on papermaking machine that makes woven or laid effects on the texture of the paper sheet; used in the manufacture of better grades of book papers.

DEAD FORM: Type that has been used and is ready for distribution.

DEAD MATTER: A typeform or plate that has been printed and for which there is no further use.

DECKLE: The bands which run lengthwise along edge of the web on a papermaking machine.

DECKLE EDGE: The untrimmed feathery edges of paper formed where the pulp flows against the deckle.

DEGLAZE: The process of removing the dried layer of ink and gum from press rollers and the offset blanket.

DELETION: In offset printing, the delibrate removal of an imaged area from a litho plate. Also: copy marked to be left out.

DELETION FLUID: Liquid used to remove unwanted image areas on an offset plate.

DELIVERY SYSTEM: The part of a printing press which transports the printed sheet from the press cylinder to the printed sheet stack.

DENSITOMETER: A sensitive photoelectric instrument which measures the density of photographic images or of colors.

DENSITY: The degree of darkness of photographic film and printed inks.

DERMATITIS: A skin disease characterized by an itching rash or swelling; sometimes caused by solvents.

DESCENDER: The part of lower case type that extends below the base line of the type such as in g, j, p, q and y.

DESENSITIZER: A liquid (usually gum arabic) applied to an offset plate to make the nonimage area of the plate nonreceptive to ink.

DETECTOR FINGER: Device on some offset presses which prevents the impression when a sheet fails to feed through.

DIE CUTTING: A shaping process which uses a sharp steel rule to cut special shapes from printed sheets. It is usually done on the press in line with the printing.

DIE STAMPING: Printing with designs cut or engraved in copper or steel dies.

DIMENSIONAL STABILITY: The ability of a substrate (printing material) to maintain size.

DIRECT PRINTING: Any printing technique where the ink transfer is direct from the image carrier (printing plate) to the sheet being printed.

DIRTY PROOF: Proof that contains many typographical errors.

DISPLAY TYPE: Type set larger than the text to attract attention.

DISTRIBUTION: The act of returning used type to the case.

DOCTOR BLADE: The blade that scrapes the excess ink from the surface of etched or engraved gravure press rolls. Ink remains in the cells that make up the gravure image.

DOT: The individual element of a halftone.

DRAWSHEET: The top sheet on the tympan of a platen press. Gauge pins or guides are attached to this sheet.

DRIERS: Materials added to speed or hasten drying of ink.

DROP-OUT: Portions of an original that are purposely not reproduced, usually colored lines or background areas. Areas of the original are dropped out on purpose.

DRYER: A mechanical device used to speed up the drying of ink.

DRY TRANSFER LETTERING: Ready-made lettering with adhesive backing which is transferred from storage sheets by rubbing the surface with a burnishing tool.

DUCTOR ROLLER: The roller (in both the inking and dampening systems) that alternately contacts the fountain roller and the vibrating roller.

DUMMY: A preliminary layout showing the probable position of illustrations and text on the finished job.

DUMPING THE STICK: Transferring hand set type from a composing stick to a galley.

DUOTONE: A term for two-color halftone reproduction from a one color photograph.

DUPLEX PAPER: Paper having a different color or finish on each side.

DUPLICATOR PAPER: A smooth, hard surface paper made for use on spirit duplicators.

EDGE GILDING: Placing gold leaf on the edge of a book.

EDGE MARBLING: Marbleizing the edge of a book.

EDITION BINDING: Case binding done on a production basis.

EGGSHELL: A paper with a finish similar to that of an eggshell.

ELECTROPHOTOGRAPHY: The image transfer systems used in copiers that make use of electrostatic forces and selenium surface or zinc oxide coating to produce images.

ELECTROSTATIC PRINTING: Printing in which inks and paper having opposite electrical charges are used.

ELECTROTYPE: A facsimile of a typeform, cut or combination of both made by an electroplating process. The thin shell is backed with type metal.

EM: The square of a type body. Name came from the letter "M" which in early type fonts, was cast on a square body.

EMBOSSED FINISH: A paper with a raised surface that resembles wood, cloth, leather or other pattern.

EMBOSSING: Impressing an image in relief to achieve a raised surface. It can be done over printing, or on blank paper. When done on blank paper it is called "blind embossing."

EMULSION: A gelatin coating containing light-sensitive silver salts.

EN: Half the width of an em.

ENAMEL: Term applied to a coated paper or to a coating material on a paper.

ENDPAPER or ENDSHEET: The sheet placed between the cover and the body of a book.

ENGRAVING: Print made from an engraved printing plate. The image is cut into the plate by hand with a graver or by mechanical or electronic means.

ETCHING: The print made from a chemically engraved plate.

EXPOSURE: Term used for the sum of the time and the intensity of illumination acting upon light-sensitive material.

EXTENDED TYPE: A type whose characters are wider than normal.

EXTENDER: A colorless substance mixed with ink to improve its covering power.

FACE: The printing surface of a piece of type.

FACSIMILE: An exact reproduction of a letter, document or signature.

FEEDER: The system on the press that separates the sheets and feeds them to the printing cylinder one at a time.

FELT SIDE: Smooth side of a paper sheet.

FILLING IN: When ink fills in the spaces between halftone dots.

FILM NEGATIVE: A photographic image that is the reverse of the original or printed copy.

FILM POSITIVE: A photographic image that is the same as the original or printed copy.

FINISHING: Any of several operations which will change the shape or appearance of printed materials. These operations may include case binding, hot stamping, trimming, die cutting, corner rounding and laminating.

FIXER: Acid used to dissolve and remove undeveloped silver salts in an exposed and developed photographic image. After fixing, the film emulsion is no longer sensitive to light. Fixer is also called the "hypo."

FLASH EXPOSURE: The supplementary exposure given to strengthen the dots in the shadow areas of negatives.

FLAT: The assembly of photographic negatives on goldenrod paper, glass or acetate film. Also: lacking in contrast and definition of tone or detail.

FLEXOGRAPHY: A printing technique that uses rubber plates and a thin-bodied ink.

FLUSH COVER: Term used when the cover is trimmed to the same size as the inside text papers.

FLUSH RIGHT (FLUSH LEFT): Type set to line up at the right or left. Most pages in this book are set flush left and right.

FLYING PASTER: An automatic pasting device, fitted to some web presses, that splices a new roll of paper onto an expiring roll without stopping the press.

FOIL: Very thin metal sheeting (less than 0.006 inch thick).

FOLD: To bend over so that one part of the sheet lies on another part.

FOLIO: A number of pages. Also: page number.

FOOT MARGIN: The blank space at the bottom of a printed page.

FONT: Complete set of one size and style of hand set (foundry) type. Consists of individual letters, numbers and punctuation.

FORE EDGE: Right hand edge of a book or pamphlet.

FORM: Matter (type and cuts) locked in a chase ready for printing.

FORM ROLLERS: The rollers (either inking or dampening) that contact the plate on an offset press.

FOUNTAIN: Name given to the ink reservoir and dampener reservoir on offset presses.

FOUNTAIN ROLLER: The roller that revolves in the ink fountain. In offset printing, it can also refer to the roller that revolves in the dampener solution.

FOUNTAIN SOLUTION: Usually a mixture of water, acid and gum used to prevent the nonimage areas of an offset printing plate from receiving ink.

FOURDRINIER: In papermaking, a large mesh web upon which the pulp is laid as it is made into paper.

FRACTIONAL PAGE: An advertisement or editorial occupying less than a full page.

"f" STOP: Fixed sizes for setting camera lens apertures (openings).

FURNISH: Bleached pulp which is ready to be made into paper.

FURNITURE: Wood or metal blocks used to fill in around type and other matter when it is locked in a chase.

FUZZ: Fibers projecting from the surface of paper.

GALLEY: A shallow metal tray used to hold type.

GALLEY PROOF: Proof taken of type standing in a galley.

GANGING: Several jobs are combined and printed on the same sheet. They are cut apart after printing.

GATHERING: The assembling of folded signatures in there proper sequence.

GAUGE PIN: Steel or brass guide used on the tympan of a platen press to position the sheet for printing.

GHOSTING: A faint image of a design that appears in areas of a printed page that are not intended to receive that portion of the image.

GLOSS INK: Ink that is not absorbed into the paper and dries to a high lustre.

GOLDENROD: Special yellow paper used in stripping up film in preparation for making offset printing plates. Being heavy and opaque, it blocks out light in nonprinting areas.

GRAIN: Arrangement or direction of fibers in paper. Paper folds easier with the grain (parallel to fiber direction).

GRAINING: Technique of roughening the printing surface of a metal offset plate with a very fine abrasive to make the surface more receptive to water.

GRAY SCALE: A strip of standard gray tones, ranging from white to black, placed on the side of original copy during photography to measure tonal range and contrast.

GRIPPER EDGE: The leading edge of paper as it passes through the press.

GRIPPER MARGIN: Blank edge of the paper on which the grippers bear. It cannot be printed.

GRIPPERS: Metal fingers that clamp on paper and control its movement as the paper passes through the press.

GROUNDWOOD: Wood pulp made by grinding.

GUTTER: The blank space between the text and the bound edge of a page.

HAIR SPACES: Very thin pieces of copper and brass used to space out and justify a line of hand set type.

HALFTONE: Photograph broken up into a fine dot pattern for printing.

HALFTONE SCREEN: Piece of film or glass placed over the film during halftone photography to produce the dot pattern in a photograph which is to be printed.

HEAD MARGIN: Unprinted space above the first line on a page.

HICKIES: Spots or imperfections in the printed portion of the page. They are caused by dried ink film, paper particles and dirt.

HIGHLIGHT: The lightest or whitest portions of a photograph. They are represented in a halftone reproduction by the smallest dots or the absence of all dots.

HONING: Using a fine abrasive stone to remove unwanted image area from offset plate.

HOT METAL COMPOSITION: Cast metal type set either by hand or by a linecasting machine.

HUE: Basic name of a color.

IMAGE AREA: Part of the plate or sheet occupied by the image.

IMAGE ASSEMBLY: Positioning and pasting down of camera-ready art and type in preparation for printing.

IMAGE GENERATION: The setting of type and production of artwork or other materials which will illustrate printed matter.

IMPOSING TABLE: Smooth, metal topped bench where type is assembled and locked in a chase before being placed in the press.

IMPOSITION: The laying out of pages in a press form so they will be in the correct order when the printed sheet is folded.

IMPRESSION: The pressure exerted as type, plate or blanket comes in contact with the paper during printing.

INK FOUNTAIN: On a printing press, the tray that stores ink and supplies it to the inking rollers.

INK ROLLERS: Rubber surfaced cylinders which pick up ink from one source and deposit it evenly across a typeform during printing.

INSERT: Printed material added to and usually bound into a publication or other printed piece.

INTAGLIO PRINTING: Printing process where the image area is below the nonimage area. Paper pressed against the image carrier picks up the ink in the image area. Also known as gravure.

ITALIC: Type style in which letters slant; often used in text for emphasis.

INTENSITY: Amount of pure color in a hue. Also called saturation, chroma or purity of color.

JOG: To align sheets into a neat pile by shaking or striking on a flat surface.

JUSTIFY: To space each line of type out to a required length so that left and right margins are even.

KEY: Usually refers to the black plate in a four color reproduction.

KNIFE FOLDING: Machine method of folding paper which uses a bar or knife to force the sheet down into the folding rollers.

KRAFT: A brown colored paper made from unbleached pulp.

LACQUER: A clear coating applied to a printed page for appearance and protective purposes.

LAID SHEET: A type of paper that has a pattern of evenly spaced parallel lines. The lines give a ribbed effect.

LAMINATION: A clear plastic film bonded to a printed piece for appearance and protective purposes.

LASER: A device that uses the natural movement of atoms to generate electromagnetic radiation. In printing it is used for making engravings and shaping dies for die cutting.

LAY OF THE CASE: Location of letters, figures and spaces in the California Job Case.

LAYOUT: Drawing or pasteup showing how the elements of a printed page are to be combined.

LAYOUT PERSON: Craftsperson whose job is to arrange the elements of a reproduction in their proper relative positions.

LEAD: In letterpress printing, thin metal strip used as spacing between lines of type.

LEADERS: Rows of dots used in tabular work, programs, menus, tables of contents and to indicate deleted material in a quotation.

LEDGER PAPER: A paper with a high degree of durability and permanence. Used for record keeping.

LETTER SPACING: Adding thin spaces between words in hand set or machine set type.

LETTERSET (DRY OFFSET): A printing technique that uses a blanket like regular offset printing but uses a relief plate. No dampening is necessary.

LETTERSPACING: Term used when extra spacing is used between each letter of a word.

LIGATURES: Pieces of hand set type on which more than one letter appears.

LIGHT TABLE: Table with a frosted glass top through which light is shone.

LINE COPY: Any copy suitable for reproduction without the need for halftone screening.

LINE GAUGE: Printers' measuring rule marked in picas and inches.

LINE MECHANICAL: An accurate diagram or pasteup of all the elements of a printed page showing the size and position desired.

LINE NEGATIVE: A contrast negative of type or line copy.

LINE SLUG: A line of type after it has been cast on a linecasting machine.

LINE SPACING: The amount of space added between lines of type; the spacing material used in letterpress printing.

LINE WORK: Artwork or photographic material which contains no tonal values.

LINOTYPE: Hot metal typesetting machine which uses a keyboard to release matrices from a storage case, then casts lines of metal type for use in letterpress printing.

LITHOGRAPHY: Art or process of printing from a flat, inked surface; based on principle that oil or grease and water do not mix.

LIVE MATTER: Type which is waiting to be printed or is to be stored for reprinting later.

LOCKUP: Positioning and clamping printing matter in a chase.

LOGOTYPE (LOGO): A special design used by a company or organization as a trademark.

LOWER CASE: The small letters in a font of type, as distinguished from capitals.

M: Abbreviation for a quantity of 1000.

MACHINE COATED: Paper coated on one or both sides on the paper machine.

MAGAZINE: Flat case which can be attached to linecasting machines for storage or retrieval of matrices.

MAKEREADY: Building up the packing on a letterpress platen so light and dark areas print with the correct impression.

MAKEREADY KNIFE: Long-handled, razor sharp knife used by compositors for cutting paper and thin cardboard during press preparation in letterpress printing.

MAKEUP: The arranging of lines of type and illustrations into pages or sections of the correct length.

MAKEUP RULE: Thin, rectangular piece of metal used by printers to tuck end of cord into wrappings after tying up hand set or machine set type.

MASKING: To cover some light-sensitive areas of a film or plate to block out or prevent exposure.

MASTER: Used to indicate the plate for a duplicating machine.

MATRIX: Mold used to cast type or typeform.

MATTE FINISH: Paper finish that has no gloss or lustre.

MECHANICAL: The final assembly of camera-ready art and type.

MILEAGE: Slang term for image life of offset plate.

MIMEOGRAPH: Type of printing which squeezes ink through a stencil onto the sheet being printed.

MIMEOGRAPH PAPER: Paper with the toothy, absorbent surface needed for mimeographing.

MOIRE (pronounced mwa-ray): An undesirable checkerboard of plaid effect that sometimes occurs when a screened reproduction of a photograph or artwork is rescreened for one of the printing processes.

MOLD AND DECKLE: A frame and strainer arrangement used to scoop up pulp while producing handmade paper.

MOLLETON: A flannel-like cloth covering used on the dampening rollers of an offset press.

MONOTONE: Black and white copy or its photographic counterpart.

MULL: See SUPER.

NEWSPRINT: Paper used in printing newspapers. It is made mostly from groundwood pulp.

NICK: The groove near the bottom front of a foundry type character. It aids in distinguishing different typefaces and permits the compositor a quick check as to whether the characters are set right side up.

OFFSET LITHOGRAPHY: Lithographic printing in which image is first transferred to a blanket and then onto the material to be printed.

OFFSET PLATE: Light-sensitive plate which carries the printing image in offset printing.

OPAQUE INK: An ink that conceals any color beneath it.

OPAQUING: The act of blocking out an area with a paint that will not permit light to pass through.

OUTLINING: To indicate the outer edges of an object. This can be done on a photograph by painting out the background with white from edges of the image to be printed. It can also be done by opaquing on the negative.

OVERHANG COVER: A cover larger than the pages it encloses.

OVERLAY: Transparent or translucent material placed upon artwork or negative or positive for the purpose of adding to or indicating the addition or position of material to be added. Often used to indicate special instructions about parts of the artwork.

OVERPRINT: Any area of one color that is superimposed upon another color, or where black type appears to have been printed over a black and white photograph in a final reproduction. Also known as surprint.

OVERRUN: Copies printed in excess of the number required.

OXIDATION: Drying of inks by contact with air. This type of ink is required on hard finished paper where there is no absorption of ink into the paper.

PACKING: Paper used to build up the tympan, impression cylinder on a letterpress or plate or blanket on an offset press to achieve a uniform pressure for printing.

PADDING: Applying liquid adhesive binding by hand to loose sheets clamped in a press.

PADDING PRESS: Device for applying pressure to stack of single sheets while they are being padded (glued).

PAPER DRILL: Hand operated or power machine which makes holes through many sheets at one time for purpose of binding.

PAPYRUS: Marsh plant of the Nile valley used by ancient Egyptians to make paperlike writing material.

PARCHMENT: Skin of a goat or sheep prepared as writing material.

PASTEUP: Process of assembling images on a page in preparation for printing.

PERFECTING PRESS: A press that prints on both sides of a sheet in one pass through the press.

PERFORATING: Cutting a series of holes or slits in paper so it will tear more easily in a predetermined way.

pH: A number used to express the acidity or alkalinity of solutions. Rating is made on a scale of 0 to 14. A value of 7 is considered neutral. A value lower than 7 is considered acid while those higher are alkaline.

PHOTOCOMPOSING: A method of placing elements in position either by projection camera, or by contact in a machine especially designed for the purpose.

PHOTOCONVERSION: Photographing the camera-ready art onto light-sensitive film and developing the film.

PHOTOENGRAVER: Skilled worker who uses photography and chemical processes to make photoengravings—metal plates for reproducing drawings and photographs in relief printing.

PHOTOENGRAVING: Process of using light and chemicals to etch a raised image on a sensitized plate.

PHOTOGRAPHY: Process of producing images on a sensitized surface by the action of light and chemicals.

PI: Type that has been mixed, spilled or otherwise disarranged.

PICA: Printer's unit of measure. One pica equals approximately 1/6 of an inch.

PICKING: Condition where the pull of the ink is greater than the strength of the paper. Tack of ink on image carrier lifts small bits from the paper's surface during the printing.

PIGMENT: Substance used to color inks and paints.

PINHOLES: Pinpoint sized holes or imperfections in developed film.

PIN REGISTER: The use of accurately positioned holes and special pins on copy, film, plates and presses to assure accurate register (position) of colors.

PLANOGRAPHIC PRINTING: Printing from a smooth surface. The image and nonimage areas are on the same plane. The process is also known as lithography and offset.

PLATEN: In printing, a flat plate or cylinder which presses paper or other printing material against an inked image for purpose of making a copy of the image.

PLATEN PRESS: Printing press which presses entire typeform against the paper at one time.

PLUGGING: Filling or bridging of halftones, dots or type by too much developer and/or ink.

PLUNGER CAN: Storage container for chemicals especially in graphic arts which has a dispensing unit that applies the contents to a cleaning rag when a plunger is pressed.

POINT: Printer's unit of measure used primarily to designate type size. There are 12 points to a pica and approximately 72 points to an inch.

PRESS LIFE: Number of usable printed sheets which an offset plate can produce.

PRESSURE-SENSITIVE PAPER: A paper with an adhesive coating that will stick without moistening. The adhesive is protected by a backing sheet until it is ready to be used.

PRINTING: The technique that transfers an image from one material to another material.

PROCESS: Commonly used term indicating the number of colors involved in a reproduction such as four-color process, three-color process, etc.

PROCESS CAMERA: A special camera used to photograph printing layouts and transfer the image to film.

PROCESS COLORS: A combination of colors printed one directly over the other to produce additional colors as represented in the original copy.

PROGRESSIVE PROOFS: Proofs of color plates showing each color by itself and then in combination with the other process colors.

PROJECTION: Making a negative or positive by exposure in the camera as opposed to contact exposure.

PROOF: A trial impression of matter to determine what, if any, corrections must be made.

PROOFREADER: One who checks copy for mistakes after it has been set in type and marks the copy for corrections.

PROOFREADERS' MARKS: A kind of shorthand or set of symbols used in marking corrections in typeset material.

PULP: The wood or other fibers used to make papers.

QUAD: Blank spacing material less than type high. It is used to fill out lines of letterpress type. Quads are thicker than spaces.

QUOIN: An expanding device used to lock (clamp) type matter in a chase.

QUOIN KEY: Small hand tool used to expand quoins with a twisting action.

REAM: 500 sheets of paper.

REFLECTION COPY: Copy that reflects light, such as drawings, paintings and photographic prints, as opposed to color transparencies.

REGISTER: Printing two or more images and/or colors in exact alignment with each other.

REGISTER MARK: A small design usually in the form of fine crossed lines scribed or marked in the same relative position on each negative to be overprinted. They assure proper alignment with each other when printed.

REGISTRATION PINS: Pins which hold printing plate and film in exact register during exposure of plate.

RELATIVE HUMIDITY: The amount of water vapor present in the atmosphere. It is expressed as a percentage of the maximum moisture that could be present at the same temperature.

RELIEF PRINTING: Reproduction method in which the image area is raised above the nonprinting area. Ink is applied to the raised surface and then transferred from the image area to the paper. The process is also known as letterpress.

REPRODUCTION PROOF: A proof of type matter suitable for photographic reproduction.

REPROS: An abbreviation of "reproduction proofs" which

means a proof of type taken on enameled or other coated paper to insure the highest quality in the final reproduction.

RETOUCHING: Refers to all methods used to correct tonal values of the negatives or positives to the proper densities required by the printing department for producing work to the customer's specifications.

REVERSE: When the black and white areas of an image are reversed. That is, black type on white paper would appear as white type on black paper.

REVISE: A change in instructions that will alter either the original copy or the final printed results.

ROLLER STRIPPING: The term used when ink does not adhere to the metal ink rollers on a press.

ROLL-UP: Inking the plate image on the press.

ROUTING: Cutting away the nonprinting areas of a letterpress plate.

RUN: Number of copies to be printed.

SADDLE STITCH: To bind a booklet by stapling from outside to inside through the fold.

SAFELIGHT: A light used in the darkroom that does not fog (expose) sensitized materials.

SATURATION: See INTENSITY.

SCALING: Determining the correct size of an illustration that will be reduced or enlarged.

SCANNER: Usually refers to an electric eye device that scans the printed web (paper) as it passes through the press for adjusting register and ink viscosity or strength.

SCORE: To crease or impress a mark with a rule to make paper easier to fold.

SCREEN: Crossed fine lines used to convert a continuous tone image into a screened image suitable for etching and printing. The number of lines per inch varies and is dependent upon the reproduction process and the quality of paper being printed.

SCREEN ANGLE: The angle at which the crosslines of a screen are positioned in relation to the horizontal axis of the copy. The screen for each color being printed in the process method has a specific angle of screen to avoid an objectionable moire pattern in the final printed product.

SCREEN HALFTONE: An image created by the use of various sized dots. Changes in tone are created by controlling the size of the dots. The larger the dot the darker the area and vice versa.

SCREEN PRINTING: Another form of stencil printing. A hand cut or photographically prepared stencil is adhered to a screen mounted on a frame. Printing is done by forcing special paints through the porous image area with a squeegee.

SCROLL: A roll of paper or paperlike material containing a written document or message; in phototypesetting, to move the lines of type on the CRT screen for purpose of editing or correcting copy.

SCUMMING: The term used to describe the problem of ink adhering to nonprinting areas of an offset plate.

SECONDARY COLOR: Mixture of two primary colors. For example: red and yellow for orange.

SELF COVER: Cover of same paper as inside text pages.

SENSITIVITY GUIDE: A black and white image consisting of several narrow panels each a different shade ranging from white to black used to judge proper exposure and development of graphic arts film. Also called a gray scale.

SEPARATION: Breakdown of colors in an illustration into primary printing colors or special colors.

SERIF: The short lines at the ends of the main strokes that make up the letters in many faces of type.

SETOFF: When wet ink on a printed sheet comes off on the next sheet printed. It is also known as offset.

SHADOW: The darkest parts of a photograph. They are shown in a halftone by the largest dots.

SHEETWISE: To print one side of a sheet with one form or plate, then turn the sheet over and print the other side with another form or plate using the same gripper and side guides.

SHOW-THROUGH: When printing on one side of a sheet can be seen through the sheet under normal viewing light.

SIDE WIRE: To staple sheets or signatures of a booklet or magazine along the side near the backbone.

SIGNATURE: A printed form after it has been folded to page size.

SILK SCREEN: See SCREEN PRINTING.

SIZING: The process of treating paper to make it resistant to moisture.

SKID: A rack or platform used to support a pile of cut sheets.

SLIP SHEET: Any paper or plastic sheet used to separate one plate from another. Also the sheet used to separate freshly printed sheets to prevent setoff.

SLITTING: Cutting printed sheets or webs by means of cutting wheels while the paper is on the press or in a folder.

SLUG: A strip of metal, usually 6 points thick, used as spacing between lines of type. Also a line of type produced on a typecasting machine (Linotype).

SMALL CAPS: Small capital letters available in most Roman type faces. The letters are about the same height as the lower case letters of the font.

SMASHING: A binding operation which applies great heat and pressure to the binding edge of the book to reduce its thickness.

SOLID MATTER: The lines of type set for reading matter as distinct from illustrations.

SOLIDS: Areas where ink coverage is 100 percent.

SPACES: Pieces of type metal less than type high which add space in a line of type. Spaces are thinner than quads.

SPINE: The back of a bound book.

SPIRAL BINDING: A book bound with a wire spiral inserted into holes punched along the binding side of the book or tablet.

SPIRIT DUPLICATING: A planographic printing process which makes copies by dissolving carbon from the image area of a master sheet in the presence of a duplicating fluid.

SPOTTING: A step in print finishing to eliminate white spots on the print surface.

SPREAD: More than a single page layout, but not more than a two page layout processed together.

SQUEEGEE: Device with rubber or plastic blade used to force ink through the screen in screen printing. Also: to remove excess water or chemical from a surface with a squeegee.

STAPLE: To fasten a number of sheets together with U

shaped wire fasteners. The open end of the staple is closed after it has been forced through all of the sheets.

STENCIL PRINTING: Printing process in which the image area is cut into thin material (sheet metal, plastic, paper, etc.). Ink is brushed or forced through the cut away portion onto the material being printed.

STEP-AND-REPEAT: The technique for repeating exposures of one image several times on the same plate according to a layout.

STEREOTYPE: A duplicate printing plate or typeform cast in metal from a paper mold or matrix.

STICK: Narrow tray held in the hand to hold hand set type during composition.

STOCK: Any material used to receive the printed image.

STONE: Steel topped table used to assemble matter for letterpress printing. Called "stone" because early tables were topped with marble or granite. See IMPOSING TABLE.

STRAIGHT MATTER: Type composition set in paragraph form.

STRIKE-ON COMPOSITION: Type set by a direct impression machine such as a typewriter.

STRIPPING: The positioning and fastening of negatives on a flat prior to platemaking.

SUBTRACTIVE COLORS: The three colors, cyan, magenta and yellow, so called because each results when a third additive primary color (red, green or blue) is subtracted from white light.

SUPER: Coarse reinforcing cloth which is glued to the bound edge of books for added strength.

TEXT: The body matter of a page or book.

THERMOGRAPHIC COPYING: Limited copy reproduction method using heat-sensitive paper.

THERMOGRAPHY: A printing technique that makes use of a special resin powder and heat to produce raised printing. The powder is sprinkled over a printed sheet while the ink is still wet. Excess powder is removed and heat is applied. The ink and resin powder fuse together and expand above the sheet's surface.

THIRTY (written-30-): Used in newspaper work to indicate the end of the story.

TINTS: Lighter variations of a solid color made by adding white to the base color.

TIP-IN: A sheet printed separately and glued into a book.

TIPPING: Process of adhering endsheets to first and last signatures of a book.

TISSUE OVERLAY: A thin, translucent sheet placed over a layout for protective purposes. Also used to indicate colors to be used, corrections to be made and instructions to camera operator.

TOOTH: A slightly rough finish on many papers that permits the paper to take ink readily.

TRANSPARENCY: A colored photograph on transparent film.

TRANSPARENT: Quality of process ink which allows light to reflect through it off the white sheet.

TRANSPOSE: To reverse position of a letter, word or line with another letter, word or line.

TRIM: To cut to size. Also: the extra paper allowance to be removed by cutting.

TRIM MARKS: Marks placed on layout to indicate where cutting is to be done.

TYPE: The characters used singly or collectively for the purpose of creating text.

TYPE HIGH: The standard height of type forms in letterpress – 0.918 inch.

VACUUM FRAME: Device used to hold copy and offset plate in contact during exposure.

VEHICLE: Liquid which carries the colors in printing inks.

VELLUM: Fine-grained calfskin or skin of a goat prepared especially for writing on or for binding of books.

VELLUM FINISH: A toothy finished paper that absorbs ink readily.

WARM COLOR: A color that is on the red side of the color chart.

WASH DRAWING: A drawing done in varying shades of black, white and gray. The paints have not been mixed with Chinese white which makes the colors opaque. Often transparent water color paintings are also called wash drawings.

WASHUP: Cleaning ink from the various parts of the press.

WEB: Paper from the roll in a printing press; the full length of paper contained in a roll of stock as it passes through the press.

WEB PRESS: Press that prints from rolls of paper.

WIDOW: Partial line consisting of a single word or partial word appearing at top or bottom of column of type.

WITH THE GRAIN: Folding or feeding paper parallel to the grain of the paper.

WOODCUT: A piece of wood on which an image has been cut for printing purposes.

WORD SPACING: Adding em spaces or thin spaces between words for better appearance or to fill out (justify) a line of type.

WORK AND TUMBLE: To print one side of a sheet, then turn the paper over from gripper to back and, using the same side guide and plate, print the second side of the sheet.

WORK AND TURN: To print one side of a sheet, then turn the sheet over from left to right and print the second side. The same gripper and plate is used to print both sides.

WOVE PAPER: A paper having a uniform unlined surface and a soft smooth finish.

WRONG FONT: The proofreader uses the mark "WF" to indicate a character of the wrong size or face.

XEROGRAPHY: A dry printing process that makes use of electrostatic forces on a selenium plate to produce the image.

ZINC ETCHING: Line engraving produced on zinc plate for relief printing process.

USEFUL INFORMATION

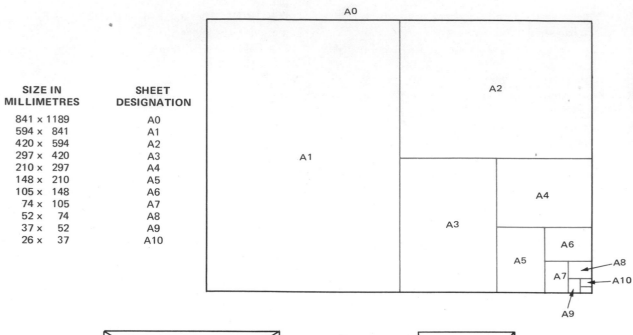

SIZE IN MILLIMETRES	SHEET DESIGNATION
841 x 1189	A0
594 x 841	A1
420 x 594	A2
297 x 420	A3
210 x 297	A4
148 x 210	A5
105 x 148	A6
74 x 105	A7
52 x 74	A8
37 x 52	A9
26 x 37	A10

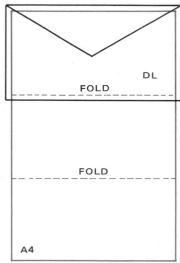

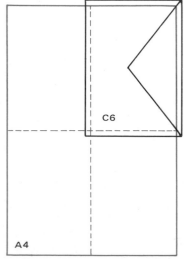

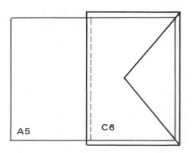

ENVELOPE SYMBOL	SIZE
C7	81 x 114 mm
C7/6	81 x 162
DL	110 x 220
C6	114 x 162
B6	125 x 176
B6/C4	125 x 324
C5	162 x 229
B5	176 x 250
C4	229 x 324
B4	250 x 353
C3	324 x 458

PRINTERS UNITS AND METRIC EQUIVALENTS IN MILLIMETRES

POINTS	PICAS	MILLIMETRES	APPROXIMATE THICKNESS
1	1/12 (0.08)	0.35	
1.5	1/8 (0.125)	0.525	
2	1/6	0.70	
2.5	5/24		
3	1/4	1.05	
3.5	7/24		
4	1/3	1.40	
4.5	9/24		
5	5/12	1.75	
5.5	11/24		
6	1/2 (0.5)	2.10	
6.5	13/24		
7	7/12	2.45	
7.5	15/24		
8	2/3	2.80	
8.5	17/24		
9	9/12	3.15	
9.5	19/24		
10	10/12	3.50	
12	1	4.20	
14	1 1/6	4.90	
18	1 1/2	6.30	
24	2	8.40	
30	2 1/2	10.50	
36	3	12.60	
42	3 2/3	14.70	
48	4	16.80	
60	5	21.00	
72	6	25.20	

PROOFREADERS' MARKS

∧	INSERT CORRECTION NOTED IN MARGIN	“/”/	INSERT QUOTATION MARK	~~	UNDER LETTER OR WORD MEANS "BOLD FACE"
×	DEFECTIVE LETTER	/?/	INSERT QUESTION MARK	○	SPELL OUT (CIRCLE ABBREVIATION)
///	STRAIGHTEN LINE	(!)	INSERT EXCLAMATION POINT	stet.	LET IT STAND, RETAIN
w.f.	WRONG FONT	/=/	INSERT HYPHEN	out s.c.	SEE COPY FOR OMISSION
✓	CORRECT SPACING	(/)	INSERT PARENTHESES	tr.	TRANSPOSE LETTER OR WORD
#	INSERT SPACE	[/]	INSERT BRACKETS	lc.	CHANGE TO LOWER CASE
¶	PARAGRAPH	1/m or 2/m	1-EM OR 2-EM DASH	caps	CHANGE TO CAPS
⊥	PUSH DOWN SPACE	⁐	CLOSE UP, NO SPACE	s.c.	CHANGE TO SMALL CAPS
⊙	INSERT PERIOD	‿	LESS SPACE	ital	CHANGE TO ITALICS
,/	INSERT COMMA	[	MOVE WORD OR LETTER LEFT	rom.	CHANGE TO ROMAN LETTERS
:/	INSERT COLON	]	MOVE WORD OR LETTER RIGHT	⋎⋎	EQUALIZE SPACING
;/	INSERT SEMICOLON	9	TURN REVERSED LETTER	Qu or ?	IS THIS CORRECT?
✓'	INSERT APOSTROPHE	₰	TAKE OUT, DELETE		

Graphic Arts Fundamentals

ELEMENTS OF DESIGN

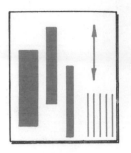

Lines give a feeling of movement or continuation. They can be straight, curved, angled, heavy or light. They help deliver the message. They move the eye from one point to another.

LINE

Form gives an element shape. It may appear as a square, rectangle, circle, triangle or a free-form shape. You see it as something that stands out in a printed message.

FORM

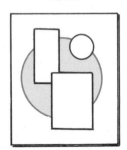

Mass refers to the size or amount of space taken up by an element. It is affected by the lightness or darkness of the element. Dark areas seem larger than light ones.

MASS

Color is attractive to the eye. This factor makes color useful in presenting visual messages. Used on a layout, it causes that part of the layout to attract attention.

COLOR

Texture is a part of every printed image whether intended or not. It can be the roughness or smoothness of the paper or cloth receiving the printed image. Sometimes the texture is printed on as in this example.

TEXTURE

PRINCIPLES OF DESIGN

Proportion is the relationship of size and shape to each other. In good proportion, the effect of the relationship is pleasing. In the example, underlines suit weight of type. Thus, the proportion, being good, pleases.

PROPORTION

Balance refers to equalizing the weight of elements in a design. Like children on a teeter-totter, equal sizes of elements will be in balance if equally distant from the center of the page. A smaller element placed further from the center of a page will still balance a larger element which is closer to the center.

BALANCE

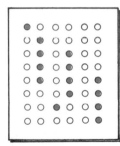

Contrast or emphasis causes some elements of a layout to stand out. This feeling can be created by a difference in size, color or appearance.

EMPHASIS OR CONTRAST

Unity is a quality that gives elements the appearance of belonging together. This appearance may be the result of likeness of shape. This is the case for the circles shown in the example. It also is the case when similar typefaces are used.

UNITY

Rhythm is a quality of a layout that moves the eye in a desired direction. The rhythm acts as a guide so the eye reads important parts of a message.

RHYTHM

Useful Information

CONVERSION TABLE — ENGLISH TO METRIC

WHEN YOU KNOW	MULTIPLY BY: * = Exact — VERY ACCURATE	APPROXIMATE	TO FIND
LENGTH			
inches	*25.4		millimetres
inches	*2.54		centimetres
feet	*0.3048		metres
feet	*30.48		centimetres
yards	*0.9144	0.9	metres
miles	*1.609344	1.6	kilometres
WEIGHT			
grains	15.43236	15.4	grams
ounces	*28.349523125	28.0	grams
ounces	*0.028349523125	.028	kilograms
pounds	*0.45359237	0.45	kilograms
short ton	*0.90718474	0.9	tonnes
VOLUME			
teaspoons		5.0	millilitres
tablespoons		15.0	millilitres
fluid ounces	29.57353	30.0	millilitres
cups		0.24	litres
pints	*0.473176473	0.47	litres
quarts	*0.946352946	0.95	litres
gallons	*3.785411784	3.8	litres
cubic inches	*0.016387064	0.02	litres
cubic feet	*0.028316846592	0.03	cubic metres
cubic yards	*0.764554857984	0.76	cubic metres
AREA			
square inches	*6.4516	6.5	square centimetres
square feet	*0.09290304	0.09	square metres
square yards	*0.83612736	0.8	square metres
square miles		2.6	square kilometres
acres	*0.40468564224	0.4	hectares
TEMPERATURE			
Fahrenheit	*5/9 (after subtracting 32)		Celsius

CONVERSION TABLE — METRIC TO ENGLISH

WHEN YOU KNOW	MULTIPLY BY: * = Exact — VERY ACCURATE	APPROXIMATE	TO FIND
LENGTH			
millimetres	0.0393701	0.04	inches
centimetres	0.3937008	0.4	inches
metres	3.280840	3.3	feet
metres	1.093613	1.1	yards
kilometres	0.621371	0.6	miles
WEIGHT			
grains	0.00228571	0.0023	ounces
grams	0.03527396	0.035	ounces
kilograms	2.204623	2.2	pounds
tonnes	1.1023113	1.1	short tons
VOLUME			
millilitres	0.06667	0.2	teaspoons
millilitres	0.03381402	0.067	tablespoons
millilitres		0.03	fluid ounces
litres	61.02374	61.024	cubic inches
litres	2.113376	2.1	pints
litres	1.056688	1.06	quarts
litres	0.26417205	0.26	gallons
litres	0.0531467	0.035	cubic feet
cubic metres	61023.74	61023.7	cubic inches
cubic metres	35.31467	35.0	cubic feet
cubic metres	1.3079506	1.3	cubic yards
cubic metres	264.17205	264.0	gallons
AREA			
square centimetres	0.1550003	0.16	square inches
square centimetres	0.00107639	0.001	square feet
square metres	10.76391	10.8	square feet
square metres	1.195990	1.2	square yards
square kilometres		0.4	square miles
hectares	2.471054	2.5	acres
TEMPERATURE			
Celsius	*9/5 (then add 32)		Fahrenheit

INDEX

Index